Introducing Communication Research

Fourth Edition

For Charlotte, James and Joseph
Luke and Owen

And for Kristina

Sara Miller McCune founded SAGE Publishing in 1965 to support the dissemination of usable knowledge and educate a global community. SAGE publishes more than 1000 journals and over 800 new books each year, spanning a wide range of subject areas. Our growing selection of library products includes archives, data, case studies and video. SAGE remains majority owned by our founder and after her lifetime will become owned by a charitable trust that secures the company's continued independence.

Los Angeles | London | New Delhi | Singapore | Washington DC | Melbourne

Introducing Communication Research

Paths of Inquiry

Fourth Edition

Donald Treadwell

Westfield State University

Andrea Davis

Western New England University

Los Angeles | London | New Delhi
Singapore | Washington DC | Melbourne

FOR INFORMATION:

SAGE Publications, Inc.
2455 Teller Road
Thousand Oaks, California 91320
E-mail: order@sagepub.com

SAGE Publications Ltd.
1 Oliver's Yard
55 City Road
London, EC1Y 1SP
United Kingdom

SAGE Publications India Pvt. Ltd.
B 1/I 1 Mohan Cooperative Industrial Area
Mathura Road, New Delhi 110 044
India

SAGE Publications Asia-Pacific Pte. Ltd.
18 Cross Street #10-10/11/12
China Square Central
Singapore 048423

Printed in the United States of America

Library of Congress Cataloging-in-Publication Data

Names: Treadwell, D. F. (Donald F.), author. I Davis, Andrea, (Andrea M.), author.

Title: Introducing communication research : paths of inquiry / Donald Treadwell, Andrea Davis.

Description: Fourth edition. I Thousand Oaks, California : SAGE, 2019. I Includes bibliographical references and Index.

Identifiers: LCCN 2019005416 I ISBN 9781506369051 (paperback : alk. paper)

Subjects: LCSH: Communication—Research—Methodology.

Classification: LCC P91.3 .T76 2019 I DDC 302.2—dc23 LC record available at https://lccn.loc.gov/2019005416

Acquisitions Editor: Lily Norton
Senior Content Development Editor: Jennifer Jovin-Bernstein
Editorial Assistant: Sarah Wilson
Marketing Manager: Staci Wittek
Production Editor: Veronica Stapleton Hooper
Copy Editor: Karen E. Taylor
Typesetter: Hurix Digital
Proofreader: Dennis W. Webb
Indexer: Karen Wiley
Cover Designer: Janet Kiesel

This book is printed on acid-free paper.

19 20 21 22 23 10 9 8 7 6 5 4 3 2 1

BRIEF CONTENTS

DETAILED CONTENTS

LIST OF EXHIBITS

PREFACE

FOR STUDENTS

Let's imagine that you are looking forward to a well-deserved break; it is time for that trip you have been dreaming about. Two inescapable questions come to mind immediately. Where will you go, and how will you get there?

Generally, you will have some goal in mind. Perhaps, as a music lover, you will be thinking about a great concert experience somewhere. Perhaps you have always been intrigued by the cultures of Asia and think of Asia as a destination. Your trip is triggered by some basic interest, but interest alone will not make it happen. To get to your destination, you must have a specific address, and you must decide how you will get there.

Automobiles can stop when you need them to, but are mostly limited to roads. Planes can provide a wonderful overview of the territory but may not take you exactly where you want to go. So it is with research methods. There is no one best method, only a most appropriate method.

Then there's the question of how you will experience your destination when you get there. Some of us like to stay in one area to experience it as fully as possible. Others are movers—every day a new attraction. The first approach gives you an in-depth experience; the second gives you a broad experience.

Of course, you will want to record and share your experiences with others, so questions of recording and communication arise. What will you record—local music, architecture, interesting people, food, landscapes? How will you record this content—video, audio, photography, drawings, written notes? How will you share this content with others—blog, social media, e-mail, postcards, Internet chat?

Most journeys are fun, interesting, and intellectually and emotionally satisfying, but you had better know where and how you are going or you won't get there.

Researching human communication is very similar. At heart, it is simply a journey from not knowing something to knowing something or to knowing something more about human communication. Certainly it is interesting and intellectually rewarding. Virtual realities, social networking, web chat, soap operas, family dynamics, podcasts, advertising, tweets, and group decision making are just a few manifestations of the complex interactions that we call human communication and that we can research.

Other travel analogies apply. Because it is difficult to take two journeys simultaneously, most researchers opt to study one area at a time. They also have a "travel plan" in the form of decisions about the phenomena they will study, the method(s) they will use, and the people they will invite to be in their study. In the form of published research reports, they will undoubtedly read advice from those who have been there before to help them avoid the pitfalls and to maximize the return on the time, effort, and intellectual energy that good research demands.

The above introduction uses travel as a metaphor for the research process, but other metaphors are possible. We might, for instance, recast research as a fight against ignorance, as a contest between what we intuit and what we can demonstrate, or between fact and senti-ment. You will find other such tensions as you read through the text; for example, should the researcher be a dispassionate observer of communication phenomena or an individual with biases and preferences for viewing the world in a particular way?

Becoming comfortable with research is therefore not just a matter of mastering method; it is also a matter of identifying and understanding the assumptions and uncertainties that underpin the methods, and that you bring to your own research.

Just as maps, websites, and guidebooks can help optimize your travel experiences, this book will guide you through the basics of communication research design while pointing out many of the decisions that will need to be made en route.

Chapters 1 through 3 begin the journey by examining some of the basic assumptions and disagreements about human communication, how best to understand it, and the ethical implications of researching human participants.

Chapter 4 will help you find out more about your areas of interest. It will help you with the detailed reading and recording you will need to do in order to get a good working knowledge of the specific area you will be researching.

Chapters 5 through 13 discuss sampling, statistics, and the qualitative and quantitative research methods you will most likely encounter in a career in communication. Metaphori-cally, these chapters will help you with your mode-of-travel decisions.

We finish with a chapter on presenting your research results so that others can get a good picture of where and how you went, what you discovered, and how you chose to interpret it.

Throughout this edition, you will find an emphasis on the Internet and social media and the problems and challenges they present as both the topic of and tool for research.

Each chapter has learning objectives to highlight the skills and knowledge you should get from the chapter, a summary of key ideas, and an ethics panel to help you think about the ethics of research. The application exercises in each chapter will help you think about research design in practice. Terminology that may be new to you is shown in boldface **like this** and defined in the glossary at the end of the book.

The ideas and questions that you run into in your communication research courses will almost certainly come back to visit you in your professional career and certainly in an academic career. Therefore, we suggest that you keep this book and find a place for it on your bookshelf.

Welcome to that most fascinating of journeys—research in human communication.

FOR FACULTY

This text aims to provide a reader-friendly introduction to the basics of communication research and to some of the assumptions and questions behind research practice.

Our experiences in teaching communication research have led us to believe that an intro-ductory text should give students looking at either academic or professional careers

- a mastery of basic communication research methods,

- an understanding of the assumptions behind research methods,

- an enthusiasm for research that will continue on into advanced research or careers in communication,

- an appreciation of the relevance of communication research to communication practice, and

- a sense of why we find human communication so fascinating as a research field.

We hope you will find that this text achieves these aims in your research courses.

Chapters 1 through 3 examine some of the basic assumptions and disagreements about human communication. Chapter 4 centers on bibliographic research and the literature review. Chapters 5 through 13 discuss measurement, sampling, statistics, and research methods. Chapter 14 covers research writing and presentation using traditional and social media for both scholarly publics and interest groups.

This edition has

- new vignettes at the beginning of each chapter, which present a student-friendly lead-in to the chapter content;

- an expanded discussion of basic research perspectives and assumptions in Chapter 2;

- an expanded discussion of online consent and permissions in Chapter 3;

- an updated and expanded discussion of statistical significance in Chapter 8;

- a new discussion of big data and its implications in Chapter 9;

- an expanded discussion of writing and presenting research via social media in Chapter 14; and

- an emphasis throughout on social media and the Internet as subjects of and tools for communication research.

Support for student learning in each chapter includes

- learning objectives to highlight the skills and knowledge students should get from the chapter;

- a chapter summary that provides an overview of chapter content;

- an ethics panel with questions to facilitate discussion of research ethics in practice;

- highlighted vocabulary words, which are defined and explained in the glossary at the end of the text; and

- application exercises to help students learn to make decisions about research practice.

Each method chapter has a practice-based organizing example that guides students through the practical and theoretical decisions a researcher faces when designing and implementing research.

The companion website has a section on APA style as well as the updated ancillary material listed below.

We hope that this text will make a useful contribution to your research courses, and we welcome your thoughts on it. Thank you for adopting it.

ANCILLARIES

SAGE edge for instructors supports your teaching by making it easy to integrate quality content and create a rich learning environment for students with:

- a password-protected site for complete and protected access to all text-specific instructor resources;

- a test bank in Word and ExamView that provide a diverse range of ready-to-use options that save you time. You can also easily edit any question and/or insert your own personalized questions;

- multimedia content that meet the learning needs of today's media-savvy students and bring concepts to life;

- sample course syllabi for semester and quarter courses that provide suggested models for structuring your courses;

- editable, chapter-specific PowerPoint® slides that offer complete flexibility for creating a multimedia presentation for your course;

- lecture notes that summarize key concepts by chapter to help you prepare for lectures and class discussions;

- recommended readings that provide instructors and students with a list of suggested books and articles for instructors and students can use to supplement the textbook;

- chapter-specific discussion questions that allow students to engage with the material; and

- class activity suggestions to help students engage with the text content in class.

SAGE edge for students enhances learning, it's easy to use, and offers:

- an open-access site that makes it easy for students to maximize their study time, anywhere, anytime;

- eFlashcards that strengthen understanding of key terms and concepts;

- quizzes that allow students to practice and assess how much they've learned and where they need to focus their attention;

- learning objectives that reinforce the most important material;

- video, multimedia, and Web links that facilitate student use of Internet resources and further exploration of topics.

- industry case studies from previous editions that can be used as a basis for "research in practice" discussions; and

- a five-minute APA guide to help students structure their papers and properly cite their sources.

ACKNOWLEDGMENTS

Every text benefits from rigorous and informed criticism, and we appreciate the constructive input provided by

Amy M. Smith, Salem State University

David Lapakko, Augsburg University

Jennifer L. Adams, DePauw University

Patricia Atkinson, Marist College

Sandra Duhé, Southern Methodist University

We thank them for their time and patience, and hope that they will recognize the results of their advice in this final product.

We are grateful for the resources available from the Pew Research Center Internet & Technology site.

Thanks go to the SAGE editorial, production, marketing, and ancillaries teams for bringing this project to fruition. In particular, we thank Karen Taylor for her contributions, suggestions, and editorial fine-tuning.

Thanks go as well to a friendly avatar, Jill Student, whose questions helped us focus each chapter on student learning.

Special thanks once again go to Jill Treadwell—editor, muse, critic, and sounding board—for her conceptual, creative, and culinary input.

Special thanks to Katy Hone for her love, support, encouragement, and coparenting.

Donald Treadwell

Andrea Davis

GETTING STARTED

Possibilities and Decisions

"Hey Luke! How was your break?"

"Great, Sofia, except now it's back to reality. I need coffee already to get me through the semester. Want to get some?"

"Sure! We're both doing Comm. Research this semester, right?"

"Looks like it. Who else is doing it? Carlos maybe?"

"Jada I know for sure, James, maybe Charlotte. Carlos did it last semester."

"What about Eric? Think he's hiding from all the math?"

"Why would he? It's not a math course."

"Well, it's got that reputation."

"We'll get some statistics I hear, but Carlos said we'll do a lot of comm. research without going anywhere near stats."

"So the whole 'research equals math' thing is wrong?"

"Not wrong; math is a tool. You pick the tool for the job, is how Carlos explained it."

"OK—that I can handle, but how do I pick a research topic? I heard you had to do that."

"Keep your eyes open, I suppose. Look around. Like, how come everyone here in the coffee bar has to watch CNN and not Fox or MSNBC or whatever? How do they know what we want to watch? Did someone run a survey? Who decided and how? Who watches network TV anyway? Come to think of it, what does anyone watch?"

"I've got some answers to those questions. First of all, just look around. You can see who's watching TV . . . and you can guess at their ages, occupations, maybe majors even. And there you have it. Those are the people that watch TV."

"Doesn't sound very scientific."

"Well, you have to start somewhere. Now, as to what everyone else is looking at, why not just walk around casually and try to see what each person's looking at?"

"That's spying on people. You can't do that."

"Why not? You can walk around campus recording how many people wear baseball caps backwards, so why can't you record what's on people's screens—like text messages or movies? Should be easy with laptops and big-screen phones like the one Joe bought."

"That's just not ethical."

"Sure it is. You're just observing what's public. You'd have no problem recording what people were looking at in a newspaper would you? Lee says he's going to record campus traffic this semester to get some evidence for more parking spaces. How's that different from walking around looking at what's on people's screens?"

"It's different because there's no personal information in a newspaper, and because parking lots are public. Mobile devices have personal information, and they're not public. You're intruding on private discussions when you look at peoples' messages."

"If it's posted, it's public I say."

"Hey speaking of Joe! Welcome back. How was your break? Where are you going?"

"Hi back at ya—and in question order—lousy and library."

"Lousy and library???"

"Yeah . . . my laptop crashed over the break. No backup, so there was the whole recovery thing, and now I'm in debt to Mom until I pay her off for a new one. This semester I'm backing up everything and booking a study space in the library. That way I'm handy to real books and journals and a library computer if I crash again. You know what they say. Crash once, maybe it's someone else's fault. Crash twice, it's on you."

"Sounds from what Carlos said, we'll be seeing you at the library while we're all trying to get our heads around comm. research."

"Guess so. Don't know why we can't all stay home and do research. Everyone and everything is online."

"Except when your laptop crashes, Joe! Plus face-to-face with library staff is good. They're credible at helping you sort out stuff you need from all the stuff you don't need. Who on line is credible—and how would you know?"

ASA Comments

ASA—your All-Seeing Authors—will drop into this discussion from time to time to make a few brief points. Communication research topics are all around us. From the preceding discussion, we can identify several. For example, what are students' preferred news sources? How are decisions about campus media made? Joe's arrival suggests additional questions. Luke and Sofia were getting into the ethics of accessing online content, but Joe seems to have redirected the conversation to laptops and libraries. How did that shift happen, and what might explain it?

Outside of specific research questions, there are broader issues framing research: for example, ethics, or the standards of behavior expected of researchers; the question of whether human communication is best understood through numbers (quantitative) or words (qualitative); and research standards, or the methods and processes that make a research study credible. We'll delve into these issues in more detail in Chapters 1 through 4, after we meet Mike . . .

"Hey it's wonder boy—Mike. Heard you got straight A's last semester! You're treating us all to lunch, right?"

"Nah, just had breakfast. Actually, I'm embarrassed about those A's. I mean, I got a "93" in two courses; if they were "92s"—just one point less—I would have had two A minuses. It's more random luck than capturing my abilities. And Caroline, who was truly running straight A's, blew one question in one test, that took one course grade down, that took her GPA down, that knocked her out of the honor society when she should have been in it more than me. I don't know what they think they're measuring with this GPA stuff. "

"Sort of like the mystery muffins you're about to treat us to, if you're not treating lunch?"

"Nice try . . . maybe I will. Wouldn't you think they'd have upgraded the menu in all the time we've been here?"

"Yeah, you'd think they'd be responsive to all the vegan-vegetarian-paleo-whatever palates on campus—not to mention all the religious do's and don'ts. The food's so 'yesterday.' It's like farm-to-table doesn't exist. They should run a survey and get a read on what we like."

"And you would be the one to survey, Mike? You think the four major food groups are cappuccino, latte, Americano, and espresso!"

"OK. So who would they ask? We'd all be graduated by the time they got around to asking the entire campus."

"Right, but let's agree that not asking you would be a good idea if they want to capture some majority opinions!"

"Fine. Don't ask me. But you can't revamp an entire campus food plan based on what a handful of volunteers like you think."

"I bet you can if you pick the right people."

ASA Comments

Hello again. Our student group has now raised two further important topics. The first is measurement, in this case, of academic excellence. How do we define and measure it? Communication research faces similar problems. For example, how might we define and measure an attitude?

The second topic is sampling. If we want an accurate survey of student food preferences, whom exactly would we survey? This is not just a theoretical question. The survey industry spends time and effort trying to get representative samples of people at a time when most people are not interested in responding to surveys. As we will see, sampling techniques combined with some knowledge of statistics can let us make generalizations about large numbers of people from a smaller sample of them.

We discuss measurement, sampling, and statistics more fully in Chapters 5 through 8. In Chapter 6, Elizabeth begins the first of some campus-based research examples when she plans her own survey of student food preferences. Right now, Lee has his own problem—parking.

"Hey, Lee! Haven't seen you in a while?"

"Right! I've been looking for a parking space."

"I sort of meant over the last few months, but I hear you on the parking problem. I don't know why commuter students even come here—the parking's so bad."

"I heard some good news though; they're bulldozing the old Hunter building to put in a car park."

"About time too. It *is* an ugly damn thing. And we need a car park."

"Hold on. Hunter's got historic value, for starters. And even if it hasn't, I can't see that bulldozing it guarantees more parking space."

"I thought we were supposed to be going all green? A car park just encourages more cars. They don't want to do that do they?"

"Sounds as if nobody knows what they want."

"Pull it down and see who shows up to protest. That'll tell you a lot about who's really committed to saving it."

"Or just read all the campus graffiti and bumper stickers. Those'll tell you. Count up all the "Save Hunter" and all the "More Parking on Campus" and there's your vote one way or the other."

"Yeah, from everyone that gets a charge out of defacing buildings . . . or likes bumper stickers."

"Beats the hassle of interviewing. Why go around interviewing people when you can just sit back and let public opinion come to you?"

"Yeah . . . well. Hey Charlotte . . . we're just talking about parking. But you're more into clubbing tonight. Right?"

"Yep! Anyone interested? There's a new dive downtown doing lo-fi hip-hop—I think."

"Now there's a communication experience, Charlotte. Maybe you can write all that up for your comm. research project."

"Too much writing. I'd have books full of stuff. Plus I'd be a part of it. So it wouldn't be good research, right? Not objective."

"Who says you have to be objective?"

"Who says you don't?"

ASA Comments

In this third discussion, we discover what many people think of as the basics of communication research—method. There are many methods to think about. Surveys (Chapter 9) and experiments (Chapter 10) are two classic quantitative methods. Campus interest groups presumably would be surveyed on the future of the Hunter building. Pulling the building down does provide a low-level "natural" (albeit impractical) experiment in that it sets up a condition and then looks to see how people respond to it. Graffiti, bumper stickers, and social media postings pertaining to the proposed demolition can be analyzed quantitatively by categorizing and counting them as either for or against the demolition (Chapter 11). A qualitative approach (Chapter 12) would be to analyze the arguments in such content for insights on why people favor or oppose the demolition.

Human interaction can of course be analyzed qualitatively, as we will see in Chapter 13 when Bonnie considers ways to research students' uses of social media.

Finally, Charlotte's thoughts about clubbing raise the important issue of objectivity. Charlotte's not sure she can be objective. Isn't research supposed to be objective? Or does it always carry the biases and assumptions of the researcher? Plus, how can she possibly report every interaction she observes at her research location. As she says . . .

"Write up everything that happened? I don't think so! Write up all that 'who said what to whom' stuff, plus what they did, what they wore, and who danced with whom, and I'll still be writing 800 pages later!"

"That's what's great about statistics. You can just write up that the average score was 42—or something like that—and you're done. Right?"

"Why not just submit a video of the whole thing and let people draw their own conclusions?

"But that doesn't explain anything. Print or video, people want to know who you researched, why you researched them, how you did it, why you did it, where you did it . . . and like that. You've got to justify yourself; got to address that big "so what" question, right?"

ASA Comments

The discussion about reporting research raises some valid questions. Why does everything have to be reported in print format? The short answer is, it doesn't. Conventionally, though, scholarly research reporting is "print heavy" and detailed so that readers can understand exactly how you did your research. Why not submit a video of the whole thing? Technology makes that possible, but what else would any researcher viewing your video want? And what about objectivity? Over time, communication research has seen a shift from striving for objectivity to recognizing that subjectivity will not go away—and addressing that fact. We'll discuss these topics and others in Chapter 14, by which time you should have your own answer to the objectivity question.

In the meantime, as Carlos might have advised, drink some coffee and read Chapter 1.

The coffee is optional.

Chapter 1 is not. It begins here.

CHAPTER OVERVIEW

Welcome to communication research. This chapter introduces some of the many ways scholars of human communication think about research, their main interest areas, and some of their research methods. It will help you with the often-difficult process of getting started and getting focused on a research project, and introduce you to some of the assumptions and decisions that every researcher makes, consciously or unconsciously.

CHAPTER OBJECTIVES

This chapter will help you

- Identify basic assumptions behind human communication research.

- Identify research questions that might be asked about communication.

- Describe some of the decisions required when planning communication research.

GETTING STARTED IN RESEARCH

Any day or any journey requires that you first wake up and then make a series of decisions to get started. Stay in bed or get up? Gym first and then breakfast? Or breakfast first and hang out with friends? Bike, bus, or walk to work, or work online from home? Each day requires that you get oriented in some direction and decide on the priorities for that day. Similarly, any research project requires that you start by getting yourself oriented toward an area of interest. Then you will need to decide what questions, assumptions, and methods will best get you the answers to your interest questions.

Communication researchers have interests ranging from interpersonal communication on up to web media reaching millions of people worldwide. Researchers often specialize in areas defined by the numbers of people they are studying, as in interpersonal communication, groups, organizations, or social media. But many research interests transcend such categories. For example, rhetoricians, those who study the use of language and argumentation, may do so in all of these areas.

Potential topics for research are all around us. Why do people prefer some music genres over others? What is the best way to deliver instructional content—the web, readings, seminars, lectures, or hands-on experience? What websites are seen as the most credible sources of advice for students downloading new "apps"? Do student behaviors in class influence instructor behavior? Do blockbuster movies shape public opinion or follow it? What can we say about the effects of violent or sexually explicit media content on people exposed to such content? What predicts whether an online video will "go viral"?

The next step after finding questions of interest is deciding how best to get answers to these questions. You will find from the scholarly literature that this can be a hotly contested issue. Choosing a research method or methods unavoidably requires making assumptions and decisions about the nature of human behavior, such as whether people are basically all alike or are unique individuals. These assumptions and decisions will help you prefer some methods to others, but you may well find that for every researcher going down your road, there is another researcher opting for a different route to answering essentially the same question.

Every research question has assumptions behind it that reflect the researcher's view of communication and how to study it. These are discussed below and in Chapter 2.

BASIC ASSUMPTIONS BEHIND COMMUNICATION RESEARCH

Several basic assumptions underpin all communication research. Consciously or implicitly, researchers bring these assumptions to their research. Several major assumptions—each of which can be contested—are outlined below.

Observations Capture/Do Not Capture an Underlying Reality

One assumption is that what we choose to look at—dress or language, for example—tells us something about an underlying reality we cannot see but assume exists. For example, "power" is not something we can actually see. When you think about it, what we see is not power as such but rather someone behaving in a particular way and other people responding. Nonetheless, "power" seems like a useful concept in our efforts to understand human communication, and generally we elect to study it by looking at behaviors that we assume represent power.

Similarly, no one has ever actually seen an attitude. What people have seen is someone behaving in a particular way or responding to a set of survey questions designed to capture this thing called "attitude." Once again, "attitude" seems too useful a concept to discard, and so we research attitudes on the assumption that they exist or at least that the concept of attitude provides a useful tool for thinking about communication processes.

Theories About Human Behavior Can/Cannot Be Generalized

A second assumption is that theories about human behavior can be generalized. It may be insightful to discover that your grandfather has a LinkedIn account and that your little sister has a Twitter account. But your research would be much more useful and rewarding if you were able to make a general statement such as "Young people are more likely than older people *example* to have a Twitter account." If true, this statement would be of interest to advertisers, educators, and disaster management agencies, the last of which might need to reach large numbers of people rapidly in an emergency. However, to make this statement, you basically have to assume that your grandfather is like other grandfathers and your little sister is like other little sisters, at least with respect to social media use.

Probably, though—and correctly—your grandfather and sister regard themselves as unique individuals, so to what extent can we assume people are basically like other people? It is an important question because if our world is full of unique individuals, we are not entitled to make any generalizations about them (except, of course, that each of them is unique!). Nonetheless, researchers using survey or experimental methods typically will want to assume that the results of their research will apply to people who are similar to the study participants but not in the study. That is, there is an assumption that people are similar in the way they behave.

Researchers Should/Should Not Distance Themselves From Their Research Participants

A third assumption relates to the researchers' level of engagement with their research participants. As researchers, we could get more involved with the students in the discussions at the beginning of this chapter—perhaps by sitting in on the conversations or by interviewing some of them. This brings up a fundamental decision. The more distant the observer becomes, the more neutral or dispassionate she can be in reporting a group's behavior, but she will be unable to get the insights she would get if she were closer to the group. On the other hand, moving closer to the group will provide her with insight, but she then becomes open to influencing the group dynamics or to seeing only the group's view of the world and becoming biased in her reporting as a result.

Research Should/Should Not Be Done for a Specific Purpose

A fourth assumption is about the purpose or reason that should underlie research. Most scholarly researchers probably began their careers with a simple curiosity about human behavior, and it is that curiosity, plus the pleasure of discovery for its own sake, that continues to drive them. Scratch the surface of that interest, though, and we will find other purposes or motivations that come into play. At a personal level, it may be need for fame or funding. At another level, researchers may see their research as helping to solve society's problems or refining a highly theoretical model of human interaction. As we will see in Chapter 2, researchers may be content if their studies lead to accurate descriptions or an understanding of human behavior, but they are more likely to see their research as worthwhile if it explains or predicts that behavior.

Researchers whose work is funded by a corporation or foundation looking for specific answers to a question as quickly as possible may find that their personal motivations for research and their preferred direction for the research take second place relative to the needs and motivations of the funding agency.

There Is/Is Not One Best Position From Which to Observe Human Behavior

A fifth assumption is simply that some aspects of a question are more important to look at than others and, related, that there is one best standpoint from which to observe human communication. A simple way to understand this is to consider an early telecommunications-based model of communication (Shannon & Weaver, 1949). Given the complexities of human communication, it is an overly simplistic model, but it does identify major components in any human interaction as follows:

- Source—the provider or initiator of content

- Message or messages—the content of communication

- Channel or medium—the vehicle for communication content; for example, social media

- Receiver(s)—the recipient(s) or consumer(s) of information

- Noise—extraneous information or distractions that can disrupt an interaction

- Context—the relationships between individuals, the situation in which the interaction occurs, and the cultural norms around that interaction

In human interaction, communication gets more complicated. Source and receiver may swap roles as a discussion proceeds. What is noise to one party may be useful information to another. Nevertheless, this basic model does indicate some possible major entry points into the study of human interaction.

For example, a major area of research on the first component of the model is source credibility. Why do some news consumers find the *Huffington Post* more credible than, say, the *New York Times*, or the *New York Times* more credible than *Al Jazeera* or vice versa? The "message" component raises any number of questions about communication content—how best to present complex scientific information to a lay public, for example. The "channel" component raises questions about the impact of process on human behavior. For example, what are the circumstances in which personal, face-to-face instruction should be preferred to online learning? Or what happens to a recipient's understanding of a complex issue when message content is reduced to 140-character tweets? The "receiver" component often raises questions about how the demographic, cultural, and psychological characteristics of people influence their comprehension of messages or receptiveness to persuasive messages.

You will likely have already decided that none of these components can be studied in isolation. Receiver and sender interact and swap roles in many interactions. In the case of advertising research, receiver characteristics affect message content and channel selection. But researchers will typically find one of these components of the communication process more interesting than others and will give that component priority in their investigations.

By way of example, let's look at how researchers might approach a specific piece of communication content—an advertisement. We shall see that there are many possible approaches to studying such content.

SOME RESEARCH POSSIBILITIES: WHAT CAN WE DO WITH AN AD?

Let's explore how a single situation can lend itself to many research questions, using public service advertisements (PSAs) as the basis for our discussion. PSAs are targeted communications designed specifically to promote positive attitudes and behaviors. They focus on public interest topics such as health, education, safety, the environment, and other social causes. Many of them are likely to be familiar to you. Most PSAs are produced under the auspices of the Ad Council, a body that links nonprofit organizations with professional agencies that produce advertisements as a public service. For this discussion, we will focus on recent PSAs that tackle the problem of impaired or distracted driving. You can find the ads mentioned in this section, as well as many others, at www.adcouncil.org.

PSAs are typically based on, and address, a strong, often alarming fact or statistic, such as "Every 51 minutes, someone is killed in an alcohol-related car accident," or "In 2016, 3,450 people were killed in motor vehicle crashes involving distracted drivers." The creative challenge is to relate these often "remote," "happens-to-other-people" statistics to individual members of a target audience. This relevance is usually achieved by a tagline that makes the message personal, encourages a behavior or attitude change, and may become the overall campaign theme.

For example, the first statistic mentioned above resulted in the following anti–drunk driving campaign themes, which you will likely find familiar:

"Friends don't let friends drive drunk."

"Drinking and driving can kill a friendship."

"Buzzed driving is drunk driving."

And the problem of distracted driving inspired this texting and driving prevention campaign:

"Stop the Texts, Stop the Wrecks."

The second statistic inspired the themes of two anti–texting-while-driving messages.

The Ad Council's anti-texting print PSA features the image of an ambulance with the message "You don't want them responding to your text." Its television PSAs show the consequences of texting while driving—social opprobrium, missing a once-in-a-lifetime sighting, and, yes, death. You can view these ads at www.psacentral.org/campaign/texting-and-driving-prevention.

You can view a further series of messages aimed at distracted driving at AT&T's "It Can Wait" campaign website: www.itcanwait.com.

Many of these ads are hard-hitting, "pull-no-punches" messages that have the potential to grab attention and, perhaps, shock the target audience into a behavior change. Others rely more on social appeals or on recruiting individuals to join the campaign and providing the resources they will need to become advocates in their own right.

Communication researchers may have a number of questions about any of these PSAs. Does it work or doesn't it? How or why does it work? Whose interests are advanced by the ad? Does the medium itself (radio, magazine, television, newspaper, Internet) have an effect on how the content is understood? The following sections introduce several approaches to researching advertising using these PSAs as examples.

Does the Ad Work?

This is a question that, essentially, focuses on the receivers of the message. We want to know what they did or how they felt as a result of exposure to the message. Applied communication researchers, and certainly advertising executives and their clients, want to know how many people adopted the recommended behavior or at least changed their attitudes as a result of exposure to this ad. The question is not that readily answered.

If statistics show that accidents associated with texting have decreased, we could assume that the anti-texting advertisement was effective. Correct? Not necessarily. There could be many other explanations for such a decrease, and these would need to be ruled out before we could conclude that the ad had a significant effect.

One way to assess the effectiveness of these advertisements is to take a scientific approach. Two characteristics of scientific method are observation or empiricism and the attempt to rule out alternative explanations. From a scientific point of view, we might measure how much advertising time or space the campaign received and the number of texting citations issued and then look for a relationship between the two. We would hope to discover that as the amount of advertising increased, the number of citations decreased. But we would also need to be sure that any observed decrease was related to our advertising and not to an increase in the number of police on the highways or to a new ad that was launched before assessing whether the old one was working effectively. All possible causes would need to be identified and ruled out before we could assume that the anti-texting advertisement and *only* the advertisement caused the decrease.

What Can Readers and Viewers Tell Us?

This question also focuses on the receivers of the message, but with a shift in emphasis toward understanding the "whys" of human behavior. Establishing that the advertisement did influence behavior or attitudes provides no insight on why it did so. One way to answer this question would be to conduct a survey, asking questions based on what you suspect made the advertisement effective—the celebrity spokesperson, the animation showing how distractions affect reaction time, or the real-life story of an "innocent victim" of a texting-related crash, for example.

It is likely that an advertising agency would ask such questions before the advertisement was released in order to make the ad as effective as possible. Of course, the audience could have totally different perceptions of what is important about the ad; for example, viewers may decide that the catchy soundtrack is really what grabbed their attention. It is important, therefore, to capture what people have to say in their own words as well as to ask the questions that you think are important.

For such public opinion research, surveys are typically used to ask questions the researcher thinks are important, and focus groups are used to capture opinions that the audience thinks are important. Historically, surveys have used mail, phone, or personal interviews to present a series of specific, predetermined questions to a predetermined group of respondents, but today, the Internet and social media are equally likely vehicles, depending on the target audience. Focus groups involve bringing together maybe 6 to 12 people in person or online and asking them to discuss their reactions to an advertisement, issue, or product. The essential focus-group strategy is listening to people in order to capture their responses in their own words.

Surveys generally produce quantitative results (48% did not like the spokesperson); focus groups generally produce qualitative results in that they capture people talking ("I really did not like the spokesperson because . . ."). Surveys and focus groups both have their advantages and limitations, as we will see in later chapters.

What Can the Content Tell Us?

This question clearly focuses on message content. So far we have analyzed the texting campaign largely in terms of audience response, but what could we learn from the ad content itself? There are many angles from which to study media content, including rhetoric, content analysis, and critical theory. These angles share an interest in media content but take different approaches for different reasons.

Rhetoricians are essentially interested in the **appeals** or persuasive tactics used to persuade an audience to adopt the behavior. For example, if you look at the Ad Council's anti-texting campaign, two appeals are apparent: the appeal of the ambulance EMTs as authority figures (in the print ad) and the real-life experience of being in the car with a driver who cannot resist just a quick look at a text (in the TV ad). As with many commercial ads, this TV ad shows a "typical" teenager in a "typical" texting situation, leading to a further appeal that "people just like us" can be guilty of dangerous texting behavior.

Rhetoricians using theory developed by Aristotle (384–322 BCE) might search for appeals based on *logos* (logic), in this case the logic of "texting + driving = crash"; *ethos* (character), in this case the use of a typical teenager with typical reactions to a text; or *pathos* (emotion), in this case the tragic consequences of a crash.

Kenneth Burke, a 20th-century theorist who analyzed human communication in terms of drama, offered a set of analytical questions that ask, essentially, "What is the act, the scene, the people, and the purpose of the act?" We could analyze our ad using Burke's questions. Looking at the ad content, we could describe the setting, the driver, and the mini-drama of a person becoming absorbed in a text, losing control, and crashing.

Rhetorical approaches to researching advertising content are essentially qualitative; they analyze the use of language.

Content analysis, by contrast, is primarily a quantitative method for assessing media content. For example, looking at ads for distracted driving, including drunk driving, buzzed driving, and texting and driving, a content analyst might set up categories of content based on his interest in representations of gender in advertising. The analyst counts the number of appearances in the ads of men and women and compares them. He could also compare his results to a known distribution of these categories in accident records. He might then be able to conclude that the advertisements overrepresent women as buzzed drivers and underrepresent them as texting drivers, for example. He would be comparing advertising's world with what we know of the real world.

Critical analysis works from a basic assumption that communication maintains and promotes power structures in society. Essentially, the focus is on the relationship, explicit or implicit, between message source and recipient rather than on just one component of the communication process. With that as a basis, the critical researcher asks "Whose interests are served by the advertising, and more specifically, how exactly do language and representations maintain the interests of such entities as corporations, colleges, or governments?" Unlike the content analyst, who looks for what is explicit and observable, the researcher may look as much for what is implicit or unsaid.

For example, the AT&T "It Can Wait" campaign referenced above is a sophisticated web-based campaign that offers a virtual reality experience, a video gallery, a social networking hub, and ways in which the visitor to the site can take action against distracted driving. A critical analyst would want to know how AT&T—at time of this chapter's writing, the second largest provider of mobile phone services in the United States—benefits from this campaign. Do the company's messages distance it from the problem, and if so, how? How are the company's interests maintained and promoted by this campaign?

What Can the Creators of the Ad Tell Us?

This question focuses on the source of the message rather than on the recipient, message, or communication medium. Our understanding of the advertisement would, of course, be enhanced if we could talk with the client and with the producers, directors, and writers in the agencies that produced the ads. In this case, we would probably be interested in finding out how and why decisions about content and production were made. For example, might a truly hard-hitting PSA have been "watered down" because the sponsor wished to avoid controversy?

Researchers interested in organizational dynamics and decision making might want to know whether the basic creative approach was worked out over the course of extended meetings involving large numbers of people or if it came about as a directive from a client or creative director. Researchers interested in decision making would want to interview members of the creative team individually so that each member feels free to talk. They might also want to interview the team as a group and probably would want to get permission to record the creative meetings as they take place. Such research could give us insight on how communication facilitates or discourages creativity, decision making, and client-agency relationships, or on the process by which professional communicators build an image of the consumers they are trying to reach.

SOME RESEARCH POSSIBILITIES: BEYOND THE AD

The previous discussion centers on advertising by way of example, but analogous questions can also be asked of interpersonal, group, or organizational communication. For example, your academic department presumably uses social media to keep its student community apprised of relevant news such as new course offerings, faculty changes, and scholarship opportunities.

We might, again, ask the "Did it work?" question. For example, can we observe that the social media messages triggered additional numbers of students to register for new course offerings or apply for scholarships? We might, by using surveys, interviews, or focus groups, determine how students feel about this use of social media to provide them with departmental information. We could analyze this social media content to see what appeals are used to promote new courses and scholarships. We might even take the perspective of a critical organizational theorist and examine how such social media content encourages student compliance with the departmental "way of doing things."

If interpersonal communication were our field, we might be interested in tracking how communication changes as two people move from acquaintances to friends to romantic partners. Again, similar questions apply. The "Did it work?" question might be reframed in terms of trying to observe what vocabulary or behaviors work to strengthen or weaken the relationship, or we could interview the two individuals themselves to see what they have to say about their communication and why it works, or doesn't. Similarly, we could examine the content of their text messages or transcripts of their phone calls to relate the content to key events in the relationship.

A SERIES OF UNAVOIDABLE DECISIONS

"Communication researchers have different agendas and assumptions that underpin the methods they use. This is explained by the complexity of human communication. Because it is almost impossible to examine and explain a communication event in its totality, researchers focus on a part of that totality and choose a method for investigating it with which they have a comfort level, be it methodological or ideological.

For example, even though the research approaches outlined above share a common focus on understanding public service advertising, researchers clearly differ in what exactly they choose to research and the reasons for doing their research.

In addition to their theoretical priorities, all researchers face the reality of limited time, limited resources, and an inability to be in more than one place at a time (web conferencing excepted). Following are some of the choices that are almost inevitable for all types of researchers, based on their theoretical predispositions and resources.

The Field of Study—Wide or Narrow?

Time is short, the topic vast, and, realistically, we must research the available and the achievable. Methodological preferences aside, a communication researcher typically focuses on one of the many specific interest areas shown in Exhibit 1.1. This list is compiled from the names of the divisions and interest groups of the National Communication Association, the International Communication Association, and the Association for Education in Journalism and Mass Communication.

The Researcher—Dispassionate or Involved?

To what extent should researchers get involved with their human "subjects"? The scientific tradition values objectivity and dispassionate observation. The "reward" to the researcher is the satisfaction of a new finding, the development of a new theory, or the confirmation or disconfirmation of an existing theory.

EXHIBIT 1.1 ■ Communication Research Interest Areas

Activism, Communication, and Social Justice	Human Communication and Technology
Advertising	Information Systems
African American Communication and Culture	Instructional Development
American Studies	Intergroup Communication
Applied Communication	International and Intercultural Communication
Argumentation and Forensics	Interpersonal Communication
Asian/Pacific American Communication Studies	Journalism Studies
Children, Adolescents, and the Media	Language and Social Interaction
Communicating Science, Health, Environment, and Risk	Latino/Latina Communication Studies
Communication and Aging	Lesbian, Gay, Bisexual, Transgender, and Queer Studies
Communication and Law	Mass Communication
Communication and Social Cognition	Media Ethics
Communication and Technology	Media Industry Studies
Communication Apprehension and Avoidance	Mobile Communication
Communication Assessment	Newspaper and Online News
Communication Ethics	Nonverbal Communication
Communication History	Organizational Communication
Communication Law and Policy	Peace and Conflict Communication
Communication Science and Biology	Performance Studies
Community Journalism	Philosophy of Communication
Critical and Cultural Studies	Political Communication
Economics, Communication, and Society	Popular Communication
Entertainment Studies	Public Address
Environmental Communication	Public Diplomacy
Ethnicity and Race	Public Relations
Ethnography	Rhetorical and Communication Theory
Family Communication	Semiotics
Feminist and Women's Studies	Spiritual Communication
Freedom of Expression	Sports Communication
Game Studies	Theatre, Film, and New Multimedia
Global Communication and Social Change	Training and Development
Group Communication	Visual Communication
Health Communication	

Sources: National Communication Association (NCA), International Communication Association (ICA) and Association for Education in Journalism and Mass Communication (AEJMC).

By contrast, **action research** engages in research specifically to improve people's lives. The action research tradition is to be closely involved with people in order to better their lives. One school sees research as a quest for knowledge, and the other sees research as an engaged contribution to bettering society. In both cases, the researcher's behavior has ethical implications, as we shall see in Chapter 3.

The Approach—Objective or Subjective?

Can research be objective? **Social scientists** often bring the assumption of an external "real" world that can be observed, understood, and agreed on to the study of human interaction. For example, they assume that concepts such as intelligence or loyalty can be found across all people and measured objectively with an "instrument" that will apply universally and perhaps even predict human behavior.

By contrast, phenomenologists and ethnographers try to understand people's subjective worlds. They have an interpretive perspective in that they seek to understand how humans interpret or make sense of events in their lives. They assume that concepts such as intelligence or loyalty are indeed just concepts and are defined subjectively by the people they are researching, not to mention by researchers themselves. Such concepts vary from culture to culture, and from individual to individual. For example, simple interpersonal behaviors such as holding hands, kissing, or embracing may have widely different interpretations from culture to culture. The phenomenologist may observe a behavior such as kissing but really want to know what that action means for the individuals involved. There is no assumption that such behavior has a universal meaning.

The Perspective—Your Questions or Their Answers?

All researchers have a fundamental perspective that frames their research. Imagine, for example, that this is your research question: "Do men and women view social media differently?" To get an answer to such a question, researchers have two basic options. The first is to ask men and women a series of specific questions that will provide an answer to the researcher's question. Often, these might be survey-type questions such as "On a scale of 1 through 10, where 1 is not at all important and 10 is extremely important, how would you rate the importance of social media in your life?" Typically, this would be one of many such questions aimed at assessing how or why social media is used, how many hours a day participants spend on social media, and so on.

This approach may well answer the researcher's question but completely fail to capture how users feel about social media. For example, if users see social media primarily as entertainment, it may never occur to them to describe social media as "important." A second option, then, is to elicit respondents' views of social media in their own words—typically a qualitative process.

Another basic research decision, then, is whether to get answers to specific questions you have or whether to elicit people's views in their own language—not quite knowing what you might get.

The Sample—Large or Small?

How many people do you need to talk to in order to know that you have "an accurate picture" of a communication phenomenon? Public opinion researchers can answer that question: For an accurate view of adult public opinion in the United States, you need about 1,200 randomly selected people—as long as you can live with something like plus or minus 3% error.

"True enough," the small-sample people might reply, "but counting gives you only numbers and knowledge, not understanding. Will a survey of the thousands of people affected by weather, hunger, or a down-sliding economy give us any more understanding of how people communicate about such events than an in-depth interview with one family? You know what's going on, but you don't know why or how people feel about it or explain it. That is why one solid series of interviews with a few people can give a better grasp on a situation than all of the thousand-people surveys that the big-sample people can conduct."

The Data—Quantitative or Qualitative?

Are humans storytelling animals, counting animals, or both?

Numbers are important; they are how democracies and committees make decisions. Count the vote; the majority wins. Numbers and counting are an important component of scientific methods, and the number of research findings in agreement with each other helps to suggest the current "truth" of the findings.

Researchers with interests in human subjectivity respond that the complexities and subtleties of interpersonal attraction or use of social media cannot be captured in mere numbers. The "truth" can best be understood by listening to what research participants and researchers themselves have to tell us. By extension, there may well be more than one "truth" or understanding of an issue or situation.

Few of the above "either-or" distinctions are clear-cut. For example, a passionately involved action researcher could use objective social science methods to study a problem. Or the survey questions that a numbers-oriented methodologist asks could be based on extensive initial qualitative interviewing. The storytelling or counting ideas have been presented here as "either-or" to help you think about where you stand on such issues. In practice, many of the seeming opposites blend together. The most obvious blending is in the approach called **triangulation** in which researchers use multiple methods providing multiple perspectives to ensure that they have a good "fix" on a problem.

For example, in trying to understand how family life interacts with television viewing, a researcher might survey several families on their use of and attitudes toward television, interview a few family members in depth, live with one family as members watch television, and conduct a content analysis of television content to determine how content shapes the family's interactions and vice versa. Advertising executives will frequently pretest or pilot a commercial with a focus group before running the advertisement and then assessing results with a large-scale survey.

Approaches such as **Q methodology** assume that it is respondents' subjective views of the world that are of interest but combine that research focus with quantitative, computational approaches to recording and assessing these views.

In Chapter 2, we will argue that "Quantitative or qualitative?" should not be an initial decision about your research but rather one that comes after you have decided on the purpose of your research and the assumptions behind it.

The Report—Subjective or Objective?

Just as there are different ways of doing research, there are different ways of writing research. Researchers interested in interpreting the subjective world of their informants may use the primarily qualitative languages of ethnomethodology and phenomenology and report what their informants have to tell them in their informants' own words. By contrast, social science researchers typically use statistics to report and interpret the data they have collected.

The involved researcher may unabashedly use "I" writing as in "I lived with Thomas and his two children for three months, and we formed a warm social bond that had us eating together, watching movies together, and exchanging seasonal gifts." Dispassionate researchers will report in a language that strives for neutrality and that removes them from the narrative altogether—thus, "Subjects were recorded on video and their facial expressions analyzed for changes in response to visual stimuli." Critics of this style will point out that such a dispassionate style is in itself a persuasive strategy aimed at convincing the reader of the author's credibility as a researcher.

The subjectively involved researcher believes that credibility and reporting are enhanced by including personal experiences and reactions. We are getting "the truth, the whole truth, and nothing but the truth." The dispassionate researcher believes credibility is maximized by objective reporting "uncontaminated" by sentiment and value judgments (ignoring perhaps the idea that to adopt this style of writing is in itself a value judgment).

Research and research reporting both are communication activities framed by disciplinary standards and expectations, ethical decisions, and personal motivations. As critical theorists would point out, published and topical research carries a "metamessage" about what research topics are "hot," what approaches are in vogue, and who the current "stars" are.

The fact that research has an argumentative component does not necessarily mean it is adversarial. The academic journals in which research is published reflect ongoing discussions about research. A research study may be followed by responses, critiques, and other studies that change our thinking about it. You can think of articles in the scholarly communication journals (some listed at the end of this chapter) as a considered, continuing worldwide conversation among researchers on how best to understand human communication.

As we will see in Chapter 2, communication research has many different starting points, purposes, and basic assumptions. It inescapably involves ethical decisions. The following ethics panel and the ones in each chapter will give you a sense of the ethical decisions you may face as a researcher. You should try to reason through to a decision for each of the ethics problems, as they are typical of the decisions you may face when doing your own research. For help with these ethics panels, read Chapter 3, "Ethics: What Are My Responsibilities as a Researcher?"

ETHICS PANEL
A HEALTH COMMUNICATION DILEMMA

Suppose that a public health agency wants to determine the best way to help people identify the symptoms of diabetes, so they can take preventive measures and better deal with the condition if they are diagnosed as diabetic.

To do this, the agency hires your research firm to find out how best to get messages about diabetes to the public. You decide to run a three-group experiment in which people in county A will receive messages about diabetes by traditional mass media (newspapers, television, and radio) and social media. People in county B will receive intensive interpersonal communication about diabetes through neighborhood meetings, counseling, and their workplaces. People in county C will receive no messages because you need a "baseline" against which to measure whether your interventions in counties A and B have any effect. As a result of this study, you will be able to develop effective communication programs for your region.

What are the ethical implications, if any, of not providing people in county C with information that might save a life?

Chapter Summary

This chapter introduced the ways scholars think about communication research, their main areas of research, and the methods they use. In summary:

- Communication research is a process of posing questions about human communication and designing and implementing research that will answer those questions.

- Communication researchers typically specialize in one aspect of communication.

- Researchers may use qualitative methods, quantitative methods, or both.

- Researchers have empirical, interpretive, or critical perspectives on communication.

- Human communication research inescapably involves ethical decisions.

Key Terms

action research 15
appeals 11

Q methodology 16
social scientists 15

triangulation 16

Application Exercises

The application exercises you will find at the end of each chapter are warm-up exercises or mental experiments you can do to help you translate the chapter principles into research practice. For example, the following application exercises will help you identify and refine your thinking about your own research interests.

Research is much more than simply finding a topic area and questions that interest you. You must also, for example, choose a research method or methods that will give you the data you need to answer your research questions.

For example, observing people, interviewing them, and analyzing message content are all valid research methods, but we must also consider the positives and negatives of each method in order to choose the one most likely to provide credible data. For example, in relation to the student conversations earlier in this chapter, you might consider such issues as these:

- If you interview a group, won't each member tell you only what he or she wants the rest of the group to hear? Would you be better off interviewing each member separately?

- Would questionnaires give you more honest answers because you are not interviewing face to face? Or could the time and effort required to complete a questionnaire mean that you would get less than full answers?

- Does listening in on a private conversation raise ethical issues? If so, shouldn't you introduce yourself and ask permission to listen in? Might your presence then change the nature of the conversation?

Exercise 1: Finding Research Questions

This chapter begins with interactions among students in a campus coffee bar. Based on these interactions, comments from the "ASA," and your reading of this chapter, identify as many research questions as you can about human communication behavior. Think freely and broadly. No question is irrelevant at this stage of your thinking, and one may well be the spark that ignites a long-term research interest for you.

Exercise 2: Exploring Communication Interest Areas

One way to develop your own interests is to go to the websites of two of the major communication research associations—the National Communication Association (NCA) and the International Communication Association (ICA)—listed in this chapter's recommended web resources. At the NCA site, on the "About NCA" menu, look for "What is Communication?" Then expand the "Areas of Specialization" section. At the ICA site, look for "Divisions" and "Interest Groups" under the "Groups" menu item. In both cases, you will find a list of the specific interest groups for each association. The interest areas that overlap will give you a sense of the "mainstream" fields of research, and either list may spark your interest in an area that perhaps you were not previously aware of.

Exercise 3: The Internet and American Life

Access the website for the Pew Research Center's Internet & Technology division, listed below under "Recommended Web Resources." Locate a March 2018 survey report titled *Social Media Use in 2018*. At the report site you will find the full report, the questionnaire, and the data from which the report was compiled. From the questionnaire, select two questions that interest you, ask the same questions of 10 people you know, convert your answers into percentages, and compare your results with the Pew Center results. For example, questions 1 and 2 in the survey ask respondents which social media they use and the frequency of use of those media. The third question asks respondents how difficult it would be to give up their televisions, smart phones, Internet, and social media.

Do your results differ from those reported by the Pew Center? If so, how? Why do you think your results differ? What might you do to improve the credibility of your results?

Exercise 4: Improving the Effectiveness of Health and Safety Messages

The Ad Council reports that its "Friends Don't Let Friends Drive Drunk" campaign began in 1983 and that alcohol-related traffic fatalities dropped to an all-time low in 1998, after which they began to rise again.

From a communication perspective, what research would you suggest would be needed to establish with confidence a relationship between anti–drunk-driving campaigns and alcohol-related traffic statistics?

The Ad Council's strategy, as of 2017, regarding "buzzed driving" is to prompt viewers to examine their own warning signs of impairment and take responsibility for their decisions behind the wheel. The focus shifts from "friends" to the driver, with the tagline "Probably Okay isn't Okay" intended to plant a seed of doubt and to remind drivers to find a safe way home if they've been drinking.

What research might you do to find out how likely it is that this message strategy will work? What alternate message strategies might be more effective?

For both questions, you can get additional information at https://www.adcouncil.org/Our-Campaigns/Safety/Buzzed-Driving-Prevention.

Recommended Reading

There are many books and journals available on communication research, as a visit to your campus library will indicate. Many journals, ranging in focus from administrative theory to women's studies, may also report on human communication. A few key journal titles are listed below. Chapter 4, "You Could Look It Up: Reading, Recording, and Reviewing Research," will move us on to developing more relevant, targeted lists of readings.

General

Communication and Critical/Cultural Studies

Communication Monographs

Communication Research

Human Communication Research

Journal of Applied Communication Research

Quarterly Journal of Speech

Mass Communication

Critical Studies in Media Communication
Journal of Public Relations Research
Journalism & Mass Communication Quarterly
Quarterly Review of Film and Video
Television & New Media

Organizational Communication

Academy of Management Review
Administrative Science Quarterly
Business and Professional Communication Quarterly
Journal of Organizational Culture, Communications and Conflict
Management Communication Quarterly

Group Communication

Group Analysis
Group & Organization Management

Group Dynamics: Theory, Research, and Practice
Group Processes & Intergroup Relations
Small Group Research

Interpersonal Communication

Human Relations
Journal of Applied Psychology
Journal of Family Communication
Journal of Research in Personality
Journal of Social and Personal Relationships

Social Media

Convergence: The International Journal of Research into New Media Technologies
Cyberpsychology, Behavior, and Social Networking
Journal of Computer-Mediated Communication
Journal of Magazine and New Media Research
New Media & Society

Recommended Web Resources

Note: The websites recommended in this and subsequent chapters are a mix of scholarly and commercial sites. They may or may not require a fee or membership for access. Inclusion does not imply endorsement, and no criticism of similar resources not listed is intended or implied.

Association for Education in Journalism and Mass Communication (AEJMC)..........www.aejmc.org
Canadian Communication Association...........www.acc-cca.ca
Human Communication Research Centre (HCRC), University of Edinburgh...........www.hcrc.ed.ac.uk
International Communication Association (ICA)...........www.icahdq.org
National Communication Association (NCA)...........www.natcom.org

Defining the boundaries of human communication studies is difficult and a debate in its own right. The ICA, NCA, and AEJMC are three of several U.S. academic associations devoted to the study of communication. Looking at their websites will give you an idea of the many areas of research specialization under the "communication umbrella." By contrast, the HCRC site shows one of many institutions in which communication studies are being reconceptualized by bringing together such fields as computing, philosophy, psychology, and language studies.

Pew Research Center, Internet & Technology...........www.pewinternet.org

The Pew Research Center's Internet & Technology division studies how Americans use the Internet and how their online activities affect their lives. The project uses nationwide random phone surveys, online surveys, and qualitative research, along with data from government agencies, technology firms, academia, and other expert venues. You should become familiar with this site, and with the Pew Research Center more generally, as we will refer to it throughout this book.

References

Shannon, C. W., & Weaver, W. (1949). *The mathematical theory of communication*. Urbana: University of Illinois Press.

$SAGE edge™

Get the tools you need to sharpen your study skills. SAGE edge offers a robust online environment featuring an impressive array of free tools and resources.

Access quizzes, eFlashcards, video, and multimedia at **edge.sagepub.com/treadwell4e**.

FIRST DECISIONS

From Inspiration to Implementation

"Prof. Michaels, I'm worried about getting a comm. research topic."

"Well, as I told Carlos last semester, start by just looking around. There's everything from social media sites involving millions of people down to looking at how two best friends interact."

"OK, but I don't see how I get focused down to one topic."

"Well, all research starts from an interest; first decide what interests you. Then look at what's doable."

"Meaning what?"

"First, you'll want to get comfortable with one or more research methods. Second, be practical. You have to get finished by the end of semester, right? Let's say you're interested in students' attitudes to current politics. I'd research just one small group instead of say an entire class year or everyone in your major. You could also decide to look at local politics only rather than national politics or vice versa.

Also think about why you're doing your research, your methods, and what use your results will be when you get them; you have to be able to justify your research.

"OK. Anything else?"

"Try to step back and figure out how your own assumptions about the world might be shaping your ideas about research."

"Now there I really need help. What's an example?"

"OK. You're an individual, right? Nobody else out there's like you?"

"So my parents keep telling me."

"So here's the question—if we're all individuals, how can you make any generalizations about people, or should you? Or think about why you believe anything. For example, can you trust your own intuition? What makes an authority an authority?"

"That's some heavy-duty stuff."

"Trust me, you're about to find more in this chapter. You do need to wrestle through stuff like this though if you're going to do defensible research."

"Thanks, Prof."

"No problem. You can catch up with me again in Chapter 10: I might need your help with some experiments I'm thinking about. See you then."

CHAPTER OVERVIEW

Getting started may be the most difficult issue of all for the beginning researcher. As we explored in Chapter 1, there are many possible starting points. Think how many questions could be generated from even the most casual overheard conversation. Of course, this is also the good news. **Research questions** are indeed all around us, and identifying some questions about topics that interest you is a good start. You might even have good ideas about how to answer those questions, especially if you have jumped ahead to some other chapters in this book.

Appropriate research methods are those that best match your theories about human communication and the type of data you intend to collect. Behind every research project are assumptions and decisions that you cannot escape about the nature of human communication and of research.

This chapter discusses four important aspects of getting to the research starting line. The first is the basic assumptions that underpin communication research. As you will see in the following sections, your research will be unavoidably based on your assumptions about human communication and people more generally. For example, a basic assumption that we are all individuals makes it difficult to argue that your research findings can be generalized to other individuals. We will discuss such assumptions and their implications for research under "Starting With Basic Beliefs and Perspectives."

Second is deciding on a focus. There are two fundamentally different ways of doing this. Just as you can dine out knowing in advance precisely what you want to eat or deciding to be open to whatever the chef's special might be, so too you can focus your research with specifically worded research questions and **hypotheses** or you can let the world come to you and be open as to what you might find. We discuss these approaches under "Deciding on a Focus."

Third is deciding on the purpose of your research. Most scholars are ultimately motivated by a desire to understand human communication, but the specific "whys" of research can be as varied as human motivations. Every research study starts with a purpose, be it testing a sophisticated theoretical concept or attempting to get an A in a research course. Peer pressure, "first-to-publish" pressure, ego, or financial incentives may all motivate researchers. This topic is further discussed under "Starting With a Purpose."

Last but not least is the question of a research topic itself. The interest areas presented in Chapter 1 will help you with this. In this chapter, under "Starting With Ideas and Observations," we suggest that you can also use the basic "who," "what," "when," "where," "why," and "how" questions to get started.

By moving between basic assumptions about human communication and your interest areas and by considering your degree of focus and the purpose of your research, you should arrive at a sound research proposal with a defensible match among theory, method, and the data you plan to collect.

This chapter will help you

- Define the terms induction, deduction, and abduction.

- Identify key reasons for doing research.

- Explain the ways we "know what we know."

- Describe major worldviews in human communication research and how each shapes the nature of research.

- Discuss the advantages and disadvantages of basing your work on the work of other researchers.

- Explain with examples the difference between a research question and a hypothesis.

STARTING WITH BASIC BELIEFS AND PERSPECTIVES

Let's start with the basic beliefs and perspectives that shape our thinking about human behavior and therefore how we might research it. What ultimately do we believe about humans and their behaviors? Are people all alike or fundamentally different—each of us an individual? Are we predictable or unpredictable; predisposed to cooperation or to conflict; living in a shared, tangible world or in our own internal, subjective worlds? Such questions underpin the assumptions about how best to study and represent human communication.

The argument for reality as an underlying, objective, concrete entity versus reality as no more than a product of our senses is almost as old as human thought.

Generalizations and predictions about human behavior often can be made with some success, but it is equally true that many predictions fail—as political pollsters can find to their dismay. Predictions are often more successful when we observe large numbers of people rather than individuals. For example, faculty can be quite confident predicting that most students will attend class on a given day. Predicting that a specific student will attend a specific class on a specific day is a different matter altogether.

As evidence can support any and all such views, ultimately we are obliged to use our own best judgment to decide which basic beliefs will inform our research, and to live with them. Basic assumptions about human behavior coalesce into broad **worldviews** or basic sets of beliefs that underpin our perspectives on communication research.

At one extreme, Worldview I sees human behavior as predictable, objectively measurable, and generalizable. Worldview I researchers aim to make generalizations about human communication that will hold true across space and time. This emphasis on measurement and generalization is called a **nomothetic** approach.

Worldview II, by contrast, sees human behavior as individualistic, unpredictable, and subjective. This view assumes that knowledge is socially constructed out of interaction between people and is subjective. Research based on these assumptions attempts to describe and assess the subjectivity and individuality of human communication, rather than aiming to discover universal laws. This emphasis on individual understanding is called an **idiographic** approach.

Worldview I privileges the researcher's perspectives; Worldview II privileges participants' perspectives. For example, the student discussions at the beginning of each chapter are what we might call "naturally generated" or "participant generated." An external observer or researcher has had no influence on this content. However, as soon as a researcher decides to impose a method, such as a survey, on the group members, the research data are researcher generated and may have little or no resemblance to the participant-generated data.

Advertising and audience researchers subscribe to Worldview I. Researchers seek to find rules that will predict the success of interpersonal relationships, direct-marketing campaigns, or the ability of group members to work together and successfully complete a project. Television infomercials, for example, are presumably based on research indicating that using a particular type of spokesperson plus showing the product plus repeated exposure of the 1–800 phone number will maximize the number of consumer call-ins. In principle, such a generalization would apply to most products and most television audiences.

By contrast, Worldview II researchers would be interested in how consumers respond subjectively to media content. They will therefore spend time listening to individuals, with a view to capturing this subjectivity. Their goal might be, for example, to understand why some people develop a close relationship to soap opera characters or to a Second Life avatar and to investigate how these people describe those relationships. Researchers make no assumption that their findings will be generalizable and typically reject counting or measuring in favor of reporting what their interviewees said. Their overall goal is understanding rather than generalization or prediction.

Exercise 2 at the end of this chapter will help you decide which of these opposite worldviews you most identify with.

Between the two extremes of Worldview I and Worldview II are more nuanced views of human communication and how to research it.

For example, Creswell and Creswell (2018) identify four worldviews, as follows:

- **Postpositive.** This worldview challenges the notion of absolute truth but emphasizes cause and effect and the idea that the world is governed by laws or theories that can be tested or verified. Big ideas are reduced to sets of data that allow hypothesis testing. Theory leads to data collection and then to testing of the theory using quantitative methods. The emphasis is on objective observation and measurement.

- **Constructivist.** This worldview is that individuals seek understanding of the world in which they live and construct their own views of it. Researchers therefore rely on participants' own, subjective views of the world and use qualitative methods to capture them. Research is interpretive and qualitative, moving inductively from observation to theory development.

- **Transformative.** This worldview is change oriented and argues for mixing research with politics to confront social oppression and change lives for the better. There is a basic interest in the marginalized and disenfranchised. The worldview embraces a variety of research interests, including action research and critical analyses.

- **Pragmatism.** This worldview focuses on solutions to problems—what works—and using all possible approaches to understanding these problems. It does not commit to any one basic philosophy and therefore embraces mixed-method research. It is "real world" and practice oriented with a focus on the problem rather than the research method. Research decisions are based on what the researchers want to do with their research—on why they are doing it.

To further fine-tune your ideas, consider Craig's (1999) communication **metatheory**—a family of concepts embracing several different traditions of communication research.

- **Rhetorical.** This tradition considers the practical art of discourse, debate, or discussion; it emphasizes the use and power of words.

- **Semiotic.** This tradition focuses on the uses and interpretations of signs and symbols; it emphasizes the study of how meanings are constructed and the relationships between words and symbols—and thought.

- **Phenomenological.** This tradition considers the experience of others; it emphasizes the study of objects and events as they are perceived, in other words, the study of the meanings that things have as experienced phenomena, as opposed to the nature of the things themselves.

- **Cybernetic.** This tradition focuses on the flow of information; it emphasizes communication as a system of information processing and feedback. The basic source-message-channel-receiver model introduced in Chapter 1 is in this category.

- **Sociopsychological.** This tradition focuses on the interaction of individuals; it emphasizes attitudes and perceptions and individuals influencing each other or working toward collective outcomes.

- **Sociocultural.** This tradition considers the production and reproduction of social order; it emphasizes the ways in which shared meanings and social structures are produced and reproduced through communication. Its focus is conflict, alienation, and the individual as products of society.

- **Critical.** This tradition focuses on power, the perpetuation of power, oppression, and emancipation in society; it challenges common assumptions.

Craig also suggests other perspectives that might be considered—for example, you might also view communication from feminist, aesthetic, economic, or spiritual perspectives.

The research method you select should follow logically from your basic assumptions about human behavior and communication. For example, a Worldview I researcher who believes that people's thinking can be measured and that careful sampling will allow her to generalize results from a small sample to a large number of people may ask "What type of survey can I run?" A Worldview II researcher interested in hearing people's subjective experiences in their own words is more likely to ask "What focus groups or interviews will I need?" and will use theory-based judgment rather than statistical sampling to select participants. The first researcher will use quantitative methods by virtue of her worldview; the second will prefer qualitative approaches.

There is no inherent reason that one perspective on human communication should be privileged over others anymore than one specific research method should be privileged. Rather, the focus and the method of research are the outcome of the researchers' interests and assumptions about research.

The first question, then, is not whether to prefer qualitative over quantitative methods. Rather, it is "What are my basic assumptions about human communication?" The answer to this question should drive the decisions about the nature of the data to be gathered and therefore the research methods to be employed.

Foundational beliefs and arguments about human behavior are issues ultimately of **ontology**, which addresses the nature of what we study. Ontological questions deal with the nature of existence and what language actually refers to. In communication studies, ontology wrestles with assumptions about the nature of human communication and what we "really" observe when we observe it.

For example, have you ever seen someone's attitude? You might answer, "Yes, many times." But what have you really seen? What you have really seen is someone behaving in a particular way, being verbally aggressive perhaps. Or perhaps all you saw were check marks on attitude scales, from which you infer an attitude. Where is the attitude itself? Is there, in fact, such as thing as an attitude?

Ontological questions for communication scholars include "To what extent do we make real choices?" For example, is your decision to attend class voluntary or not? Is human experience primarily individual or societal—what would you know of the world and of yourself if you had no interaction with other people? Is communication contextual or universal—does a smile always mean the same thing to everybody or does the meaning depend on who is smiling and under what conditions?

The Relationship Between Theory and Observations

A theory or generalization about communication is weak if not supported by evidence, so researchers move between theory and observation. They may start with a theory that needs testing with observations, or they may have observations that lead them to construct or reconstruct a theory. Three thought processes that link observations with theories are induction, deduction, and abduction.

Induction

Induction is reasoning from observations to a theory that might explain your observations. Induction moves from the specific to the general. Let's go back to Chapter 1, in which we dropped in on students socializing. As an observer, you might make a note of communication behaviors such as the following:

- Gender clustering—males are more likely to sit with males, and females to sit with females.

- Class distinction—upper-class students are more likely than first- or second-year students to socialize in the coffee bar.

What theories might explain these observations? You might think of several. For your gender-clustering observation, you might theorize that

- Students have a greater comfort level with same-sex than with opposite-sex conversations.

- Male and female students have already formed separate social groups by virtue of being in separate campus housing units.

For your class-distinction observation, you might theorize that

- Upper-class students are more likely to have jobs, grants, or fellowships, so they can afford to socialize and drink handcrafted coffees.

- Upper-class students are more likely to live off campus, and meeting on campus is the only way to get group projects done.

Having generated several such theories, you could then design a study that would help you decide which theory offers the best explanation of the phenomenon.

Deduction

By contrast, **deduction** moves from a theory to defining the observations you will make to test the theory; it moves from the general to the specific. For example, you might have some reason to theorize that women are more likely than men to discuss grades and academic performance. You would then design a study to capture the observations that would test this idea. In this case, your research might involve recording the conversations of both men and women and counting for each group the number of times words such as *grade, grade point average,* or *assignment* occur. If you could then show that the frequency of these words is greater in women's conversations than in men's, your theory would be supported—except for two big "ifs."

First, you will want to be confident that your statement is true for all female students, not just the small group you observed. Second, you will want to know that this pattern you observed is true at all times, not just for the one discussion you happened to observe, perhaps as final examinations were approaching. This is where appropriate sampling (Chapter 6) can help us.

Deduction is in a sense more efficient than induction in that it leads to a specific observation that will test your **hypothesis**—the statement about the relationships you expect to find. Having completed that test, you can then move on to another hypothesis. With induction, you have a further step: finding a way to decide which of the many possible theories you induced from your observations are correct. Induction requires the confidence that you have enough observations to support your conclusion and that you can rule out all the other conclusions that might also be derived from your observations.

Abduction

In the context of research, **abduction** refers not to being kidnapped by aliens from the planet Zog but rather to reasoning from an effect to possible causes. For example, a large group of young children in the campus coffee bar would be an unusual sight. That occurrence might raise some questions, but a perfectly plausible answer might be that university employees are participating in a "bring your children to work" day. With abduction, your starting point is an effect from which you reason back to possible causes. In this example, your research project would be to find out whether there is such an event on campus that explains your observation or if there are other events that offer a more plausible explanation.

STARTING WITH A FOCUS

Starting with a focus is a broader question than just deciding on a specific method. It is a question of being open to whatever the world of human communication might have to tell us versus approaching that world with very targeted preformulated questions.

You can opt to begin your study with no prior assumptions—to the extent that this is possible. For example, here is how organizational culture researchers Evered and Reis (1981) described their process of finding out about a new organization:

> We were "probing in the dark" into the hidden organizational realities around us, in many directions simultaneously. . . . We did not form and test explicit hypotheses, we did not do a literature search, we had no elaborate instruments, and we did not use sample statistics or draw inferences at the ".05 level of significance." In comparison to the idealized scientific method, the process we used to make sense of our organization was a messy, iterative groping through which we gradually, though quite rapidly, built up a picture of the organizational system of which we were a part. (p. 387)

This is an approach that has almost no initial focus other than being theoretically informed, but it builds a picture of human communication, impression by impression, until the researchers have a full picture that allows them to make statements confidently about the topic that interests them.

Research Questions: Less Certainty; More Room to Move

One way to focus more precisely on a topic is to pose research questions, as shown below. (In this text, we follow a style of *RQ* and *H* to denote research questions and hypotheses, respectively.)

Open-ended research questions basically ask whether there is a relationship between variables. Here's an example:

RQ_1: Is there a relationship between involvement in video gaming and academic performance?

Closed-ended research questions focus on a direction of the relationship, as does this example:

RQ_2: Does academic performance decline as involvement in video gaming increases?

Starting with an open-ended research question, such as RQ_1, is appropriate for the exploratory study you would conduct when you don't have a lot of evidence as to what might be going on. With additional evidence, you can question the direction of the relationship between variables, as in RQ_2.

With still further evidence or theoretical support, you may be able to predict a relationship and to write that prediction in the form of a hypothesis.

Hypotheses: Statements of Prediction

Hypotheses are statements about the relationship that we expect to find between variables.

Two-tailed hypotheses state that there is a relationship between variables but do not specify the direction of the relationship. For example:

> H_1: There is a relationship between level of involvement in video gaming and academic performance.

One-tailed hypotheses require extra confidence because you commit to predicting the direction of the relationship between the variables, as in the following:

> H_2: As time spent in video gaming increases, academic performance decreases.

Null hypotheses, usually symbolized as H_0, specify that there is no relationship between variables. Here is an example:

> H_0: There is no relationship between level of involvement in video gaming and academic performance.

Isn't a null hypothesis self-apparent? Yes and no. Basically, the null hypothesis makes explicit the notion that we are always working with two hypotheses—the first that the relationship we suspect exists; the second that it does not (the null hypothesis). The null hypothesis proposes there is no relationship between variables other than what we would find by chance. The probability of getting the results we did can be calculated, as we shall see in Chapter 8. Based on that probability, we can then decide which of these two hypotheses to accept, and which to reject.

Preferring a hypothesis over a research question gives you the advantage of focusing your study because you have said with some level of confidence "I know what's going on." Your study then becomes an exercise in determining whether or not your hypothesis is supported.

A research question, on the other hand, is more speculative. You sense that something is going on, but you may need to be more open-minded in your research design in order to capture relationships you had not anticipated.

Hypotheses and research questions have the advantage of focusing your research and, importantly, telling you what you do not need to focus on. But both may do so at the cost of blinding you to relevant and important phenomena outside your immediate focus. This essentially is the argument for the Evered and Reis (1981) "probing in the dark" approach outlined previously.

Operationalizing Constructs

If you are concerned with measurement and precision in your observations, getting started requires that you identify key **constructs** and **operationalize** them. Constructs are ideas or concepts. Operationalizing them means to define them in such a way that they can be measured. For example, let's suppose that you are interested in the relationship between playing video games and academic performance. You observe individuals who are heavily involved in such games. You conclude inductively that such people keep weird hours and some have peculiar personal habits, but that could be true for any group of people, gamers or not.

Deductively, you reason through to two contrary conclusions. First, time spent on gaming must detract from time spent on studying. Therefore, gaming must be detrimental to academic performance. On the other hand, gaming appears to need mental agility, the ability to think fast and to make decisions, and imagination. Deductively, it seems that gaming ought to have a positive effect on academic performance.

You have identified two important ideas or constructs—involvement in gaming and academic performance. You think that there is a relationship between them; you're just not sure what that relationship is.

To operationalize these constructs means to define them in a way that other researchers could replicate your study. Now comes a question of how we operationalize these constructs—that is, define what they mean in practice.

Exhibit 2.1 shows some of the ways the two constructs could be operationalized or made measurable. We have taken ideas (mental constructions or "constructs") and translated them into observable operations that can be measured.

At the heart of many studies is a decision as to what measures will be used. Intuitively, some of the measures shown in Exhibit 2.1 appear to do a better job than others. Grade point average, for example, is a widely though not totally accepted measure of academic performance. On the other hand, membership in a gaming club or amount of money spent on games may have little or no relationship to whether an individual is an active game player. Of all the options, a best guess might be that time spent on gaming is the best measure of involvement as long as we can measure it accurately. (Note, however, the assumption that objective measurement of time spent is going to be the most relevant or useful measure. It could well turn out that gamers' subjective ratings of time spent [e.g., "not much time" or "most of my time"] have greater explanatory power than an objective measure such as "hours per week.")

EXHIBIT 2.1 ■ Operationalizing Constructs	
Construct	
Involvement in Gaming	**Academic Performance**
Operationalizing the Constructs	
Time spent on gaming	Class rank
Money spent on gaming	Number of academic awards
Number of memberships in gaming clubs	Current grade point average
Number of online "personas" or avatars	Cumulative grade point average
Percentage of time spent with other gamers	Class participation as rated by faculty
Number of gaming software titles owned	Class attendance as recorded by faculty
Percentage of gaming terms used in conversation	Number of memberships in academic honor societies

These constructs or concepts have now been operationalized into **variables**. Variables are capable of being measured or taking on a value. In other words, they can vary. The constructs "gaming" or "academic performance" cannot be measured; the variables "time spent on gaming" and "grade point average" can.

Hypotheses and, more specifically, the process of operationalization have the advantage of focusing your research, but you may not be able to focus your research initially, or indeed want to.

For some researchers, the specificity of hypothesis testing is its own weakness. Researchers out of the **ethnomethodology** and **phenomenology** traditions especially would argue that complex human behavior cannot be simplified into variables as we did with our hypothetical video game study. They may further argue that finding a relationship between two variables provides no explanation of why the relationship exists and oversimplifies complex relationships by focusing on a few variables rather than on the multitude of influences on human behavior. Fundamentally, they are interested in rich description that provides understanding rather than a simple "yes, there is a relationship" answer to their questions. We will examine such approaches to communication more fully in Chapter 13.

"My method beats your method" arguments take place repeatedly and heatedly in research circles, but your reading of this chapter should have you understanding that one method never "beats" another method except in the context of the research. The real question is this—"Is your research method theoretically and practically appropriate for the research you want to do?" Or, to put it another way, "Can you make defensible connections among your theory, your method(s), and the data you plan to collect?"

As you will see from Exhibit 2.2, there should be a match between assumptions about human communication and the most appropriate approaches to studying it. This does not preclude mixing methods. For example, researchers in health communication may spend a great deal of time with adolescents who drive and text in order to understand fully and qualitatively what texting means in the adolescents' own terms. This subjective information could then be used to develop **scaled questions** for quantitative analysis in a broader survey of young people's risky driving behavior.

STARTING WITH A PURPOSE

In addition to the personal motivations that may drive an individual's research, research has several broad purposes—exploration, description, explanation, prediction, control, interpretation, and criticism.

Exploration

Exploration is curiosity-based research. You start down a path that may lead who knows where, but that's OK. You have a commendable curiosity to learn more. Good starting points here will be targeted library research (so you don't "reinvent the wheel"), discussions with those who share your interests, and your own initial observations.

"I wonder why the residents of two dorms have such different lifestyles" or "Students don't phone each other nearly as much as they used to" could be the beginning of your research career in organizational cultures or communication and technology, respectively.

Exploratory research typically results in descriptions of what you are interested in. The description may be quantitative or qualitative. For example, based on observations and surveys of a student group, we might summarize them statistically in terms of gender, major, class year, choice of drink, topic of conversation, or campus address. But the study could also be qualitative as we interview each person and report, in the words of the students themselves, what it means to be a student, what it means to socialize with others, or how the ambience of a preferred coffee bar helps them get work done.

At this beginning phase of a research program, a researcher is more likely to be writing broad questions than specific hypotheses. Hypotheses—specific statements about what the researcher expects to find—will come later as the researcher gathers the data and develops the theory that will form the basis for such a statement.

Description

Description, especially rich descriptions of people's lives, can be compelling reading. Indeed, one test of a good description of human behavior is that it *is* compelling reading. But description does tend to leave us wanting more—in particular, wanting an answer to the "why" question. For example, reporting that women are more likely than men to discuss their grades is informative but does leave us wondering why.

Explanation

Studies focused on **explanation** attempt to answer the "why" question. For example, your observations might indicate that women are more likely than men to socialize over coffee after class. Your interviews with them might lead you to the discoveries that more women than men live off campus and that socializing after class is the easiest way to get group projects organized. Thus, what was observed to be a primarily female social behavior is explained in terms of housing status and meeting face to face as a preferred way of getting work organized.

Prediction

Generally, our explanations have greater credibility if they are capable of **prediction**. There is an intellectual satisfaction in obtaining research results that predict human behavior and confirm a theory. There is also an understandable demand from almost every sector of society for research that allows the prediction of human behavior. For example, political communication consultants want to know what appeals will predictably move swing voters toward a particular candidate.

The conclusion we arrived at about female students drinking coffee is reasoned and verifiable based on observation, but our theory would be even more impressive if it could predict this behavior. In principle, testing the predictive power of this theory is easily done. We could devise an experiment in which we give the same group project to equal numbers of on- and off-campus students. If our theory is correct, we should see more off-campus students in the coffee bar, discussing how to get the project done. Note, though, that this design is weak because it does not rule out other explanations. For example, we cannot rule out the possibility that the students we see meeting have bad Internet access, and it is this fact rather than housing status per se that explains their need to meet in person. We discuss how to strengthen such experimental designs in Chapter 10.

Control

Another goal of research may be control. In the physical world, control means researching with a view to being able to predict and manipulate physical processes such as digital recording, combustion, or space flights. In the case of human communication, advertisers, for example, want to be able to control audience responses to advertising, broadcasting, or direct mail. Their interest is in knowing how best to motivate viewers to watch a particular program, purchase a product, or open a piece of direct mail. Industry journals such as *Advertising Age*, *Marketing News*, *Broadcasting & Cable*, and *Adweek* contain such advice on how to "control" audiences, frequently in the form of "if-then" ideas. "If you make your direct mail piece an unusual shape, then it will attract more readers" is an example of this genre of advice given to establish audience control.

Interpretation

Interpretive studies can be understood as attempts to place yourself "in the other person's shoes." In other words, the researcher attempts to understand human communication from the point of view of the people doing it. For example, what does meeting with student colleagues to get coffee really mean for those doing it? Is this an opportunity to set up dates for the weekend, to engage in intimate conversation with significant others, to clarify a difficult concept in the communication theory course, to get work organized, or some combination of these? Our interest as researchers is not to impose our own interpretation but to capture the interpretations of those involved and to present these interpretations so that our research audience will get an accurate understanding. Almost by definition, this overarching purpose will mean reporting the results of your research in the language of your research participants.

In the interpretive frame of mind, the researcher's questions focus on the language in use and its meaning.

In the case of a student group working on a class project, the research interest thus becomes "What does the group mean by 'meeting for coffee'?" Obviously, a campus coffee bar provides a common meeting place and the coffee provides a social lubricant, but tea, fruit juice, and soda will also be on the drinks list, so "meeting for coffee" is to be understood not literally as a thirst-quenching experience but, most likely, as a metaphor for something else. What is that something else? Careful listening of the type discussed in Chapter 13 will tell us.

Under the interpretive umbrella, we are more likely to write open-ended research questions because we need to be open to whatever our research participants may want to tell us rather than seeking a simple confirmation or disconfirmation of a hypothesis generated by the researcher.

Criticism

The basic quest of critical theorists is to understand and explain the way in which communication is used to exercise and maintain power in groups, organizations, and societies. To this end, critical researchers might look, for example, at the way in which organizational structures and processes prevent or facilitate the progress of certain groups within the organization. In the case of our campus coffee bar, the critical researcher might ask these questions. Do coffee-drinking rituals perpetuate and reinforce class or gender distinctions? Can males join a female discussion group? Are there informal rules that say first-year students cannot mix with senior

EXHIBIT 2.2 ■ Assumptions About Human Communication and Their Research Implications	
Assumptions About Human Communication	**Research Implications**
People are generally similar, predictable, and motivated by events, personality type, and other people. We can make generalizations about their behavior.	Surveys, experiments, and other quantitative methods allow for precision in reporting and generalizations to populations from smaller samples.
Each person is unique, unpredictable, and self-motivated. We cannot make generalizations about his or her behavior.	Ethnography, interviews, and observations allow for insight, understanding, and the authenticity of each research participant's own language.

students? Does an individual's language define him or her as a member of an in-group or an out-group?

The basic starting point of critical research is the assumption that power structures exist in society or organizations and are reinforced and perpetuated by behavior and language. This basic assumption allows the critical researcher to start with general exploratory questions or to propose specific hypotheses about communication behavior and language.

The research starting points outlined here may mix to a greater or lesser degree. It is possible to have explanation without prediction, and vice versa. For example, we may have a very good understanding of the dynamics of small groups but be unable to predict whether a new group will be a success or not. Or we may be able to predict the changes in language that a couple uses as they become more intimate, without necessarily understanding why this change is taking place.

STARTING WITH THE "WHAT" QUESTION

The most obvious what questions are "What shall I study?" or "What's going on here?"

Communication phenomena in the form of song lyrics, interpersonal behavior, group dynamics, social media, news coverage, and virtual realities are all around us. So a good starting point is to observe the communication phenomena you are interested in.

"Communication" is a large umbrella under which many research interests find a home. Your career interests and academic electives likely already have you heading toward a general interest area. You may find a more specific focus by looking at the websites of the scholarly communication associations listed at the end of this chapter and revisiting the communication research interest areas shown in Chapter 1, Exhibit 1.1.

Reading relevant scholarly articles is a "must." See Chapter 4, "You Could Look It Up: Reading, Recording, and Reviewing Research," for a discussion of one of your most important starting points—your academic library. Often, our interest may be triggered by a news item, a casual observation, or an occupational interest. For example, the following scholarly research may have been triggered by a casual question—"Do men and women view online dating differently?"

McGloin, R., & Denes, A. (2018). Too hot to trust: Examining the relationship between attractiveness, trustworthiness, and desire to date in online dating. *New Media & Society, 20*(3), 919–936. doi: 10.1177/1461444816675440

An interest in social media and the contentious 2016 U.S. presidential election no doubt triggered the following:

Lee, J., & Xu, W. (2018). The more attacks, the more retweets: Trump's and Clinton's agenda setting on Twitter. *Public Relations Review*, 44(2), 201–213. doi: 10.1016/j.pubrev.2017.10.002

By way of a complete contrast, how about the following?

Haynes, J. (2018). Looking for (women's) rights in all the wrong places? Country music and hillbilly feminism in the 1990s. *Feminist Media Studies, 18*(2), 315–318. doi: 10.1080/14680777.2018.1436900

While popular news and entertainment media and events plus your own observations and experiences might trigger a research interest, your academic library will provide the best examples of theoretically sound research using research methods appropriate to the task and reviewed by other researchers before publication. As Chapter 4 explains, the scholarly articles in academic databases will give you ideas about topics and appropriate research methods, point you to other relevant articles, and help you decide whether your research would help test an existing theory or be pioneering new research.

STARTING WITH "WHO," "WHERE," AND "WHEN" QUESTIONS

"Who?" pinpoints a person or a group of people as a starting point. It may suggest your interest in the rhetoric of a political or religious leader, sports celebrity, or an advocacy group. If you elect to research one person, the "who" is apparent, but with large groups of people there is usually a sampling decision, for both practical and theoretical reasons. For example, almost 20 million students attend U.S. colleges and universities (National Center for Education Statistics, 2017)—an impossible number to survey. How many of these students would you need to sample in order to be confident that your sample accurately reflects that huge population, and how would you select them? Sample and population each have a specific meaning in communication research, and we will discuss both in more detail in Chapter 6.

"Where?" suggests a geographic starting point such as how U.S. news media coverage of U.S. presidential elections differs from the coverage in, say, France or China. It may suggest a more specific location such as employee-management communication in one specific factory setting. Under the "where" umbrella, we find rhetoricians' interest in the "**rhetoric of place**"—studies that examine how public places such as museums or memorials can shape public memory and shared understandings of history and events. "Where?" may also suggest a broad disciplinary starting point, such as critical theory rather than applied communication.

"When?" suggests a point-in-time start. For example, you are interested in discovering how or if newspaper portrayals of women's suffrage differ before and after World War I or how the Vietnam War was portrayed in movies produced during the sixties and seventies. The "when" question means that you see time as a critical concept in your research. "Time" may be long term, as in examining the behavior of adolescents exposed to particular media content as children, or short term, as in analyzing how communication within a family changes over the course of a day.

STARTING WITH THE "HOW" QUESTION

"How?" may be a specific research question: "How does a web-based collaborative writing project get coordinated?" From a getting started point of view, the "How" question is more "How do I do my research; what method or methods should I select?" Many researchers start with a method preference. For example, a political communication consultant may know that monitoring Twitter or Facebook postings is the best way to track rapid changes in voter preferences and to make some generalizations about them. Or a brand consultant making recommendations on what a new product should be named may know that focus groups offer the best chance of capturing all the (mis)understandings that a new product name is capable of generating.

On its own, this "method start" is really not intellectually defensible. It is the equivalent of saying you will make a digital recording of human behavior because you know how to use the video camera on your smartphone. For experienced researchers, however, a method start is grounded in a concept of what about human communication is important to know and how best to know it. It is the track record of the method and its "fit" to the researcher's interests that make the method start defensible.

Method decisions are rooted in **epistemology**—the question of how we know what we know. We might know as a result of **tenacity**—we've always done it or understood it that way; **intuition**—the hunch or the gut instinct; **authority**—because a credible source said so; **rationalism**—logical reasoning; or **empiricism**—observation.

Scientific methods typically combine empiricism, rationalism, and **positivism** (the idea that phenomena are governed by, and can be explained by, rules). Two strengths of this approach are openness and self-correction. Openness means that a researcher's methods and data are open to inspection by other researchers, most typically in peer-reviewed publications. Self-correction means that other researchers can replicate a study. If a second study supports the first, researchers can have increased confidence in the findings.

STARTING FROM THE WORK OF OTHERS

Starting a research project without regard to the work of others is risky business. You run the risk of doing research that has already been done and therefore making no new contribution to knowledge. You will also miss out on knowing about especially relevant research methods, advances in research, and findings that might help you. Most important, perhaps, you will miss out on knowing about the research that most scholars agree is well designed and professionally executed and that makes a significant contribution to knowledge.

The easiest way to join the community of scholars who share your interests is to access academic journals regularly. Academic journals (**serials**) record in the form of articles and letters ongoing conversations among researchers. Browsing communication journals regularly will keep you up to speed with current research and ideas in your interest area.

Chapter 4 discusses this essential starting point in more detail.

ETHICS PANEL
DO SOME RESEARCH METHODS HAVE MORE ETHICAL IMPLICATIONS THAN OTHERS?

The subjectivity in human communication requires that you explore the subjective life of individuals as they report it. Typically, this means interviewing people and "probing" as to why they see things the way they do. To facilitate this process, you assure your interviewees that their confidences will be respected and that nothing you report will identify them.

As you explore the complexities of organizational culture in a major corporation, one informant, based on your assurances of confidentiality, "lets loose." You hear all about his unsatisfactory working conditions, personal life, and prospects in general. The veiled threats that emerge from the informant's interview suggest that he may become a danger to his colleagues, if not himself. What do you do?

As you walk away with a voice recorder full of statements that you have chosen to interpret as veiled threats, you contemplate the fact that, had you asked simple yes-no or multiple-choice questions, the troubling information you now have may never have surfaced.

Could it be that some research methods raise more ethical problems than others?

What is your obligation to those who might be harmed in some way if the threats you detect were to translate into action?

What is your obligation to the individual you interviewed?

What is your obligation to the research process in general? For example, should you stay away from such research because of its potential complications or be prepared to break your assurances of confidentiality when you detect potential danger to your participants or others?

You can jump ahead to Chapter 3 for some help with these questions.

Chapter Summary

- Communication researchers differ in ontology (how to define communication) and in epistemology (how best to understand communication).

- Generally, researchers assume either that human communication is objectively measurable and can be summarized in rules and generalizations or that communication is subjective and individualistic and must be described as such.

- The processes of induction, deduction, and abduction link observations to theory.

- Ways of understanding communication include tenacity, intuition, authority, and empiricism.

- The general purposes of research are description, explanation, prediction, control, interpretation, and criticism.

- Research may begin with specific hypotheses, general research questions, or no specific questions at all.

- Credible research has a logical link between the methods chosen and the assumptions that underpin them.

Key Terms

abduction 28
authority 37
closed-ended research
    questions 29
constructivist 25
constructs 30
critical 26
cybernetic 26
deduction 28
description 33
empiricism 37
epistemology 37
ethnomethodology 32
explanation 33
exploration 32
hypothesis 28

idiographic 25
induction 27
intuition 37
metatheory 26
nomothetic 24
null hypotheses 30
one-tailed hypotheses 30
ontology 27
open-ended research
    questions 29
operationalize 30
phenomenological 26
phenomenology 32
positivism 37
postpositive 25
pragmatism 26

prediction 33
rationalism 37
research questions 29
rhetoric of place 36
rhetorical 26
scaled questions 32
scientific methods 37
semiotic 26
serials 37
sociocultural 26
sociopsychological 26
tenacity 37
transformative 25
two-tailed hypotheses 30
variables 32
worldviews 24

Application Exercises

Exercise 1: Identifying Your Interests

In practice, research is often an intersection of topic interest and the appropriate methods for that topic. Use the following checklist to identify your broad topic interests and the types of research that most appeal to you.

Context
(a) Mass media and social media
(b) Organizations
(c) Groups
(d) Interpersonal
(e) Other (name it)
Data Collection
(a) Count behaviors or media content.
(b) Observe behaviors.
(c) Interview and listen.
(d) Survey.
Reason for Research
(a) Get practical results that can be used.
(b) Get results that test ideas and theories.
(c) Get results that explain power structures in society.

Relationship to Research Participants
(a) Observe objectively from a distance.
(b) Engage closely with people.

Focus of Research
(a) Study large numbers of people or media.
(b) Study a few people or media in depth.

Level of Research
(a) Study messages at "face value."
(b) "Unpack" hidden meanings behind messages.

Exercise 2: Finding Your Worldview

As discussed in this chapter, all researchers bring to their research a worldview or basic assumptions about human communication and therefore how best to study and report it.

This exercise is an opportunity for you to explore and identify your own basic worldview. Following are a number of statements about human behavior and ways of understanding it formatted as polar opposites. Think through each pair of statements and put a check mark on the line next to the statement with which you most agree. If you cannot decide, put a check mark in the middle column (B).

When finished, total the number of check marks for each column. If you have the most check marks in column A, you have a Worldview I perspective; if most marks are in column C, you have a Worldview II perspective. Having the most marks in column B suggests that you see advantages to both perspectives or have yet to take a position. In this case, you might try the exercise again, this time forcing yourself to select from either column A or column C. Review this chapter for a discussion of each worldview and its implications for research.

Worldview I	A	B	C	Worldview II
People are basically alike.				Each person is unique.
People are predictable.				People are not predictable.
It is possible to make generalizations about human behavior.				It is not possible to make generalizations about human behavior.
People's behavior is determined by events and circumstances.				People's behavior is determined by the choices and decisions they make.
People live in an objective world that makes sense to any observer.				People live in a subjective world that makes sense only to the individual.
Human communication is best understood by examining one aspect at a time, in depth.				Human communication is best understood by examining all aspects simultaneously, or holistically.
The best understanding of human communication comes from keeping an objective distance from participants.				The best understanding of human communication comes from getting as close as possible to participants.

Worldview I	A	B	C	Worldview II
The most accurate reports of human communication come from quantitative methods such as surveys and experiments.				The most accurate reports of human communication come from qualitative methods such as interviews and observations.
The best understanding of human communication comes from reports written in the scholarly language of research.				The best understanding of human communication comes from reports written in the language of the research participants.
TOTALS				

Exercise 3: Fine-Tuning Your Worldview

In Exercise 2, you located yourself relative to two fundamentally different assumptions about human behavior: Worldview I and Worldview II. You are now in a position to fine-tune your perspectives on human communication and how it might be studied. Revisit Creswell and Creswell's four worldviews and Craig's seven communication research traditions outlined previously. Based on your consideration of worldviews and research traditions, decide which one of the Creswell worldviews you most align with. Then rank Craig's seven research traditions according to their relevance to your own view of human communication. These exercises will help you narrow down the communication research literature to something aligned with your own view of human communication and how it might best be studied.

HINT: A starting point would be to review Craig (1999), referenced at the end of this chapter. You might also use the tradition and worldview names as search terms to see examples of research based on each tradition or worldview.

Recommended Reading

Afifi, T. D. (2018). Advances in methods and statistics: An introduction to an invited special issue. *Communication Monographs*, *85*(1), 1–3. DOI: 10.1080/03637751.2017.1421816
Introduction to a special issue of *Communication Monographs* on methods and statistics in communication theory.

Anderson, J. A., & Baym, G. (2004, December). Philosophies and philosophic issues in communication, 1995–2004. *Journal of Communication*, *54*(4), 589–615.
A review of many of the issues discussed in this chapter.

Becker, H. S. (1998). *Tricks of the trade: How to think about your research while you're doing it.* Chicago, IL: University of Chicago.
Discusses ways of thinking about research in practice.

Huffman, T. P. (2018). Paradigmatic tools for communication scholar–activists: Toward a pragmatic and relational epistemology.

Review of Communication, *18*(1), 19–36. DOI: 10.1080/15358593.2017.1405460
Argues for pragmatism rather than interpretive or critical perspectives as a paradigm for communication scholars who are committed to activism and social justice. Pragmatism focuses on the connection between ideas and action.

Littlejohn, S. W., Foss, K. A., & Oetzel, J. G. (2017). *Theories of human communication* (11th ed.). Long Grove, IL: Waveland Press.
Provides coverage of major communication theories, their intellectual origins, and their relationships.

Walther, J. B. (2018). The emergence, convergence, and resurgence of intergroup communication theory in computer-mediated communication. *Atlantic Journal of Communication*, *26*(2), 86–97. DOI: 10.1080/15456870.2018.1432616
Discusses the refinement of intergroup communication theory to explain the social effects of computer-mediated communication.

Recommended Web Resources

Communication Research (SAGE Publications).........http://crx.sagepub.com
  You can sign up for free content alerts from this journal at this site.

Communication Institute for Online Scholarship.........www.cios.org
  Offers access to a variety of online resources including the Idea Monkey and the Visual Communication Concept Explorer. Use these tools to explore the relationships between key concepts in the communication literature. An individual or institutional membership is required to access most services.

Scholarly Organizations

Association for Education in Journalism and Mass Communication.........www.aejmc.org
International Communication Association.........www.icahdq.org
National Communication Association.........www.natcom.org

The above sites are for three of the many academic interest groups in communication. Visit them to explore the diversity of academic research areas and method interests.

Pew Research Center Internet & Technology.........www.pewinternet.org
  See Chapter 1.

Applied Communication Research

American Association of Advertising Agencies.........www.aaaa.org
American Marketing Association.........www.marketingpower.com
The Data and Marketing Association.........www.the-dma.org
  This was formerly the Direct Marketing Association.
National Association of Broadcasters.........www.nab.org
Public Relations Society of America.........www.prsa.org

The above five websites are for major communication industry groups. You will not be able to access all aspects of these sites, but you will be able to browse for insights on current research, research issues, and possible careers.

References

Craig, R. T. (1999). Communication theory as a field. *Communication Theory* (1050–3293), 9(2), 119–162.

Creswell, J. W., & Creswell, J. D. (2018). *Research design: Qualitative, quantitative, and mixed methods approaches* (5th ed.). Thousand Oaks, CA: Sage.

Evered, R., & Reis, M. (1981). Alternative perspectives in the organizational sciences: "Inquiry from the inside" and "inquiry from the outside." *Academy of Management Review, 6*(3), 385–396.

National Center for Education Statistics. (2017). *Table 303.10—Total fall enrollment in degree-granting postsecondary institutions, by attendance status, sex of student, and control of institution: Selected years, 1947 through 2027.* Retrieved from https://nces.ed.gov/programs/digest/d17/tables/dt17_303.10.asp.

⑤SAGE edge™

Get the tools you need to sharpen your study skills. SAGE edge offers a robust online environment featuring an impressive array of free tools and resources.

Access quizzes, eFlashcards, video, and multimedia at **edge.sagepub.com/treadwell4e**.

3

ETHICS

What Are My Responsibilities as a Researcher?

"What's that you were up to in the car park, Lee?

"Demolishing the Hunter building."

"Well, watch it! There's a webcam somewhere watching you! What's this demolition thing?"

"Well, that's the goal. We want parking space more than we want an old building they should have bulldozed years ago."

"Who is 'we'? Some of us like that building. Anyway, what were you doing?"

"Recording license plates, arrivals, departures, how long people take to find a parking spot, how many drive away because they can't find one."

"Isn't that a bit old fashioned?"

"How so?"

"Why not just set up a webcam and do the whole thing on your laptop? Even better—get into online discussions on the parking thing and find out exactly who's saying what. Read the comments and find out who's for demolition, who's for saving Hunter. You could even figure out who the activists are on either side. . . . like who's going to meetings or picketing."

"But that's spying on people without their knowledge; I'd need their permission."

"You're already spying on people—recording their vehicle movements."

"That's anonymous; I don't know who owns the vehicles."

"But other people, like campus security, know, and you could find out. Actually, online, people will save you that trouble and mostly identify themselves."

"But online discussions are private or at least people assume privacy. I can't just go around quoting their views about Hunter or anything else."

"I say if you can access a discussion it's public. If participants don't want to go public, they shouldn't post to the Internet. Besides, you're not really spying on people's behavior. The people aren't there. You're just looking at web content. You don't need permission to read a billboard and report on it. So why would you need permission to read and report on online content?

"Because I don't want anyone taking my online stuff public without my permission, so . . ."

"OK, I get the 'do unto others' thing. But what about your greater good of getting a car park?"

CHAPTER OVERVIEW

Researching human communication means interacting with people, and there is no escaping the fact that this has ethical implications. Your relationship with research participants will be guided by your personal ethical standards, by organizational and sector standards, and by codes of ethics and laws designed to protect research participants from psychological and physical harm. This chapter focuses on some of the ethical issues in human communication research, on codes of ethics that govern research on human subjects, on approval procedures for human communication research in a scholarly setting, and on some of the many issues and problems that arise with research on the Internet.

CHAPTER OBJECTIVES

This chapter will help you

- Identify major ethics issues in human communication research.

- Explain some of the classic ethical positions that inform communication research.

- Describe some of the major contemporary codes of ethics.

- Discuss the concepts of peer review and of institutional review boards.

- Describe how the level of involvement with research participants can shape a researcher's relationship with them.

- Identify some of the ethical issues unique to researching human communication on the Internet.

INTRODUCTION: SOME ETHICAL DECISIONS

Ethical decisions in human communication research are inescapable. Consider the decisions that might need to be made in the course of designing communication research. For example, would you expose research participants to sexually explicit or violent material? Deliberately deceive participants? Ensure that some people receive important information while denying it to others? Accept research funding from a source that hopes your research results will help promote its products or services? Start false rumors? Monitor people's behavior without their knowledge or consent?

The following sections set out some of the ethical issues for communication researchers, some of the "classic" ways of resolving ethical dilemmas, and some specific ethical standards and practices that anyone researching human communication should be aware of.

Sex, Violence, and Deception

Sex, violence, and deception may sound like the elements of a reality show or a crime show, but each can be the focus of serious research in communication, and each clearly has ethical implications.

Debates, often politically fueled, rage over sexually explicit and violent media content, as well as over the nature of their effects. From a research point of view, there are two major questions. First, what are the effects (if any) of viewing such content, and second, what causes these effects? In other words, can we claim that exposure to such content causes some particular condition, or is it possible that some condition itself leads to voluntary exposure to such content?

Many studies and research designs have addressed these two questions, but suppose there comes a point in your own research at which you decide that you need to expose participants to explicit content so that you can assess their responses to it. With respect to minors, this exposure could well become a legal question, the answer to which is "you can't." For adults, you may be able to, but should you? Answers will be determined by the age and other characteristics of the research participants, the specific research experiences that the participants will be going through, the sponsoring agency behind the research, and, of course, the personal values and ethical standards of the researcher.

You may be interested in how audience feedback influences a speaker. For example, does a supportive audience improve a speaker's performance? Can a hostile audience weaken a speaker's performance? To answer such questions, you decide to expose speakers participating in your study to an audience made up of **confederates**. Confederates are participants in a study who have been briefed to behave in a particular way. In other words, they are "faking it" and deceiving the speaker. The speakers then address audiences who are faking a response such as enthusiasm or disinterest. Legal? Sure. Ethical . . . ?

Or perhaps you are interested in how information travels in organizations. The only way you can study this in a controlled fashion is to start a rumor, ask around to find out who heard it, and then "back track" to see from whom individuals first heard the rumor. This allows you to track the speed and the patterns of informal communications in an organization. To begin the experiment, you sit with a couple of strangers in your campus coffee bar and, conversationally, announce that your university's trustees are planning a 30% hike in tuition effective next semester. You are, of course, lying. Does the value of your research outweigh the need to deceive people?

Many health communication studies seek to establish the most effective means of getting health information to groups of people. One basic research design is to provide information to one community by interpersonal means, to another by social media, and to a third by a combination of the two. In order to establish that there have been any effects at all, you need a fourth, control, community that receives no information. As part of your study, then, you deny the control community information that could perhaps save or extend a life. Legal? Sure. Deceptive? Maybe. Ethical . . . ?

Money and Relationships

If sex, violence, and deception can feature in our list of ethical considerations, can money and relationships be far behind?

Let's take look at the hypothetical ClickAQuiz educational technology company. The company makes software that allows multiple-choice quizzes to be downloaded to smartphones; students can answer the questions in their own time and space and then upload their answers for grading. Your interest is in how such technology affects academic performance, and you have designed survey questions that focus on technology and academic performance. ClickAQuiz has a keen interest in your research in interactive technologies. In fact, the company offers to write a check to support your research. In return for the check, ClickAQuiz wants you to include several additional questions about how and where students might use this technology, what they would be willing to pay for the service, and how they feel about banner advertising on their phones. Do you incorporate these questions into your survey or reject them as an unnecessary commercial "intrusion" unrelated to the focus of your research? Could the ClickAQuiz questions, if used, affect student responses to the questions you want answered by, for example, "framing" the technology as "user pays" rather than free? On what basis might you change or refuse to use any of the ClickAQuiz questions?

In the "relationships" department, researchers may relate to their research participants in ways that range from dispassionate observation to psychological closeness.

Unobtrusive measures is an approach that by definition observes people's behavior without their being aware of it. This approach is often used to check on the reliability of the information people provide. For example, most people would probably say when interviewed that they wear seat belts when driving. One unobtrusive-measures check on this is simply to observe people driving and to record the percentage you see wearing seat belts.

At the other extreme, as someone researching family dynamics, you may find that you need in-depth, face-to-face interviews to gain an understanding of a family's culture and communication patterns. As you question family members in depth, you may find that the questions you ask are distressing to your interviewees. Or you may find that they are revealing confidences about other members of the family, who would be hurt if they knew that this information was going outside the family to a stranger—you.

Less dramatic decisions such as simply listening in on a conversation also have an ethical component. In Chapter 1 of this book, we listened in on a discussion among a group of students. From a research point of view, this eavesdropping seems an interesting thing to do, but it seems intuitive that, just as we would ask permission to join the group physically, so also would we ask permission to record the conversation of group members and, in due course, to publish our report and interpretation of their discussions. This issue becomes especially important when we study human communication on the Internet and is discussed more fully later in this chapter.

The overriding question in all the hypothetical cases outlined here is "What standards of behavior should apply to my research?" Typical issues in communication research are discussed in the following section. These issues relate to your relationships with research participants and with the readers who will depend on you for an accurate account of your research. Both are important to your career as a researcher.

ETHICS ISSUES IN COMMUNICATION RESEARCH

Honesty

It seems axiomatic that honesty is always the best policy, but deception can be part of legitimate and professional research studies. To be honest and reveal the deception "up front" may be to weaken the whole research design. Professional codes of ethics generally address this dilemma by allowing deception in some research designs as long as the participants are made aware of the deception immediately after the study is concluded, in a process known as debriefing. The American Psychological Association (APA) states that psychologists do not use deception unless they have determined that deception is justified by the study's significant prospective scientific, educational, or applied value and that no effective nondeceptive alternatives are feasible (American Psychological Association, 2017).

Honesty is also a significant consideration in areas other than research design. Researchers have an ethical responsibility to their readers as well as to their research participants to report results honestly. In this case, honesty means reporting possible flaws in your research and negative results as well as the good news. Most research papers have a section in which the author discusses possible weaknesses in the study. Such a section is helpful, not an embarrassment, because it provides a launchpad for further research. Finding "nothing" or results that are counterintuitive may not do a lot for your ego, but it does not invalidate your study. The fact that something you expected to find was not found still contributes to our knowledge, and you can honestly report that finding. With funded research, the conduct and reporting of research may wittingly or unwittingly favor the funding agency. Honest disclosure of a researcher's relationships to funding agencies is therefore another ethical consideration and may also be a legal one.

Confidentiality and Anonymity

To protect the individuals who may be disclosing personal information, the researcher customarily assures them of **confidentiality**. This means that you, the researcher, will not release any information that identifies your participants even if you know what information each participant provided you.

To protect and reassure participants fully, you may need to offer **anonymity**. Anonymity goes a step further in protecting people in that the data you collect from them absolutely does not identify them. Even you do not know which participant provided the information you collected. Typically, you ensure anonymity by instructing respondents not to put their names on any information they provide. Any consent forms that they sign are turned in separately, so there is no link between those documents that identify them and any other document. Depending on what method you use, anonymity might not be an option. For example in face-to-face interviews, you could not offer anonymity.

Violating any anonymity or confidentiality agreements when you report your research results is an ethical issue and may well become a legal one. Researchers usually protect their respondents' anonymity in qualitative studies by referring to them as "Respondent A" or by using a false and typically neutral name such as "Bob Smith" or "Jane Jones." Quantitative studies typically report statistical summaries for a group of people, so there is no need to identify specific individuals.

Making Generalizations

The professional codes of practice discussed in this chapter require that research participants be volunteers. If only willing volunteers are recruited to your study, you will be recruiting individuals who have a bias toward your study in the sense that they are willing to participate in it. Generalizations from your study, then, can be made only to this type of individual.

Because all of your participants are volunteers, you cannot make generalizations about the "nonvolunteer" type. For certain types of research, such as ethnography (Chapter 13), generalizability is not a goal; therefore, you should not attempt to generalize beyond your actual research results.

Debriefing

If your participants have been exposed to deception, you have an ethical obligation after the study is over to ensure that you contact them, explain the deception, and invite any follow-up questions they may have. Failure to do so means that your participants will leave the research assuming that they have been involved in a real event when in fact they have not. The APA ethics code referenced previously calls for any deception to be revealed to participants as early as possible, preferably at the conclusion of their participation but no later than at the conclusion of data collection, at which point participants can withdraw their data.

More generally, researchers should respond promptly to participants' requests for information about the nature, results, and conclusions of the research. Most researchers need to ask their participants to document their agreement to be in a research study by signing a consent form, increasingly in some web-based format. Consent forms describe the study and emphasize the right of participants to leave it at any time and to access the results of the study. Because consent forms must be signed in advance of a study, they will not explain any deceptions that are a part of it. As noted, participants who have been subject to deception should be made aware of that deception as soon as possible, and readers of your research report will want to know that your results were obtained under conditions of deception.

The Literature Review

A large part of any research project is the literature review—discussed in Chapter 4. This is your summary and evaluation of what other researchers working on your topic have published. You review this literature to get ideas on how best to do your own research and, importantly, to demonstrate to others how your own research will contribute to our shared knowledge.

There is a voluminous literature on communication research. You will have to read and report it selectively. This means that your readers' view of the field, as well as your own, will be shaped by both what you choose to write about and how you write about it. Following are some of the questions you might have about a literature review.

How far back in time should I review? Can I use secondary (summary) articles rather than primary (original) sources? Should I report articles that do not support my viewpoint?

Can I report research that is relevant but proprietary (i.e., "owned" and I do not have permission to publish it)?

Views about communication change over time, as they should. Just as it is possible to misrepresent the current state of knowledge by selecting only certain authors to review, so it is possible to misrepresent by selecting particular time periods for review. Reviewing summaries of research rather than the original reports can give you an initial overview of the field, but summarizing summaries could lead to dangerous oversimplifications and further magnify any biases of interpretation in the summaries you are reading. Articles that do not support your ideas and methods should be reported because your readers need to be aware of any debates and controversies in your area of interest, and you have a responsibility to summarize the debates.

Proprietary information is information that is owned, typically by corporations, and may not be published without the owner's permission. As a researcher, you may have access to proprietary information, but publishing that information may be both an ethical and a legal violation.

In summary, your writing may or may not accurately represent the work of other researchers and therefore requires that you be ethically sensitive.

Acknowledging Others

Authorship of a published paper implies more than just writing it; it implies taking responsibility for the project reported. To the extent that others contributed to your project, it may be appropriate to list them as coauthors or at least to acknowledge their contributions.

The basic decision is what constitutes "others." Researchers reporting summary data for hundreds of survey respondents are unlikely to acknowledge specific individuals. Researchers who work closely with one or two collaborators may well want to acknowledge them but may be unable to do so if they have been promised anonymity.

Appropriate Language

Members of the research community who share your interests will want to see your literature review, research methods, results, and conclusions all written in a professional scholarly style.

Scholarly writing may become ethically problematic, however, if your research participants cannot understand it. You should always approach participants at their level of understanding, whether you are seeking permission from them or communicating results to them. The Office for Human Research Protections (OHRP) of the U.S. Department of Health and Human Services (1993) recommends that informed consent documents "be written in 'lay language' (i.e., understandable to the people being asked to participate)."

"Understandable to the people being asked to participate" implies not only language but also level of the language. In other words, consent documents may need to be written in the language best understood by the participant (not necessarily English) and at the level of comprehension of that participant. Often, your university's institutional review board (IRB) will request a draft of your consent documents to determine if the level of writing is appropriate for your audience.

Plagiarism

There are a number of reasons to dislike plagiarism. Primarily, of course, it is an unethical (and may well be an illegal) representation of others' work as your own. In essence, plagiarism is fraud, which can be defined as intending "to deceive others, typically by unjustifiably claiming or being credited with accomplishments or qualities" (https://en.oxforddictionaries.com/definition/fraud). If the plagiarist is publishing proprietary research, the issue could also become one of copyright violation. From the point of view of your busy research colleagues, however, plagiarism also represents the problem of "used goods." Representing others' work as your own means that readers may end up reading both the original research and the plagiarist's version of that research. It does a disservice to researchers trying to stay current because they may be misled into reading two different versions of the same research.

SOME CLASSIC ETHICAL POSITIONS

All the above issues pose questions that must be answered in order to design ethically defensible research studies. For many researchers, the answers come in the form of specific codes of ethics that must be followed, with penalties such as loss of funding if they are not.

More generally, researchers may turn to one or more of the following "classic" ethical positions for guidance.

The **Judeo-Christian ethic** of doing unto others as you would have others do to you or, conversely, not doing to others what is hurtful to you suggests a very simple test of ethical behavior. Would you be willing to be a participant in your own study? If not, your project may be ethically suspect as it affects other people.

Philosopher Immanuel Kant proposed a **categorical imperative**—that a behavior is valid if you are willing to see it applied as a universal rule. For example, if you are willing to use deception as part of a research design, then you should be prepared to accept deception as a universal value.

The **principle of utilitarianism**, associated with philosophers Jeremy Bentham, John Stuart Mill, and David Hume, argues for the greatest good for the greatest number. It suggests that research designs that may hurt a minority of people are justified if there is an overall greater good. For example, we might argue in communication research that misinforming a few people via a false rumor is defensible if out of that research emerges a fuller understanding of how best to use informal communication networks in an emergency.

Philosopher John Rawls's "**veil of ignorance**" approach asks us to take a dispassionate perspective, reviewing all sides of a decision equally. We are asked to wear a veil that blinds us to all information about ourselves that might cloud our judgment. For example, suppose our research design has the potential to cause severe psychological distress to our research participants. We need an ethical decision as to whether this is acceptable or not. The "veil of ignorance" blinds us to the role we would be playing in the research; that is, we could be researchers, or we could be participants. Recognizing that psychological distress is undesirable and could happen to us, we would probably decide that our research ought not to cause any distress to our research participants.

TWO BRIEF HISTORIES—OR WHY WE CARE ABOUT RESEARCH ETHICS

It's a long way from Nazi Germany to monitoring people's behavior on the Internet, but Nazi medical experiments during World War II were the 20th-century impetus for codes of ethics covering research on human **subjects**. After the war, at the Nuremberg trials, a number of Nazi physicians and administrators were charged with crimes against humanity, more specifically with conducting without consent medical experiments that caused death and inflicted injury on concentration camp inmates.

From 1932 to 1972, the U.S. Public Health Service ran a study in Tuskegee, Alabama, to learn more about syphilis. In doing so, it withheld adequate treatment from a group of Black men who had the disease and were participants in the study. In 1972, a panel reviewing the study concluded that it was ethically unjustified and that the knowledge gained was sparse compared with the risks the study posed for its subjects. The review of the study led to the 1979 *Belmont Report*, discussed below, and to the establishment of the OHRP.

CONTEMPORARY CODES OF ETHICS

Professional concern for human subjects dates back to at least the 4th century BCE oath of Hippocrates, and the two brief histories described in the previous section indicate why such a concern is still warranted. It is unlikely that most communication research would have the potential for physical harm. However, there is always the possibility of psychological harm, for example, as a result of exposure to graphic content or from requiring participants to behave in a way contrary to their beliefs. Codes of ethics seek to protect research participants from any form of harm by prescribing professional standards of behavior for researchers.

The Nuremberg Code

One outcome of the Nuremberg trials was the 1948 **Nuremberg Code**, the first international code to emphasize that

- research subjects must consent to the research in which they are involved and
- the benefits of the research must outweigh the risks.

The Declaration of Helsinki

In 1964, the World Medical Association's **Declaration of Helsinki** established international ethical guidelines for medical professionals researching human subjects. The Declaration of Helsinki continues to be revised and emphasizes that

- research protocols must be reviewed by an independent committee prior to the research,
- **informed consent** must be obtained from research participants,
- research must be conducted by medically or scientifically qualified individuals, and
- research risks should not exceed the benefits.

The *Belmont Report*

The National Commission for the Protection of Human Subjects of Biomedical and Behavioral Research prepared the *Belmont Report* in 1979. The report outlines three basic ethical principles surrounding research with human subjects. These are **autonomy, beneficence**, and **justice**. The principles and their applications in practice are summarized in Exhibit 3.1.

REGULATIONS

Many nations have regulations that implement principles such as those set out above. In the United States, Health and Human Services (HHS) regulations that implement these principles have been adopted by many other agencies that fund or conduct research on human subjects. These shared standards are known as the Federal Policy for the Protection of Human Subjects, or the "**Common Rule**."

EXHIBIT 3.1 ■ The *Belmont Report*—Principles, Applications, and Questions for Internet Research

Principle	Application	Questions Related to Internet Research
Autonomy Individuals should be treated with respect. Persons with diminished autonomy are entitled to protection.	**Informed Consent** Subjects must be given the opportunity to choose what shall or shall not happen to them. The consent process must include three elements: • Information • Comprehension • Voluntariness	• Are avatars human subjects? • How do researchers verify the following factors? 　○ The identity of participants 　○ Participants' understanding of informed consent 　○ The validity of "signed" consent forms • Could pseudonyms "mask" vulnerable individuals such as minors? • Should consent forms inform participants about special risks from Internet research (e.g., anonymity may not be guaranteed)? • How can researchers debrief all participants and do long-term follow-up when the online population is constantly changing?
Beneficence Human subjects must not be harmed, and efforts should be made to secure their well-being. Research should maximize possible benefits and minimize possible harm.	**Assessment of Risks and Benefits** The nature and scope of risks and benefits must be assessed systematically.	• Are all possible risks and benefits to research participants actually known? • Can researchers guarantee anonymity? • How can long-term risks and benefits be assessed when the online population is constantly changing?
Justice The benefits and risks of research must be distributed fairly.	**Selection of Subjects** There must be fair procedures and outcomes in the selection of research subjects. Consider these guidelines, for example: • Subjects ought not to be recruited simply on the basis of accessibility. • Some individuals and groups must not bear disproportionate risks while others reap the benefits of research.	• The Internet population is different from the population at large, so how can the risks and benefits of online research be distributed equitably?

Source: Adapted in part from Office of Human Subjects Research (1979).

The Common Rule addresses requirements for ensuring compliance by research institutions, requirements for obtaining and documenting informed consent, **institutional review boards (IRBs)**, and special protections for vulnerable research subjects such as pregnant women, prisoners, minors, and participants with disabilities.

PEER REVIEW AND INSTITUTIONAL REVIEW BOARDS

Peer review at its simplest consists of qualified researchers with similar interests assessing each other's work.

Informally, researchers brainstorm over coffee cups, swap ideas at conferences, and put together project research teams. Such interactions can provide an informal peer review of ethics and research design more generally before any project is launched. This, of course, can be a hit or miss operation, depending on how actively the researcher networks.

Formal review is required when researchers undertake any human subjects research for the federal government or are employed by any institution that receives federal funding.

The most typical method of formal peer review with respect to ethics and treatment of human participants is the IRB. The IRB is a panel established to review research proposals specifically for their impact on any human participants. There is an IRB in some form on almost every campus where human subjects research is conducted.

The fact that most communication research does not involve physical impact on participants does not exempt it from IRB review. Protection involves psychological protection as much as physical protection.

That said, nonmedical researchers have questioned why protocols designed essentially to protect participants in medical research need apply to researchers investigating, say, students' use of social media or responses to advertising.

In 2017, the HHS's Office for Human Research Protections revised its rules to exempt research involving "benign behavioral interventions" such as having subjects play an online game or decide how to allocate a nominal amount of cash among themselves. The stated intent of this revision was "to better protect human subjects involved in research, while facilitating valuable research and reducing burden, delay, and ambiguity for investigators" (Federal Policy for the Protection of Human Subjects, 2017, p. 7149).

Shweder and Nisbett (2017) argued that risk-averse university administrators had allowed IRB "mission creep" to reach the point of requiring IRB approval for all human subjects research and that the new regulations provided an opportunity to exempt all low-risk research from IRB review. More cautious researchers and administrators wondered about the ability of researchers to self-regulate, the impact on research funding if IRB approvals were not obtained, and the potential problem of an unapproved study "gone wrong" on the reputation of an institution and on other researchers. Some argued that, legalities aside, the IRB approval process can be positive and provide useful ideas that improve the original research design.

In an application exercise at the end of this chapter, you are invited to further consider the implications of exempting everyday social science research from IRB approval.

WHAT SHOULD I CALL YOU? THE ETHICS OF INVOLVEMENT

The individuals participating in the research may be known as subjects, informants, participants, or collaborators.

Traditionally, researchers used the term *subjects,* with the connotation of an omniscient white-coated professional observing an acquiescent group of human subjects in the cause of a

EXHIBIT 3.2 ■ Researcher-Participant Relationships in Communication Research		
	Researcher's Involvement With Participants	
	Low	**High**
Researcher's Orientation to Participants — Dispassionate observer: "Stranger"	Measure people objectively	Explore people's subjective views
	Not involved	Involved in order to elicit subjective information
	Behavior motivated by regulations and codes of ethics	Behavior motivated by regulations, codes of ethics, and need to establish trusting relationships
	People: "Subjects"	People: "Informants"
Involved in participants' condition: "Friend"	Involved in lives only as a means of observing them	Involved, with participants' views driving research design and implementation
	Behavior motivated by regulations, codes of ethics, and need to access participants successfully	Behavior motivated by regulations, codes of ethics, and research goals important to participants
	People: "Participants"	People: "Collaborators"

greater good. *Informant* and *collaborator* may have negative connotations outside research, but within it both terms recognize that researchers would be nowhere without the information provided by research participants. *Participant* recognizes the active and voluntary role that research participants play in making research possible.

As you can see from Exhibit 3.2, terminology, research design, and the nature of the researcher's relationship with research participants are closely related. All researchers are bound by relevant regulations and professional codes, but as research participants move from being subjects to being collaborators, the ethical dilemmas can increase. It is unlikely that a researcher out of the "let's survey 1,200 people" school of thought would need to be professionally concerned with each subject's private life. At the other extreme, a researcher working with a small group of collaborators is more likely to assume an ethical responsibility for their well-being because they are part of the team that has shaped the nature of the research from the beginning and may well continue to do so.

THE INTERNET AND RESEARCH ETHICS

Research on the Internet can be an ethical gray area, complicated by the fact that relevant human subjects regulations were written essentially for biomedical research and long before virtual realities, avatars, and social media came into existence. The following sections set out some of the theoretical and practical issues with Internet research, as well as their ethical implications.

What Is the Internet?

The big theoretical question fueling discussion about research ethics on the Internet is "What is the Internet?" The ambiguity in the very term *Internet research* captures the basic definitional problem.

Internet research may include research on Internet content with no direct human subjects contact, research that uses the Internet as a tool for recruiting subjects, research about the Internet itself, research about Internet users, and research that uses the Internet as an intervention tool. It is a tool for research and a venue of research, with social media blurring the distinction between tool and venue (U.S. Department of Health and Human Services, 2013).

Simplistically, the Internet can be regarded as process and as content. If it is regarded as a process of interaction or a virtual space within which human interaction occurs, then the argument has to be made that social science research standards apply because the communication behaviors of individuals are being studied. That obligates researchers to respect the human subjects and seek the institutional approvals outlined earlier in this chapter.

The case can also be made that the Internet is fundamentally content and that researchers studying web behavior are simply studying published content. This raises the proposition that because individuals are not being studied directly, the researcher has no impact on their lives and therefore no research approvals are required. Internet research in this light becomes essentially a type of content analysis.

The issues are more complicated than the simple process-versus-content distinction sketched out above. Even if the view is taken that the Internet is fundamentally content, an issue that remains is that much Internet content is intellectual property and subject to copyright law.

Anonymity and Identification on the Internet

Many Internet residents post content on the assumption that their identity is protected by virtue of posting anonymously or posting to a discussion area that is not open to the public. However, an important ethical issue with respect to human subjects research is that Internet content may have the names of identifiable individuals attached to it or be such that determined "web sleuths" can find or deduce an individual's identity.

Web surveys cannot guarantee respondents anonymity because identifying information may be linked to documents they are transmitting and to their e-mail addresses. This issue becomes important as funding agencies and others may require experimental data to be publicly available. Data sets can have names, addresses, and phone numbers of individuals removed, but there is debate as to whether individuals can be "re-identified" using other information associated with them (De Montjoye, Radaelli, Singh, & Pentland, 2015; Sánchez, Martínez, & Domingo-Ferrer, 2016).

The U.S. Department of Health and Human Services (2013) notes that while the regulatory definition of "human subjects" has not changed, new forms of identity such as avatars exist in the Internet and personally identifiable information about living individuals may be obtainable through such virtual representations. The HHS identifies the verification of identity as a major issue in Internet research. While low-risk studies may require only minimal identity verification, high-risk studies involving sensitive information may call for "multiple-factor authentication."

Privacy on the Internet

The regulatory definition of "private information" means "information about behavior that occurs in a context in which an individual can reasonably expect that no observation or recording is taking place, and information which has been provided for specific purposes by an individual and which the individual can reasonably expect will not be made public" (U.S. Department of Health and Human Services, 2013, p. 5).

The HHS notes that all information that is legally available to any Internet user could be considered public information. Alternatively, the privacy policy created by the site could be used to establish whether its online information is public or confidential, with investigators operating in accordance with the privacy expectations that the site offers and requests from members. Another approach would be to consider as private any venue where authorization for membership or participation is necessary.

Thelwall (2010) argues that academic researchers should not have any restrictions placed on the kinds of (legal) data that they investigate on the public web and that they should be able to conduct these investigations without obtaining informed consents, if the information researched is on the public web. He argues that the web is a venue where individuals may expect that their postings are private but ought not to assume that their privacy is protected. For example, a posting to a work group of colleagues may be regarded as private to that group, but the group has no reason to assume a guarantee of privacy given the rights and abilities of employers to monitor employee e-mail.

A further privacy issue is cross-national data storage. For example, Canadian research ethics boards may include a statement that SurveyMonkey survey data are held in the United States and are subject to U.S. law, in particular to the USA PATRIOT Act that allows U.S. authorities to access the records of Internet service providers.

Informed Consent and Debriefing on the Internet

Informed consent becomes a much more complex issue because the individuals providing that consent cannot necessarily be easily identified. For example, two or more people may share one e-mail address. Which person at that address agreed to participate in the survey, and is that the same person who actually answered the survey questions? Similarly, how is the researcher to determine and verify that any person answering the survey is not a minor? (You will recall that research on minors and other special groups particularly requires IRB approval.)

Informed consent requires that participants be informed about the research and that the researcher ensures that participants comprehend the research and obtains their signed voluntary agreement to the research. Each of these steps presents a difficulty on the Internet. For example, risks to the participants may not be fully known to researchers because they do not know what effect participating in the research will have on a respondent's relationship with other individuals in cyberspace. While, in principle, the researcher is available to answer any questions about the research, knowing that respondents fully comprehend the research can be made more difficult by the fact that "signing" consent forms often means that respondents use electronic signatures or click an "agree" box on an online form. This process of agreeing gives researchers less confidence, perhaps, that the respondent is fully aware of the research and its implications than a signed document would provide. A further question related to informed consent is "From whom?" For example, does a researcher need the permission of every participant in a discussion group to access the discussion or would the permission of a discussion leader be sufficient?

One problem related to the consent process is the difficulty of authentication or determining and confirming the identity of the participant who signed a consent. Researchers therefore increasingly need to consider using researcher-assigned usernames and passwords, digital signatures, ID verification services, scanning and transmittal of government-issued IDs, and biometric identification processes.

Kozinets (2013) argues that for research that involves no risk to participants an "implied consent" may be appropriate. Implied consent occurs online when a participant agrees to continue in a study by clicking an "accept" button on a web page or by providing information.

Then comes the problem of **debriefing**. How to ensure that everyone who participated in a study receives a follow-up explanation of the study? In principle, this can be done by e-mailing a debriefing document to every participant, but again the researcher cannot know exactly who has access to an e-mail account and therefore whom such a mailing will reach. Releasing sensitive or controversial material to an e-mail address may place participants in an emotionally difficult situation the researcher is unaware of.

Guidelines and Questions for Internet Research

Townsend and Wallace (n.d.) propose a three-step process for ethical research with social media. First—review the terms and conditions of the social media platforms you will be working with and ensure that you are compliant with your own institutional IRB or other terms and conditions. Second—review whether the data you will be accessing or generating are private or public. Start by assessing whether social media participants could reasonably expect to be observed by strangers. Private data obviously require the appropriate consents, which may not be straightforward given that you may be trying to access confidential information, sensitive information, or information originated by or about minors. Third—consider your publication of results and the possible reuse or republication of "your" data. For example, your research participants may have allowed you access to sensitive information, but that does not mean that they have given you permission to publish their information or to identify them in any way.

The Association of Internet Researchers (AoIR) proposes guidelines for Internet research rather than a specific code that may not fit every eventuality (Markham & Buchanan, 2012). Because the ethical questions may be different at different stages of the research process, the AoIR recommends a process of posing different questions at each stage of the research. These questions include the following:

> How is the [research] context defined and conceptualized? How is the context (venue/participants/data) being accessed? Who is involved in the study? What is the primary object of the study? How are data being managed, stored, and represented? How are texts/persons/data being studied? How are findings presented? What are the potential harms or risks associated with this study? What are the potential benefits associated with this study? How are we recognizing the autonomy of others and acknowledging that they are of equal worth to ourselves and should be treated so? What particular issues might arise around the issue of minors or vulnerable persons? (Markham & Buchanan, 2012, pp. 8–11)

An AoIR summary chart that presents commonly asked ethical questions for different types of Internet contexts such as direct contact, special interest forums, and avatar-based social spaces is listed under "Recommended Web Resources" below.

Questions related to Internet research rapidly become much more complex than whether the Internet is a tool, such as a **search engine**, or a medium or a social space. The same issues that arise with non-Internet studies—privacy, consent, participant risk, method appropriateness, sampling, recruitment, and anonymity—are all compounded by the size of the Internet, its ever-shifting population, and its special problem areas of authenticity and security.

The AoIR and HHS both remind us that the *Belmont Report*'s fundamental principles of respect for persons, beneficence, and justice apply to Internet research as much as to any other form of human subjects research. As the HHS report reminds us, adherence to these fundamental principles is important to encouraging public trust in the ethical conduct of Internet researchers.

Dr. Mary Gray, a senior researcher at Microsoft Research and professor at Indiana University, proposed a simple test for researchers: "If you're afraid to ask your subjects for their permission to conduct the research, there's probably a deeper ethical issue that must be considered" (Goel, 2014).

The AoIR summary, the HHS "Considerations and Recommendations" document, and the classic ethical positions and codes of ethics outlined in this chapter will help you with research ethics and with this chapter's application exercises.

ETHICS PANEL
DATA SECURITY AND ACCESS

In 2014 a company, Cambridge Analytica, offered Facebook users $1 or $2 each to download and use a personality quiz app called "thisisyourdigitallife." In 2018, the *New York Times* and the UK's *Guardian* revealed that the app had "harvested" detailed information not only from the two hundred and seventy thousand people who installed the app but also from their Facebook friends for a total of over 80 million Facebook users.

Facebook provided this data to the makers of the app, who turned it over for use by Cambridge Analytica, a political consulting firm involved with the 2016 U.S. presidential campaign. Facebook argued that users had knowingly provided their information and given their consent. Tufekci (2018) argued that, legally, not all people whose data were provided did give their consent and that if these users of the app did, it was certainly not an informed consent.

It would be tempting to view the Cambridge Analytica case as a uniquely corporate problem, but hundreds of Facebook data sets are also in use by academic researchers. These data sets have differing institutional protocols for security. For example, a 2006 Facebook data set compiled by Harvard University researchers allowed other researchers to trace the data back to identifiable Harvard freshmen (Frenkel, 2018).

Thinking first as an individual, what level of protection would you want on your own social media data—totally public, totally private, or somewhere in between? Does your answer depend on who might seek to access your data? Does it depend on the type of data, for example, whether it is your basic demographic information, a chat with an intimate friend, "selfies," or your web-browsing history? Would your thinking change if you knew that your personal data would be analyzed or published anonymously, that is, never associated with your name?

Think now as a researcher. For example, imagine you have a research interest in how online discussions of sexual harassment have changed over time. Specifically, what types of social media content from what types of individuals would you want to access? What level of access would you need? For example, would just knowing the groups an individual belongs to be enough, or would you want to access the contents of these groups' discussions?

How do your interests in protecting your personal data differ from your interests as a researcher in accessing such data?

As a researcher, how might you solve the problem of maximizing your access to individuals' online data while at the same time maximizing their privacy protections? Note that the guiding principles of the *Belmont Report* and the Common Rule acknowledge both the rights of research participants and the interests of scholarly researchers.

HINT: You should be able sign into your own web services to explore their privacy policies and your own privacy settings and permissions.

SOURCES: Many articles discuss Facebook, Cambridge Analytica, and the 2016 U.S. presidential election. See Herrman (2018), the Cambridge Analytica files of *The Guardian* (n.d.), and, for a perspective from professional Internet researchers, the Association of Internet Researchers (2018).

Chapter Summary

- Ethics is the study of right and wrong; responsibility; and, in the context of this chapter, appropriate behavior toward research participants.

- Communication research ethics share with medical and psychological ethics a basic concern to protect the well-being of human participants.

- The formal mechanism for reviewing the protections for human subjects at most institutions is an institutional review board.

- Peer review and publication also provide a check on the ethics of research.

- Ethical decisions are involved in the treatment of human participants, in research design, and in research reporting.

- Formal codes of ethics include the Nuremberg Code, the Declaration of Helsinki, the *Belmont Report*, the Common Rule, and the APA's *Ethical Principles of Psychologists and Code of Conduct*.

- The Internet as both research site and research tool raises questions and challenges related to participant selection, anonymity, informed consent, and debriefing.

Key Terms

anonymity 47
autonomy 51
Belmont Report 51
beneficence 51
categorical imperative 50
Common Rule 51
confederates 45
confidentiality 47

debriefing 57
Declaration of Helsinki 51
informed consent 51
institutional review
    board (IRB) 52
Judeo-Christian ethic 50
justice 51
Nuremberg Code 51

peer review 53
principle of
    utilitarianism 50
proprietary 49
search engine 58
subjects 50
unobtrusive measures 46
veil of ignorance 50

Application Exercises

Exercise 1: The Ethics of Internet Research

You have been asked to advise your campus IRB on whether campus-based Internet research implies a special set of "e-ethics" specific to research on the Internet and its users. There is some thinking that the basic principles of human subjects research protections cover Internet research adequately and that no specific guidelines for such research are required. List the sources of information you might go to in order to write a report and recommendations for your board.

Exercise 2: IRBs Revisited

As of 2019, the HHS's Common Rule exempts "benign behavioral interventions" such as social science interviews and surveys from IRB oversight.

The stated intent of this amendment is to better protect research subjects while facilitating valuable research and reducing delay and ambiguity for researchers.

The rule does not specify what is and is not a benign behavioral intervention. What examples of research can you think of that might be regarded as benign . . . or not? More generally, how would you define "benign"? Absent IRB oversight, is it sufficient that researchers themselves should decide that their research is benign? What mechanisms, if any, are needed to protect your interests as a participant in online or classroom-based research? How does the presence or absence of a campus IRB affect your feelings about participating in a professor's research? Can the *Belmont Report*'s ethical principles of autonomy, beneficence, and justice with respect to research participants be maintained in the absence of IRB oversight? Research the current IRB guidelines followed on your campus to determine what exemptions, if any, exist for the types of research you might be interested in.

Exercise 3: "#MeToo" and Research Ethics

The "#MeToo" movement was founded in 2006 to help survivors of sexual violence. More recently, the #MeToo discussion of sexual harassment and assault became viral internationally and launched more sector-specific discussions focused on churches, sports, military, entertainment, and government. *Time* magazine chose the #MeToo movement as its Person of Year in 2017.

As a researcher you are interested in answering the many questions that might be asked about #MeToo as a communication phenomenon. On the #MeToo publicly accessible Facebook site, victims of sexual harassment may self-identify, post the nature of the assault, and "name names." To what extent ought you to be able to use such data, publish it, and make the data you gathered available to other researchers for further use and publication? What consent, if any, to the use of such data should you seek?

Do your answers to these questions change with respect to the nonpublic postings of a group of Facebook friends of which you are a member?

HINTS: Facebook privacy policy currently says that "you have control over who sees what you share on Facebook." The #MeToo movement has a web presence at https://metoomvmt.org.

Recommended Reading

Beaulieu, A., & Estalella, A. (2012). Rethinking research ethics for mediated settings. *Information, Communication & Society, 15*(1), 23–42. DOI: 10.1080/1369118X.2010.535838

Discusses how e-research can shape ethical issues and the relations between researchers and their constituencies and stakeholders. Focuses on ethnography in mediated settings.

Emery, K. (2014). So you want to do an online study: Ethics considerations and lessons learned. *Ethics & Behavior*, *24*(4), 293–303. DOI: 10.1080/10508422.2013.860031

Discusses the advantages and disadvantages of online psychological research and especially the limitations and ethical implications of fully automated online research.

King, C. S. T., Bivens, K. M., Pumroy, E., Rauch, S., & Koerber, A. (2018). IRB problems and solutions in health communication research. *Health Communication*, *33*(7), 907–916. DOI: 10.1080/10410236.2017.1321164

Discusses the challenges of health communication research stemming from communication in highly protected, private spaces such as medical exam rooms, online patient forums, and electronic health records.

Recommended Web Resources

Formal Ethics and Codes of Practice

American Association for Public Opinion Research Code of Professional Ethics and Practices (revised 2015).........https://www.aapor.org/Standards-Ethics/AAPOR-Code-of-Ethics.aspx

Data and Marketing Association (DMA) / Association of National Advertisers (ANA) Guidelines for Ethical Business Practice.........https://thedma.org/accountability/ethics-and-compliance/dma-ethical-guidelines/

The above two websites provide the codes of ethics for two areas of applied communication—public opinion research and marketing.

American Psychological Association Ethical Principles of Psychologists and Code of Conduct.........www.apa.org/ethics/code/index.aspx
Many of the ethical principles set out by the APA apply to communication research. APA style is the publication style used to format many communication research papers.

Association of Social Anthropologists of the UK and Commonwealth Ethical Guidelines for Good Research Practice.........www.theasa.org/ethics/guidelines.shtml
This site, in addition to providing ethical guidelines, sets out all the parties that can impact and be impacted by human subjects research—research participants; sponsors, funders, and employers; colleagues and the discipline; and governments and society at large.

Illinois Institute of Technology Center for the Study of Ethics in the Professions.........http://ethics.iit.edu

This site has hundreds of codes of ethics from a variety of disciplines, including communication. In addition to the codes, you can find discussions on the value of having such codes and guidelines on constructing a code for your own organization.

National Communication Association Code of Professional Responsibilities for the Communication Scholar/Teacher.........www.natcom.org/publicstatements
This code of professional responsibilities for a major U.S. academic communication association sets out professional standards for research, teaching, and publication.

National Institutes of Health (NIH), Department of Bioethics, Resources.........www.bioethics.nih.gov/resources/index.shtml

U.S. Department of Health and Human Services, Office of Human Research Protection.........www.hhs.gov/ohrp

The above two sites provide information on a variety of topics related to human subjects research in the United States.

Internet Research Ethics

Association of Internet Researchers (AoIR).........www.aoir.org
The AoIR is a cross-disciplinary association of scholars and students and the source of the AoIR guide on ethical decision making and online research, at www.aoir.org/ethics.

AoIR's Charting Ethical Questions by Type of Data and Venue (a summary table to help decision making).........https://aoir.org/wp-content/uploads/2017/01/aoir_ethics_graphic_2016.pdf

This chart presents commonly asked ethical questions for different Internet contexts, such as special interest forums and avatar-based social spaces.

O'Riordan, K. (2010, July 22). Internet research ethics: Revisiting the relations between technologies, spaces, texts and people. *eHumanities News*.......... www.ehumanities.nl/internet-research-ethics-revisiting-the-relations-between-technologies-spaces-texts-and-people/
This e-news article discusses the differences between the Internet as social text and as social space, and the notion that new media genres may not sit neatly under either the assumption of informed consent or the assumption that there are no human subjects.

e-Consents

The following examples show online information and consents for two web-based health studies. Note the FAQs, privacy policies, "what happens to my data," and the information about consent and participation.

MyHeart Counts.........https://med.stanford.edu/myheart counts.html
A Stanford University smartphone- and activity-tracker-based heart health study.

ADAPTABLE trial.........https://www.adaptablepatient.com /en/auth/code
A trial comparing two different doses of aspirin.

Human Subjects Protection Training

Protecting Human Research Participants.........https:// humansubjects.nih.gov/
A National Institutes of Health course in protecting human research participants.

References

American Psychological Association. (2017). *Ethical principles of psychologists and code of conduct.* Retrieved from https://www.apa.org/ethics/code/

Association of Internet Researchers. (2018, April 25). Facebook shuts the gate after the horse has bolted, and hurts real research in the process. *AoIR Community, Ethics, Publications* [post]. Retrieved from https://aoir.org/facebook-shuts-the-gate-after-the-horse-has-bolted/

Federal Policy for the Protection of Human Subjects. (2017, January 19). *Federal Register 82*(12). Retrieved from https://www.govinfo.gov/app/details/ FR-2017-01-19/2017-01058/summary

De Montjoye, Y.-A., Radaelli, L., Singh, V. K., & Pentland, A. S. (2015). Unique in the shopping mall: On the reidentifiability of credit card metadata. *Science, 347*(6221), 536–539. doi: 10.1126/science.1256297

Frenkel, S. (2018, May 6). Scholars have data on millions of Facebook users. Who's guarding it? Retrieved from https://www.nytimes.com/2018/05/06/technology/ facebook-information-data-sets-academics.html

Goel, V. (2014, August 12). As data overflows online, researchers grapple with ethics. *The New York Times.* Retrieved from https://www.nytimes. com/2014/08/13/technology/the-boon-of-online-data-puts-social-science-in-a-quandary.html

The Guardian. (n.d.). The Cambridge Analytica files. Retrieved from https://www.theguardian.com/news/ series/cambridge-analytica-files

Herrman, J. (2018, April 10). Cambridge Analytica and the coming data bust. *The New York Times Magazine.* Retrieved from https://www.nytimes. com/2018/04/10/magazine/cambridge-analytica-and-the-coming-data-bust.html

Kozinets, R. V. (2013). *Netnography: Doing ethnographic research online.* London: Sage Publications.

Markham, A., & Buchanan, E. (2012). *Ethical decision-making and Internet research: Recommendations from* the AoIR Ethics Working Committee (Version 2.0). Retrieved from http://aoir.org/reports/ethics2.pdf

Sánchez, D., Martínez, S., & Domingo-Ferrer, J. (2016). Comment on "Unique in the shopping mall: On the reidentifiability of credit card metadata." *Science, 351*(6279), 1274. doi: 10.1126/science. aad9295

Gibbs, J., & Knoblock-Westerwick, S. (2018). Statement of correction. *Communication Research, 45*(4), 628–629. https://journals.sagepub.com/doi/pdf/10.1177/0093650218776754

Shweder, R. A., & Nisbett, R. L. (2017, March 17). Long-sought research deregulation is upon us. Don't squander the moment. *Chronicle of Higher Education.* p. A44.

Thelwall, M. (2010, July 12). Researching the public web. *eHumanities News.* Retrieved from https://www.ehumanities.nl/researching-the-public-web/

Townsend, L., & Wallace, C. (n.d.). *Social media research: A guide to ethics.* Aberdeen, UK: The University of Aberdeen. Retrieved from https://www.gla.ac.uk/media/media_487729_en.pdf

Tufekci, Z. (2018, March 19). Facebook's surveillance machine. Retrieved from https://www.nytimes.com/2018/03/19/opinion/facebook-cambridge-analytica.html

U.S. Department of Health and Human Services. (1993, March 16). *Tips on informed consent.* Rockville, MD: Office for Human Research Protections, Office for Protection from Research Risks. Retrieved from http://www.hhs.gov/ohrp/policy/ictips.html

U.S. Department of Health and Human Services. (2013, March 12–13). *Considerations and recommendations concerning Internet research and human subjects research regulations, with revisions.* Rockville, MD: Office for Human Research Protections. Retrieved from http://www.hhs.gov/ohrp/sachrp/mtgings/2013 March Mtg/internet_research.pdf

⑤SAGE edge™

Get the tools you need to sharpen your study skills. SAGE edge offers a robust online environment featuring an impressive array of free tools and resources.

Access quizzes, eFlashcards, video, and multimedia at **edge.sagepub.com/treadwell4e**.

YOU COULD LOOK IT UP

Reading, Recording, and Reviewing Research

"Joe, looks like a nice, quiet little library area you have here. Getting a head start on comm. research?"

"Yes and no. Caroline got me thinking about that old Hunter building. She's all for keeping it—historic value, unique architecture, and all that sort of thing. And I think even if it is a wreck why replace it with a car park? I'm all for a green campus—not more vehicles all over the place."

"So?"

"So I said I'd research other scenarios like this—what the arguments were, who won, who lost—that sort of thing. I was just going to Google 'building demolition.'"

"That'll pick up everything. You'll get a zillion articles on how to bulldoze, dynamite, or otherwise destroy buildings. And you won't need or want any of them. I'd be thinking seriously about search terms, for starters. Like do I really want to search for 'building demolition'? Maybe it would be better starting off with something like 'campus protests' or—even more specific—'campus building protests.'"

"And then?"

"And then sign into the library databases that focus on communication. That way you'll avoid all the engineering and architecture stuff related to buildings. Take a look on your smartphone. Databases have search fields so you can search by subject, date, author, or combinations of those—and a whole lot more."

"Sounds like work."

"Sort of. But here's how I think of it. You can work at locating a few good, relevant articles in a database, or you can work at reading through the zillion hits you'll get from a web search, trying to decide which ones you really want."

"OK, so I'm thinking search terms and databases. That about it?"

"Actually, there's more. You might be doing this on a smartphone, but you're the one that has to be smart. You need to be able to identify credible sources. And then there's Boolean logic of course."

"Boo who?

"Read the chapter, Joe."

CHAPTER OVERVIEW

All good research is built on a foundation of previous research. Reviewing and synthesizing this research is an essential start to any scholarly paper. Your review of the research **literature** should suggest research topics, ways of doing research, and, most important, how your proposed research will contribute to our collective understanding of human communication. Additionally, the review should help you find a "gap" or space for your own proposed research. This is an early step in creating new knowledge. Finding relevant information may be easy, but scholarly research requires that you prefer information that is credible as well as relevant. This chapter will help you identify the most credible sources of information and discusses how to search for them in a way that gets you the most relevant and credible results.

CHAPTER OBJECTIVES

This chapter will help you

- Explain why library research is a necessary preliminary to your own research.
- Illustrate the difference between relevant information and quality information.
- Describe with examples the difference between search engines and databases.
- Summarize the difference between scholarly, popular, and trade publications.
- List the differences between primary and secondary sources.
- Summarize the difference between search terms and search fields.
- Identify key questions you might ask to assess whether an item of information is credible.
- Discuss the concept of Boolean logic and its use in database research.
- Explain the purpose and nature of a scholarly literature review.
- Identify bibliographic software available for assisting a literature search.

LIBRARY RESEARCH: WHY BOTHER?

If I have seen further it is by standing on the shoulders of giants.

This quotation, attributed to Sir Isaac Newton (1642–1727), the British physicist and mathematician, refers to his dependency on Galileo's and Kepler's previous work in physics and astronomy (Newton, 1676).

The purpose of any research is to add to knowledge. The operative word is *add*. Unless you know what has gone before, you cannot know if your research will add to knowledge or merely replicate what others have already done. You must know the past if you are to contribute to the future.

Knowing the published scholarly research in your area—or, in research jargon, "the literature"—will stimulate your own research, give you a broader vision of your field, suggest appropriate research methods, and show where your own research fits into the broader body of knowledge.

Once you know what has been researched, you will be able to assess what needs to be researched and be confident that your efforts will result in a further contribution to our knowledge of human communication. You will also be able to identify other people working in your area of interest, the research methods used, and the debates surrounding your interest area and how best to research it. By synthesizing and thinking about previous and current research in your field, you will be able to see much farther than you ever would have seen on your own.

In most cases, the place to find published relevant literature is your academic library—your one-stop shop for scholarly research reports. Academic libraries will also have other material such as newspaper and video archives of potential relevance to communication researchers. You may want to look at such resources to identify the breadth of material that might be relevant to you. Ultimately, though, you will want to focus on "the literature"—the published scholarly research that has been done according to academic standards and is available most typically through the databases in academic libraries.

A thorough review of the scholarly literature will help you in the following specific areas, as well as providing the obvious benefit of a **bibliography**, or list of published sources on which you will build your own research.

Methods

Focus group or field interview? Ethnography or experiment? Your readings of the literature will identify accepted methods of research in your area of interest. A good review of the literature should also reveal methods that challenge conventional wisdom and the debates about how best to do the research that interests you.

Theory

What theories or ideas are being used to frame the communication phenomena you plan to study? How do the different theories apply to different research questions or hypotheses? Reviewing theory in your literature search can help give your study direction and suggest appropriate methods. For example, the constructivist theory that individuals make their own views and understandings of their world implies the use of research methods that capture participants' unique subjective ideas about the world, and these methods are qualitative rather than quantitative. A review of relevant theories may also help strengthen your arguments for the significance or relevance of your research and help you answer the "so what" question about it.

Ethics

Most communication research is research on human subjects. As discussed in Chapter 3, how people are recruited, treated, and debriefed is important to them psychologically and to you professionally. The research literature can suggest how to ensure your research is conducted ethically.

Language and Style

Each research specialization is a community defined by its own language and way of writing. From your own readings, you will see the somewhat formulaic format that most research papers have and the language that typifies each subfield and its specific style for citations, abbreviations, and use of tables and graphics. Just as reading generally is a good way to develop your general vocabulary and writing skills, so reading research is a good way to develop your research vocabulary and writing skills.

Inspiration

An unpredictable but joyous outcome of a literature search is discovering that one great "breakthrough" paper that suddenly makes a difficult concept clear, shows precisely how to use a specific method, or takes you off in a whole new direction. You will know it when you see it. You may find it out of a random search, but a systematic, thorough search will maximize your chances of finding it.

In summary, a targeted, systematic search for relevant journal articles, books, and other media will have you "standing on the shoulders of giants" and able to envisage your research project, how to go about it, and the contribution it will make to our collective understanding of human communication.

FINDING RELEVANCE, FINDING QUALITY

We want two things from a literature search—relevance and quality. The two are not the same.

Relevant information is information that is immediately useful to you. Quality information is information that is credible, can be relied on, and, in the case of scholarly research, meets the standards of the research community. Information can be highly relevant but not of any academic quality, or it can be highly credible but irrelevant. For example, you may find that the *National Enquirer* has information about communication with extraterrestrials that is highly relevant to your interests but not of any scholarly merit. The *New England Journal of Medicine* publishes research that is highly credible but probably irrelevant to your interest in corporate rhetoric. The art and science of a good literature search is finding out how to overlap relevance and quality.

Identifying Relevant Information

"Out there" is a lot of information that will be highly relevant. There is also a significantly larger volume of information that is irrelevant. Example? Use *communication* as a **search term**, and you will get material on mass, group, interpersonal, and organizational communication. You will also get information on telecommunications, animal communication, and communication with extraterrestrials. If your interest is in, say, rhetoric and public address, you will drown in information you don't need even though it all relates to communication.

The strategy of the search for relevance is simple. You want to find all relevant information—only. You do not want to find irrelevant information, and you do not want to miss relevant information. In communication research, this can be difficult because many other fields ranging from evolutionary psychology and web design to computer systems and marketing could be relevant to your interests. One key to obtaining relevant information is to develop a good vocabulary and to appreciate the difference in results that different search terms may bring. For example, *groups* and *teams,* though similar in concept, may produce quite different results when used as search terms.

Identifying Quality Information

Quality information means information that has been obtained in a way that meets scholarly standards. These standards include a clear, defensible, ethical research design; data collection methods and analyses that logically fit the research design; and results and conclusions that make an original contribution to our understanding of communication. Academic journals put all the research reports they receive through a process of peer review or **refereeing**. A refereed article is one that has been reviewed or refereed by other researchers in the author's field (peers) before being accepted for publication. Academic journals by definition contain refereed articles that meet scholarly standards; most other journals do not.

SCHOLARLY DATABASES VERSUS SEARCH ENGINES

Search Engines

Search engines such as Google, Yahoo, Bing, Lycos, and Dogpile are popular if for no other reason than their elegantly simple interfaces or, in the case of DuckDuckGo, the emphasis on user privacy. A one-line box allows you to type in search terms and get results, usually far more than you can cope with. The pluses of search engines are ease of use, ease of access, and a simple interface. The minuses can be a totally unmanageable number of search results, many of questionable quality.

Search engines can be useful in giving you a sense of what's "out there" and what's popular. For example, the web resources listed at the end of this chapter include the Google Trends site, which allows you to monitor Google searches by topic, by country, or by time period. This site provides one way of accessing what is of current interest to Internet users, but any understanding of Internet users based on these rankings will obviously be superficial.

Databases

With the important caveat that not all scholarly and relevant research findings are online, the scholarly **databases** typically hosted by or accessible through academic libraries are good places to find scholarly research.

Databases have a defined number of entries, and many databases consist of scholarly articles that have been peer reviewed. You will not get millions of irrelevant hits as the result of a search, and your research results should have a high level of credibility. You can automatically improve the quality of your search results simply by preferring databases to search engines. Proof? A search using the Google search engine for *communication* resulted in over 2.8 billion hits. Now look in the "All Fields" column of Exhibit 4.1, which shows the results of using different search terms in the scholarly database Communication & Mass Media Complete (CMMC). Just by preferring this database to Google, we reduced the number of hits for *communication* from millions down to about 290,000.

Databases are similar to phone directories in that a wrong search term or misspelling will give you the "wrong" results, or no results.

Scholarly databases have more sophisticated interfaces than search engines. Their **search fields** allow you to search for an article by author, date of publication, title, keywords, subject matter, or any combination thereof, resulting in a much more targeted search. A well-executed database search should give you the results you want and none of the results you don't want.

Because different databases contain different content, you can make your search for relevant literature even more focused simply by selecting the most relevant database. For example, CMMC might be a good starting point for a literature review unless you are specifically interested in business communication, in which case a database such as Business Source Premier might be preferable. In some circumstances, you can search several databases at the same time. For example, because EBSCO hosts Communication & Mass Media Complete as well as other databases relevant to communication studies, such as the Psychology & Behavioral Sciences Collection and Academic Search Premier, a researcher can select and then search these three databases together.

Don't forget CIOS, the Communication Institute for Online Scholarship, introduced in Chapter 2. You can use a keyword system, the Visual Communication Concept Explorer, or the Idea Monkey to get started on your research project.

By combining a search of relevant academic databases with a focus on refereed articles, you can maximize your chances of getting relevant, quality search results. Two cautions are in order, though. First, you should not restrict yourself to refereed journals exclusively. Books, news media, and websites may all be relevant—especially, perhaps, in communication

EXHIBIT 4.1 ■ Focusing Search Results by Combining Search Terms and Search Fields

Search Terms	Search Fields		
	All Fields	Subject Search	Title Search
Communication	289,559	89,440	32,061
Communication in organizations	3,162	2,776	31
Communication in nonprofit organizations	5	5	2

research. Second, communication studies are wide ranging. You may find the articles you need in political science, international affairs, psychology, journalism, or business databases. Your initial searches will require both a broad vision and a narrow focus.

Again, always remembering that not all relevant scholarly information is necessarily online, you should be able to optimize your research results simply by preferring specific search terms in a scholarly database to general search terms in a search engine.

SCHOLARLY JOURNALS: A GOOD STARTING POINT

Scholarly journals will give you a more specific start on a search because most of them focus on a specific area of interest. Once you find one issue of a journal with a high percentage of articles that are relevant to you, you may well find that other issues of the same journal will also have relevant content.

Communication Research could be a good general starting point because it reports research in a variety of fields.

More focused sources might include, for example,

International Journal of Business Communication, if you are interested in communication in business contexts;

Journal of Applied Communication Research, if you are interested in applying research in a campus or workplace setting;

Language and Speech, an interdisciplinary journal, if you are interested in how individuals perceive use of language as well as studies of disorders of language and speech;

Critical Studies in Media Communication, if you are interested in communication as an expression of power; or

Convergence: The International Journal of Research Into New Media Technologies, if you are interested in social media.

Revisit Chapter 1 for a more thorough although not comprehensive list of communication journals you might select as starting points for your literature review.

Assessing Scholarly Journals

One way to assess scholarly journals is to look at each journal's **impact factor**. In essence, the impact factor is a measure of the number of times the articles in a journal are cited by other scholarly articles. An impact factor of two would indicate that, on average, the articles in a journal were cited twice by other authors; a factor of three indicates that, on average, the articles were cited three times. The impact factor is the subject of debate, as with any such **metric**, but journals with a high impact factor can be regarded at least as publishing articles that are influential in their field.

The impact factor is, of course, irrelevant if the journal's content is irrelevant to your interests. Given two journals covering essentially the same interest area, though, you may decide to focus on the one with the higher impact factor. Some scholarly journals and academics have noted that impact factors can be problematic in some contexts. For example, *Nature*, one of the world's most cited academic journals, queried the idea of impact factors as a reliant metric. "Being an arithmetic mean, it gives disproportionate significance to a few very highly cited papers, and it falsely implies that papers with only a few citations are relatively unimportant" ("Time to Remodel," 2016, p. 466). That said, many journals still heavily rely on impact factor as a determinant of success.

Examples of sites that list journal impact factors or allow you to search for them are listed under "Recommended Web Resources" at the end of this chapter.

SCHOLARLY, POPULAR, AND TRADE PUBLICATIONS: WHAT IS THE DIFFERENCE?

What is the difference between scholarly and popular material? **Scholarly articles** go through a process of peer review before publication. Peer review, as discussed in Chapter 3, means that before journal editors will accept an article for publication, they will seek the opinions of other scholars doing the same kind of research as the author of the article. These reviewers read the article to determine whether the research has been done to professional standards, makes a contribution to knowledge, and appears to exhibit no ethical violations such as plagiarism.

How Will I Know a Scholarly Article When I See One?

The title *Journal of* . . . is one good clue but does not automatically flag a journal as refereed. Another clue is the format of the article. If you see headings such as "Abstract," "Method," and "Literature Review" and a list of references at the end of the article, there is a good chance that the article is refereed. Frequency of publication is also a clue. Refereed publications are typically quarterly, perhaps monthly, but not daily or weekly.

By contrast, **popular articles** are published without a refereeing process, typically in daily or weekly media, and are targeted to a lay audience. They do not have the formal subheadings noted above or a list of references as scholarly articles do. Newspaper and magazine stories are typical examples of popular articles.

Between these two extremes are the so-called **trade publications**. Trade publication articles, like academic articles, are written by experts, but the experts are more likely to be practitioners than academics, and their articles are not usually peer reviewed or refereed.

Articles in the trade press are more topical than academic articles because they appear daily, weekly, or monthly and do not get held up by a review process. However, information important to you as a scholarly researcher, such as a review of topic-specific literature, a detailed description of methods, a discussion of findings, and a list of references will not be included as a matter of course.

One reason to prefer scholarly, refereed journals and books is that they give you access to primary (original) research. Popular and trade articles may give you a summary of the research published by other authors, but you will need to go to scholarly sources to read what each original author wrote. Scholarly articles always provide citations ("cites") at the end of the article to let you find out what their sources wrote. Popular and trade articles do not do this; you have to accept what one author is telling you about other authors' research.

PRIMARY VERSUS SECONDARY SOURCES

A **primary source** is an original article; a **secondary source** is another author's summary of the primary source. Consider the two articles referenced below on sleep. If you go to the first, the *Journal of Sleep Research,* the primary source, you will find that it is several pages in length and has the subheadings typical of scholarly research papers—"Introduction," "Materials and Methods," "Results," "Discussion," and "References." By contrast, the second article, from the *Washington Post,* is a secondary source. It summarizes the 10-page primary source in a relatively short newspaper column with no subheadings. (Both articles are cited at the end of this chapter in the list of references.)

Sleep duration and mortality—Does weekend sleep matter?

Åkerstedt, T., Ghilotti, F., Grotta, A., Zhao, H., Adami, H., Trolle-Laggeros, Y., & Bellocco, T. First published 22 May 2018: https://doi.org/10.1111/jsr.12712

Sleeping in on the weekends can compensate for lack of sleep during the week, study suggests.

By Ben Guarino

Published May 23, 2018: https://www.washingtonpost.com/news/speaking-of-science/wp/2018/05/23/people-who-sleep-in-on-weekends-avoid-dying-young-study-suggests/

Note that the secondary source gets right to the point with the heading "Sleeping in on the weekends can compensate for lack of sleep during the week" because the author is summarizing the findings of the primary source as far as possible.

Secondary sources may be credible, as with the *Washington Post* article shown above, or, from a research point of view, have no credibility whatsoever. What all secondary sources have in common is that they summarize other people's research. They therefore omit detail that other researchers may need if they are to understand the research fully; a secondary source might also omit specific details that the original authors wanted published, as it provides only a summary of what someone other than the original authors thinks is important.

Secondary sources can be a quick way to get an overview of research, but making your own summary based on secondary sources is a bad idea because your summary of the summaries can magnify any biases and misinterpretations in the secondary sources. You can use secondary sources as a starting point, but as a professional, scholarly researcher, you will want and need to go to the primary sources and write your own summaries of this research.

SEARCH STRATEGIES: GENERAL TO SPECIFIC AND SPECIFIC TO GENERAL

Often, your **bibliographic** research will take the profile of a champagne glass, as shown in Exhibit 4.2. You start with a wide-ranging search and a large number of search results. You then narrow down your findings to a few highly relevant sources whose reference lists then provide a larger number of relevant sources.

On the other hand, you can start by finding or being assigned one "breakthrough" article that summarizes the history of a topic, explains how to research it, and inspires you to research it further. From the citations in that one article or by searching a relevant database for the authors of that article or for other articles tagged with the key terms the database uses to describe that one article, you will be able to generate a bigger set of relevant readings.

SEARCH TERMS AND SEARCH FIELDS

Search terms are the logical start to a search. They are also an exercise in using your vocabulary to expand or refine your search, for example trying the search term *virtual world* or *hyperreality* if the term *fantasy world* does not produce credible results.

Another way to expand or refine a search is to use the search fields in scholarly databases. Typically, you will be able to search by name of author, title of article, subject, date of publication, and many other fields. You can search for these alone or in combination. The results for any given search term will vary according to whether you do a general search of the database or restrict the search to the title or the subject of articles.

Subject terms such as *health communication* are assigned by authors and publishers to help the search process. They are important because they help locate an article in an area of interest but are not necessarily words that appear in the title. Think of a title as the name or label of an article. The subject is what the article is about, so a subject search will capture more articles than a title search because it is less specific and is likely to be a better starting point for a search.

An example of combining search terms and search fields to get more and more specific is shown in Exhibit 4.1. Note how selecting a specific search field such as "Subject" or "Title" makes a difference in search results. The "All Fields" column of the exhibit shows how the number of results becomes smaller as the search term becomes more and more specific.

EXHIBIT 4.2 ■ The Champagne Glass Model of Bibliographic Research
(1) Wide-ranging findings from your initial search
should lead you to
(2) very specific
citations,
which
generate
(3) still more highly relevant readings.

You can see from Exhibit 4.1 that a general search using a broad search term such as *communication* produces an unmanageable number of results. On the other hand, the very specific search term *communication in nonprofit organizations* in a title search produced only two scholarly articles. The five results from using this search term in a search of all fields in the CMMC database were

- two conference papers given at annual meetings of the International Communication Association;

- an article from the serial publication *Communication Arts* on the design and printing of nonprofit publications; and

- two scholarly journal articles, cited below, that together list 73 references.

If you had a specific interest in nonprofit communications, this search would give you 73 immediately relevant references, at least according to these articles:

When the "Stakes" are Communicative.

By: Lewis, Laurie K.; Richardson, Brian K.; Hamel, Stephanie A. Human Communication Research. Jul2003, Vol. 29 Issue 3, p400. 31p. 6 Charts.

Subjects: COMMUNICATION; STOCKHOLDERS; NONPROFIT organizations; ORGANIZATIONAL change; STOCKS (Finance)

Discourse, Identity, and Power in International Nonprofit Collaborations.

By: Murphy, Alexandra G.; Dixon, Maria A. Management Communication Quarterly. Feb2012, Vol. 26 Issue 1, p166–172. 7p. DOI: 10.1177/0893318911424374.

Subjects: FIRST person narrative; UGANDA; KENYA; GROUP identity; POWER (Social sciences); NONPROFIT organizations

Obviously, some judgment is required here; two seems a suspiciously small number of results. A search that is too specific may be "overfocused" and miss articles that might have been relevant to your interests. Also, these two articles are not the newest articles dealing with communication in nonprofit organizations; sometimes backing out a bit to a wider number of articles will increase both recency and relevance in your findings. Note also that apparently minor changes in spelling may influence your search results. For example, the above search results come from using the word *nonprofit*; different results come from using *non-profit* or the two words—*non profit*.

Note that the above citations are reproduced from the original search result. They are not formatted in the American Psychological Association (APA) style frequently used to cite communication research materials. Also, the examples presuppose that we were looking for scholarly articles. Scholarly databases may also let you search for other types of material such as editorials, books, magazines, or nontext resources such as photographs, maps, and graphs.

HOW CAN THE LIBRARY OF CONGRESS HELP MY LITERATURE SEARCH?

The answer is subject headings. You will want to be familiar with Library of Congress Subject Headings (LOCSH). The source is a standard reference item in academic libraries. The subject headings show you how information is categorized by the Library of Congress (LOC), but more to the point, they give you alternative search terms and perhaps a reminder of how your own vocabulary can limit or expand your search. Let's look at an example from the LOC's own website:

> If you search the Library's online catalog for the keywords "battered women," you find more than one hundred entries and may be perfectly satisfied. But by not identifying the Library's correct subject headings—"Abused women," "Abused wives," and "Wife abuse"—you may miss the best materials for your topic. A search combining these three terms yields more than one thousand records. (Library of Congress, n.d.)

In other words, thinking of alternative words to *women* and to *battered* can substantially multiply the number of relevant "hits" you get.

OTHER RESOURCES

Journals, books, and databases are not the only resources available. Other resources include catalogs, dictionaries, encyclopedias, indexes, annuals, yearbooks, handbooks, bibliographies, and abstracts. Some of these are listed as resources at the end of this chapter.

BEING SKEPTICAL ABOUT INFORMATION: WEBSITES AND FAKE NEWS

Your initial search results may vary in quality between refereed journal articles and web sources of extremely dubious quality. When anyone with a website can post to the world the "fact" that his or her parents were Martians, a touch of skepticism is required in evaluating websites. The following questions will help you identify good scholarship in web as well as print formats.

Stage 1: Think Book or Journal

Ask of the website the same questions you would ask of a book or journal.

- Author's credentials (e.g., Prof., Dr., PhD, MD)?

- Author's affiliation (e.g., university, college, corporation, think tank)?

- Date of publication and edition or revision? Remember that a book that has been frequently reprinted and is now into its 20th edition may have scholarly credibility or may simply be popular.

- Publisher? University presses and academic associations are academically respectable, as are academic publishers. This does not mean that their books and journals are unbiased; it means merely that there is a level of credible scholarship behind them.

- Title? "Lost tribes of Israel found at South Pole" versus "Conceptualizing and assessing organizational image: Model images, commitment, and communication" will give you some clue as to academic credibility.

- Intended audience? From the style of writing (word and sentence length and language), you will be able to guess at the intended audience and also whether the authors' intent is persuasive or informative.

- Objectivity—subjectivity? What biases can you discover?

- Coverage? Is the coverage comprehensive or selective? Credible sources will discuss all research relevant to the topic rather than "cherry-picking" only research that supports a particular perspective.

- Writing style? Is the writing style popular, technical, or academic?

- Reviews (if any)? Use the name of the author or the title of the article as a search term; you may pick up reviews of the article that will give you some critical insight on it.

- Citations? What references (credible or otherwise) are drawn on by the authors?

Stage 2: Additional Questions for Websites

- What does the URL tell you? Is it .com, .edu, .org, .mil, .gov, or another extension?

- Does the site tell you the criteria by which information is accepted or rejected? Does it accept all contributions, or is there some review process?

- What organization or people wrote the page? Do they have demonstrable expertise? Note that *expert* does not have to mean *unbiased*. We expect the XYZ company's website to be an authoritative source of information on XYZ products and predictably biased toward them.

- Could the page be a satire or comedic? It doesn't happen often in academia, but it does happen. Check out the *Journal of Irreproducible Results* by way of example (www.jir.com).

- Is contact information provided?

- Can you verify what is said or shown on the website? If not, it is academically suspect.

- Are documents in the site dated, and when was the site last updated?

- How does the site compare to others that are similar? If you do a web search for sites with a similar name, URL, or content, what is the quality of the information you get? Can you detect malicious or fake sites that are designed to appear credible but are actually phishing for information or pushing propaganda?

Many library websites demonstrate with examples how to distinguish quality sites from the more suspect ones. Some of these are listed at the end of this chapter.

Assessing Fake News and Other Nonscholarly Sources

Closely related to the issue of web site credibility is that of **fake news**. Fake news has been around as long as news itself, but the term has developed a special potency since the 2016 U.S. presidential election campaign.

Lazer et al. (2018) define fake news as "fabricated information that mimics news media content in form but not in organizational process or intent." They characterize it as lacking traditional news media editorial norms and processes for ensuring accuracy and credibility.

In popular usage, fake news may refer to information that is totally fabricated and false or accurate but written to deliberately mislead or make specious connections. It could be written by "imposters" pretending to be someone else or using "fake" credentials, or it could simply be humor or satire that should be self-apparently untrue. In some cases, news may be credible and trustworthy but labeled "fake" by those who disagree with it.

Although the term has been used to derogate credible, professional news sources, it does usefully raise the notion of questioning news and other information sources as to their accuracy and credibility. Identifying and evaluating fake news is not necessarily an easy task, especially when our own biases and beliefs may lead us to prefer and accept certain content uncritically, without looking for opposing information or perspectives.

The suggestions listed previously in this section and related to evaluating websites apply equally well to assessing the credibility of news articles and other nonscholarly sources. An end-of-chapter exercise asks you to suggest further questions that might help identify suspect news and other dubious sources.

MR. BOOLE AND THE THREE BEARS

One way to reduce the number of search results to something manageable is to ask the right combination of questions.

George Boole (1815–1864), an English mathematician, invented a type of linguistic algebra, the three most basic operations of which are AND, OR, and NOT. The relevance of these "**Boolean operators**" is this. Suppose you were unwise enough to use the search term *communication* in a search. As we have seen, you would likely drown in the number of largely irrelevant results, even from a database. You might similarly drown in the results of using the term *Smith* for an author search. But if you search for "*communication* AND *Smith*," you will reduce the number of results significantly. Similarly, "*communication* OR *social media*" will expand your search results if you need to, and "*communication* NOT *social media*" will narrow your search.

Exhibit 4.3 demonstrates the use of Boolean operators in a search of the CMMC database using all fields. You can see that combining search terms with the AND operator can reduce the number of search results significantly.

As with the story of Goldilocks and the three bears, literature searches can produce results that are too big, too small, or just right. Mr. Boole's operators can help you fine-tune a search to "just right."

EXHIBIT 4.3 ■ Use of Boolean Search Terms	
Search Term	**Number of Results**
communication	289,559
feminist	4,754
Search Term Combinations	
communication OR *feminist*	292,152
communication NOT *feminist*	287,398
communication AND *feminist*	2,161

SAVING YOUR SEARCH RESULTS

Ways of recording your search results include pen and paper, dumping everything to print or "flash drive," bookmarking websites, and using citation management software, discussed below. Saving search results electronically saves trees and makes sense because you will record citations accurately and you can edit your saved content as necessary for your literature review. In many cases, you're also able to annotate directly in your file. Note, however, that recording citations accurately does not necessarily mean that you will be recording them in the style that you will need for writing your report. Most scholarly databases will allow you to select the style in which you want citations saved (APA, Chicago, or MLA), and you should check for this option. Old-fashioned pen and paper still are helpful because they allow you to sketch out and visualize relationships that may be important in your search, as well as summarize details that are important to you.

Information You Must Record

Record *full* bibliographic information. Bibliographic information is information that uniquely identifies a specific book, journal or newspaper article, website, or specific quotation so that your readers can immediately locate it. For print media, bibliographic information includes the following items. Make sure to record them all as fully as you can; you will need them for your literature review and list of references at the end of your research report.

- Author—full name. Note that APA citation style uses each author's first initials and last name; other styles use the author's full first name. Play it safe and record full names initially so that you have them if you need them. Keep in mind that other citation styles may use first names, so it is always better to record first names than not.

- Title of the book; title of the chapter within the book, if the book consists of separately authored chapters; or title of the article and of the journal in which the article appears.

- Date of publication and, if a journal, volume and issue number.

- Edition, if a book.

- Page numbers that locate a journal article in a periodical or a separately authored chapter in a book.

- Page numbers that locate any direct quotation that you wish to reproduce from a book or periodical.

- For websites, additionally record the URL (web address), the **DOI** (digital object identifier) if available, and the date you downloaded the information. Style guides are becoming less insistent on reporting the download date for documents because the DOI or URL will adequately identify many Internet resources. For example, the article on sleep from the *Journal of Sleep Research* has its own DOI, which will lead to the source document or object.

Information You Should Record

The information that you should record is in some respects the information that most interests you. It is the information that explains why and how the research was done and the results and conclusions from the research.

In addition to author, title, and publication details, you will typically want to record the following:

- Method—how the research was conducted

- Results and conclusions—the results of and conclusions from the research

Results are the qualitative or quantitative new information generated by the research. Conclusions are how the researcher opts to interpret that information.

- Participants and/or media content—who or what (in the case of critical analyses or content analyses) was studied

- Unique aspects of the study—what is special about it

- The "ah-ha" factor—what, specifically, about this article makes it relevant for your research

Exhibit 4.4 shows one possible design for summarizing and recording the results of your searches. The example is based on an interest in searching for research on news media bias.

When starting your search, you might prefer to use such headings until you have a more specific sense of the headings you will need to best summarize your findings. Setting up as a table or a database, either the form as shown in Exhibit 4.4 or your own version, will allow you to sort your records by author, date, or title and search for words just as you would in an online database search. Many database services allow you to build your own portfolio of search results online and to format the results of your research in a particular scholarly style, such as APA style.

EXHIBIT 4.4 ■ One Way to Summarize Your Bibliographic Research		
Title	*Author(s)*	*Publication Details*
Visual War: A Content Analysis of Clinton and Trump Subreddits During the 2016 Campaign	Hale, Brent J. and Grabe, Maria Elizabeth	*Journalism & Mass Communication Quarterly*; 2018, Vol. 95, Issue 2, pp. 449–470. From CMMC database (Issue published June 1, 2018; accessed online July 13, 2018)

Summary

Examined subreddits for Clinton and Trump in order to find how they were framed by supporters in terms of gender (masculinity / femininity / gender-neutral). Basically found both Clinton and Trump showed more masculine leadership qualities than feminine leadership qualities.

Method

Collected samples from Reddit subreddits for Clinton and Trump from September 1 to Election Day 2016. Sample was selected by taking the "five most highly scored posts for each subreddit" during the time period. This study used posts with visual images of the candidates / spouses / VP candidates. Data were collected at different times of the day (between 8 a.m. and 8 p.m.). Coding was done on manifest content (Reddit pages) and latent content (visuals).

Participants and/or Media Content

Reddit pages for Clinton and Trump

Results/Conclusions

Clinton was scored positively in masculine characteristics by supporters, but only slightly positively in gender-neutral and feminine characteristics. Trump supporters scored Clinton negatively in all three. Trump was scored positively in masculine, gender-neutral, and feminine characteristics by supporters. Clinton supporters referenced Trump's "masculinity in positive ways."

My Notes/Unique Aspects of Study

Looks exactly like what I want. Presents an interesting basis for studying candidate preference, although still depends on coders' judgments and the social media platform used. Content analysis good idea. Should also look for news analyses (newspaper or television) of gender and candidates. Follow up on the citations in this article.

Bookmarking articles and websites is another way to organize and retain information although that process provides no summary of the information you have identified. For some people, handwritten notes of the type shown in Exhibit 4.4 are helpful because the writing process helps them think about the content of the material and its implications. Others find that an effective way of summarizing information is to type their research notes into a personally constructed database and to flag their own searchable key words for easy retrieval.

Typically, resources such as scholarly databases will allow you to set up a personal file in which you can collect selected resources at the click of a "save" button. Often, you will be able to save your search history, which is useful in reviewing what combination of search terms did or did not work for you and which journals provided the most relevant content. An important bonus for many users is the ability to view and save the citation for any article in the scholarly style you need—APA, MLA, or Chicago, for example. Online tools may or may not let you record your own notes and interpretations of what you are reading. Ensuring you have some mechanism that lets you record your own notes is therefore essential.

Citation Management Software

Citation management software lets you organize and retrieve citations for books, articles, websites, and the like by interfacing with library databases. The software can then work with word-processing software to insert properly formatted citations into your paper and create a properly formatted reference list. Most citation management software also allows you to take notes and annotate articles; this is cloud-based software, so you're able to access your files and notes on your own computer but also elsewhere, from a library computer, for example. Examples of this software include wizdom.ai, EasyBib, EndNote, Mendeley, RefWorks, Sorc'd, and Zotero. You can find out more about each of these from the websites listed at the end of this chapter.

REVIEWING THE LITERATURE

It is useful to make a distinction between reviewing the literature and the literature review. Reviewing the literature is the process by which you get from a perhaps mind-numbingly large number of relevant scholarly materials to a final product—a literature review.

Reviewing the literature means assessing the results of your literature search item by item and deciding which items will be in your literature review and what you will write about each item. This means assessing, for its theoretical and methodological relevance and its importance with respect to other items in your search results, each seemingly pertinent source you have found and saved from your search.

Exhibit 4.5 shows the questions an investigative journalist might ask when reading a research report. They will help you to assess scholarly literature and develop your own sense of what articles are credible and relevant to your own needs.

THE LITERATURE REVIEW: WRITING YOUR SEARCH RESULTS

You are now poised to write your literature review—your organized synthesis, analysis, critique, and summary of the literature most relevant to your research. This means turning your bibliographic notes into a summary and review of relevant literature that will convince readers that your own research is built on a sound theoretical foundation and will advance our comprehension of human communication.

A literature review may be very brief or constitute an entire paper, the purpose of which is to capture the history and current status of a discipline or a research method.

Generally, a literature review is a prelude to a research report. When you come to write up your research, your readers will first want to know your justification for doing the research and how it contributes to existing knowledge. In both cases, this means summarizing and analyzing your search results in the form of a literature review.

The literature review is more than a summary of the relevant literature; it is also your assessment of each article and its significance. A well-written literature review will support your own research while at the same time demonstrating gaps in our knowledge, some of which your own research demonstrably will fill. A literature review is a persuasive document; it is just one part of a research proposal or a research report, but it is an essential part in that

EXHIBIT 4.5 ■ Reviewing Scholarly Literature as Investigative Journalism

General Question	Specific Questions	Why Ask?
WHO	did the research?	A literature search using the authors' names may generate more relevant articles. Authors' credentials and institutional affiliations provide clues to the credibility of the research.
	was researched?	The number and nature of the research participants will indicate the sampling strategy and whether the research was done with a large sample, with a view to making generalizations, or with a small sample so as to be focused more on in-depth understanding.
	published the research?	Is the publication from a university, think tank, interest group, advocacy group, commercial organization, or political party? The publisher provides clues to credibility, expertise, and possible bias of the study.
WHAT	was researched?	For communication content studies, the media and the content and how they were selected and analyzed will provide insight on the generalizability of the findings and the researchers' theoretical framework.
	were the results?	For example, are the results qualitative, quantitative, empirical, critical, or generalizable? The nature of the results reported, independent of the specific findings, provides insight on the assumptions behind the research.
WHEN	was the research done?	The date of the research tells you whether you are looking at current research, research that may be outdated because of advances in the field, or a "classic" well worth reading and reviewing even though dated.
	was the research published?	Many scholarly journals publish the editorial histories of their articles. The time between the date of acceptance and the date of publication of an article may indicate whether the original paper needed substantial revision or had questionable content that required further research to clarify.
WHERE	was the research done?	This question should have you thinking about generalizability. For example, would research done in a college classroom be generalizable to a factory workforce or a military setting?
WHY	was the research done?	Did researchers want to test a theory, explore a new concept, or solve a marketing problem? Thinking about the "why" question may help identify bias and strengths and weaknesses in the study.
HOW	was the research done?	This is basically a methods question. Did researchers use focus groups, surveys, ethnography, observation, or data mining? Answering the "how" question will give you insight on the assumptions behind the research. In the case of human subjects research, you should also get insight into the ethical standards influencing the research.
	important is this research, theoretically and methodically?	Relative to other articles, does this paper stand out in terms of helping you to theorize about a research topic or to design a research project?
HOW WELL	was the research done?	Answering all of the above questions will help you decide whether the research merits inclusion in your literature review, as well as what and how much you need to write about it.

it should lead readers to understand that the methods you have used or propose to use are appropriate to your research question and that the results of using those methods do indeed contribute to our knowledge of human communication.

Structuring the Literature Review

There are several ways to structure a literature review.

Many reviews are written as a history; that is, they describe and evaluate selected research reports in order from oldest to most recent. This gives the reader a sense of how thinking about the topic has changed over time.

If there is little consensus among scholars, a review might be written with a "pro-con" structure, analyzing where the research articles agree and disagree and then coming to a conclusion. You could, for example, base your review on method, discussing all the studies that were done as surveys and all those done as experiments and then coming to conclusions about why your proposed method will be the most appropriate to answer your research question.

At times, you might structure your review topically. That is, when your study covers multiple areas, you might discuss each of them individually. For example, a study on ethics in political ads online might have a literature review begin with ethics in advertising, then consider political ads, and focus last on political ads in social media. In that structure, the author will show the "gap" where the proposed study will fit.

Most likely you will use one of the above structures for your literature review, but other structures are possible. For example, a study of censorship internationally might be prefaced by a literature review that reviews current research country by country rather than chronologically or with a pro-con structure. Various arrangements can be used conjointly as well. For example, a country-by-country review of censorship might use chronology or the pro-con structure within the review of the literature about each individual country.

Questions of Style

Scholarly papers have specific ways of setting out information or styles that clearly mark them as scholarly and not as trade or popular publications. The most common style in the social sciences is **APA** (American Psychological Association) style, the style used in this book for formatting references. Two others that you may encounter are **Chicago** and **MLA** (Modern Language Association).

All styles agree on the requirement for specific subheadings that flag the literature review, research method(s), results, discussion, conclusions, and a listing of other people's work. They also all insist on consistency of language and style so that readers are not confused and on accurate citation so that readers can easily find the cited works.

For specifics of APA style, see the APA style resources listed at the end of this chapter under "APA, Chicago, and MLA Style Guides." You should consult the websites and stylebooks available in any academic library for specific guidance in all three styles.

Use the checklist shown in Exhibit 4.6 to help ensure that your literature review meets scholarly standards.

EXHIBIT 4.6 ■ Literature Review Questions

1. Does your review
   - Explain how your readings agree and disagree?
   - Identify gaps in our knowledge of human communication?
   - Summarize the current status of research on the topic being reviewed?

2. Does your review have a logical structure that helps the reader understand it?

3. Does your review set the scene for readers to understand that a logical next step would be one or more of the following?
   - Test a hypothesis.
   - Describe or explain a phenomenon.
   - Replicate previous research in a different setting.
   - Explore a new research method or combination of methods.

4. Are all your reviewed articles cited accurately in the required scholarly style?

ETHICS PANEL
THE ETHICS OF SCHOLARLY PUBLICATION

Behind the scholarly research you are accessing, most likely through your academic library's online databases, there are competing intellectual and business models of scholarly publication.

You can get a sense of these debates as you review textbook purchase options each semester—hardcover, paperback, or electronic version; rent or buy; bundled or not bundled; purchased directly from the publisher, from your campus bookstore, from a student cooperative, or maybe even from a shady online site selling pirated copies at suspiciously low prices.

To a large extent, such options have been made possible by the same developments in web technology that are challenging the traditional model of scholarly publishing. Traditionally, a final research report is submitted by the authors to the editor of a scholarly journal, who then seeks a peer review of the research. If the review is favorable, the report will be published in an issue of the journal. The journal is available for a subscription fee that covers the costs of editing, printing, and distribution, as well as a profit margin for the publisher, which often is a for-profit business. Likely, the publisher also holds copyright on the published articles. This means that the publisher's permission has to be obtained by anyone seeking to reproduce any of the published content, usually for a fee.

The Internet has fundamentally challenged the traditional model in two ways. First, web publishing lowers the cost of publication by virtually eliminating printing and distribution costs. Second, the personal and institutional connections the Internet made possible increased scholars' ability to contact each other directly and bypass traditional publishers. Why must I wait three months for your research to appear in a print journal when I can just request that you e-mail me your research report?

A further challenge to the traditional publishing model comes from the open access movement—a coalition of individuals and interest groups arguing for better access to research and critiquing the traditional subscription model for journal access. The open-access model argues that research findings should be freely available so that research progress is not hindered by financial barriers or copyright restrictions.

One model of open access is "author-pays"—that is, the author, or more likely her or his employer, pays publication expenses per manuscript published or manuscript submitted, an arrangement used particularly for submissions to scientific and medical journals. Open-access journals may also be subsidized by grants, advertising, membership dues, and/or volunteer labor, and there are hybrid models in which both author and journal subscribers are charged.

A troubling subspecies of open-access publishing is the so-called "predatory journal," which makes its money by charging authors but without regard to the conventional review processes. The result, as *The Economist* points out, is that "a journal that need not induce readers to pay can publish rubbish, as long as authors will pay for the presumed prestige . . ." (B.S., 2018).

Some researchers may be duped into publishing in these less than credible journals; others may opt in knowingly as a painless way to boost their résumés. Some may opt to cite articles from these journals thereby reinforcing a false credibility and multiplying the impact of unreviewed research.

One important implication of these different publishing models is the need for you to be able to distinguish between apparently credible research, truly credible research, and the fun, ironic, and totally fictitious content published in, for example, the *Journal of Irreproducible Results.*

There are few legal constraints on predatory publishing, but what are the ethical implications of publishing unreviewed research in such "predatory" journals, and of citing research from such journals in your own work?

Review the ethical principles outlined in Chapter 3 to help you arrive at your answers.

At the end of this chapter, you will find Beall's website listing predatory publishers and journals along with a checklist to help you identify such journals.

Chapter Summary

Library research, well done, will guide you on

- What other researchers in your field have discovered

- Research methods

- Research ethics

- Language and style

You should know

- The difference between databases and search engines

- The difference between primary and secondary sources

- The differences among scholarly, trade, and popular publications

- How to focus your library research by using appropriate databases, search terms, and search techniques

- The basics of formatting and style for scholarly papers

- The bibliographic software available for recording and formatting the results of a literature search

Key Terms

APA 83
bibliographic 73
bibliography 66
Boolean operators 77
Chicago 83
citations 72
databases 69

DOI 79
fake news 77
impact factor 70
literature 65
metric 70
MLA 83
popular articles 71

primary source 72
refereeing 68
scholarly articles 71
search fields 69
search term 68
secondary source 72
trade publications 71

Application Exercises

Exercise 1: APA Style

Under the heading "Primary Versus Secondary Sources" above, locate the referenced article "Sleep Duration and Mortality—Does Weekend Sleep Matter?" taken from the *Journal of Sleep Research*. Rewrite the citation so that it conforms to APA style.

Exercise 2: Comparing Primary and Secondary Sources

Locate the original *Journal of Sleep Research* and *Washington Post* articles on sleep cited above under the heading "Primary Versus Secondary Sources." Carefully compare these two articles and answer the following questions:

* What information in the original *Journal of Sleep Research* article is missing from the *Washington Post* article? What content, if any, in the *Washington Post* article cannot be found in the *Journal of Sleep Research* article?

* Assuming the *Washington Post* article is written to help and inform readers with sleep disorders, what writing techniques can you identify that are used to interest and motivate such readers and maintain their interest?

Exercise 3: Nonscholarly Sources and Fake News

Much of this chapter offers techniques and tips related to finding and evaluating scholarly sources. But the Internet also offers a vast range of nonscholarly content that may potentially contribute to a literature review or become a focus of a research project in its own right. The question arises of how to evaluate nonscholarly sources, particularly as reports of "fake news" in the media remind us to assess all sources of information critically.

What resources and services does your campus library offer to assist you with identifying problematic sources during your research?

Review the "Being Skeptical About Information, Especially Web Information" in this chapter and identify additional questions you might ask to help identify nonscholarly sources such as news sites as credible or not.

HINT: Scholars tend not to yell at each other in caps—LIKE THIS!!!!!!!

Exercise 4: Search Terms and Boolean Operators

Write down all of the search terms you might use to get a comprehensive listing of scholarly papers on social media.
Combine these search terms using Boolean operators to then focus your research on

* social media and youth,

* social media and romantic relationships, and then

* social media and public relations.

Note that this is not just an exercise in Boolean operators; it is also an exercise in vocabulary. For example, *social media* may prove to be too broad a search term. What terms other than *social media* could you use to narrow your search? Note also that *youth*, *romantic*, and *public relations* all have analogous terms that might give you better or worse search results. For each of these three terms, identify an alternative word or words that you might substitute to narrow or expand your search.

Exercise 5: Writing a Literature Review

Search the Pew Research Center Internet & Technology website—www.pewinternet.org—for the topic "elections and campaigns." You will find a series of reports on U.S. elections for the years 2000 through 2016. Write a brief literature review summarizing how the role of the Internet and social media in U.S. elections has changed since 2000. Cite all sources correctly using APA style. For most years, you will find several different reports, so you will need to be selective in your reading and writing.

HINT: You can use the "Refine Results" menu to limit your search by research area (e.g., Internet, Science & Tech") and by date (e.g., by using "Custom Date Range").

Recommended Reading

Communication Yearbook

An annual review of communication research, published by the International Communication Association. The series provides in-depth articles on research on such aspects of communication as interpersonal, health, organizational, intercultural, international, technology, politics, and rhetoric.

Cull, N. J., Culbert, C., & Welch, D. (2003). *Propaganda and mass persuasion: A historical encyclopedia, 1500 to the present*. Santa Barbara, CA: ABC-CLIO.

Surveys key propaganda campaigns, people, concepts, techniques, and current research.

Danesi, M. (2000). *Encyclopedic dictionary of semiotics, media, and communications*. Toronto, ON: University of Toronto Press.

Describes the terms, concepts, personages, schools of thought, and historical movements related to these fields.

Lievrouw, L. A., & Livingstone, S. (Eds.). (2009). *New media*. Thousand Oaks, CA: Sage.

Covers historical, economic, social, and behavioral issues related to new media.

Rubin, R. B., Rubin, A. M., & Haridakis, P. M. (2010). *Communication research: Strategies and sources* (7th ed.). Belmont, CA: Wadsworth.

This book will help you learn library research skills, scholarly writing, and the basics of APA style.

Siapera, E. (2018). *Understanding new media* (2nd ed.) Thousand Oaks, CA: Sage.

Discusses new media as they relate to politics, security, surveillance, journalism, identities, gaming, mobile media, and social media.

The above resources provide an overview of some key areas in communication. Use your own academic library to find more specialized resources such as the *Broadcasting and Cable Yearbook* or the *Handbook of Political Communication Research*.

Recommended Web Resources

Academic Serials in Communication..........www.ascus.info

Academic Serials in Communication—Unified System (ASCUS) is a not-for-profit, society-governed, full-text database of academic publications in communication. ASCUS is a collaboration between academics, societies, and publishers in which content is widely distributed at low cost.

American Psychological Association..........www.apa.org

Provides insights and resources on psychological aspects of human communication and on APA style.

Beall's List of Predatory Journals and Publishers..........www.beallslist.weebly.com/

One listing of predatory publishers and journals along with a checklist to help identify such journals.

Electronic Journal of Communication..........www.cios.org/www/ejcmain.htm

One of the first peer-reviewed and electronically distributed scholarly journals.

Journal of Irreproducible Results...........www.jir.com

A magazine of humor about science and scientists.

Library of Congress Classification Outline..........www.loc.gov/catdir/cpso/lcco

This site shows the Library of Congress's classification outline. Clicking on any category will show you potential search terms in that category.

Voice of the Shuttle (VoS): Media Studies..........http://vos
.ucsb.edu
*Provides annotated links to resources in media theory
and theorists, media histories, TV, film or video, new
media, popular music, journalism, radio, comics, telecom
issues, consumerism and advertising, censorship,
journals, and departments, programs, and professional
associations (VoS "is woven" by Alan Liu of the University
of California, Santa Barbara).*

APA, Chicago, and MLA Style Guides

APA style resources..........www.apastyle.org
Chicago style...........www.chicagomanualofstyle.org/home
.html
MLA style..........www.mla.org/style

Evaluating Websites

Cornell University Library, "Evaluating Web Pages"..........
http://olinuris.library.cornell.edu/ref/research/
webeval.html
Cornell University Library, "Fake News, Alternative Facts
and Misinformation Workshop"..........http://guides
.library.cornell.edu/c.php? g=636325&p=5176823
Purdue University, "Evaluating Print vs. Internet
Sources"..........https://owl.purdue.edu/owl/research

_and_citation/conducting_research/evaluating_
sources_of_information/print_vs_internet.html

Citation Management Software

wizdom.ai.....................................https://www.wizdom.ai
EasyBib..www.easybib.com/
EndNote...www.endnote.com
Mendeley..www.mendeley.com
RefWorks...www.refworks.com
Sorc'd...www.sorcd.com/
Zotero...www.zotero.org

Journal Impact Sites

CiteFactor...www.citefactor.org
Impact Factor Search.........www.impactfactorsearch.org

Miscellaneous

Code of Ethics of the American Library Association.........
www.ala.org/advocacy/proethics/codeofethics/
codeethics

What Is Everybody Else Searching For?

You can find out the most popular nonacademic search
terms by time, category, or country at https://trends
.google.com/trends/.

References

Åkerstedt, T., Ghilotti, F., Grotta, A., Zhao, H., Adami,
H., Trolle-Lagerros, Y., & Bellocco, R. (2018). Sleep
duration and mortality–Does weekend sleep matter?
Journal of Sleep Research, 28(1), e12712. https://doi.
org/10.1111/jsr.12712

B.S. (2018, July 10). The Economist explains:
What are "predatory" academic journals? *The
Economist.* Retrieved from https://www.economist.
com/the-economist-explains/2018/07/10/
what-are-predatory-academic-journals

Guarino, B. (2018, May 23). Sleeping in on the weekends
can compensate for lack of sleep during the week,
study suggests. *Washington Post.* Retrieved from
https://www.washingtonpost.com/news/speaking-
of-science/wp/2018/05/23/people-who-sleep-in-on-
weekends-avoid-dying-young-study-suggests/

Lazer, D. M. J., Baum, M. A., Benkler, Y., Berinsky, A. J.,
Greenhill, K. M., Menczer, F., Metzger, M. J., Nyhan,

B., Pennycook, B., Rothschild, D., Schudson, M.,
Sloman, S. A., Sunstein, C. R., Thorson, E. A., Watts,
D. J., & Zittrain, J. L. (2018, March 9). The science
of fake news: Addressing fake news requires a
multidisciplinary effort. *Science, 359*(6380),
1094–1096. DOI: 10.1126/science.aao2998

Library of Congress. (n.d.). *The library's catalogs.*
Retrieved from http://memory.loc.gov/ammem/
awhhtml/awsearchcat.html

Newton, I. (1676, February 5). Letter to Robert
Hooke. In *Oxford Dictionary of Quotations* (5th
edition). Original attribution is from H. W.
Turnbull (ed.) *Correspondence of Isaac Newton*
(vol. 1).

Time to remodel the journal impact factor. (2016, July
28). *Nature, 535*, 466. Retrieved from https://www
.nature.com/news/time-to-remodel-the-journal-
impact-factor-1.20332

$SAGE edge™

Get the tools you need to sharpen your study skills. SAGE edge offers a robust online environment featuring an impressive array of free tools and resources.

Access quizzes, eFlashcards, video, and multimedia at **edge.sagepub.com/treadwell4e**.

5

MEASUREMENT

Research Using Numbers

"Hey, here's our grade-A guy, Mike."

"Knock it off; I got a couple of A's . . . that's all. Couple of points less and I'd be in A-minus territory. Reality is, I'm sort of a B plus person overall, so I have no idea what these A's are all about—not that I'm complaining."

"So what are they measuring? Like if I do a brilliant job explaining comm. theory, why get downgraded for misspelling? The theory test was supposed to measure my knowledge, not my spelling ability, right? Tests should measure what they're supposed to measure."

"It doesn't matter what they measure if your test results are all over the place. You can't rely on tests; they have a dumb-luck component. If we all sat our last semester's tests again, we'd all get different grades."

"That is if you still remembered everything from last semester!"

"OK, but all things being equal, don't you think a test ought to produce the same results each time—sort of like you can rely on a good barista to make the coffee you like each time?"

"That might be true except for the reality that there are good and bad baristas, and good and bad tests I suppose."

"So you're one of those people who thinks there are two kinds of people in the world—those who divide the world into two kinds of people and those who don't?"

"Very funny . . . not! This campus does it all the time—like pass/fail grading."

"I suppose pass/fail does tell you something—like the 'passes' did better than the 'fails.'"

"Except you wouldn't put every 'pass' in our honor society. You've got to be more discriminating than pass/fail."

"So we're back to measuring stuff, numbers and whether Mike gets a 93 instead of a 92. And what does a 93 mean anyway?"

"Maybe that's what this chapter is all about."

"And more, I bet. We'll need coffee!"

"You bet. Now I think about it, how do they grade coffee?"

CHAPTER OVERVIEW

This chapter introduces quantitative approaches to the study of human communication. If we are to have faith in research numbers, however obtained, they must measure what they are supposed to measure (validity) and do so consistently (reliability). This chapter introduces these two important concepts; the nominal, ordinal, interval, and ratio levels of measurement; and two **scales** commonly used in communication research—the Likert and semantic differential scales.

CHAPTER OBJECTIVES

This chapter will help you

- Discuss the concept of measurement and its use in communication research.
- Differentiate, with examples, nominal, ordinal, interval, and ratio measurement.
- Explain the concepts of validity and reliability.
- Identify ways of assessing reliability.
- Identify ways of assessing validity.
- Compare and contrast, with examples, Likert and semantic differential scales.

WHAT DO YOUR HEAD SIZE, ATTITUDES, AND READABILITY HAVE IN COMMON?

Nineteenth-century **phrenologists** argued that there was a relationship between cranial size and shape and mental attributes such as, perhaps, the ability to comprehend language or mathematical concepts. After all, if you have a big head, you must be brainy, right? Twenty-first-century wisdom rejects such a connection, but head size, readability, and attitudes do have one thing in common. They have all been subject to measurement, the focus of this chapter.

Many of us have experienced using numbers to make sense of the world and believe that measuring and assigning numbers to phenomena are good ways to make sense of the world, even if numbers perhaps leave us short of fully understanding it. Think of the numbers in your life. Vehicles are advertised on the basis of miles per gallon. Committees make decisions on a "six for; two against" basis. Academic careers and financial aid are predicated on such numbers as grade point average (GPA) and GRE and SAT scores. Broadcast programs live or die on audience share and ratings. Politicians live or die on approval ratings, opinion polls, and of course the vote count. Web advertisers count click-throughs. You buy clothes and shoes based on a measurable body size. And then, of course, there's hang time, yardage, RBIs, assists, and golf handicaps.

Assigning numbers to things seems to lend precision to an imprecise world and is, of course, the basis of all statistical analysis.

This chapter discusses **measurement** as it is understood in communication research. To begin with, a couple of definitions:

- **Numerals** are labels. On their own, "13," "2013," and "64" are not numbers but labels for phenomena. They could be street addresses, a brand name, a commuter jet, or a cologne.

- **Numbers** assign value and relativity to phenomena. For example, the numbers 1 through 5 can indicate increasing levels of agreement with a statement if people are asked to rate their agreement on a scale where 1 = strongly disagree and 5 = strongly agree. As an age, "64" signifies that someone has been on this earth longer than someone who is "13."

Numbers give us the ability to make accurate discriminations and to generalize. That ability is important when trying to decide whether there are "real" differences between groups. For example, a survey shows that 48% of a group of women and 52% of a group of men prefer candidate X. Can we assume that, in the wider voting population, candidate X would win the male vote and lose the female vote, or is there a probability that both groups are much the same in their attitudes?

Numbers and statistical methods can allow us to generalize with varying levels of confidence. Intuitively, if the above groups consisted of 10 men and 10 women, we would have some difficulty predicting the outcome of a national election. If the groups were each 100 people, we would feel more confident, and if 1,000 people, perhaps more confident still. Statistical calculations, as we will see, allow us an ability to generalize based on numbers, and tell us the level of confidence that we are entitled to in those generalizations.

One major advantage of numbers in applied communication fields such as marketing, political communication, advertising, employee communication, and public-opinion tracking is the ease of processing the answers. If 2,000 people each write one page explaining their views on media violence, you are in for a lot of reading. If the same 2,000 people each position themselves on a scale between 1 (*strongly disagree*) and 5 (*strongly agree*), with respect to a statement about media violence, their responses can be readily collected by e-mail, phone, website, or optical scanners and, once collected, computer-analyzed in seconds.

Of course, those who argue that adopting a "numbers only" approach ignores qualitative evidence and therefore loses a great deal of information and the potential for an in-depth understanding of human communication are correct. We will explore the advantages of qualitative methods more fully in Chapters 12 and 13.

AN INTRODUCTION TO SCALES

Measurement is essentially the process of finding out whether people or media content have more or less of an attribute we are interested in. For example, we might be interested in whether people have 5 or 500 social media contacts, whether they score high or low on a measure of religious intolerance, or whether they are rich or poor. It is clear that these questions vary in the level of precision with which they can be answered, and in the extent to which the answer requires a subjective judgment by the researcher.

For example, it is conceptually easy to measure how much time a person spends online. You could simply record his or her time online (ignoring, for the moment, how exactly we might do that) and get an answer. If two independent observers did this and agreed on their results, we would have even more confidence in the measurement.

On the other hand, measuring whether someone is rich or poor is problematic. We could measure the person's wealth, but that raises two questions. First, how do we measure wealth precisely? Is it a bank balance? The value of real estate? The potential for inheritance? Second, assuming we have a good measure of wealth in, say, dollars, how do we decide what counts as rich and what counts as poor? The number of dollars in a bank account can be counted and verified. *Rich* and *poor* are relative terms. Even though the criteria may be clear, for example earning over or under $50,000 a year, the decision to establish such categories and to assign individuals to them is ultimately a subjective, and perhaps political, one.

Measurement requires answers to three questions:

What exactly shall we measure and record?

Does the measure capture what we're interested in?

Can we be sure that our measurements, when repeated, will give the same results?

For example, communication researchers often record **demographic** information such as political affiliation, level of education, or sex. These are legitimate and common "measurements," but what is it that Republicans have more of than Democrats, seniors more than sophomores, females more than males? The questions are not that readily answered, and some of these demographic variables are really little more than labels—a very low level of measurement, as we will see.

RESEARCH NOIR

We don't cover film noir in this book, but research NOIR is a handy acronym to help you remember the basic levels of measurement. NOIR stands for four basic levels of measurement —**nominal**, **ordinal**, **interval**, and **ratio**.

Measures can be nominal—essentially labels; ordinal—allow rank ordering; interval— allow statistical calculations; or ratio—allow more sophisticated statistical operations.

Nominal Measurement

Examples: New York, Nevada, Idaho, California, Ontario, Quebec
Newspapers, radio, television
Basketball, curling, football, cricket
Facebook, Twitter, Instagram, Tumblr

Nominal measurement is really nothing more than labeling or classification. For example, male and female; Buddhist, Christian, Muslim, and Hindu; and area codes 413, 508, 415, and 775 are all sets of nominal "measures." Even when urban, suburban, and rural, for example, are assigned a code or transformed into numbers for computer processing, they remain nominal. Coding *urban* into "1" and *suburban* into "2" and *rural* into "3" does no more than substitute labels because, in this instance, 1 and 2 and 3 are numerals, not numbers. Similarly, the 413, 508, 415, and 775 characters representing area codes are also numerals, not numbers. They don't "measure" anything. You can't add them up or come up with an "average area code." The 775 area code is not inherently bigger or better than the 413 area code (except perhaps subjectively to those who live in Nevada).

The only numbers we can really generate from nominal variables are counts or percentages, as in "75 respondents (30%) were female; 175 (70%) male."

Ordinal Measurement

Examples: Freshman, sophomore, junior, senior
First, second, third place
BS, MS, PhD
Private, corporal, sergeant

Ordinal measures indicate some level of progression; in some sense, one category has "more" of something than another. Second graders have "more" education than first graders. Sophomores have "more" education than freshmen. Generally, parents, faculty, and students are comfortable with such a ranking, but it is imprecise. Is the difference between freshmen and sophomores time at school, number of credits, or a combination of the two? If the difference is credits, how many credits make a difference—one, three, six, nine? The distinction is not a clear one. We cannot say that a sophomore has X times more education than a freshman; we can say only in some less than precise way that a sophomore has been at school "longer" and perhaps has "more" credits.

In public opinion polling, rank order questions are an example of ordinal measurement. If you rank order restaurants on some attribute such as value for money, convenience, or hygiene, you are telling the researcher that you believe that your top-ranked restaurant has "more of" that attribute—but not "how much more of" it. As researchers, we get a sense of difference or proportion, but we still have no numbers with which we can compute. You cannot determine from such a ranking that restaurant X is twice as good as restaurant Y; you can determine only that X is "better than" Y.

Interval Measurement

The basic characteristic of interval measures is the assumption of equal intervals between points on a scale. In our NOIR hierarchy, we finally have instruments to which we can attach numbers rather than numerals, and results we can analyze quantitatively.

Two classic interval scales in communication research are the Likert scale, named after its developer, Rensis Likert, and the semantic differential scale, pioneered by Osgood, Suci, and Tannenbaum (1957). Examples of both are shown later in this chapter. Interval measurement is common in quantitative communication research. You will almost certainly be familiar with such scales from completing course evaluation forms at the end of each semester.

Ratio Measurement

Ratio scales contain a "true" zero that captures the absence of an attribute. There are authentic zeros, for example, zero speed on a speedometer, zero heartbeat or brain activity, and an absolute zero temperature. There are some authentic zeros in human communication as well. Class attendance and going to the movies, for example, can both be zero if they never happened. It is possible to have zero income, zero employment, or zero formal education if you never attended school.

Why Do We Care?

The reason we care about categories of data is that the type of data we collect determines what we can or cannot do with the data statistically. Nominal data limit us to reporting only numbers and percentages. We can do nothing more than report, for example, that in a sample of 20 individuals, 12 (60%) were female and 8 (40%) were male, or that 3 (15%) preferred print news, 7 (35%) preferred radio, and 10 (50%) preferred social media.

The same is true for ordinal data. We cannot calculate an average of private, corporal, and sergeant anymore than we can calculate an average of freshman, sophomore, junior, and senior. Again, we can really report only the numbers and percentages of each class year. Note, however, that if we defined class status in terms of number of years at college, we could use that number from each individual in our sample to get an average number of years for the sample.

There are two broad categories of variables (attributes that vary) within the NOIR family. Nominal and ordinal data fall into the category of "discrete" variables; interval and ratio data fall into the category of "continuous" variables.

Discrete data "jump" from category to category. That is, a person is either a freshman or in another class year, a sergeant or another rank, a graduate or not a graduate, and so on.

Continuous variables change incrementally. Age, for example, changes by the day, the hour, the minute, the second, and the fraction of a second; income changes by the dollar or cent; speed changes by miles per hour, feet per second, and inches per second. It is obvious that continuous variables offer a greater level of precision in measurement and therefore can capture more subtle differences and changes than do discrete variables. Importantly, they also permit the use of the most sophisticated statistical tools. With ratio and interval data, we can explore relationships and differences in ways that are not possible with discrete variables.

Typically, we need questions that use interval or ratio scales because attitudes are rarely expressed in black-or-white, yes-or-no terms. We need to give people the opportunity to express the strength of their feelings in more graduated terms using, for example, a Likert scale—discussed below.

Ratio scales are at the top of our NOIR hierarchy for these reasons. Note that while discrete variables cannot be treated as continuous variables, it is possible to treat continuous variables as discrete ones. For example, a researcher may collect demographic data such as age but decide that he is really only interested in whether students are over or under the legal drinking age. In this case, the age of each individual would be examined, and each person would be labeled as either "over the drinking age" or "under the drinking age" on that basis. In effect, there are now two discrete groups: "over" and "under." We now have an ordinal scale, and the continuous variable, "age," has disappeared.

The advantage of converting a continuous variable—age in this case—into a discrete variable is that the original age variable remains available if the researcher needs to do more sophisticated analyses related to age in years. The technique works in only one direction, though; discrete variables cannot be converted into continuous variables. If we ask research participants only whether they are under or over the drinking age, for example, we have no way of knowing how old they were when they took the survey. We will have only two discrete age groups and cannot convert these data to the continuous type of variable.

In practice, researchers are likely to default to continuous variables whenever possible because they allow the most sophisticated statistical analyses. In principle, we should be thinking about getting the best match of theory (what ideas we are exploring), method (how we can best capture the data we are interested in), and data (what data best provide insight on our research problem). If categorical variables suffice, there is no theoretical reason to use continuous variables, but the latter often offer "the best of both worlds."

NOIR in Action

The following shows how the variable of age might be measured at the four different levels of NOIR:

> Nominal: Parent, child (note that *a* child could be older than *a* parent)
> Ordinal: Child, adolescent, adult
> Interval: Age (years): __ 0–4 __ 5–9 __ 10–14 __ 15–19
> Ratio: Age in years _____

The reason to remember NOIR is that statistical calculations assume a particular type of underlying measurement. To revisit an example, you cannot code *male* as "1" and *female* as "2," discover that you have seven women and three men in your sample, average the scores, and report that the average gender for the group was 1.3. "Gender" as a variable is nominal. It lends itself to classification but not to computation.

This is not a mistake most people make, but the danger comes with the use of statistical analysis software, which by and large requires information to be coded numerically. While it is possible to code *male* as M and *female* as F, the temptation is to use numbers for everything and code *male* and *female* as 1 and 2, respectively. Computers do exactly what they are told to do and will "average" men and women together and report a "mean" of 1.3 if you ask them to do so.

TO NOIR IS NOT ENOUGH: RELIABILITY AND VALIDITY

Credible research results demand the use of credible research instruments. *Credible* in a general sense means trustworthy or believable. You must use instruments that you and the readers of your research can have confidence in. In research, confidence is maximized, though never ensured, by knowing that your measures have both **reliability** and **validity**.

RELIABILITY

Imagine the frustration of having an erratic watch. You arrive at 9:59 a.m. for a 10 a.m. class, to discover that the time on everyone else's watch is 10:15. You set your watch correctly and arrive in class the following day at 9:59 to discover that everyone else thinks the time is 9:45. This brings up the epistemological question of whether or not truth is ultimately that which most of us agree on; perhaps everyone else is wrong. But the important issue for now is that your watch appears to be unreliable; you cannot trust it.

Obviously, we cannot rely on the results this watch is giving us, and equally we cannot rely on the data provided by a research device that is not reliable. We will trust the 10:00 a.m. time displayed by this watch when every other timekeeping device we can access also tells us it is 10:00 a.m., when independent observers each looking at the watch agree that it says 10:00 a.m., and when an agreed-on independent standard such as official "atomic time" says it is 10:00 a.m. when the watch is reporting 10:00 a.m. In other words, we want to see and hear again and again from multiple sources that it is 10:00 a.m. when the watch is reporting 10:00 a.m.

Reliable instruments are a must. Unreliable speedometers can get you into trouble, and so can unreliable measures of communication. A measure of interpersonal intimacy that captures a couple in love on Monday, mutually homicidal on Tuesday, and indifferent on Wednesday may be capturing the natural swings in any relationship, but if we assume the couple has some level of steadfast mutual regard, then it appears the measure is behaving unreliably.

As researchers, we work toward eliminating errors of reliability in measurement as far as possible. If we can reach that ideal state, we will know that any variations in our research data are due to variations in the phenomena we are measuring and not to instability in our measuring instruments. The tests for reliability described below check for reliability across time and across space. For example, a **test-retest** check seeks to establish that a measure of communication will produce the same results at two different times, all other things being equal. A test for **intercoder or observer reliability** seeks to establish that two observers of the same phenomenon at the same time will record the same results, all other things being equal.

Conceptually, the reliability of a measure is established by repeating measurements on the same phenomenon and looking for similar results each time. If this does not happen, the reliability of the measure is questionable. The following paragraphs outline ways of assessing reliability.

Test-Retest

A common test for reliability is test-retest. A test is administered to a group of people and then repeated with the same group a week or two later. The test scores are then compared using a process called correlation. Correlation scores in this particular case are referred to as **reliability coefficients** and range between 0 and 1.0, with 1.0 being perfect and, typically, unobtainable. Most communication researchers regard anything over 0.95 as close to perfection, a score over 0.85 as acceptable, and anything under 0.75 as perhaps indicating questionable reliability.

The administration, timing, and interpretation of test-retest scores are matters of judgment. Retesting within 24 hours of the first test can result in a high correlation because people probably remember how they replied the first time around and will repeat that. They will also find the retest easier to do because they have already done the test. Retesting a month later, we may find that a number of people will have changed their minds, will have developed other priorities, or will find the test a challenge because they don't recall how to answer. Thus, most test-retests typically take place within a week or two.

Intercoder or Observer Reliability

Just as you want a measure to be reliable over time, so you would want different observers to agree that they are observing the same thing and are consistent in their observations. In other words, we want to be assured that Observer A and Observer B are recording the same thing if they are both meant to be observing it.

Two typical research scenarios that require observer reliability are the observation of human interaction and the content analysis of news media. Let's say that, in both cases, you are interested in measuring aggression. As a starting point, you need to define aggression in a way that all observers can agree that they have or have not seen it. This is the process of operationalization introduced in Chapter 2. You might then develop two broad categories of aggression, armed and unarmed, and instruct your observers to classify each incident of aggression they see as either armed or unarmed. Armed aggression seems obvious enough. Assertive behavior with firearms or knives would count—once you have an agreed-on, operational definition of *assertive.* But how about when a researcher observes aggressive domestic behavior involving a pan full of hot spaghetti sauce? Observers could easily disagree on whether the gesture is armed or unarmed, or even whether it is or is not aggressive.

The secret to high intercoder or observer reliability is thorough training of observers and clear definitions and classifications of behavior. That done, you will still want to know that your observers are categorizing the same content in the same way, and so you calculate a correlation between the coding of observers to see whether this is happening.

Two other checks are needed if we are to have full confidence in the reliability of our measures. These are a check on the **internal reliability** of our measures, and a check against other established measures that measure the phenomena we are interested in.

Inter-Item or Internal Reliability

Typically, we need more than one question to measure something, an attitude or whether a student understands NOIR, for example. One question may not fully capture what the researcher (or professor) is trying to ask, or it may oversimplify the concept. For example, asking a question about war specifically may not capture attitudes toward the more general concept of violence or perhaps vice versa.

A check on **inter-item reliability** is a check that the individual questions in a question set are consistent in their results and capture the same concept. We need a check on internal reliability because we want to be as sure as possible that all the questions basically operationalize the same concept. If the questions operationalize different concepts, then any variation we see in our results may be a result of question design and not of variation in the attitudes of individuals in our sample.

Suppose, for example, we had a set of questions that were designed to capture attitudes toward social media. We might develop questions that ask individuals how they feel about using generic social media such as blogs, wikis, and photo sharing and perhaps specific media such as Facebook, Twitter, and Second Life. If we developed a set of 12 such questions, we should expect each question to elicit approximately the same level of response; that is, there should be a strong correlation among the responses to these 12 questions because they were designed to measure the same thing. One way to check on this is the **split-half technique**, in which the results from 6 of our 12 questions would be correlated with the results from the other 6. If the measure has an overall high level of reliability, there should be a high split-half reliability. Another way is to compute the correlation between scores from randomly selected pairs of questions in the measure.

Computing inter-item reliability allows researchers to modify their question sets to ensure that each question is addressing the same concept but is not duplicative to the point that each individual respondent is scoring identically on every question. After checking inter-item reliability in this way, researchers can be comfortable that any variation in scores they see from a sample of people is due to respondents' having varying attitudes toward the same concept and not to respondents' having varying responses to different concepts.

Established Measures Reliability

Established measures reliability is simply a comparison. You compare 1) the results obtained from the measure you are developing and 2) the results obtained from a known, tested measure that has been designed for the same purpose. A high correlation between your measure and an established, credible measure should add to the level of confidence you can have in your measure.

So why not just use an existing measure? Perhaps you should if it appears to address your needs. You will know its history and its reported reliabilities from published research that has used the measure. By using such a measure, you may also be able to compare your results directly with those from earlier research or across different cultures. Often, though, a measure may not successfully cross cultural boundaries, and yesterday's measures may not be an exact match for today's research. For example, questions designed for use in the United States may need serious rewording for use in other countries. A measure designed to capture attitudes toward online banking, movie viewing, dating, or working in virtual organizations will almost inevitably need changing, and testing, as Internet technology changes.

You can improve the reliability of measures by rewording specific questions, adding or dropping questions based on inter-item correlations, pretesting instructions for observers, training observers, and trying to ensure that a measurement, when repeated, is repeated under the original conditions as far as possible.

VALIDITY

A 100% reliable instrument that measures the wrong thing is 100% useless. This is obvious in the physical sciences. We do not expect barometers to measure wind direction or thermometers to measure air pressure, but life is not so simple in the social sciences. Take a simple Likert question such as the following:

	Strongly Agree	Agree	Neutral	Disagree	Strongly Disagree
I enjoy watching television.	_____	_____	_____	_____	_____

If respondents reply to this by marking their answers online or on paper, all that you have actually recorded are marks on a scale. Because you have used an interval-level measure, you can make some summary statements such as "13% disagreed or disagreed strongly, 50% were neutral, and 37% either agreed or strongly agreed." But what has the question actually captured?

Enjoyment could mean enjoyment of specific content. So while 37% agree or strongly agree that they like watching television, in fact some are really telling you that they like watching football, others cooking shows, and others 24-hour news or weather. For some people, *enjoyment* could mean enjoying having the television on all day without caring about content. Just having another voice and maybe some background music in the house while people do something else altogether (maybe even read a book) could count as their definition of enjoying television viewing. So *watching* television can mean different things too. Some research suggests that people may be attracted to television by production values such as cuts, zooms, and changes in volume, voices, or lighting. In other words, there is a vaguely hypnotic quality to television that attracts some people quite independent of content.

What, then, has the "I enjoy watching television" question captured? If the question was intended to capture the television-viewing experience and instead captured a content preference, it has little validity. It is in a sense "misreporting" a communication phenomenon.

Consequently, we must be confident that our measures really do capture what we set out to capture and that our readers can be assured, for example, that we are really measuring attitudes toward a political candidate and not toward the candidate's party. This match between the measure and the concept it attempts to capture is called validity.

There are several kinds of validity. The literature has somewhat different names for them and ways of classifying them, but we can think basically of three kinds of validity—content validity, construct validity, and criterion validity.

Content Validity: Looks OK

A measure has **content validity** if it matches or covers all aspects of the concept under investigation. For example, the above "I enjoy watching television" question and other questions centered on the word *television* could be faulted for lacking content validity if the question set was actually designed to capture individuals' responses to viewing video content. As video content is increasingly viewed on smartphones and tablets, the question set does not cover all video-viewing scenarios and therefore lacks content validity.

Content validity is something of a judgment call. It might be established by the reviewer as the result of an extensive literature review or by pretesting with research participants—for example, asking a group of web designers if the questions appear to capture fully the concept of "interactivity" if interactivity is the concept being researched. A determination by experts gives the questions "**expert validity**" or "**panel validity**." Expert validity is preferred because it means that your questions have passed the test of peer approval. Other experts in the field agree with what you are doing.

Face validity, a closely related concept, means basically that the questions appear to measure what they measure. Face validity can, however, vary from group to group. For example, a nonexpert might regard the above question about television viewing as having face validity. A group of communication theorists might disagree and decide that "I enjoy watching television" is really measuring a level of desire for escapism and fantasy.

However, face validity can be important. A series of questions about people's attitudes to sex may have no face validity to respondents who think they have been recruited to answer questions about romance; they may not see the two as related. The politics of research may also require face validity. For example, you may suspect that a high level of involvement in online chat rooms negatively affects students' academic performance, and you want a whole series of questions exploring that aspect of students' lives. However, agencies or foundations funding your research may expect to see questions that directly capture classroom activity. Your "chat" questions may have little face value to them and render the relevance of your study suspect to them.

Construct Validity: Theoretically OK

Construct validity means that there is a demonstrable agreement between the concept or construct you are trying to measure and other related concepts. In organizational communication studies, for example, one would expect employees to show a high correlation between their scores on measures of identification, loyalty, and commitment. This is **convergent validity**. Each of these measures captures somewhat different concepts, but all live under one broad conceptual umbrella called something such as "willingness to stay with my organization."

Conversely, we might expect employees who score highly on measures of loyalty to score low on measures of individuality or independence. The theory is that highly individualistic, self-centered individuals are not attracted to the group ethos required by many organizations. If scores on commitment to an organization have a low correlation with the scores on individuality, we can argue that we have good **divergent validity**. In other words, valid measures should not only have a close relationship to similar measures (convergent validity); they should not show any relationship to dissimilar measures (divergent validity).

Criterion Validity: Tests OK

Criterion validity relates your measures to other specific measures in two ways.

You have high **concurrent validity** if scores on your measure correlate highly with other measurements of exactly the same construct. If you construct a measure of leadership, for example, you would expect scores on your measure to correlate highly with other measures of leadership.

You have high **predictive validity** if your measures predict "real-world" outcomes. For example, SAT scores should predict success in college; GRE scores should predict success in graduate school; vocational preference tests should predict comfort if not success in a particular career field. If they do, they have high predictive validity. The personal interests questionnaire you filled out when applying for college or university may have been used to match you with a roommate. If the relationship is still flourishing, the questionnaire had good predictive ability (maybe!).

Frequently, the reason for such tests is to predict outcomes in the workplace and in relationships. Private enterprise, government agencies, schools, career and psychological counselors, dating services, and the military all use tests with presumably high predictive validity to help identify people who will perform in a particular way. Implicitly, there is another reason for testing, and that is to rank order people on their scores in an attempt to predict who will be most or least successful in a particular job, graduate school, or profession. There are many proprietary tests available, each marketed on the basis of its predictive validity.

Who Wins in the Reliability-Validity Shootout?

An ideal instrument has both reliability and validity. It should measure what it measures well and consistently. But validity has a theoretical priority. It does not matter how reliable an instrument is; if it is measuring something other than what you have in mind, it is, in a sense, capturing irrelevant data and has no value. That said, reliability has a claim also because if an instrument is unreliable, you can never properly assess its validity.

TWO COMMON MEASUREMENT SCALES

There are many ways of capturing human communication behavior that will be discussed in subsequent chapters. In terms of scaled measurements, you should know two scales commonly used in attitude research in academia and industry—the Likert scale and the semantic differential scale. There are many other scales, but these two are common in scholarly and applied research, as you may have discovered if you have ever filled in a class evaluation form or participated in a market research study. In this chapter, we introduce these two scales as measurement devices. In Chapter 9, we will revisit these scales.

The Likert Scale

Note, as in the following examples, that the Likert scale is framed as a statement, not a question. Each statement has its own scale.

The scale may vary between 5 and 7 points. It most commonly has 5 points, and the response options are always the same—"strongly agree" through to "strongly disagree." Respondents are asked to check the answer that best describes their level of agreement with the statement. Each answer is given a numerical value between 1 and 5 for a 5-point scale, and the answer from each person for each question is recorded as a score.

Suppose, for example, we are interested in consumers' attitudes toward social media. We might ask Likert-formatted questions such as the following:

	Strongly Agree	Agree	Neutral	Disagree	Strongly Disagree
1. Social media are essential.	_____	_____	_____	_____	_____
2. Social media are secure.	_____	_____	_____	_____	_____
3. Social media content can be trusted.	_____	_____	_____	_____	_____
4. Social media violate people's privacy.	_____	_____	_____	_____	_____

The Semantic Differential Scale

The semantic differential scale pairs opposite ideas toward a concept or object and invites each respondent to decide where between the two opposites her or his opinion lies. There may be multiple word scales for each concept.

The semantic differential shown below explores attitudes to social media, capturing concepts similar to those in the Likert example above. It has a 5-point scale, and each point is assigned a value between 1 and 5. Scores are recorded for each person for each question after each respondent marks on each scale a position representing his or her opinion.

Social Media					
Friendly	_____	_____	_____	_____	_____	Unfriendly
Inexpensive	_____	_____	_____	_____	_____	Expensive
Safe	_____	_____	_____	_____	_____	Dangerous
Trustworthy	_____	_____	_____	_____	_____	Untrustworthy

A semantic differential scale can be more difficult to construct in that words that form authentic opposites have to be found and pretested for meaning before use. For example, how do people see the opposite of *expensive? Cheap, inexpensive,* or *affordable?* Likert statements require no such effort. Of course, neither type of question is exempt from the requirement that it have good reliability and validity. Significant pretesting time and effort may be required to establish these.

Both the Likert and semantic differential scales have "steps," to which we can assign numbers that will allow us to make some summary claims about the data.

For example, Exhibit 5.1 shows a basic Likert-scale question, the answers from five respondents, and, in a sneak preview of Chapter 7, the simple descriptive statistics that summarize those answers. Looking at the five responses we received, we can make some statements after inspection and some elementary calculations:

- Scores ranged between 1 and 5.

- The most frequent score was 5.

- The average score is 3.2, or $(1 + 2 + 3 + 5 + 5) / 5$.

We can summarize these data by saying that while there is some collective disagreement with the statement, the average score of 3.2 is closer to agreement than disagreement, and therefore, overall, our respondents are more likely to agree than disagree with the statement.

EXHIBIT 5.1 ■ Example of Likert Question, Responses, and Basic Descriptive Statistics

(Statement) Social media are essential.

	Strongly Disagree	Disagree	Neutral	Agree	Strongly Agree
Score	1	2	3	4	5
Value assigned to statement by respondents					
Respondent 1		X			
Respondent 2			X		
Respondent 3					X
Respondent 4	X				
Respondent 5					X
Descriptive Statistics					
Sample size					5
Minimum score					1
Maximum score					5
Range of scores					(5 – 1) = 4
Average score (sum of scores / sample size)					3.2

While we can make statements about the distribution of results with nominal and ordinal variables (for example, 65% of respondents were male; 35% female), interval measures allow us for the first time to make summary statements such as "The average score was 3.2."

Note that the assumption of equal distances between points on a Likert or semantic differential scale is just that—an assumption. Mathematically, the distance between any two adjacent points on the scale is the same. Psychologically, however, this may not be the case for respondents. People can be reluctant to take extreme positions and may be more likely to favor middle-ground positions such as "agree" more than "strongly agree." There is also a question of what precisely the midpoint of a Likert scale means to the respondent. It may mean "undecided," "don't know," "neutral," or "both agree and disagree." Related is the broader question of whether a respondent's complex feelings on such issues as reproductive rights, same-sex marriage, or freedom of speech can ever be captured adequately in the form of a check mark on a 5-point or a 7-point scale.

In summary, measuring communication phenomena at the nominal and ordinal levels allows us to classify and rank communication phenomena. Measuring at the interval and ratio levels allows us to use statistics as a reporting and decision-making tool.

The downside of such quantification is the loss of all information that cannot be turned into a number and the danger of **reification** or turning the measure itself into the reality it is supposed to measure. As evolutionary scientist Stephen Jay Gould (1996) pointed out in his excoriating review of attempts to measure human attributes, the first problem is that scales and tests can lead us to assume that the test is the thing. The map is not the territory, but the fact that there is an IQ test leads us to assume, unwisely, that there is a single measurable entity called "intelligence." The second problem is the danger of ranking based on such scales. Given the existence of an IQ scale that is supposed to measure a unitary entity called intelligence, how wise is it to rank people on the basis of a single score?

This question is the focus of this chapter's Ethics Panel.

ETHICS PANEL
THE ETHICS OF MEASUREMENT SCALES

Major problems with the development of measures such as the IQ test include the assumptions that there is a single human ability or entity called intelligence, that a test can be devised to assess it, and that individuals can be accurately ranked and their futures perhaps determined on the basis of such a test (Gould, 1996). A familiar example is the SAT, intended to predict (academic) success in college. In a general sense, academic success is a product of many factors—the quality of high school preparation, socioeconomic status, personal "drive," study habits and ambition, and, of course, the college environment itself. On what basis, then, should a student with high SAT scores be preferred for college admission over another student with lower scores?

Questions

- How ethical is it to rank or evaluate students based only on the results of a single set of tests such as the SATs?

- More generally, how wise is it to classify people on the basis of any single measure such as authoritarianism, conservatism, loyalty, commitment, or dogmatism?

- What nonscaled methods might you propose that capture, for example, intelligence, conservatism, or loyalty?

Chapter Summary

Measures of communication must have

- Validity—measure what they are supposed to measure.

- Reliability—produce the same results consistently.

Measures exist at four levels:

- Nominal—essentially labels.

- Ordinal—allow rank ordering.

- Interval—allow statistical calculations.

- Ratio—allow more sophisticated statistical operations.

Two frequently used scales in communication research are the

- Likert scale—ranges between "strongly disagree" and "strongly agree."

- Semantic differential scale—ranges between polar opposites such as "strong" and "weak."

Key Terms

code 94
concurrent validity 101
construct validity 100
content validity 100
convergent validity 101
criterion validity 101
demographic 93
divergent validity 101
established measures
    reliability 99
expert validity 100
face validity 100

inter-item reliability 98
intercoder or observer reliability 97
internal reliability 98
interval 93
Likert scale 94
measurement 92
numbers 92
numerals 92
nominal 93
ordinal 93
panel validity 100
phrenologists 91

predictive validity 101
rank order questions 94
ratio 93
reification 104
reliability 96
reliability coefficients 97
scales 91
semantic differential
    scale 94
split-half technique 98
test-retest 97
validity 96

Application Exercises

These application exercises ask you to develop questions in nominal, ordinal, interval, and ratio formats so that you can develop an understanding of the strengths and weaknesses of each format. They will also have you thinking about how best to operationalize the concept you are hoping to measure and the relationships among concepts.

Exercise 1. NOIR Revisited

Under "An Introduction to Scales," the perhaps-questionable statement was made that it is relatively easy to measure how much time a person spends online. List as many ways you can think of to measure time spent online; then identify each measure as nominal, ordinal, interval, or ratio. Which of these measures do you consider to be most valid, and which do you consider most reliable?

Exercise 2. Teens, Social Media, and Technology

At www.pewinternet.org locate a May 31, 2018, survey report titled "Teens, Social Media, & Technology." Click on the "Topline Questionnaire" icon to access the specific questions asked in this survey. You can also click on the "Complete Report" icon and find them at the end of the report. Categorize each question as nominal, ordinal, interval, or ratio. You will find that one level of measurement is predominant. What are the advantages and disadvantages of operating at this level of measurement? What types of information about how teens use social media and technology might not be available as a result of operating at this level of measurement?

Exercise 3. Parlez-moi d'amour

Let's consider love. Generally, love is held to be a good thing. We might expect people in love to be happy, considerate of others, altruistic, and motivated and generally to have a positive outlook on life. A reliable and valid measure of love might allow us to predict, for example, individuals' success in romantic relationships, their success as members of a team, or their willingness to engage in antisocial behavior. There are good theoretical and practical reasons that a researcher might want to measure love.

- Develop a set of nominal, ordinal, interval, and ratio questions that measure love.

- Assess the validity and reliability of your measures.

- Identify other measures and other concepts.

Identify specific reasons you might want to measure an individual's level of love. For example, might a high level of love of country predict willingness to enlist for military service, to be active in politics and civic affairs, to be caring of one's fellow citizens, and more generally to be willing to contribute time and resources to building a better nation? Intuitively, this seems like a concept of love that is different from the passionate love for a significant other, warm familial love, the gourmet's love of fine food, or the extreme-sports enthusiast's love of rock climbing.

Given the reasons you identified for wanting to research love, would questions that focus not on love as you first operationalized it but on another concept such as patriotism be more appropriate to your research interest? Can measures that capture love of food, one's country, or rock climbing be used successfully to establish the validity of measures of romantic love? How likely is it that your questions developed in response to the first assignment in Exercise 3 will work successfully as a measure of love in a different culture?

Recommended Reading

Fikkers, K. M., Piotrowksi, J. T., & Valkenburg, P. M. (2017). Assessing the reliability and validity of television and video game violence exposure measures. *Communication Research, 44* (1), 117–143.

This article considers the reliability and validity of self-report measures of media violence exposure. Multiple measures were assessed for test-retest reliability, criterion validity, and construct validity.

Rubin, R. B., Palmgreen, P., & Sypher, H. E. (Eds.). (2009). *Communication research measures II: A sourcebook.* Mahwah, NJ: Erlbaum.

This book shows many scales used in communication research and discusses scale development.

References

Gould, S. J. (1996). *The mismeasure of man.* New York, NY: Norton.

Osgood, C. E., Suci, G. J., & Tannenbaum, P. H. (1957). *The measurement of meaning.* Urbana: University of Illinois Press.

⑤SAGE edge™

Get the tools you need to sharpen your study skills. SAGE edge offers a robust online environment featuring an impressive array of free tools and resources.

Access quizzes, eFlashcards, video, and multimedia at **edge.sagepub.com/treadwell4e**.

6

SAMPLING

Who, What, and How Many?

"Pizza, pasta, and a sad-looking salad bar. Ugh. I can't stand this. We've gotta do something about the food they offer on this campus."

"What do you mean, Elizabeth? I like the food."

"I just don't think it's very good. For one, it's same old same old—same stuff every day—boring!! Also, there aren't a lot of options for people with dietary restrictions, like people who have gluten allergies or are vegetarians or anything."

"Well, even if that's true, what can we do about it?"

"I'm not sure, but we could start by asking people what they think about it . . . their likes and dislikes on the menu and how they think it could be improved. Once we find out what's not working, we can ask for changes. But nobody will do anything unless we get some evidence—so we really need to do a survey and get some campus opinion."

"Liz, there are thousands of students on this campus. You're going to survey thousands of students about the lunch buffet?! Besides, how would that even work? Do you care about what the seniors think? They're about to graduate. And would commuters and residents need the same things? And the same for people with dietary restrictions—how would you even know who they are?!"

"No, I don't think I can survey thousands of students. But I can survey some of them. Prof Michaels is talking about sampling in methods this week. It's about how you pick people for your survey. There are different ways to do it and some of them let you choose people based on groups, like commuters and residents or freshman and seniors."

"So you can get good information without surveying everyone?"

"According to this chapter!"

CHAPTER OVERVIEW

We cannot study the entire universe of human communication in one research project, much as we might want to. The universe is too large, and the questions too numerous.

What we can do, however, is define populations from that universe and study samples from those populations. The process of selecting the individual units for study is called sampling.

This chapter discusses two types of sampling—probability and nonprobability. Probability sampling strives to obtain samples that statistically represent the overall population. Studies using probability sampling can, at times, be used to generalize to a larger population. Nonprobability sampling is not statistically representative of the population being sampled but may have greater theoretical relevance and the advantage of convenience.

Sample size—an important issue—depends on the homogeneity of the population and on the level of confidence you want when making generalizations from your data.

CHAPTER OBJECTIVES

This chapter will help you

- Compare and contrast probability and nonprobability sampling.
- Identify and explain major nonprobability sampling methods.
- Identify and explain major probability sampling methods.
- List the factors influencing the size of a sample.
- Describe the concept of a sampling frame.
- Discuss the advantages and disadvantages of the different types of sampling frame.

INTRODUCTION

A decision to do research is a decision to sample. As soon as you have a research question, you automatically have questions about who or what and how many you will study in order to answer it. This is true both for quantitative and qualitative research.

A **population** is defined not by size but by the fact that it contains every one of the units the researcher has elected to study, for example every licensed driver in the United States, every U.S. edition of a Harry Potter book, or every woman working for a minority-owned public relations agency. Large populations can be difficult to study because their exact size and nature may be unknown. This is one reason we combine sampling and the inferential statistics discussed in Chapter 8. Together, they help us make intelligent estimates from a sample when the population's exact size and nature are unknown or the population is too large to conduct a **census**—a study of every member of a population. A **sample** is a selected segment of a population presumed to represent that population.

Nonprobability samples are based on a judgment by the researcher; probability samples are generated by randomly selecting the sample units. Both approaches have advantages and disadvantages.

In this chapter, we follow a student, Elizabeth, as she thinks about her sampling options for a campus survey on food preferences.

NONPROBABILITY SAMPLING

The advantages of **nonprobability sampling** include convenience and providing insight. Statistically, nonprobability sampling does not permit generalizations to a wider population, but that does not make it a second-class citizen of the sampling world. There are situations in which it can be the most logical method. For example, a researcher may make a professional judgment that one particular informant or item of text will provide the insights he or she is looking for or that seeking out volunteers is the only way to build a relevant sample of people. As outlined below, there are several approaches to nonprobability sampling.

Convenience Sampling

As the name implies, **convenience sampling** is based on convenience to the researcher. You may have been part of a convenience sample when an instructor requested your consent to participate in a survey or an experiment; that is, you were part of a group convenient to the instructor. Constraints on time or money may lead researchers to use convenience sampling. It can be useful when pretesting a study or when the results of the research are not intended for scholarly publication. As a matter of convenience, Elizabeth may initially survey her class colleagues about their eating habits and their perceptions of campus food services. She makes no assumption that her survey results would apply to the student body as a whole or that her research will contribute to new theoretical models of human communication. She just wants some basis for her inquiries. After all, she has to start somewhere.

Purposive or Judgmental Sampling

Purposive sampling is based on the idea that a specific person or media content will meet specific criteria the researcher may have. For example, Elizabeth may decide that the director of campus dining services and only the director of campus dining services can provide the insight on the economic, nutritional, and scheduling decisions that lead to the menu options that students see on a day-to-day basis. She will therefore deliberately seek out that individual as part of her research.

She may also seek to interview students who can make a special case or who exemplify a special problem—for example, students who cannot eat at campus facilities for religious reasons or whose health may be at risk because the ingredients in campus food are not clearly documented and displayed. Such students may not represent majority opinion, but the stories they have to tell may be just as enlightening as a survey finding of "78% of females and 58% of males want more vegetarian offerings." In-depth interviews with such students could generate new ideas, insights, and research questions that Elizabeth might not be able to obtain from conventional-diet students. She might even elect to interview such students specifically *because* they do not represent conventional wisdom.

Quota Sampling

Quota sampling was one of the first attempts to bring a scientific approach to survey research. It attempts to replicate in a sample the features that the researcher thinks are important in the population. Let's suppose that Elizabeth has decided to interview students who live on campus and those who live off campus because she suspects that the attitudes of these two groups will differ with respect to eating and to campus food services.

She decides to interview 10 students. She knows that 80% of students live on campus, so she decides to interview eight resident students plus two students who live off campus. She has successfully replicated one important feature of the student community in her sample, but the 10 students she interviews are her choice. They have not been randomly sampled, as discussed below under "Probability Sampling." Something other than chance has put them in the sample. That something is the researcher's judgment, which may be biased. For example, she may knowingly or unknowingly sample the students living in a housing unit that—uniquely—has kitchen facilities.

Network or Snowball Sampling

Network or snowball sampling is a form of volunteer sampling that occurs when you rely on members of a network to introduce you to other members of the network. Let's suppose that Elizabeth is especially interested in getting the opinions of vegetarians. Despite her best efforts, she can find no campus listing of vegetarians or any links to a local vegetarian group. She decides that the only way to identify such students is to post on campus bulletin boards or her Facebook page a request that any vegetarians contact her to discuss possible participation in her research.

One such person contacts her, and Elizabeth realizes that the only way to recruit more vegetarians into her study is to ask this person to identify other vegetarians who might be willing to be interviewed. If she is lucky, the size of her sample will grow exponentially as more and more vegetarians introduce her to more and more vegetarians. The quality and size of any such sample depends on the willingness and ability of others to identify other people in their networks to you. One potential problem with snowball sampling is that because friends tend to recommend friends, the snowball sample may consist of individuals with essentially the same opinion and will not capture any diversity of opinion or demographics within the broader student body. Conversely, relative isolates may not be recruited and will be underrepresented as a result.

Volunteer Sampling

Network or snowball samples are obtained by an initial group of volunteers linking to other potential volunteers whom they identify. Volunteers may also be recruited directly by the researcher.

Calling for volunteers may be the only way you can obtain research participants. If, for example, Elizabeth is seeking student members for a focus group to discuss possible changes in campus meal offerings, she has little choice but to use volunteer sampling. The focus group method, as we will see in Chapter 13, requires the active participation of people prepared to express opinions.

You may well want volunteers and volunteer enthusiasm if you intend to translate the results of your research into action. For example, the vegetarian volunteers Elizabeth recruits using her snowball sampling may provide her not only with the information she needs but also with the volunteer enthusiasm needed to develop educational materials or with help in lobbying efforts supportive of changes to the campus food offerings.

The bad news is that volunteer samples can be problematic because, by definition, you are recruiting one type of person—volunteers! Research findings from volunteer samples will be biased because you have not captured what nonvolunteers might have said.

Of course, in a general sense, anyone participating in a research project is a volunteer, as our discussion of ethics and institutional review board (IRB) procedures in Chapter 3 should make clear. Intuitively, though, we can sense a distinction between an individual who has simply agreed to participate in a research project and another who is aggressively determined to see that his or her viewpoint dominates the research findings.

Web-based public opinion polls such as those hosted by local news media can be particularly prone to this problem because they attract people willing, by definition, to visit a website and volunteer a vote—or multiple votes. Other people are not willing to do this, and so these web polls represent only the opinions of a particular personality type. Unless the website has some control over access, the enthusiasts who decide that if one vote is good, two votes would be twice as good may vote repeatedly, further compounding any bias in the results.

Volunteer sampling obviously applies only to human participants. Convenience, judgment, and quota sampling can be used with nonhumans, most typically to select media content for content analysis. In all cases, the researcher would be the one deciding what media content goes into a sample. There will inevitably be some bias behind that decision. For example, Exhibit 6.1 shows the class year and food preferences of a student population that Elizabeth might sample. Exhibit 6.2 shows how a convenience sample (highlighted) could seriously

EXHIBIT 6.1 ■ Population

Class Year										Percent of Population
1st		2nd			3rd			4th		
B	B	B	B	B	B	B	B	B	B	
B	B	B	B	B	B	B	B	B	B	40%
B	B	B	B	B	B	B	B	B	B	
B	B	B	B	B	B	B	B	B	B	
P	P	P	P	P	P	P	P	P	P	
P	P	P	P	P	P	P	P	P	P	30%
P	P	P	P	P	P	P	P	P	P	
V	V	V	V	V	V	V	V	V	V	20%
V	V	V	V	V	V	V	V	V	V	
R	R	R	R	R	R	R	R	R	R	10%
20%		30%			30%			20%		100%

The above exhibit shows a population containing 16 subgroups.

Reading down the columns, we see four sets of food preferences:
B = Balanced diet
P = Pizza diet
V = Vegetarian diet
R = Medically restricted diet

Reading across the rows, we see four class levels: first-, second-, third-, and fourth-year.

The right-hand column shows the percentage of each food-preference group in the population. The bottom row shows the percentage of each class year in the population.

This exhibit could equally well represent ethnic or occupational subgroups of a human population or subgroups of a media population (corporate websites, nonprofit websites, talk radio, or lifestyle magazines, for example).

EXHIBIT 6.2 ■ Convenience Sample

Class Year										Percent of Population
1st		2nd			3rd			4th		
B	B	B	B	B	B	B	B	B	B	
B	B	B	B	B	B	B	B	B	B	40%
B	B	B	B	B	B	B	B	B	B	
B	B	B	B	B	B	B	B	B	B	
P	P	P	P	P	P	P	P	P	P	
P	P	P	P	P	P	P	P	P	P	30%
P	P	P	P	P	P	P	P	P	P	
V	V	V	V	V	V	V	V	V	V	
V	V	V	V	V	V	V	V	V	V	20%
R	R	R	R	R	R	R	R	R	R	10%
20%		30%			30%			20%		100%

Exhibit 6.2 represents a convenience sample obtained by arbitrarily selecting 10 individuals from the right "corner" of the population. The selected units are highlighted.

Convenience sampling may overestimate or underestimate the population. In this case, all *P*s, *V*s, and *R*s have been eliminated from the sample, as have all first- and second-year classes.

The sample is 100% *B*s, who make up only 40% of the population.

Of that sample, 30% are third-year students, who make up 30% of the population, and 70% are fourth-year students, who make up 20% of the population.

misrepresent the population by leaving out first- and second-year students and three of the four food preference groups.

Ideally, we need some mechanism that reduces or eliminates researcher bias so that the sample reflects the population and not the researcher's biases. That mechanism is probability sampling.

PROBABILITY SAMPLING

Basically, **probability sampling** means assigning the selection of sampling units to a mechanism over which the researcher has no control, so every unit has an equal chance of being selected.

Probability sampling permits us to make statistical generalizations from our results. A major contribution of sampling theory to communication research is to tell us that we do not necessarily need huge samples as long as we are prepared to live with a level of uncertainty— which can be calculated as discussed in Chapter 8.

Researchers, especially in such applied fields as political communication, marketing, broadcasting, and public relations, want to be able to make generalizations to large audiences or markets and therefore put considerable effort into probability sampling.

The master list from which a probability sample is selected is referred to as a **sampling frame**—for example, a list of graduates held by your college or university's alumni office, the membership list of a club, or all registered members of a political party. In practice, and especially in the case of large populations, we sample from sampling frames because we cannot identify every member of the population. **Sampling units** are the units selected for study. Frequently in communication research, the unit will be individuals, but the unit could also be couples, corporations, comic strips, athletic teams, *Deadpool* movies, or editorials from the *Chicago Sun-Times*.

There are several approaches to probability sampling.

Random Sampling

Random sampling is the most obvious and perhaps most common example of probability sampling.

Examples of random sampling include throwing dice, drawing names out of a hat, and lotteries. In each case, there is no predicting what specific names or numbers will be sampled. You may control how many names or numbers will be selected, but you cannot control what each specific name or number will be. Random sampling removes the researcher as the agent of selection and replaces him or her with "luck of the draw."

For example, Elizabeth may be able to obtain a list of all students signed up for the campus meal plan (recognizing that students who do not participate in the plan are ignored even though their reasons for doing so should interest her). To get a genuinely random sample of students who will represent all participants in the plan, she would assign each student a number beginning at 1 and number each individual systematically. Then she would use a table of randomly generated numbers—or a **random numbers generator**, such as the one available at http://randomizer.org—to generate the list of students who would form her sample. Random number generators allow you to specify how big you want your sample to be and how you want your sample numbers computed and presented. You can have the generator pull numbers randomly, pull every fifth or every tenth number (see "Systematic Sampling" below), or begin sampling at a number you define. For example, to randomly generate a series of phone numbers for the 212 area code, you can instruct the generator to produce randomly a series of 10-digit numbers beginning with 212.

A common misconception of random sampling is that it will produce a sample that is diverse. This is not automatically so. For example, married Asian women over the age of 40, living in New Mexico with two children and a household income of between $100,000 and $150,000, would be a very homogeneous population demographically. Random sampling from such a population would produce an equally homogeneous sample; we would not expect the sample to be diverse.

Stratified Random Sampling

Paradoxically, one problem with purely random samples is that they may not reflect the population from which they are drawn. Because "anything can happen" with random sampling, there is always a possibility that an important subgroup could be entirely missed or overrepresented. For example, Elizabeth may have decided that she needs vegetarians in her survey sample, and she knows that this group constitutes a small minority of students. But random sampling is blind; a random sample of all students living on campus may not select any vegetarians.

Randomness does not respect the fact that you may need all categories of people in your sample and that random sampling might eliminate some categories from your sample. **Stratified random sampling** is a way to "force" such groups into your sample.

To ensure that all the groups of interest are proportionately represented in a sample, you set aside a number of places in your sample relative to the size of the groups in the population you are drawing from. Then you fill those places by random sampling from those specific subgroups, as shown in Exhibit 6.3.

For example, if Elizabeth needs both resident and nonresident students in her sample, and knows that nonresident students make up 20% of the student population, she needs to ensure that 20% of her sample consists of such students. Suppose she decides on a final sample size of 100 students. She would then randomly select 20 nonresident students from a list of such students and randomly select 80 from a list of resident students. This is similar to nonprobability quota sampling, the key difference being that the individual units in stratified random sampling are selected by a process of randomization, not by the researcher.

EXHIBIT 6.3 ■ Stratified Random Sample											
Class Year											**Percent of Population**
1st		**2nd**			**3rd**			**4th**			
B	B	B	B	B	B	B	B	B	B		40%
B	B	B	B	B	B	B	B	B	B		
B	B	B	B	B	B	B	B	B	B		
B	B	B	B	B	B	B	B	B	B		
P	P	P	P	P	P	P	P	P	P		30%
P	P	P	P	P	P	P	P	P	P		
P	P	P	P	P	P	P	P	P	P		
V	V	V	V	V	V	V	V	V	V		20%
V	V	V	V	V	V	V	V	V	V		
R	R	R	R	R	R	R	R	R	R		10%
20%		30%			30%			20%			100%

In this example, the selected units are highlighted.

40% of the sample is Bs.

30% of the sample is Ps.

20% of the sample is Vs.

10% of the sample is Rs.

These percentages are the percentage of each food preference group in the original population. Within each of these groups, random sampling takes place to select individuals for the overall sample so that the original percentage of each group in the population is protected in the final sample.

Note that this sample overrepresents first-year students (30% of sample; 20% of the population) and second-year students (40% of sample; 30% of the population). The sample underrepresents third-year students (10% of sample; 30% of the population).

Systematic Sampling

Systematic sampling means sampling every *n*th person on a list—for example, taking every 10th or every 100th person listed in a phone book. The interval that you select (10, 100, etc.)

is the **sampling interval**. The method is based on random sampling because typically you use a random number or numbers to locate a starting point. For example, if you were sampling from a telephone directory, you might generate a random number to decide at which page to start sampling and then another random number to decide at which name on that page to start. Having identified a starting point, you then take every *n*th name until you have the sample size you need. The random starting point means that you have no control over which names get selected, and any researcher bias in who gets selected is therefore avoided.

Systematic sampling is diagrammed in Exhibit 6.4.

One problem with systematic sampling is that if a pattern in the original population matches the sampling interval, you can get an overweighted or underweighted sample. For example, suppose you want to interview residents of a dormitory on their attitudes to safety and security. You use a random numbers generator to select one dorm room as a starting point and then systematically sample every 10th room after that. It so happens that every 10th room selected has an emergency alarm button outside it that residents cannot help but see as they enter and leave

EXHIBIT 6.4 ■ Systematic Sample

Class Year											Percent of Population
1st		2nd			3rd			4th			
B	B	B	B	B	B	B	B	B	B		40%
B	B	B	B	B	B	B	B	B	B		
B	B	B	B	B	B	B	B	B	B		
B	B	B	B	B	B	B	B	B	B		
P	P	P	P	P	P	P	P	P	P		30%
P	P	P	P	P	P	P	P	P	P		
P	P	P	P	P	P	P	P	P	P		
V	V	V	V	V	V	V	V	V	V		20%
V	V	V	V	V	V	V	V	V	V		
R	R	R	R	R	R	R	R	R	R		10%
20%		30%			30%			20%			100%

Here, a starting point is randomly selected (top row, third unit); then every *n*th individual is selected, in this case every 6th. Using this method, we have 17 individuals in our sample. The selected units are highlighted. If we wanted a larger or smaller sample, we would need to adjust the sampling interval (*n*).

41% of the sample is *B*s (40% of the population).

29% of the sample is *P*s (30% of the population).

18% of the sample is *V*s (20% of the population).

12% of the sample is *R*s (10% of the population).

Based on the sample size of 17.

Second-year students are overrepresented (41% of sample; 30% of population).

Third-year students are underrepresented (18% of sample; 30% of population).

First-year (18%) and fourth-year (24%) student percentages approximated those in the population (20%).

their rooms. It is possible, then, that your findings will be biased because every student in your sample will have a greater (or possibly lesser) sense of security than others in the same dorm.

Multistage Cluster Sampling

Suppose you wanted a representative sample of a country's population. In practice, this would mean trying to sample from a list of every resident of that country, assuming in the first place that you could get such a thing. There has to be an easier way, and there is. Multistage cluster sampling works by first sampling larger units such as states or provinces. Towns and cities are then sampled from the state, province, or county sample. City blocks are then sampled from the town or city sample, and finally individual addresses are sampled from city blocks.

At the campus level, Elizabeth might consider multistage cluster sampling if she were unable to obtain a student directory from which to sample. In that case, she might randomly select housing units, then floors within the selected units, then rooms within the randomly selected floors, and possibly individuals within each room.

The advantage of this method is the relative ease of identifying people, or at least households. It is much easier to go from state to city to city block to household than it is to find a comprehensive listing of millions of people. The catch is that, at every stage of sampling, the potential for bias in the final sample increases. No two states are identical, so any sample of states will have some attributes overrepresented or underrepresented.

Clearly, sampling is more complicated than it may first appear and involves a number of decisions—some theoretical, some practical. Exhibit 6.5 summarizes the advantages and disadvantages of different sampling methods.

EXHIBIT 6.5 ■ Advantages and Disadvantages of Sampling Methods

	Advantages	Disadvantages
Nonprobability Sampling	Overall: Convenience.	Overall: Sample does not represent the population being sampled.
Convenience	Speed, cost.	Cannot generalize from sample to population.
Purposive/Judgmental	Meets a specific need of the researcher.	Sample may not represent the population.
Quota	Attempts to replicate features of the population in the sample. More readily done than random sampling.	Sample may not represent the population.
Network/Snowball	Identifies research participants the researcher would not otherwise be aware of.	Depends on ability of researcher to network. Sample may over- or underrepresent aspects of the population. Possible loss of diversity in sample.
Volunteer Sampling	Identifies willing participants the researcher might not otherwise be aware of.	Agendas and interests of volunteers may influence the research. Sample may over- or underrepresent characteristics of the population.

(Continued)

EXHIBIT 6.5 ■ (Continued)

	Advantages	Disadvantages
Probability Sampling	Overall: Sample represents the population being sampled.	Overall: Consumes time and resources.
Random Sampling	Ability to generalize from sample to population.	May eliminate individuals who should be in the sample.
Stratified Random Sampling	Minority groups that should be represented in the sample are forced into it.	Need to identify and sample a sampling frame for each subgroup to be represented in the sample.
Systematic Sampling	Only one or two random number starting points are needed to start sampling.	Sample may over- or underrepresent features of the population.
Multistage Cluster Sampling	Eliminated need for a comprehensive sampling frame of every individual to be sampled.	Sampling frame needed for each stage of sampling. Sample may over- or underrepresent features of the population.

HOW BIG DOES MY SAMPLE HAVE TO BE?

At a practical level, sample size depends on your resources. Time and money place constraints on research and on sample size. If Elizabeth decides to survey graduating seniors during the spring semester, she needs to complete her survey by the end of that semester. If she has no money, she will be unable to entice people into her focus group with the offer of food and drink or to offer the chance to win a prize for participating. Every research project is a balancing act between striving for the ideal sample and working within the constraints of resource limitations and deadlines.

A second "it depends" is the nature of your research. Ethical considerations may constrain the size of your sample. For example, if deception is involved, you may decide that you want to minimize the number of participants even though the deception has been approved by an IRB. You might have a sample of any convenient size if you are just **piloting** a survey; that is, you are testing it out to identify any possible problems with questions and question wording before running it "for real." Sample size is also less of an issue if your survey is an informal one aimed at just getting a sense of what people are thinking or has no official or policy implications and is not intended for scholarly publication.

A third "it depends" is the level of confidence—statistical confidence in this case—that you want or need in your research results. If you want absolute 100% confidence in your results, then you will not be sampling at all; you will be conducting a census. Given a small population, you might conduct a census—a survey of every member of a population, but as we will see in Chapter 7, a census is often impractical and unnecessary. Most researchers elect to sample and to accept a (calculable) level of error in return.

A fourth factor is the **homogeneity**—the degree of "sameness"—of the population.

Assume, for a moment, that the population is 100% homogeneous; that is, every unit in the population is identical on whatever variables you are researching. In that case, you would need a sample size of only one!

The less homogeneous a population, the more likely you are to need a bigger sample to ensure that its full range of diversity is captured. The homogeneity of the population, sample

EXHIBIT 6.6 ■ Relationships Among Standard Error, Homogeneity, and Sample Size		
	Standard Error	
	1%	5%
Homogeneity	Sample Size	Sample Size
90:10	900	36
50:50	2,500	100

size, and **standard error** are related. Standard error is a measure of the extent to which the scores in a sample vary and is discussed further in Chapter 8. If you know or assume two of these, statistical tables, software, or a relatively simple calculation will tell you the third. Exhibit 6.6 shows how standard error, homogeneity, and sample size relate. The first two websites listed in the "Recommended Web Resources" section at the end of this chapter will help you calculate a sample size based on your needed confidence level and confidence interval.

Calculating either a desired sample size or a level of error helps the researcher make the trade-off between level of confidence, on one hand, and getting the research done expeditiously, on the other. That decision is ultimately driven by the purpose of the research. Elizabeth, for example, will most likely be concerned with getting some defensible research results by the end of the semester. Her sample size and the sampling error may be of lesser concern for a report that will be used only internally to stimulate thinking and local action. On the other hand, a research project on student dietary habits that is headed for publication in a refereed scholarly journal will likely have a minimum required sample size because the journal's publication standards may require reporting results at the 95% confidence level, and that confidence level will then determine the sample size the researcher needs.

SOME ISSUES WITH SAMPLING FRAMES

The basis of almost every good sample is a good sampling frame—the full list of individuals, groups, or media content from which the sample will be drawn. However, for survey research in particular, the nature of the sampling frame may constrain your ability to develop an appropriate sample, as discussed below.

Postal Sampling Frames

Postal addresses presuppose a residence, which not everybody has. Sampling postal addresses, then, is likely to eliminate the homeless and the transient from the sample. Furthermore, as people move and zip code demographics change, we may find that we are not reaching the individuals we intended to reach. Additionally, underrepresentation of some locations can lead to coverage bias (Amaya, Zimmer, Morton, & Harter, 2018.)

Despite these and other problems, interest in postal sampling has returned with the development of **address-based sampling (ABS)**, largely in reaction to decreasing response rates from traditional telephone surveys. "Arguably, address lists updated via the United States

Postal Service (USPS) Computerized Delivery Sequence (CDS) file are the best possible frames for today's household surveys in the United States. National coverage estimates vary, but are very high overall and nearly 100% in many areas, and coverage continues to improve" (Harter et al., 2016, p. 1). For researchers wishing to use such lists, list vendors may "add value" by appending additional information such as phone numbers, names, geographic coordinates, ages, races, ethnicities, and household incomes (Iannacchione, 2011).

ABS has a relatively slow turnaround and can be problematic in rural areas and in geographically locating households with P.O. boxes rather than street addresses. It may result in overcoverage of households with both street addresses and P.O. box addresses, but it can be helpful with in-person surveys and multimethod surveys and is obviously useful in mail surveys. "Once the exclusive realm of direct mailers, the use of residential mailing addresses now influences the development of sampling frames for surveys regardless of mode" (Iannacchione, 2011, p. 570).

Telephone Sampling Frames

Telephone surveys became attractive to survey organizations and researchers once the majority of U.S. households had a phone. The ease of dialing a number relative to having to knock on doors or mail out surveys and wait for a response was obvious. Autodialing technology made telephone sampling even easier. But that was then. Now there are problems, outlined below, with sampling from phone directory listings.

Unlisted phone numbers will not get into a sample taken from directory listings. Survey researchers attempt to overcome this problem with **random digit dialing (RDD)**—that is, dialing computer-generated random numbers in the hopes of reaching unlisted numbers. This technique has its problems because many sequences of numbers are not put into use by phone companies, as well as because people are increasingly giving up traditional landline phones in favor of mobile phones.

Over 90% of U.S. households have mobile phones. A 2017 survey found that over 50% of U.S. households are wireless only. For some subgroups, this percentage can be much higher or lower. For example, 73% of the age group 25–29 lived in wireless-only households versus 24% for those over 65. Hispanic adults are more likely than non-Hispanic Whites or Blacks to be wireless only (Blumberg & Luke, 2017). This means that, in traditional landline surveys, the age group 25–29 and Hispanic adults may be significantly underrepresented and the "over 65s" overrepresented.

Traditional landline phone numbers identified the owners' area codes and exchanges and therefore their geographic locations. With mobile numbers, this is not necessarily the case, so information about an owner's location may be lost, or researchers may assume incorrectly that individuals sampled from a specific area code are living in that area code. Between 10% and 12% of people with cell phones live in a different state from that suggested by their phone numbers (Cohn, 2014). Because of the challenges in linking cell phones to location, RDD is difficult to use when trying to sample on "geographically-clustered characteristics of the target population such as race/ethnicity. These inaccuracies result in undercoverage, sampling inefficiencies, and increased data collection costs" (Shook-Sa, Currivan, Roe, & Warren, 2016).

Telephone surveys have low response rates because many people use caller ID and voice mail to filter out marketing and research calls and put their names on "do not call" lists.

Even if you reach a working number, people may decline to participate in your survey. The percentage of households in a sample that are successfully interviewed fell to 9% in 2012 from, typically, 36% in 1997 (Pew Research Center, 2012). Even with a successful contact, you have no guarantee that the individual answering the phone is the person you were trying to reach.

Even among households that use landlines and mobile phones, nearly 40% received all or nearly all of their calls on their mobile phone, further limiting the use of RDD on landlines (Blumburg & Luke, 2017). In response to this shift to mobile phones, researchers are looking at limiting or even eliminating landlines as a sampling frame. One study simulated a cell phone only design by removing landline data and determined that estimates changed less than one percent, arguing that cell phone only sampling is certainly one viable option for telephone sampling moving forward (Kennedy et al., 2018).

Finally, having any telephone account implies the means to pay for it. Sampling phone directories therefore tends to "sample out" lower income households. Conversely, households with more than one phone number will get those homes disproportionately represented in the sample.

Telephone surveys become even more problematic as phone users abandon both traditional phones and cell phones in favor of Internet services such as Skype; individuals may not have accessible phone numbers at all.

Internet Sampling Frames

Sampling from the Internet offers both advantages and disadvantages. Participants can be recruited globally, and social media platforms can be particularly effective for snowball sampling. Recruits can link to large numbers of other potential recruits unknown to the researcher. A related benefit is that social media can reach hidden populations, such as drug users or the homeless, people who might not otherwise be accessible (Barratt, Ferris, & Lenton, 2015). In principle, the large samples that the Internet makes possible can help reduce sampling bias and the chance that a few abnormal individuals could overly affect the results. Sterrett, Malato, Benz, Tompson, and English (2017) note that representativeness is less a concern with online sampling now that so many individuals have access to the Internet. However, concerns about bias still exist. According to Sterrett et al. (2017), "potential coverage bias of web-only surveys is declining for several demographic groups, but Americans without Internet access remain a distinct segment of society that should be included in any survey designed to make precise inferences about the broader public" (p. 355).

Kim, Mo Jang, Kim, and Wan (2018) compared simple random sampling to **constructed week sampling** in Twitter content. A constructed week sample is a type of stratified sample wherein media items are separated by the day on which they were published or posted. Then a number of items are chosen randomly from all of the Monday posts, all of the Tuesday posts, and so on to construct a week's sample. Kim and colleagues determined that simple random sampling was a more efficient process for getting a representative sample than constructed week sampling.

Ruths and Pfeffer (2014) identify several problems with sampling social media platforms. For example, a social media platform's publicly available information may not accurately represent its overall data. Spam and "bots" masquerade as humans on the Internet. Online behaviors may be platform specific; for example, the way individuals view a particular social media platform as a space for political discussion will affect how representative its political content will be.

The biggest theoretical problem with Internet sampling is that we cannot develop an Internet sampling frame because we do not know who or what the Internet population consists of. For example, there is no universal list of e-mail addresses to sample; this means that not every e-mail user has an equal chance of being sampled. The relationship between what one assumes to be the population and the actual population is unknown.

By definition, Internet users are different from those in the population who cannot or will not link to the Internet. Even though Internet use is increasingly widespread, any online survey sample is likely to include younger, more educated, and higher income individuals than are samples from the population at large. The economically disadvantaged; older people; the less educated; and those with limited computer access, interest, or capability will be underrepresented.

Unless your study population is specifically defined as Internet users, it is questionable whether the results from any online sample will be generalizable to the wider population. Even then, it is questionable whether the results from any one social media platform will be generalizable to the wider Internet population. Although social media use continues to increase across demographics, there are demographic differences among the users of different social media platforms. For example, 78% of 18-to-24-year-olds use Snapchat and 71% use Instagram, but among 30-to-49-year-olds only 25% use Snapchat and about 40% use Instagram. Pinterest is much more heavily used by women (41%) than men (16%).

Overall, 73% of adults use more than one social media platform. Facebook is the most widely used: 68% of adults in the United States use it regularly, and 75% of those users are accessing it daily. Interestingly, nearly 60% of adults think giving up social media would be easy (Smith & Anderson, 2018).

The practical problem with Internet sampling, then, is how to combine its advantages (notably speed, reach, and economy) with some level of assurance that your sample has in fact captured the attributes of the population you are really trying to sample. Fortunately, there are some solutions to the problem.

Couper and Miller (2008) propose two basic approaches to the problem. The "design-based" approach attempts to build probability samples using traditional means such as RDD and then providing Internet access to the sampled households that do not have it. Basically, you add to your online sample by recruiting from outside the Internet.

The "model-based" approach uses volunteer or opt-in panels of Internet users and then corrects such panels for any representational bias. With estimates of how the Internet population differs from your research population, you can estimate what the research results would have been had your actual research population been sampled. Suppose, for example, that you used traditional mail or phone techniques to sample a population of interest and found that 60% of those sampled were over the age of 65; then you sampled online and discovered that only 30% of those sampled were over the age of 65. You can then weight the results from your online sample by calculating what your results would have been if 60% of that sample had been over the age of 65.

It may be possible to check your findings against the results from analogous surveys that used probability sampling. For example, Bhutta (2012) recruited 2,788 study participants via Facebook. The sample was nonrepresentative, but she was able to show that many of the statistical relationships she found among variables were also found in similar surveys that used traditional probability sampling.

Barratt and colleagues (2015) suggest that generalizability may be improved by using population sampling as a complement to purposive sampling. Also, ethnographic, qualitative studies of research participants can yield a better understanding of online sites and networks and allow researchers to better interpret survey findings. (See Chapter 13 for further discussion of ethnographic research.)

Best, Krueger, Hubbard, and Smith (2001) suggest that Internet sampling should be limited to circumstances providing clear evidence that the hypotheses being tested are uniformly applicable across the entire population; that is, participants' Internet usage should not alter the hypothesized relationships among variables.

For example, Bhutta (2012) argues that Facebook has some specific advantages over other social media platforms as a sampling frame. If, however, your study involves social media use as a variable, then sampling only from Facebook will bias your results because the characteristics of users vary from platform to platform.

Much depends upon your need to generalize. Researchers are often content to explore the relationship among variables without necessarily being interested in the distribution of those relationships in a wider population. If you have no reason to generalize from your research results to a larger population or if you are just pretesting a survey, then concerns about the representativeness of Internet samples can take a backseat relative to your theoretical interests.

Special Population Sampling

Sampling or even accessing special populations such as military families, immigrant communities, prisoners, or people with a particular medical condition can be tricky. Listings of special populations exist, but typically and with good reason, organizations will not release members' names and contact information. On the other hand, organizations that see a potential benefit to your research and that it is legitimate may be happy to cooperate once they have approved your research design and been assured of the protections, such as confidentiality, that you have in place for the participants.

As noted, Internet-based snowball sampling can be an effective way of reaching special populations. For traditional mail surveys, the list rental industry can provide specifically targeted mailing lists, often developed from information about subscribers to special interest publications.

The Future of Survey Sampling

Where do the above considerations leave us with respect to survey sampling? Brick (2011) suggests that due to costs, the era of traditional probability sampling may be over. That said, there appears to be no generally accepted method of sampling from the Internet. Brick argues that a well-conducted probability sample with a low response rate is likely to be of higher quality than a sample of volunteers; others argue that a probability sample with a low response rate is itself a volunteer sample and therefore has no advantages over a nonprobability sample. Couper (2017) notes that nonprobability online sampling is often the only affordable option. He argues that these samples have a higher likelihood of error, which needs to be discussed when using nonprobability sampling.

In the meantime, new approaches such as sample matching are evolving. In sample matching, a "target" sample from a known sampling frame such as the U.S. Census is selected and then compared to different web panels—that is, groups of online participants. The closest matching web panel is then selected for research. Another probability option is sampling from known populations, such as college students or members of a particular organization (Couper, 2017). See "Recommended Web Resources" below for a probability panel example.

ETHICS PANEL
CHECKING THE ETHICS OF SURVEY RESEARCH

Just as statistics can be used to misrepresent as well as to represent, so too abuses of sampling or shoddy sampling can contribute to misrepresentation.

First, there is the issue of convenience. Under pressure of time, researchers may sample a student class, friends, or local media. Such sampling may be defensible, but generalizations from such samples probably are not.

Second, there is the pressure to get results. In applied fields such as audience research, marketing, and political communication, research companies can come under client pressure to get the "right answer." This pressure can lead to sample selections that give clients the results they want to hear. If the research results get further summarized by news media using a "get to the point" writing style, the research data can become further simplified and overgeneralized.

Questions

Check local and national newspapers for reports of public opinion polls.

- What populations can you detect were sampled?
- How were the samples obtained?
- What sampling procedures, if any, raise ethical questions with respect to representing or perhaps misrepresenting the original population? Why?
- Could this poll be reported in a scholarly journal? Why or why not?

Chapter Summary

- A census is a study of an entire population.

- A sample is a part of a wider population selected for study.

- The two major categories of sampling are probability and nonprobability.

- Probability sampling includes random, stratified random, systematic, and multistage cluster sampling.

- Nonprobability sampling includes convenience, purposive or judgmental, quota, network or snowball, and volunteer sampling.

- Probability sampling is required in order to make generalizations to a population from a sample.

- Larger sample sizes reduce sampling error, but the extent to which they do so depends on the homogeneity of the sample.

- Internet samples may be obtained rapidly and inexpensively but may not reflect characteristics of the wider population.

Key Terms

address-based sampling (ABS) 119
census 110
constructed week sampling 121
convenience sampling 110
homogeneity 118
multistage cluster sampling 117
network/snowball sampling 111
nonprobability sampling 110

piloting 118
population 109
probability sampling 113
purposive sampling 110
quota sampling 111
random digit dialing (RDD) 120
random numbers generator 114
random sampling 114

sample 110
sampling frame 113
sampling interval 116
sampling units 114
standard error 119
stratified random sampling 114
systematic sampling 115
volunteer sampling 111

Application Exercises

Exercise 1. Systematic Sampling

Using Exhibit 6.1 as your population, change the starting point and sampling interval, and create a systematic sample. How does the resulting sample reflect the original population?

Exercise 2. How Does Sampling for One Variable Affect Another Variable?

Using Exhibit 6.1 as your population and a random numbers generator such as that found at http://randomizer.org, draw a stratified random sample that reflects the proportion of dietary preferences in the population. Calculate the proportion of each class year in your sample and decide whether the sample reflects the population with respect to class year.

Exercise 3. Multistage Cluster Sampling

You decide to survey communication majors across the country with respect to their views on required courses in communication research. Design a multistage sampling procedure that identifies the stages you will sample and how you will sample at each stage.

Exercise 4. Pew Research Center Internet Knowledge Survey

The 2018 Pew Research Center Internet & Technology Report titled "Declining Majority of Online Adults Say Internet Has Been Good for Society" asked a sample of Internet users questions such as these: Has the Internet been good for you personally? Has the Internet been good for society? What is the main reason the Internet has been good/bad for society? (See Smith & Olmstead, 2018; available online at http://www.pewinternet.org/2018/04/30/declining-majority-of-online-adults-say-the-internet-has-been-good-for-society/.)
   Determine the following for each question:

- How might you expect the results from your own web-based convenience sample of college students to differ from the results reported here, and why?

- How might you expect the results from a traditional landline telephone survey of Internet users to differ from the results reported here, and why?

- How might you expect the survey results to vary as the age of the sample varies, for example, sampling those over the age of 65 or under 18? Why?

Recommended Reading

Battaglia, M. P., Dillman, D. A. Frankel, M. R., Harter, R., Buskirk, T. D., McPhee, C. B., DeMatteis, J. M., & Yancey, T. (2016). Sampling, data collection, and weighting procedures for address-based sample surveys. *Journal of Survey Statistics and Methodology, 4*(4), 476–500. DOI: 10.1093/jssam/smw025

Discusses address-based sampling (ABS) and how it can be used in lieu of random digit dialing.

Crespi, I. (1998). Ethical considerations when establishing survey standards. *International Journal of Public Opinion Research, 10*(1), 75–83.

Discusses the tension between ethical and practical considerations in survey design.

Recommended Web Resources

Creative Research Systems. . . . . . . https://www.survey-system.com/sscalc.htm

National Statistical Service (Australia). . . . . . . http://www.abs.gov.au/websitedbs/D3310114.nsf/home/Sample+Size+Calculator

The two sites above provide sample size calculators that help you calculate a sample size given your inputs such as standard error, confidence interval, and homogeneity of the sample. Commercial survey sites such as SurveyMonkey can also help with sample size calculations.

Pew American Trends Panel Datasets. . . . . . . http://www.pewresearch.org/methodology/u-s-survey-research/american-trends-panel/
This is an example of a probability panel as discussed by Couper (2017).

Pew Research Center, Internet & Technology. . . . .
www.pewinternet.org
Click on "Datasets" at the above site to get current statistics on Internet use and on the characteristics of Internet and other technology users.

Pew Research Center, U.S. Politics and Policy. . . . . . .
www.people-press.org

Click on "Methodology" for discussions of survey sampling. Recently, Pew has made its American Trends Panel the main data source for reports on U.S. political and social attitudes and behaviors. There is a 2019 article on that panel and its methods at http://www.pewresearch.org/methods/2019/02/27/growing-and-improving-pew-research-centers-american-trends-panel/.

Research Randomizer. . . . . . . http://randomizer.org
One online site for generating random numbers.

StatPac. . . . . . . www.statpac.com/surveys/sampling.htm
A commercial survey software site with tutorials on sampling and other survey procedures.

Survey Sampling International. . . . . . . www.surveysampling.com
A commercial site providing sampling services internationally.

WebSM. . . . . . . www.websm.org
A European site on web survey methods and sampling.

World Association for Public Opinion Research (WAPOR). . . . . . . http://wapor.org
Provides a code of professional ethics and practices at https://wapor.org/about-wapor/code-of-ethics/.

References

Amaya, A. E., Zimmer, S., Morton, K., & Harter, R. (2018). When does undercoverage on the United States address-based sampling frame translate to coverage bias? *Sociological Methods & Research.* DOI: 10.1177/0049124118782539

Barratt, M. J., Ferris, J. A, & Lenton, S. (2015). Hidden populations, online purposive sampling, and external validity: Taking off the blindfold. *Field Methods, 27*(1), 3–21. DOI: 10.1177/1525822X14526838

Best, S. J., Krueger, B., Hubbard, C., & Smith, A. (2001). An assessment of the generalizability of Internet surveys. *Social Science Computer Review, 19*(2), 131–145. DOI: 10.1177/089443930101900201

Bhutta, C. B. (2012). Not by the book: Facebook as a sampling frame. *Sociological Methods & Research, 41*(1), 57–88. DOI: 10.1177/0049124112440795

Blumberg, S. J., & Luke, J. V. (2017, December). Wireless substitution: Early release of estimates from the National Health Interview Survey, January–June 2017. National Center for Health Statistics. Retrieved from https://www.cdc.gov/nchs/data/nhis/earlyrelease/wireless201712.pdf

Brick, J. M. (2011). The future of survey sampling. *Public Opinion Quarterly, 75*(5), 872–888.

Cohn, N. (2014, October 30). Why polls tend to undercount Democrats. *New York Times*, October 13, 2014.

Couper, M. P. (2017). New developments in survey data collection. *Annual Review of Sociology, 43*, 121–145.

Couper, M. P., & Miller, P. V. (2008). Web survey methods: Introduction. *Public Opinion Quarterly, 72*(5), 831–835. DOI: 10.1093/poq/nfn066

Harter, R., Battaglia, M. P., Buskirk, T. D., Dillman, D. A., English, N., Fahimi, M., Frankel, M. R., Kennel, T., McMichael, J. P., McPhee, C. B., DeMatteis, J. M., Yancey, T., & Zukerberg, A. L. (2016, January 7). *Address-based sampling.* Report prepared for AAPOR Council by the Task Force on Address-based Sampling, operating under the auspices of the AAPOR Standards Committee. Oakbrook Terrace, IL: American Association for Public Opinion Research.

Iannacchione, V. G. (2011). Research synthesis. The changing role of address-based sampling in survey research. *Public Opinion Quarterly, 75*(3), 556–575.

Kennedy, C., McGeeney, K., Keeter, S., Patten, E., Perrin, A., Lee, A., & Best, J. (2018). Implications of moving public opinion surveys to a single-frame cell-phone random-digit-dial design, *Public Opinion Quarterly, 82*(2), 279–299. DOI: 10.1093/poq/nfy016

Kim, H., Mo Jang, S., Kim, S.-H., & Wan, A. (2018). Evaluating sampling methods for content analysis of Twitter data. *Social Media + Society, 4*(2). DOI: 10.1177/2056305118772836

Pew Research Center. (2012, May 15). Assessing the representativeness of public opinion surveys. Pew Research Center For the People & the Press. Retrieved from http://www.people-press.org/2012/05/15/assessing-the-representativeness-of-public-opinion-surveys/

Ruths, D., & Pfeffer, J. (2014). Social media for large studies of behavior. *Science, 346*(6213), 1063–1064. DOI: 10.1126/science.346.6213.1063

Shook-Sa, B. E., Currivan, D., Roe, D., & Warren, L. (2016). Random digit dialing versus address-based sampling using telephone data collection. *Survey Practice, 9*(3).

Smith, A., & Anderson, M. (2018, March 1). Social media use 2018. Pew Research Center, Internet & Technology. Retrieved from http://www.pewinternet.org/2018/03/01/social-media-use-in-2018/

Smith, A., & Olmstead, K. (2018, April 30). Declining majority of online adults say the Internet has been good for society. Pew Research Center, Internet & Technology. Retrieved from http://www.pewinternet.org/2018/04/30/declining-majority-of-online-adults-say-the-internet-has-been-good-for-society/

Sterrett, D., Malato, D., Benz, J., Tompson, T., & English, N. (2017). Assessing changes in coverage bias of web surveys in the United States, *Public Opinion Quarterly, 81*(S1), 338–356. DOI: 10.1093/poq/nfx002

⑤SAGE edge™

Get the tools you need to sharpen your study skills. SAGE edge offers a robust online environment featuring an impressive array of free tools and resources.

Access quizzes, eFlashcards, video, and multimedia at **edge.sagepub.com/treadwell4e**.

7

SUMMARIZING RESEARCH RESULTS

Data Reduction and Descriptive Statistics

"So, Lee, how's your car park campaign coming along?"

"Good news; bad news. On Thursday I counted over a hundred vehicles driving out of the car park because there were no parking spaces. That's good news because it's proof positive we need more parking space."

"So what's the bad news?"

"On Friday I got nobody driving out."

"So there goes your case for more parking."

"Not so. Per week we've got over a hundred vehicles without a park."

"But what about the days?"

"Monday's got maybe 10 vehicles can't park. Two days—Tuesday and Wednesday—are the same; we've got around 20."

"So four out of five days a week the worst case scenario is only 20 spaces needed. Looks to me like the no-more-car-parks people win. We're talking maybe 20 spaces needed and none at all on Fridays?

"I say a hundred vehicles looking for a park demolishes that argument. We need more parking. Weekly, there's a big problem."

"I say four days a week you don't have a problem."

"Why can't we agree that my maximum of 100 is the most important number?"

"Because there's also a minimum of zero out there?"

"Luke, help us out here."

"Sure! Why not average the numbers? Over the week you've got . . . let's see . . . 150 divided by five days is an average of 30 vehicles can't get a park?"

"No good; an average doesn't capture what's really going on. We have to consider that 100 value."

"And the zero!"

"OK. How about your most important number is the most frequent number? You have two twenties and one of everything else. So use 20. Don't like that? Then how about the number in the middle if you rank order all your numbers? That would be 20 again. Or you could . . ."

"Luke, stop! You're no help at all."

"So read the chapter."

CHAPTER OVERVIEW

The word **statistics** refers generally to the formulae that help us process and understand the raw data of research and more specifically to the resulting numbers that summarize the raw data, the relationships among variables, and the differences among groups.

Descriptive statistics, introduced in this chapter, describe and summarize the data from a research sample. Inferential statistics, discussed in Chapter 8, help us make probability-based inferences about the wider population from which we obtained our sample.

This chapter focuses on understanding and describing research data. **Data reduction** is basically a process of reducing the raw data of research—perhaps hundreds or thousands of individual responses—into a much smaller number of categories to make the research data more comprehensible. Descriptive statistics help us describe the distribution of data in a **data set**, look for relationships within those data, and understand the numbers we have in front of us.

We begin this chapter with a discussion of data reduction and then move on to descriptive statistics. But first, a quick vocabulary check. Remember that a *sample* consists of individuals selected by the researcher to represent a much larger group. This larger group is referred to as the *population*. A population is defined simply as all of the individuals who fall into the category the researcher ideally wishes to research. A population, by definition, is larger than a sample, but it is not necessarily immense. In fact, it could be relatively small, such as Asian special education teachers working in private schools.

Statistical formulae help us process the raw data of research into summary numbers that can tell us a lot about the raw data, the relationships among variables, and the differences among groups. Strictly speaking, statistics describe a sample. The numbers that describe a population are referred to as **parameters**. As we will see in Chapter 8, one important use of statistics is to estimate a population's parameters.

CHAPTER OBJECTIVES

This chapter will help you

- Describe the concept of descriptive statistics and provide examples.

- Describe the concept of data reduction and provide examples.

- Explain and calculate the following statistical measures:
  - ○ mean, median, and mode;
  - ○ minimum, maximum, range, variance, and standard deviation;
  - ○ *z* score; and
  - ○ chi-square

INTRODUCTION

The data from a research project can be unwieldy and incomprehensible without some form of processing. A 20-question survey of 50 people means 1,000 answers to be analyzed. The same survey administered in a typical national opinion poll of 1,200 people will result in 24,000 answers that have to be analyzed, summarized, and understood. If each question were formatted as a 5-point scale, we would have 120,000 response options ($1{,}200 \times 20 \times 5 = 120{,}000$).

There are two major ways of reducing such data to comprehensible terms—**tables** and descriptive statistics. Tables summarize the data and relationships within the data. Descriptive statistics describe the distribution of data in summary numbers that will tell you a lot about the nature of the raw data if you have a basic understanding of statistics.

It is wise to understand the concept behind any statistic so that you can select the statistics most relevant to your research questions. Even though most statistical calculations are done with calculators or data-processing software, you should work through the calculations shown in this chapter to get an understanding of what each statistic is trying to capture. To this end, the data in Exhibit 7.1 are much simplified relative to the data you would normally capture in a quantitative study. For example, the gender (GEN) and political preference (POL) questions each limit respondents to only two choices—male or female and liberal or conservative, respectively.

Data, by the way, is a plural—as in "the data are," not "the data is."

In this chapter, we will examine the communication behaviors of 20 people. We have gathered data on their use of the Internet and social media, their political orientation, their knowledge of world affairs, and their gender.

Our results are shown in Exhibit 7.1. The columns, in order, show the names of respondents (NAME), an identifying number we have assigned each respondent (ID), their gender (GEN), their political preference (POL), their estimate of the hours per week they spend on social media (HSM), their estimate of the percentage of their time they spend on social media (PSM), their score on a test of knowledge of world affairs (KWA), and their self-reported number of social media contacts (SMC).

Note that the columns are numbered to facilitate chapter discussions; such numbering does not normally appear in research reports.

Exhibit 7.1 shows a small number of people and variables, simple data, and some numbers that may appear anomalous because they have been selected to illustrate some specific points. Otherwise, this set of raw data, or data set, is typical for a quantitative study in which we measure a number of variables and look for relationships among them.

Typically, we would start with a hypothesis or with research questions linking these variables. Here are two:

H_1: Women spend more time than men on social media.

H_2: Individuals with more social media contacts will score higher on a test of world affairs knowledge than those with fewer social media contacts.

In conducting such a study, our first step would be to gather data from each respondent and to record it in the form shown in Exhibit 7.1. We would then input the data into a computer for statistical analysis using proprietary software such as **IBM SPSS® Statistics**, open source software such as **R**, or a spreadsheet such as Excel. Normally, any letters designating answers, such as M/F for male/female or L/C for liberal/conservative, would be replaced by numerals (not numbers—remember Chapter 5) in the coding process. We would also be dealing with thousands of units of information, or **data points**, rather than the few shown here.

Preliminary Considerations: Missing Data and Anomalous Data

The first step in data analysis is to decide what data to use. You are not obligated to analyze all your data. There are several reasons you might not use data you have. For example, ethically you may need to exclude data from individuals from whom you have not obtained a consent to participate in research.

Missing data can be a problem. Suppose we have respondent X, whom we know from information she provided is female, is politically liberal, and has a score of 4 on her knowledge of world affairs. However, we have no response to our questions about use of social media.

If our theoretical interest is in the relationship between gender and political orientation, we obviously have relevant data. If our data have been collected as part of a study related to the use of social media and political orientation, the data become problematic for two reasons. If the data are missing—no response—obviously we cannot use them. If, however, the social media data exist but are all zeros—that is, the respondent shows "0" for the variables HSM, PSM, and SMC—we have the more difficult judgment of whether or not to use the data. It is possible that respondent X truly never accesses social media, in which case her zeroes can be analyzed as valid data. On the other hand, if she never accesses social media, why would we analyze her data as part of a project on social media users? Although there is no clear-cut answer to this dilemma, one possible solution is to analyze our data set excluding her data and then to consider her data separately as an "outlier" case. Doing so may prove to be theoretically interesting and could provide new insights, especially if we also have qualitative comments from her—perhaps from a follow-up interview—about why she does not use social media.

Anomalous data are those that appear "out of line." For example, Exhibit 7.1 shows that Louise and Caroline each spend 80 hours a week on social media—a suspiciously large amount of time given that this is almost 50% of the total number of hours in a week. Louise

EXHIBIT 7.1 ■	Survey Results for 20 Respondents						
1	2	3	4	5	6	7	8
Name (NAME)	ID NUMBER (ID)	Gender* (GEN)	Political Preference* (POL)	Hours per Week Social Media (HSM)	% Time on Social Media (PSM)	Knowledge World Affairs (KWA)	Social Media Contacts (SMC)
Helen	01	F	L	07	1	4	2
Kiri	02	F	L	100	90	6	450
Lin	03	F	L	30	25	4	150
Miriam	04	F	C	40	20	10	250
Lakesha	05	F	L	60	10	2	350
Marie	06	F	L	60	5	6	250
Louise	07	F	L	80	80	6	350
Bonnie	08	F	L	40	60	8	150
Caroline	09	F	C	80	20	10	250
Elizabeth	10	F	C	10	10	2	100
Thomas	11	M	L	20	40	6	100
Harry	12	M	L	60	60	4	150
Wiremu	13	M	C	40	20	8	130
Jacques	14	M	C	80	80	4	350
Carlos	15	M	C	60	40	8	130
Gordon	16	M	C	40	40	6	100
Alfonso	17	M	L	60	60	4	100
Rafael	18	M	C	90	20	8	90
Joseph	19	M	C	80	80	4	350
Joseph	20	M	C	60	40	4	130

*F=female; M=male; L=liberal; C=conservative

estimates spending 80% of her time on social media whereas Caroline estimates her 80 hours as only 20% of her time. Such responses should trigger questions and follow-up.

Might the discrepancy be due to question wording we failed to pretest? For example, Louise may have interpreted the question to mean percentage of her time awake in a week whereas Caroline interpreted it to mean percentage of the total hours in a week. Regardless, Caroline appears to have dramatically underestimated the percentage of her time she spends on social media. Might we have an interesting new theory here? For example, if Louise is obligated to spend time on social media for work reasons and Caroline's use is purely social, might they each estimate the percentage of their time spent on social media differently?

Following up with Caroline might capture her subjective view of how much time she spends on social media—"Honestly, it really does feel like only 20 percent of my time!"—or it might reveal a totally mundane explanation, such as that she mistakenly hit "2" instead of "5" on her keyboard.

Such discrepancies may also indicate that measurement tools need closer examination. For example, an app that records a device's time online may measure "connected" time online as a full 168 hours a week whether there is a human present or not.

Anomalous data cannot be ignored just because it is convenient to do so. They may be analyzed separately, with the potential payoff of a new discovery, or they may be consciously excluded from analysis with the criteria for exclusion or separate analyses explicit so that readers can understand what happened to your data.

The criteria for excluding individuals may be one variable—no one is 128 years old. Or you could use a combination of criteria—no one is 15 years old and has a medical degree.

Such questions, issues, and decisions may arise from an initial inspection of data or become apparent in the course of data analysis, the first step of which is data reduction.

DATA REDUCTION

As shown in Exhibit 7.1, we have data for 20 respondents on eight variables ("NAME" through "SMC") for a total of 160 data points.

How can these data be summarized so they are easily understood?

The first basic approach is to do data reduction using summary tables. The second is to compute summary statistics such as the measures of central tendency and the measures of dispersion described later in this chapter.

The goal of data reduction is to present data in summary form. In survey and experimental research in particular, we are interested in groups more than we are in individuals. To select a couple of names at random from Exhibit 7.1, we have little theoretical interest in Lakesha or Gordon as individuals. What we are interested in, however, is whether and how males as a group and females as a group differ in social media use, political preference, and knowledge of world affairs, or perhaps we want to discover how variables such as political preference and number of social media contacts relate to each other.

Hard-hearted though it may be, Lakesha, Gordon, and 18 other individuals effectively disappear from our thinking when it comes to data analysis.

One clue to this "people as data" approach is the fact that in most data analyses the names of individuals (Column 1) disappear, to be replaced by a code number (Column 2). Our sample has two "Josephs," so one good reason for providing a unique identification number for each individual is to avoid the problem of duplicate names. Another function of an ID number is to provide some anonymity to individuals.

Typically, data for one individual would not be reported from such a data set unless he or she had such a unique combination of characteristics that the researcher saw a truly compelling reason to report them—for example, respondent X discussed above. The first step in data reduction, then, is simply to see what the data look like at the level of the group rather than the individual. (Compare this approach with the view you will find in Chapter 13 that the best insights on human communication come from an in-depth understanding of one individual or a small group.)

Research data such as those given in Exhibit 7.1 show that the researcher is specifically interested in six variables—gender through number of social media contacts—and has captured data about each of them. Statistical software will compute both descriptive and inferential statistics on request. In this chapter, we work through the thinking behind descriptive statistics.

Data Reduction and Univariate Data

Typically, researchers will start by looking at each variable on its own. This approach is called **univariate analysis**, as in one variable at a time.

A first step when inspecting data is to sort the values from lowest to highest as shown in Exhibit 7.2a for the variable HSM and then to establish the frequency with which each score occurs.

The term **frequency** refers to the number of times or the frequency with which a particular value occurs. To produce **frequency tables**, we construct categories that include all the values we expect to find on a test or a survey and then report the number of values that fall in each category.

Exhibit 7.2b shows an intermediate stage in data reduction. Rather than reporting individual values as in Exhibit 7.2a, we have set up categories of values—0–20, 21–40, and so on to a category of 81–100—so that we now can assign each individual value to one of five categories and count the number of values in each category.

The number of categories is a judgment on the part of the researcher. Exhibit 7.2b shows five categories, and Exhibit 7.2c shows further data reduction down to two categories. We could equally well have had 10 categories ranging from 0–9, 10–19, and so on to 90–100. The fewer categories we have, the more data reduction or simplification we have, but the more information is lost in the process. Three would be a defensible number of categories if you wanted to capture and differentiate only low, midrange, and high values.

EXHIBIT 7.2a ■ Data Reduction: Hours of Social Media Use per Week (HSM) Initial Data
HSM (Raw Scores)
7, 10, 20, 30, 40, 40, 40, 40, 60, 60, 60, 60, 60, 60, 80, 80, 80, 80, 90, 100

EXHIBIT 7.2b ■ Data Reduction: Frequency of Individuals Reporting Hours of Social Media Use per Week (HSM) in Five Categories

HSM	0–20	21–40	41–60	61–80	81–100
Frequency of Responses	3	5	6	4	2

EXHIBIT 7.2c ■ Data Reduction: Frequency of Individuals Reporting Hours of Social Media Use per Week (HSM) in Two Categories

HSM	0–50	51–100
Frequency of Responses	8	12

Sometimes the number of categories will be self-apparent. For example, categorizing individuals as male or female, or Democrat or Republican, means that there will be only two categories.

Presenting tables for variables such as gender and political preference are usually unnecessary. For example, gender data from Exhibit 7.1 would simply be reported as "10 (50%) respondents were female, and 10 (50%) were male." However, when we move on to bivariate analysis and want to show how gender interacts with another variable, gender will become part of a bivariate table. See Exhibit 7.5 for an example.

Note that the numbers in Exhibits 7.2b and 7.2c are not the actual values obtained from individuals but rather the number or frequency of these values. Exhibit 7.2b, for example, simply shows that three people had values between 0 and 20, and five people had values between 21 and 40. Do not make the mistake of reading such a table as people with values between 0 and 20 having an average value of 3. Carefully constructed and labeled tables indicate what their content represents, but research papers may report frequencies of values, such as shown above, as well as summary statistics, such as means, so it is wise to read tables carefully.

The distribution of values can also be plotted graphically; one such plot for the distribution of HSM values is shown in Exhibit 7.3.

Data Reduction and Bivariate Data

Communication research is ultimately the study of relationships, be it among people or among variables. So researchers, typically, are more interested in how two or more variables relate to each other than in the nature of one variable on its own. Take, for example, one hypothesis set out at the beginning of this chapter:

H_1: Women spend more time than men using social media.

Here, the hypothesis frames our data reduction. Implicitly, we are interested in only two variables—gender and time spent on social media (the variables GEN and HSM in Exhibit 7.1)—so for the moment we can ignore the other variables and concentrate on the relationship between these two. Exhibit 7.4 shows the HSM data from Exhibit 7.1 plotted to show the results for males and females separately.

Now we can start to explore the relationship between two variables. We can see, for example, that females' values on HSM range between 7 and 100 whereas males' values range between 20 and 90.

EXHIBIT 7.3   ■   Distribution of Individuals Reporting Hours of Social Media Use per Week (HSM)

	7	10	20	30	40	50	60	70	80	90	100
							X				
							X				
					X		X		X		
					X		X		X		
Frequency of Values					X		X		X		
	X	X	X	X	X		X		X	X	X
Values	7	10	20	30	40	50	60	70	80	90	100

With the values plotted from lowest to highest, Exhibit 7.4 shows that our respondents appear to cluster into two or perhaps three separate groups. Assuming two groups for purposes of discussion, we see that the first group has values ranging between 7 and 40; the second group's values range between 60 and 100. Inspection also indicates that although females are equally represented in both groups, more males are in the group with the higher values. Possibly, males and females are two separate groups with respect to time spent on social media or, to rephrase it as a tentative hypothesis, level of social media use can be predicted by gender.

To make this more apparent, we can do further data reduction and make a simple "two by two" summary table that summarizes the relationship between gender and HSM. Such tables are known as **cross-tabs** because the values of one variable are cross-tabulated against the values of another variable. Another name for this sort of table is a **contingency table** because its formatting shows how the values of one variable are contingent on another. Such tables can become more complex than a simple "two by two," as we shall see.

Exhibit 7.5 shows a simple summary table with the summary data highlighted. Here, we have defined low values for HSM as anything 50 or less and high values as anything 51 or more. Gender has the two categories of male and female.

There are several things to remember about tables such as Exhibit 7.5. First, the numbers in the body of the table are not values for HSM; they are the count or frequency of values. To some extent, this is self-apparent; we know that the HSM values range between 7 and 100, so it is unlikely that we would look at the category labeled 0–50 and interpret a 3 or a 5 as an average for HSM.

In effect, we have reduced our HSM values to **categorical data**—high and low. This means that we can use only the statistical formulae that apply to categorical data. Using formulae that apply to **continuous data**, such as age or grade point average (GPA), would be inappropriate. We will look more closely at how we examine relationships between continuous variables, such as knowledge of world affairs and social media use, in Chapter 8.

EXHIBIT 7.4 ■ Distribution of Individuals Reporting Hours of Social Media Use per Week (HSM) by Male (M) and Female (F)

Frequency of Values	F	F	M	F	F M F M		M M F M F M		F M F M	M	F
Values	7	10	20	30	40	50	60	70	80	90	100

EXHIBIT 7.5 ■ Summary Table of Hours of Social Media Use per Week (HSM) by Gender

HSM Values	Male (Out of 10)	Female (Out of 10)	Total (Out of 20)
0–50	3 (30%)	5 (50%)	8 (40%)
51–100	7 (70%)	5 (50%)	12 (60%)
Total	10 (100%)	10 (100%)	20 (100%)

A second point to be aware of is that any table can be rotated; that is, Exhibit 7.5 could have been set up with "Male" and "Female" labeling the rows and HSM values as the columns. This raises the question of how to read such tables. Because the initial research hypothesis proposed a difference between males and females in terms of social media use, we need to read across the table to get that difference. Line 2 of the table compares the number of low HSM values by gender, and Line 3 compares the number of high HSM values by gender. Obviously, we would examine the overall distribution of values in determining how males and females differ in terms of time spent on social media, but looking at males only by reading down Column 2 and discovering that they have more high values of HSM than low values, and similarly looking down Column 3 for the distribution of values for females, is a secondary interest.

Note also that the table shows both row totals and column totals. Most statistical software will report both sets of totals by default, but you are likely to have some control over which of these totals are reported. If you look at percentages rather than raw numbers in Exhibit 7.5, you will see that they add up to 100% only in the columns. In Exhibit 7.5, the Row 2 total number of values in the row is 8—only 40% of the total. The Row 3 total number of values is 12—only 60% of the total. On the other hand, the Column 2 and Column 3 numbers each total to 100%.

HINT: A rule of thumb for reading tables is to identify the "100%" columns or rows. If the columns each total to 100%, read across the rows. If the rows each total to 100%, read down the columns. In Exhibit 7.5, each column totals to 100%, so we read across the rows. If each row totaled 100%, we would read down the columns.

Data Reduction and Multivariate Data

A further level of analysis, **multivariate** analysis, is used to study the interaction of three or more variables.

You can see that Exhibit 7.6 has expanded on Exhibit 7.5 by adding the distribution of scores for another variable—knowledge of world affairs (KWA). Our aim is to determine

EXHIBIT 7.6 ■ Summary Table of Knowledge of World Affairs (KWA) by Hours of Social Media Use per Week (HSM) by Gender		
	Male	Female
HSM 0–40		
KWA 0–5	–	3
KWA 6–10	3	2
HSM 60–100		
KWA 0–5	5	1
KWA 6–10	2	4
Total	10	10

whether there is a relationship between level of social media use and knowledge of world affairs, as well as between gender and these two variables. Accordingly, under each HSM category, we have added the distribution of scores for the KWA variable. We classified the KWA scores as either low (0 to 5) or high (6 to 10). We have taken each category shown in Exhibit 7.5 and for each of the four categories (male and female by HSM 0–40 and HSM 60–100) reported the distribution of scores for KWA. We can see, for example, that no males with low HSM values had low KWA scores and that only one female with high HSM values had a low KWA score.

We could continue this multivariate analysis by adding still further subcategories to our table. For example, we could look at the KWA variable and for each KWA category report the distribution of data for the POL or PSM variables. It is obvious, though, that increasingly complex tables become increasingly difficult to comprehend and that we must look for more understandable ways to summarize the distributions of data and the relationships among variables.

This is where descriptive statistics and the inferential statistics described in Chapter 8 come to our aid.

Descriptive statistics help us

- Summarize complex data.

- Show how the data vary, for example whether everyone checked "5" on a 5-point scale or whether "1," "2," "3," and "4" also got votes.

- Show if different groups of people differ in some way.

- Show if there are relationships among variables we are interested in.

MEASURES OF CENTRAL TENDENCY: MEAN, MEDIAN, AND MODE

The three basic statistics used to summarize data are mean, median, and mode. They are called measures of central tendency because they describe the central features of a data set rather than its extreme or outlying values.

- Mean is often called the average value. Calculate it by adding all the individual values and dividing by the number of values. For the variable HSM, the mean is the total of all 20 values (1,097) divided by 20 = 54.85; that is, the respondents averaged 54.85 hours per week on social media.

- Mode is the most frequent value. It is commonly, but not necessarily, in the midrange of scores. As shown in Exhibit 7.3, we have more 60s than any other value for HSM, so the mode for this group is 60.

- Median is the midrange value. When all the values are arranged from lowest to highest, we find the value that has an equal number of values on either side of it. When the number of values is even, find the value halfway between the two middle values when the values are ordered from lowest to highest. For the variable HSM, the median value is halfway between the two middle values of 60 and 60. What is

EXHIBIT 7.7 ■ Measures of Central Tendency for Hours of Social Media Use per Week (HSM)			
	Measures of Central Tendency for HSM		
	Mean	**Mode**	**Median**
Female	50.7	40, 60, 80	50
Male	59.0	60	60
Female and Male	54.85	60	60

halfway between 60 and 60? Answer? 60! Plots such as Exhibit 7.3 can be a quick way to assess basic descriptive statistics for a sample, but obviously, counting and calculation are necessary to get precise numbers.

We can also identify the minimum and maximum values (7 and 100) and calculate the range between them (100 – 7 = 93). Range is a measure of dispersion, discussed below.

Generally, we need all three measures of central tendency because any one of them may be misleading.

For example, a group of 10 people that includes one millionaire and nine other people, each with an income of $1,000, has a mean income of $100,900. The mean in this case does not portray the group's individual incomes accurately. The median income is $1,000 because half the incomes are over $1,000 and half are under it. We might decide that the best descriptor in this case is the mode, which by definition states that the most frequent income is $1,000. However, we could also get a mode of $1,000 if only two people each had an income of $1,000 and everyone else had a uniquely different income in the millions. Obviously, none of these measures on its own summarizes the unique characteristics of this group of people well. We need additional measures to do this, and these are discussed below under "Measures of Dispersion."

As summarized in Exhibit 7.7, there appears to be some difference between males and females with respect to measures of central tendency for HSM. Statistical confirmation of this hypothesis will come from such tests as the **chi-square** (χ^2), as well as the *t* tests described in Chapter 8. Note also that for women, the scores of 40, 60, and 80 appear most frequently and with equal frequency. Because there are three modes for females, we refer to their HSM scores as having a **trimodal distribution**. Two scores appearing with equal frequency would result in a **bimodal distribution.**

MEASURES OF DISPERSION: MINIMUM, MAXIMUM, RANGE, INTERQUARTILE RANGE, VARIANCE, AND STANDARD DEVIATION

Mean, median, and mode summarize the central features of a distribution but do not describe the range of scores. The range and variability of scores are described by **measures of dispersion**. Metaphorically, if measures of central tendency are taking an interest in what most people are wearing, measures of dispersion are taking an interest in the extreme "fashionistas" who are dressing differently from everyone else, and perhaps indicating a new trend or fashion subgroup. Measures of dispersion include the minimum, maximum, range, interquartile range, variance, and standard deviation.

Minimum, Maximum, Range, and Interquartile Range

- **Maximum** = highest value.

- **Minimum** = lowest value.

- **Range** = maximum value minus minimum value.

For our variable HSM, the values range between 100 and 7, so the range is 93 (100 – 7 = 93). If all scores were identical, say 75, the range would be 0 (75 – 75 = 0).

- **Interquartile range** is a way of looking at the "middle ground" of dispersion. This range is calculated simply by ignoring the highest 25% of values and the lowest 25% and then identifying the highest and lowest values remaining under consideration, in other words, the range for the middle 50% of values. For example, if we look at Exhibit 7.2a and remove the five lowest values and the five highest values (highlighted), we are left with the middle 50% of values, which range from 40 to 80. The interquartile range, then, is 40 (80 – 40 = 40).

Variance and Standard Deviation

Variance and **standard deviation** allow us to compare different measures "on a level playing field."

The range statistic, for example, provides no basis for comparing different sets of values. Suppose a class has test scores ranging between 5 and 48 out of a possible 50. The scores have a range of 43 (48 – 5 = 43), but so do the scores for another class with scores ranging between 53 and 96 on a test scored out of 100. Clearly, we cannot directly compare the two sets of scores and the way in which they vary. Variance, standard deviation, and z scores help us to do this.

Variance and standard deviation are measures of the extent to which values in a data set vary. Standard deviation is the square root of variance. The larger the standard deviation of a variable, the wider the range of values on either side of the mean.

Variance: Formula

Computing variance is a four-step process with Steps 1 and 2 repeated for each value of the variable in your sample—as shown in Exhibit 7.8.

1. Subtract the mean value for the group from each individual value.

2. Square each result (to eliminate the problem of dealing with negative numbers).

3. Add the results.

4. Divide the sum of these squares by the number of values minus one to get an average of the squared variations from the mean.

This is expressed in the following formula.

Formula for Calculating Variance

$$s^2 = \frac{\Sigma(X - \overline{X})^2}{(N-1)}$$

s^2 = variance

Σ = "the sum of"

X = each individual score

$\overline{X}$ = the mean score for the group

N = the number of scores

Standard Deviation: Formula

Standard deviation (SD) is the square root of the variance. The formula for calculating standard deviation is

$$SD = \sqrt{s^2} = \sqrt{\frac{\Sigma(X - \overline{X})^2}{(N-1)}}$$

Variance and Standard Deviation: Example

Let's calculate the variance and standard deviation for the current variable of interest—hours per week on social media (HSM). The data for this calculation come from Column 5 of Exhibit 7.1.

As we computed previously, the mean for the HSM variable is 54.85. Using the 20 values for this variable, we compute the variance and standard deviation for the group as shown in Exhibit 7.8.

As a quick check, note that the numbers shown in Column 4 of Exhibit 7.8—the differences between each individual score and the group mean—should always add to zero. The sum of the squared differences is 12,978.55, which divided by the number of scores minus one (19) gives us a variance of 683.08.

The standard deviation, the square root of the variance (683.08), is 26.14.

We will revisit this important statistic in Chapter 8. A sneak preview of the importance of standard deviation is that it allows us to make generalizations about the wider population from which we have drawn our sample and to calculate the probability of any particular result occurring.

For example, for the variable HSM "hours per week social media," our sample of 20 people has a mean of 54.85. We know this is true for the 20 people we sampled, but how likely is it that these numbers represent the population from which the sample was drawn? To get a sense of how likely our calculated mean of 54.85 is true for the bigger population, we use the standard deviation of the sample: 26.14.

Similarly, if we look at the HSM standard deviations for males and females separately, as shown in Exhibit 7.9, it is clear that females have more variability in their scores than do males. This is apparent from the ranges (93 versus 70) and variances (949.40 versus 454.44) shown for the sample.

With standard deviation we can move beyond sample statistics and estimate the distribution of values in the sampled population. This estimation of parameters for the sampled population involves some basic assumptions about the distribution of values in the population. These assumptions and the use of standard deviation to estimate the population are discussed more fully in Chapter 8.

EXHIBIT 7.8 ■ Computing Variance and Standard Deviation for Hours of Social Media Use per Week (HSM)

ID	HSM	Group Mean	Hours per Week – Group Mean	(Hours per Week – Group Mean)^2
1	07	54.85	−47.85	2,289.62
2	100	54.85	45.15	2,038.52
3	30	54.85	−24.85	617.52
4	40	54.85	−14.85	220.52
5	60	54.85	5.15	26.52
6	60	54.85	5.15	26.52
7	80	54.85	25.15	632.52
8	40	54.85	−14.85	220.52
9	80	54.85	25.15	632.52
10	10	54.85	−44.85	2,011.52
11	20	54.85	−34.85	1,214.52
12	60	54.85	5.15	26.52
13	40	54.85	−14.85	220.52
14	80	54.85	25.15	632.52
15	60	54.85	5.15	26.52
16	40	54.85	−14.85	220.52
17	60	54.85	5.15	26.52
18	90	54.85	−35.15	1,235.52
19	80	54.85	25.15	632.52
20	60	54.85	5.15	26.52
		Sum =	0.00	12,978.55
		Variance (s^2) =		12,978.55/(20 − 1)
		=		683.08
	Standard Deviation (SD) = $\sqrt{\text{Variance}}$ =			26.14

EXHIBIT 7.9 ■ Measures of Dispersion for Males and Females on Hours of Social Media Use per Week (HSM) Variable

	Measures of Dispersion		
	Range	Variance	Standard Deviation
Female	100 − 7 = 93	949.40	30.81
Male	90 − 20 = 70	454.44	21.32

Z SCORE

Once we have computed a group's standard deviation for a variable, we can compute a *z* **score** for any individual in the group. A *z* score is the number of units of standard deviation any one value is above or below the mean. In our data, we have a measure of how many hours per week respondents spend on social media. Obviously, there are other ways of asking about social media use. For example, we asked them this question: "What percentage of your time do you spend on social media?" There is no easy way to compare the two sets of answers—hours spent and percentage of time spent—even though they address the same question. The two questions use different metrics (units of measurement) and are of a different order of magnitude. The first question uses absolute numbers with a maximum possible answer of 168 hours (7 days × 24 hours = 168). The second question uses percentages with a maximum possible of 100. The two sets of answers cannot be compared unless we standardize them in some way.

A statistic that allows us to compare results from two or more different measures would be desirable, and this is what the *z* score accomplishes. Expressing each individual value in terms of standard deviation allows us to compare data obtained using different metrics. The larger a *z* score, the further its value from the group's mean; the smaller the *z* score, the closer it is to the mean. A *z* score of 0 means that the individual's unstandardized score is equal to the mean—that is, there is zero deviation from the mean. The *z* score is to an individual's value as standard deviation is to a group's values.

z Score: Formula

Calculate the *z* score for each individual by subtracting the individual's score from the group mean and dividing that result by the standard deviation for the group. Using the notations shown previously in the formula for calculating variance, the formula for *z* is as follows:

Formula for Calculating a *z* Score	
$$z = \frac{X - \bar{X}}{SD}$$	z = *z* score X = individual score $\bar{X}$ = mean score for the group SD = standard deviation

z Score: Example

The calculation below uses the data from Column 5 of Exhibit 7.1. Remember the group mean for HSM is 54.85.

Taking the first two individuals from the group of 20 scores shown in Exhibit 7.1, we can compute their *z* scores as follows:

$$\text{Helen: } z = \frac{7 - 54.85}{26.14} = -1.83 \qquad \text{Kiri: } z = \frac{100 - 54.85}{26.14} = 1.73$$

We know already that Helen's score is below the group mean and that Kiri's score is above it, but more specifically, we now can say that Helen's HSM value is 1.83 standard deviations below the group mean, and Kiri's HSM value is 1.73 standard deviations above the mean. The z score represents a standard deviation for individuals. As we will see in Chapter 8, we can use an individual's z score to estimate the probability of that response occurring in the total population.

Most z scores are somewhere between –2 and +2—that is, between plus and minus two standard deviations of the mean. Scores greater than 2, whether positive or negative, have a 5% or lower probability of occurring. You might also intuit this from the observations that Helen's and Kiri's HSM scores are at the extreme range of scores for the group and that each score occurs only once, relative to the more frequent midrange scores of 40 and 60.

THE CHI-SQUARE TEST

What happens when we have variables such as religion that are essentially labels?

Remember "NOIR" from Chapter 5? Variables such as *religion*, *political affiliation*, and *gender* are nominal, that is to say, basically labels. We can count them, but we cannot work with them mathematically. They are categories rather than values. We may code *male* as 1 and *female* as 2, but "1" and "2" are simply labels; they do not imply that the two sexes are quantitatively different on some scale that measures gender.

We cannot calculate a mean of male and female or of liberal and conservative. All we can do is look at the distribution of their values. To assess group differences on such nominal or ordinal variables, we need a test based on the distribution of their values. This is where the chi-square test comes in.

For example, suppose we want to know if there is a relationship between gender and political affiliation. In other words, do males and females differ significantly in political affiliation?

We interview 10 females and 10 males, and ask them for their political affiliation. The results are shown in Exhibit 7.10a.

From Exhibit 7.10a, it appears that males are more likely to be conservative than females. To get a more precise reading, we would want to compare their scores on a conservatism scale with the scores for females on the same scale.

EXHIBIT 7.10a ■ Observed Values (*O*) of Political Affiliation by Gender		
	Male	Female
Liberal	3	7
Conservative	7	3

EXHIBIT 7.10b ■ Expected Values (*E*), Assuming No Difference Between Groups		
	Male	Female
Liberal	5	5
Conservative	5	5

But wait! There are no scores. Exhibit 7.10a shows numbers of people, not the values of a variable. What to do? All we can do is compare the pattern of responses shown in Exhibit 7.10a with the results we would expect if there were no pattern—that is, if each category had the same number of people in it. This is called the expected pattern, and it is shown in Exhibit 7.10b.

The chi-square test is based on computing the difference between the observed result for each cell in a table and the expected result if there was no difference between the groups. A table showing the distribution of chi-square values will then tell us whether the calculated value of chi-square can be attributed to chance.

Chi-Square: Formula

The chi-square formula is shown below. Note that χ denotes the Greek letter *chi*, not an *X*.

Formula for Calculating Chi-Square	
$$\chi^2 = \Sigma \frac{(O-E)^2}{E}$$	$\chi^2 = chi$ squared $\Sigma =$ "the sum of" $O =$ observed value in each cell of table $E =$ expected value in each cell of table

Chi-Square: Example

Exhibits 7.10a and 7.10b show the distribution of observed values (O) along with the expected values (E) if no difference between the groups existed. Putting these values in the above formula results in a chi-square value of 3.2 as shown below.

$$\chi^2 = \frac{(3-5)^2}{5} + \frac{(7-5)^2}{5} + \frac{(7-5)^2}{5} + \frac{(3-5)^2}{5}$$

$$= \frac{4}{5} + \frac{4}{5} + \frac{4}{5} + \frac{4}{5}$$

$$= 3.2$$

To interpret the chi-square result, we need to know the **degrees of freedom (df)**. Degrees of freedom (df) is an estimate of the number of independent pieces of information on which an estimate is based. Simplistically, an estimate based on a sample size of 1,000 can be expected to differ from the same estimate based on a sample size of 100, so we need to know and report the degrees of freedom.

For the chi-square test, df is the number of columns multiplied by number of rows, minus one, in this case 3 because $(2 \times 2) - 1 = 3$.

We would go to a table of chi-square values, part of which is shown in Exhibit 7.11. Such tables are available in many research texts and on the web. Alternatively, statistical software will calculate the value of chi-square and the probability of it occurring.

Exhibit 7.11 shows that our computed value of chi-square = 3.2 at df (3) is well below the value of 7.82 needed to demonstrate significance at the 95% (.05) **confidence level**. In spite of what appears to be a difference between males and females with respect to political leaning, we conclude that if the study were to be repeated, in 95 cases out of 100 we would find no significant difference in frequencies between gender and political preference.

More formally, we calculated 3.2 as the value of chi-square with 3 degrees of freedom and opted to use the conventional .05 probability level as the criterion for rejecting the null hypothesis that men and women do not differ in political preference. The table of chi-square values tells us that, for the above degrees of freedom and probability level, a value of at least 7.82 is needed to reject the null hypothesis of no difference between groups. Because our value of 3.2 is well below 7.82, we accept the null hypothesis that there is no statistically significant difference. That is to say, the results we obtained could have been obtained by chance.

We report our findings as follows. There was no significant difference between men and women with respect to political affiliation: $\chi^2(3) = 3.2, p < .05$.

Exhibit 7.12 summarizes the statistical tests described in this chapter. See the recommended websites at the end of this chapter for details on the assumptions behind these tests, their specific applications, and their limitations.

EXHIBIT 7.11 ■ Part of Chi-Square Table				
	Level of Significance			
(df)	**.10**	**.05**	**.01**	**.001**
2	4.60	5.99	9.21	13.82
3	6.25	7.82	11.34	16.27
4	7.78	9.49	13.28	18.47

EXHIBIT 7.12 ■ Summary of Basic Statistics		
Statistic	**Purpose**	**Example Research Question**
Variance	To measure the variation of individual values from the mean.	How far are test scores spread out from the mean? Low variance means that individual values are close to the mean; high variance means the individual values are spread out. Are respondents' ratings of product reliability concentrated around the mean or polarized, with some rating reliability at the high end of the scale and others giving the lowest rating?
Standard deviation (square root of variance)	To estimate the probability of a value occurring	Jack spends 30 hours a week on social media. Knowing the distribution of all such values in Jack's group, what is the probability of his value occurring?
z score	To express different units of measurement in a standard way for purposes of comparison.	Jack spends 30 hours a week on social media. Jill spends 65 percent of her time on social media. How can we compare Jack and Jill's use of social media?
Chi-square test	To assess the relationship between categorical variables.	Do men and women differ significantly with respect to being either liberal or conservative? Do faculty and students differ significantly in preferences for rap, rock, reggae, and rumba?

See the recommended websites at the end of this chapter for further details on statistical tests, their assumptions, applications, limitations, and the type of data used.

ETHICS PANEL

CAN RANKINGS BE MISLEADING?

The *U.S. News & World Report* provides annual rankings of colleges and universities, and these became controversial when some educational institutions were caught attempting to improve their rankings by manipulating or even falsifying their institutional data (Slotnik, 2012).

Manipulating data with the intent to deceive is obviously an ethical problem and may well be criminal behavior, depending on the circumstances. In this case, however, you are invited to consider the ethical implications of ranking, per se. The *U.S. News & World Report* lists colleges and universities in several categories—for example, national and regional universities, national and regional liberal arts colleges, best undergraduate business programs, and best undergraduate engineering programs. In each such category, the institutions list out as rankings—number one, number two, number three, and so on.

Such rankings are ordinal. That is, they rank institution A as "better than" institution B but not how much better. "How much better" would be represented by a rating system that uses scores rather than a rank. For example, using a 1–5 scale to rank a campus on its food service might result in hypothetical scores of 4.2 and 4.5 for each of two institutions.

The National Association for College Admission Counseling (NACAC) has drawn attention to this distinction between rankings and ratings. A 2010 survey of its members showed that a majority of college admission counseling professionals held negative opinions of the *U.S. News & World Report* undergraduate rankings (NACAC, 2011).

On a scale of 1 (*strenuously object to rankings*) to 100 (*strongly support the rankings*), high school counselors rated the ranking system a 29, and college admission officers rated the system a 39. A large majority of respondents believed that the rankings offer misleading conclusions about institutional quality.

Some respondents also emphasized that there is little statistical difference between schools and that placing colleges in ordinal rank therefore creates the illusion of differences where there are none.

And, of course, the questions of "best for whom?" and "best for what?" arise. The best college for student A will not be the best college for student B. Nor will the criteria most important to student A be the criteria most important to student B.

In the context of this chapter on basic statistics, think about these questions:

Questions

- How might readers of college rankings be misled by looking only at rankings?

- What attributes of colleges and universities should be measured in order to help a potential student make the most appropriate decisions about his or her education?

- At what level should the attributes you identify be measured—nominal, ordinal, interval, or ratio? Why?

- Would it be helpful or confusing to present readers with every institution's score on every measure so that each reader can develop his or her own "best" ranking? Why?

Websites for the *U.S. News & World Report*, NACAC, and the U.S. Department of Education's "College Navigator" are listed below under "Recommended Web Resources."

Chapter Summary

- The basic aim of data reduction is to make large data sets comprehensible.

- Descriptive statistics describe and summarize the data recorded from a research project.

- Measures of central tendency—mean, median, and mode—describe the "center" of a data distribution.

- Measures of dispersion—range, interquartile range, variance, and standard deviation—describe the range and extreme values of a data distribution.

- The *z* score is a standardized measure of how far an individual value is from the mean for its group.

Key Terms

anomalous data 132

bimodal distribution 140

bivariate 136

categorical data 137

chi-square (χ^2) 140

confidence level 146

contingency table 137

continuous data 137

cross-tabs 137

data points 132

data reduction 130

data set 130

degrees of freedom (df) 146

descriptive statistics 130

frequency 135

frequency tables 135

IBM SPSS® Statistics 132

interquartile range 141

maximum 141

mean 139

measures of central
   tendency 139

measures of dispersion 140

median 139

minimum 141

mode 139

multivariate 138

parameters 130

R 132

range 141

standard deviation 141

statistical formulae 130

statistics 130

tables 131

trimodal distribution 140

univariate analysis 135

variance 141

z score 144

Application Exercises

Exercise 1: Basic Statistics

For the variables SMC and KWA in Exhibit 7.1, compute mean, median, mode, range, variance, and standard deviation.

Exercise 2: Brand, Color, and Gender Preferences

Let's hypothesize that there are gender preferences with respect to clothing brands and color. In a setting such as a classroom, cafeteria, or library, look at the T-shirts and sweatshirts people are wearing. For each person, record your observations of gender and the shirt color and "brand" (e.g., Gap, Nike, name of a university or music group), if any. Produce two contingency tables—gender by color preference and gender by brand.

What conclusions can you come to about how color and brand preferences differ by gender?

Note that this assignment is not quite as simple as it appears because as soon as you start recording color, you will need to make a typical research decision—setting up your own categories. The number of color categories is potentially almost unlimited, so you will want to make that number manageable. Nor is gender necessarily a binary variable. How many categories will you set up, and how will you categorize "could be this; could be that" observations? How will you handle clothing that promotes a cause or a political candidate rather than a brand? For some help with this assignment, you can jump forward to Chapter 13.

Exercise 3: "The Internet of Things"

Find the June 6, 2017, Pew Research Center, Internet & Technology report on "The Internet of Things Connectivity Binge" (Raine & Anderson, 2017; see http://www.pewinternet.org/2017/06/06/the-internet-of-things-connectivity -binge-what-are-the-implications/).

The Internet of Things, or IoT, is considered the next technology megatrend in which anything from fitness bracelets to jet engines will be connected to the Internet to transmit and share data. In the Pew summary of expert opinion on the future of connectivity, you will find seven major themes, for example: "People crave connection and convenience, and a tech-linked world serves both goals well." Select one of the themes you will find in the Pew report and write it as a Likert-type question (revisit Chapter 5 for help). You may also want to jump ahead to Chapter 9 and consider whether a statement such as "People crave connection and convenience, and a tech-linked world serves both goals well" should be presented as one question or more than one. Get responses to your question from two different categories of people (for example, two different academic majors or two different class years). Get at least five people in each category. Assign each point in your scale a number so that you can record a score on the question for each respondent. Compute measures of central tendency and of dispersion for each category of respondent and report how these statistics are similar or differ.

Exercise 4: A Social Media Study

Visit LinkedIn.com—the social media site for professionals. Information for some members that is publicly available includes academic qualifications, employment history, group or organizational affiliations, and number of individual connections. Select at least two individuals and look at such information.

Formulate your own research questions (at least two) about LinkedIn members. For example, are women likely to have more connections than men? Are members with PhDs likely to have more group or organizational affiliations than members with bachelor's degrees?

Note that some of the information displayed can be treated as continuous (the number of academic degrees or jobs) and some as categorical (the type of degree or job). Which type of data should you prefer to best answer your research questions? Produce a table of descriptive statistics that will answer your research questions. What confidence do you have that your results accurately reflect all LinkedIn members of the type you sampled? Revisit Exhibit 7.1 for examples of categorical and continuous data.

Note that this mini-assignment includes almost all the elements of a full communication research study—developing a focus for your study, writing a specific research question, planning your statistical analyses, deciding what type of data to collect and how to collect it, and presenting your results. Note also that deciding what type of statistical analyses and reporting you will do precedes your data collection. If you are interested in continuous data, you will not design a study that collects only categorical data. You need a defensible and demonstrable connection between your initial theory and research questions, the data you are interested in, and your research methods.

Note: You can access the information you will need for this project in two ways:

- Search for someone you know or think may be a member of LinkedIn using the "Find a Colleague" window on the home page: www.linkedin.com. This option avoids having to register, but limits you to publicly available information.

- Register with LinkedIn using the "Get Started" window on the home page. This option will give you access to more—members-only—information, as well as enable you to post your own information.

Recommended Reading

Huff, D. (1954). *How to lie with statistics.* New York, NY: Norton.

A statistical "best seller" since 1954. Be guided by the content, not the title!

Paulos, J. A. (1997). *A mathematician reads the newspaper.* New York, NY: Random House.

This book discusses how research results and statistics are reported or misreported in newspapers.

Recommended Web Resources

The many statistical resources on the web range from easy interactive tutorials on the basic statistics discussed in this chapter to advanced routines of interest only to a specific discipline. They range from "click and go" to "installation required" and often come with a "no guarantees" warning.

Because statistics is a language that transcends discipline, you will find statistical help at many different academic and commercial sites.

The following list errs on the side of brevity. To see the vast range of statistical websites, do your own search or check out the Statpages web page below.

EasyCalculation.......www.easycalculation.com
A site for a variety of calculators, including statistics.

GraphPad.......www.graphpad.com/guides/prism/7/statistics/
Presents essential concepts of statistics.

Statpages.......http://statpages.org
The starting point for statistical websites.

StatSoft.......www.statsoft.com/textbook/stathome.html
An online textbook/tutorial on statistics.

UCLA Statistics Online Computational Resource (SOCR).......http://socr.ucla.edu/Applets.dir/OnlineResources.html

College Rankings

National Association for College Admission Counseling (NACAC) College Rankings.......https://www.nacacnet.org/knowledge-center/college-rankings/

U.S. Department of Education "College Navigator".......https://nces.ed.gov/collegenavigator

U.S. News & World Report article "About the *U.S. News* Education Rankings Methodologies".......https://www.usnews.com/education/articles/rankings-methodologies

References

National Association for College Admission Counseling. (2011, May). A view of the *U.S. News & World Report* rankings of undergraduate institutions from the college admission counseling perspective. Survey report from the National Association for College Admission Counseling Ad Hoc Committee on *U.S. News & World Report* Rankings. Retrieved from https://www.nacacnet.org/globalassets/documents/knowledge-center/college-rankings/usnewrankingsreport-survey.pdf

Raine, L., & Anderson, J. (2017, June 6). The Internet of Things connectivity binge: What are the implications? Report from the Pew Research Center, Internet & Technology. Retrieved from http://www.pewinternet.org/2017/06/06/the-internet-of-things-connectivity-binge-what-are-the-implications/

Slotnik, D. E. (2012, February 1). Gambling a college's reputation on climbing the rankings. *New York Times.* Retrieved from https://thechoice.blogs.nytimes.com/2012/02/01/playing-the-rankings-game/

$SAGE edge™

Get the tools you need to sharpen your study skills. SAGE edge offers a robust online environment featuring an impressive array of free tools and resources.

Access quizzes, eFlashcards, video, and multimedia at **edge.sagepub.com/treadwell4e**.

8

GENERALIZING FROM RESEARCH RESULTS

Inferential Statistics

"What's with the calculations, Mike?

"Budget crunch. Trying to save some money, starting with coffee. I'm drinking about three cups a day—that adds up."

"Three sounds like most of us. Charlotte's minimal. She does one cup occasionally to be sociable. Owen's the opposite. He does about seven a day but argues they're all espressos so he's not drinking as much as the rest of us."

"Those two are extremes, I'd say . . . out on their own, with most if us in the middle. We could probably figure out the likelihood that someone's more like them than like the rest of us."

"How so?"

"Well, you know just from hanging around with us that most of us drink three or four cups a day, a smaller number drink five or six, a much smaller number drink seven or eight and so on."

"Right. You can see that with grades too. Most people have middle grades; then you see decreasing numbers of people as the grades get lower or higher."

"So, I bet you could use that general pattern to estimate the likelihood of drinking any given amount of coffee. The probability of drinking three cups a day would be greater than the probability of drinking eight cups, right?"

"You might need to ask a different question than coffee consumption though. No one remembers how much they drink. Maybe ask how much money they spend on coffee. That relates directly to how much they drink."

"Maybe not, different coffees have different prices."

" I suppose you could relate coffee consumption to anything that interests you—grades, hours of sleep, time spent in coffee shops—not just expenditure on coffee."

"I wouldn't bet much on some of those relationships."

"Maybe there are relationships that research doesn't find."

"Or maybe research finds relationships that aren't really there."

"Would one of those be worse than the other?"

"Now that's got my head spinning."

"The logic or the question?"

"Both. I think I'll get a coffee and read the chapter."

CHAPTER OVERVIEW

Analyzing a sample is done to gain insight on a larger population that the sample is presumed to represent. This means that we want to know whether the results obtained from a sample reflect the results we would get if we studied the entire population. We can, of course, never know this for certain except by researching the entire population, so our next best option is to estimate the probability that our sample represents the entire population. This is what inferential statistics do; they help us make probability-based inferences about the wider population from which we obtained our sample.

More specifically, inferential statistics help with three major tasks—estimating the probability that a sample represents a population, deciding whether there are significant differences between and among groups of people, and deciding whether there are significant relationships between and among variables. In the context of statistics, **significance** has a special meaning. Significance means that there is a better than random chance that a relationship exists.

Because inferential statistics are based on assumptions about the distribution of data in populations, this chapter begins with a discussion of an important underlying concept—the assumption of a normal distribution of values in a population.

CHAPTER OBJECTIVES

This chapter will help you

- Explain the concept of inferential statistics and how they differ from descriptive statistics.

- Describe the normal curve and its significance to inferential statistics.

- Explain the concept of statistical significance and its relevance to interpreting research findings.

- Describe and compute a *t* test.

- Explain the concept of analysis of variance.

- Compare and contrast the concepts of correlation and regression.

- Define Type I and Type II errors.

INTRODUCTION

The *descriptive statistics* described in Chapter 7 go a long way toward helping us to simplify and understand research data and toward identifying patterns and relationships in data. However, researchers looking at the data from a sample of people or of media content have one major question that descriptive statistics cannot answer: "To what extent do my sample data reflect the wider population from which I obtained my sample?"

The question is a very practical one. For example, political communication consultants want to be confident that if 53% of a sample of voters express an intention to vote for candidate X, then 53% of the broader voting population that was sampled will also likely vote for candidate X. If we cannot have confidence in sampling, then the alternative is to survey the entire study population—that is, to conduct a *census*.

A census is likely to be difficult, expensive, and time consuming, so we must find ways to give ourselves as much confidence as possible that data from a sample do reflect the data that would be obtained from a wider population. That means being able to estimate as precisely as possible the probability that our sample findings do reflect the population parameters. This, essentially, is the role of inferential statistics.

To illustrate the calculation and use of inferential statistics, we will revisit some of the data shown in Chapter 7, Exhibit 7.1. First, though, let's visit data distributions and the language of curves.

The Language of Curves

Inferential statistics are based on the assumption of a **normal distribution** of values in a population. This means that when plotted out, the frequency of values in a normal distribution form a symmetrical curve from the lowest to the highest value with the majority of values peaking in the middle.

Not all distributions are normal, however. For example, we discovered in Chapter 7 that our data might plot out with a *bimodal* profile that approximates two curves, not one. Distributions can also be *trimodal* (three peaks) or *multimodal*, or have no particular pattern.

Data may plot out as an asymmetric curve with most of the values to the left of the plot and a "long tail" of values to the right, in which case we describe the curve as having positive skew or being positively skewed. Conversely, a plot with most of the data points to the right of the plot and few data points to the left is described as having negative skew. **Skew** describes where the "tail" of a distribution is. Positive skew means the tail is in the high numbers; negative skew means that the tail is in the low numbers. When a quiz is easy, a high percentage of students will score 80 or 90 out of a possible 100, producing a so-called negative skew. If the class has the toughest grader in history, most scores will plot out at the low end, and the skew will be positive.

When data are skewed, mean, median, and mode can differ considerably, and all three become necessary to describe the distribution adequately.

A curve that is flat relative to the normal curve is described as **platykurtic**; a curve that is taller, relatively speaking, is described as **leptokurtic**. (You can remember the difference by thinking platykurtic = flat-ykurtic and leptokurtic as leapt [up]-okurtic.) A platykurtic distribution means that the values are more widely spread; a leptokurtic distribution has most values concentrated within a narrow range.

GENERALIZING FROM DATA: INFERENTIAL STATISTICS

Inferential statistics help us generalize (make inferences) about a wider population from a smaller sample of it. They are based on two assumptions:

- The population sampled has normally distributed characteristics.

- The sample is randomly selected; that is, every individual in the population has an equal chance of being selected.

The Normal Curve and the Central Limit Theorem

In a statistically perfect world, data conform to a symmetrical, so-called normal curve or bell curve. Test results, for example, may approach this pattern; one or two people may score 0, one or two will achieve that magic 100, and a large number of people will score around the 50 mark, with fewer numbers scoring in the 80s and in the 30s.

Chapter 7, Exhibit 7.3—our plot of the frequency of values for the variable hours of social media use per week (HSM)—approximates a normal curve, although positively skewed. If we accept that this distribution of values approximates a normal distribution, we can use the characteristics of the normal distribution to calculate the probability of obtaining any given value in the distribution.

A further assist comes from the central limit theorem, which, in summary, states that the distribution of the averages or sums of a large number of samples of a variable will be approximately normal regardless of the shape of the underlying distribution.

By way of example, let's revisit data from Chapter 7, Exhibit 7.1. Look at the knowledge of world affairs (KWA) variable and assume that Exhibit 7.1 shows the data for an entire population. We will attempt to estimate the mean value of KWA for this population of 20 by looking at samples drawn from that population.

We will randomly sample the variable KWA, keeping our sample size constant—three for ease of calculation—and calculate the value of the mean for each sample we take. The individuals in each sample will be randomly selected by using a random numbers generator (revisit Chapter 6, "Sampling"). We will take one, two, four, eight, and sixteen samples and record the mean for each sample. The number and size of samples is arbitrary; we could demonstrate the same principles with five, ten, fifteen, and twenty samples, just as we could have selected a sample size of 2, 4, 5, or more.

Exhibit 8.1 shows the distribution of the means calculated for every sample of three as we increase the number of samples from 1 to 16.

The first random sample of three has a mean value of 5.3. It is a problematic value because we have no idea how well this sample represents the mean for the population. Next, we randomly select two more samples of three, compute their means, and get the values of 6.3 and 9. This suggests that the mean for the population may lie between 6.3 and 9. With results from four random samples, we might guess that the population mean lies between 5 and 6.7 with the actual value lying somewhere around 5.5. Results from eight samples suggest that the mean lies between 3 and 8.3 and, again, is perhaps around 5.5 as that seems to be the median value for our set of four samples and for our set of eight samples. Results from sixteen samples approximate a normal curve when plotted out and suggest that the population mean

EXHIBIT 8.1 ■ Distribution of Means of Knowledge of World Affairs (KWA) for Samples of Three With Increasing Number of Samples

Number of Samples	Means for Random Samples of Three Scores on KWA																
One								5.3									
Two											6.3						9.0
Four							5.0	5.3	5.7			6.7					
Eight	3.0		3.7	4.0				5.3			6.3			7.3	8.0	8.3	
Sixteen									5.7								
									5.7	6.0		6.7					
		3.3			4.3	4.7	5.0	5.3	5.7	6.0	6.3	6.7	7.0	7.3	8.0		

lies between 3.3 and 8 with a high probability that the mean is 5.7 as that value occurs most frequently and also approximates the median value.

The results we obtained with sixteen samples approximate what the central limit theorem proposed. The distribution of the means is approaching a normal distribution; that is, most of the means are in the middle of the distribution with greater and lesser values tapering off in number to each side. Looking at the approximately normal distribution of means for our sixteen samples, we can at least feel confident that 5.7 has a greater probability of being the population mean than does an extreme value such as 3.3 or 8.

We can never get the population mean value with 100% certainty, but our level of certainty increases as we increase the number of samples. Our first sample mean of 5.3 leaves us somewhat clueless as to what the population mean might be, but sixteen samples give us much more confidence that it lies somewhere between 3.3 and 8 and is probably around 5.7.

As it happens, our estimate is 100% correct; the mean value for KWA for our small population of 20 is 5.7. However, without population information, we would not normally know that. So our estimate of 5.7 remains just that—an estimate. Unless we have data for the entire population, we will never be 100% confident that we have the true mean.

This is where the *z* distribution comes to our rescue. Even though we don't have population data, if we assume a normal distribution of values in the population we are sampling, we can calculate the probability that our sample has captured the characteristics of the population.

The Normal Curve, *z* Scores, and the Return of Standard Deviation

As discussed in Chapter 7, *z* scores are a way of standardizing values of variables so that they can be compared. A standardized normal curve, based on *z* scores, is symmetrical with a mean of 0, a standard deviation of 1, and a total area under the curve equal to 1. Conveniently, *z* scores equal standard deviations; a *z* score of 1.5, for example, is 1.5 standard deviations from the mean. The area under the standardized normal curve allows us to calculate the probability of obtaining any given result. For example, the probability of sampling any value under this curve is 100% or 1.0 because you must pull some value if sampling. Any value greater than or less than the mean has a 50% or .5 probability of occurring because half the values lie above the mean and half below it.

A standardized normal curve with two z scores plotted from our Chapter 7 data is shown in Exhibit 8.2. Exhibit 8.3 shows a more precise distribution of values under the normal curve. Importantly, under any normal curve,

- 68% of the values occur within ± one standard deviation from the mean—the white area under the curve in Exhibit 8.2. This means that a result greater than one standard deviation, plus or minus, occurs in only 32% (100% – 68%) of the samples or has a .32 probability of occurring.

- 95% of the values occur within ± two standard deviations from the mean—the white plus light blue areas under the curve in Exhibit 8.2. A result greater than two standard deviations, plus or minus, occurs in only 5% (100% – 95%) of the samples or has a .05 probability of occurring.

- 99.7% of the values occur within ± three standard deviations from the mean—the white plus light blue and darker blue areas under the curve in Exhibit 8.2. A result greater than three standard deviations from the mean, plus or minus, occurs in fewer than 0.3% (100%–99.7%) of the samples or has less than a .003 probability of occurring.

EXHIBIT 8.2 ■ Normal Curve Showing Two z Scores

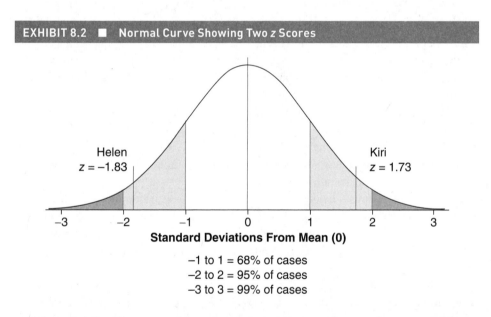

Helen
$z = -1.83$

Kiri
$z = 1.73$

Standard Deviations From Mean (0)

−1 to 1 = 68% of cases
−2 to 2 = 95% of cases
−3 to 3 = 99% of cases

EXHIBIT 8.3 ■ Percentage Distribution of Values Under the Normal Curve by Standard Deviation (SD) From the Mean

	> −3 SDs	−3 SDs	−2 SDs	−1 SD	+1 SD	+2 SDs	+3 SDs	> +3 SDs
By SD From Mean	0.13	2.15	13.59	34.13	34.13	13.59	2.15	0.13
Cumulative SD From Mean	50.0	49.87	47.72	34.13	34.13	47.72	49.87	50.0

Source: Adapted from Coolidge, F.L. (2000)/ Statistics A Gentle Introduction. Sage Publications; London.

The characteristics of the standardized normal curve allow us to calculate a specific level of confidence in our results and help us decide whether any given result should or should not be attributed to mere chance. Let's look at some examples.

Calculating Probabilities Based on the Normal Distribution

Let's revisit the KWA variable, whose mean we calculated to be 5.7. Earlier in this chapter, we estimated its mean to be between 3.3 and 8.0 and more likely to be 5.7 than other greater or lesser values. Following the example of calculating a standard deviation shown in Chapter 7, Exhibit 7.8, we calculate the standard deviation for KWA to be 2.36. We can now estimate specific probabilities of the mean for the KWA population as follows. There is a

- 68% probability that the population mean lies between 3.34 and 8.06, that is, ± one standard deviation (2.36) from 5.7;

- 95% probability that the population mean lies between 0.98 and 10.42, that is, ± two standard deviations (4.72) from 5.7; and

- 99% probability that the population mean lies between –1.38 and 12.78, that is, ± three standard deviations (7.08) from 5.7.

Of course, a score of –1.38 makes little sense when we consider that it is capturing knowledge of world affairs. It is difficult to see how anyone could have negative knowledge or score less than zero on a test. We need to remember that we are now looking at a theoretical distribution of values and the statistical probability, not the commonsense probability, of a value occurring.

From Exhibit 8.1, we might guess that the population mean is around 5.7, but we don't know what results other samples would provide. Knowing the standard deviation, having calculated our mean for the sample, and assuming the KWA values are normally distributed, we can, however, now say that if we repeat our sampling, 95 times out of 100 the mean for the sample will lie between 0.98 and 10.42.

Let's now look at how individual z scores can be used to estimate the probability of any given score occurring. Exhibit 8.2 shows the HSM z scores for Helen and Kiri that we calculated in Chapter 7. Helen's z score of –1.83 lies between minus one and minus two standard deviations from the mean and is closer to minus two standard deviations. What is the probability of her score occurring?

Half the scores under the normal curve are negative, so just by knowing that Helen's score is negative, we can say that it has no more than a 50% or .5 probability of occurring. We can get more specific than that, though. Looking at Exhibit 8.3 (bottom line) and the negative scores on the left side of the curve, we can calculate that z scores below –1 have a .1587 probability or less of occurring (50% – 34.13% = 15.87% = .1587). And z scores below –2 have a .0228 probability or less of occurring (50% – 47.72% = 2.28% = .0228). So just by knowing the normal curve, we can say that the probability of a z score of –1.83 occurring is between .0228 and .1587.

To get the exact probability, we can go to tables of z scores. Part of such a table is shown in Exhibit 8.4. It shows the area under the standardized normal curve to the left of any given z score. The probability of a z score of –1.83 occurring is located at the intersection of row –1.8 and column .03. The result is .0336—within the range of values we had estimated just by

	Standard Normal Distribution. Values Represent Area Under the Normal Curve to Left of the z Score									
z	**.00**	**.01**	**.02**	**.03**	**.04**	**.05**	**.06**	**.07**	**.08**	**.09**
–1.9	.0287	.0281	.0274	.0268	.0262	.0256	.0250	.0244	.0239	.0233
–1.8	.0359	.0351	.0344	.0336	.0329	.0322	.0314	.0307	.0301	.0294
–1.7	.0446	.0436	.0427	.0418	.0409	.0401	.0392	.0384	.0375	.0367
1.6	.9452	.9463	.9474	.9484	.9495	.9505	.9515	.9525	.9535	.9545
1.7	.9554	.9564	.9573	.9582	.9591	.9599	.9608	.9616	.9625	.9633
1.8	.9641	.9649	.9656	.9664	.9671	.9678	.9686	.9693	.9699	.9706

EXHIBIT 8.4 ■ Part of a Table of z Scores

knowing the attributes of the z distribution—and closer to .0228 than to .1587, because the z score is closer to –2 than –1, as we had noted.

Note also that z scores can help us understand the distribution of values in a population. For example, what percentage of the population is on social media between Helen and Kiri's values of 7 and 100 hours a week? Exhibit 8.4 shows their z scores of –1.83 and 1.73 highlighted. The table tells us that .9582 of the HSM values lie to the left of 1.73 and .0336 of the values lie to the left of –1.83. The difference between these two values is .9246 (.9582 – .0336 = .9246); that is, over 92% of the scores lie between 7 and 100 hours a week. We can verify this from a quick glance at Exhibit 8.2, which shows that these two z scores mark a range of scores ranging from almost two standard deviations below the mean to almost two standard deviations above the mean; that is, almost 95% of the scores fall between them.

(Note that some z tables use different conventions for showing the distribution of z and need to be read differently; for example, they may show the area between a z score and the mean.)

z Scores, Hypotheses, and Decision Making

Conventionally, we use a .05 probability cutoff to decide whether to accept or reject a null hypothesis of "no difference." This means we accept a null hypothesis that all scores lying between plus and minus two standard deviations from the mean—95% of the scores—belong to members of the same population.

There is only a 5% probability of getting values that lie beyond plus or minus two standard deviations from the mean. We assume, therefore, that something other than chance explains these values. That "something" is that these values belong to another population.

Remember that we do not know the real values for the population because we have not conducted a census of the whole population. All we have is a calculated range of possibilities. This range of values is called the **confidence interval**. In our KWA example above, we calculated the confidence interval to be 0.98 to 10.42 at the 95% confidence level.

For a **sampling distribution** (the distribution of the sample results), the standard deviation is called the standard error.

When we report results, we report the confidence level and the standard error. For example, public opinion polls often publish a statement to the effect that in 19 out of 20 cases the sample results will differ by no more than 3% from the results that would be obtained from a census of the entire population. In other words, they are reporting that at the 95% confidence level (19 out of 20 = 95%) the standard error for their results is plus or minus 3% given their sample size of, typically, 1,200. This means that we can be statistically confident that if the survey were repeated 100 times under the same conditions, we would find that 95 times out of 100 the results would vary by less than 3% (or by more than 3% only 5 times out of 100).

Used together, inferential statistics, random sampling, and the assumption of a normal distribution of data help us calculate our level of certainty when we project results from a sample to a wider population. Conveniently, inferential statistics also tell us that as long as we are prepared to accept a known level of uncertainty in our projections, we do not need huge sample sizes.

All these calculations of probability are based on the assumption of normal distribution. Statistical procedures based in these assumptions are called **parametric statistics**. When we cannot make the assumption of normal distribution or have categorical rather than continuous variables, **nonparametric statistics** must be used.

Confidence Level and Sample Size

There is a trade-off among confidence level, standard deviation, and sample size. Let's revisit the formula for standard deviation, shown in Chapter 7 and again below.

Formula for Standard Deviation	
$SD = \sqrt{\dfrac{\Sigma(X - \overline{X})^2}{(N-1)}}$	SD = standard deviation $\overline{X}$ = the mean score for the group X = each individual score N = the number of scores

Revisit the calculation of standard deviation (SD) for the HSM variable, shown in Chapter 7, Exhibit 7.8. If you recall, the sum of the squared differences was 12,978.55 (which we will round off to 12,978 here). Filling in our calculations for the standard deviation, we have the following for HSM:

$$SD = \sqrt{\frac{12,978}{N-1}}$$

Exhibit 8.5 shows how the value of the standard deviation or standard error decreases as the sample size increases.

The square root in the formula indicates that the sample size needs to be quadrupled to halve the standard error. For example, our sample size of 20 needs to be quadrupled to 80 to halve the standard error to 12.82, and it needs to be quadrupled again to 320 to further halve the error to 6.38. It would take an increase to 1,280 to halve the error again (to 3.19). For a national survey of public opinion, a sample of 20 people intuitively seems too small; 1,280 perhaps reasonable; and 5,120, which would halve the standard error yet again, a lot of work! There is obviously a law of diminishing returns here. You could put time and effort into obtaining a sample of 5,000 people (or, in the ultimate, to surveying an entire population),

EXHIBIT 8.5 ■ Relationship of Sample Size to Standard Deviation for Hours of Social Media Use per Week (HSM) Variable	
Sample Size (*N*)	Standard Deviation (SD)
20	26.14
40	18.24
80	12.82
160	9.03
320	6.38

but it is usual to settle for the convenience of a smaller sample and to accept some level of error (which you will be able to calculate) as a trade-off.

Obviously, larger sample sizes become important when a smaller level of error is needed.

Knowing the level of error and the confidence level we can afford allows us to work back to the sample size we need.

TESTING FOR DIFFERENCES BETWEEN AND AMONG GROUPS

A frequent question in communication research is "Do two groups differ on some variable of interest?" The chi-square test introduced in Chapter 7 is used when we have categorical data. With continuous data, one way to answer this question is to compare each group's mean score on our variable of interest using the *t* test, described below.

The *t* Test

The *t* test compares the mean scores of two groups on the same variable to determine the probability that the groups are different.

Let's return to Chapter 7, Exhibit 7.1, and look at two groups—the politically conservative and the politically liberal. Let's hypothesize that the groups' knowledge of world affairs (KWA) will differ based on their political preference (POL).

Column 7 of Exhibit 7.1 lists the scores of the 20 respondents for KWA on a 1-to-10 scale. Column 4 shows the POL for each respondent. We can plot the distribution of scores for the 10 individuals who are politically liberal and the 10 individuals who are politically conservative, as shown in Exhibit 8.6.

The distribution of scores suggests something like a normal distribution of scores for the liberal group and a bimodal distribution of scores for the conservative group, with the conservative group having a greater range of scores and more high scores than the liberal group.

The mean score for KWA for the liberal group is 5.0 (50/10), and for the conservative group it is 6.4 (64/10).

Based only on the means, we might conclude that the conservative group has a greater KWA than does the liberal group, but look at the distribution of the two sets of scores in

EXHIBIT 8.6 ■ Distribution of Scores on Knowledge of World Affairs (KWA) by Political Preference (POL)

Liberal (Mean = 5.0)		4	6		
		4	6		
		4	6		
	2	4	6	8	
Conservative (Mean = 6.4)		4		8	
		4		8	10
	2	4	6	8	10

Exhibit 8.6. The two groups have scores of 2, 4, 6, and 8 in common. The only score unique to any one group is the conservatives' two 10s.

The question then becomes did *all* of the conservatives score higher than *all* of the liberals, suggesting that we have two groups from two different populations? Or, if many of the individual scores are the same in both groups, are we basically looking at two groups from the same population? Clearly, the latter appears to be the case in our example.

The question is one of **statistical significance**, as in "Do the means of the two groups differ significantly?" More precisely, what we are asking is "What is the probability that the mean score for one group falls within one, two, or three standard deviations from the mean score for the second group?"

If we conclude that we are looking at samples from two different populations, we can say that the two groups are significantly different. If we conclude that we are looking at one population with two subgroups in it, we reject the hypothesis that the two groups are significantly different (in this case that the liberal group differs significantly from the conservative group on KWA scores).

The *t*-test calculation results in a value that is then compared against a table showing the probability of the calculated *t* value occurring. Basically, the *t* test shows whether our observed difference in means, corrected for the number of observations and the range of scores, is of low or high probability.

t Test: Formula

Conceptually, the *t* test is based on the differences in means for a variable common to two groups but also takes into account the range of scores for each group and each group's size, as shown below. Tables of *t* values or statistical software show the probability of the calculated *t* value occurring.

$$t = \frac{\textit{difference in group means}}{\sqrt{\dfrac{\textit{correction for group variance}}{\textit{correction for group size}}}}$$

The calculation requires three inputs from each group—the group's mean, the group's size, and the group's sum of the squared differences of each score from the group mean. You will recognize from Chapter 7 that this sum of the squared differences from the mean for each score is the variance.

The formula to calculate the value of t where two different groups are compared is called a *t* **test for independent samples**.

Exhibit 8.7 shows the group means, the size of each group, the calculation of the sum of squared differences of each score from its group mean, and the calculation of the t value.

Formula for Calculating t for Independent Variables	
$$t = \frac{\overline{X}_1 - \overline{X}_2}{\sqrt{\left[(n_1 + n_2 - 2)/(n_1 + n_2)\right]*\left[(n_1 n_2)\right]}}$$	$\overline{X}_1,\ \overline{X}_2$ = means for group 1 and group 2 $\Sigma d_1^2, \Sigma d_2^2$ = sum of squared differences of each score from its group mean n_1, n_2 = number of scores in group 1 and group 2

EXHIBIT 8.7 ■ Calculation of t for the Variable Knowledge of World Affairs (KWA) on Liberal and Conservative Groups

Data for Liberal Group			Data for Conservative Group		
KWA scores ($n_1 = 10$)	Difference between score and group mean (5.0)	Squared difference between score and group mean	KWA scores ($n_2 = 10$)	Difference between score and group mean (6.4)	Squared difference between score and group mean
2	−3	9	2	−4.4	19.36
4	−1	1	4	−2.4	5.76
4	−1	1	4	−2.4	5.76
4	−1	1	4	−2.4	6.76
4	−1	1	6	−0.4	0.16
6	1	1	8	1.6	2.56
6	1	1	8	1.6	2.56
6	1	1	8	1.6	2.56
6	1	1	10	3.6	12.96
8	3	9	10	3.6	12.96
Mean for KWA = sum of scores/10 = 50/10 = 5.0		Sum of Squared Differences = Σd_1 = 26.00	Mean for KWA = sum of scores/10 = 64/10 = 6.4		Sum of Squared Differences = Σd_2 = 71.4

$$t = \frac{5.0 - 6.4}{\sqrt{\left[\frac{(10+10-2)}{(10+10)}\right]*\left[(10*10)\right]}} \cdot \frac{(26.0+71.4)}{} = \frac{-1.4}{\sqrt{\left[\frac{(18)}{(20)}\right]*\left[(100)\right]}} \cdot (97.4) = \frac{-1.4}{\sqrt{\frac{97.4}{90}}} = -1.35$$

EXHIBIT 8.8 ■ Part of a Table of *t* Values					
		Level of Significance for One- and Two-Tailed Tests			
df		.10	.05	.01	.001
17	Two-tailed	1.740	2.110	2.898	3.965
	One-tailed	1.333	1.740	2.567	3.646
18	Two-tailed	1.734	2.101	2.878	3.922
	One-tailed	1.330	1.734	2.552	3.610
19	Two-tailed	1.729	2.093	2.861	3.883
	One-tailed	1.328	1.729	2.539	3.579

t Test: Example

The negative value of *t* in this case simply indicates that the mean for the second group is higher than that for the first group. The actual value of 1.35 tells us nothing in itself. It is a measure of the difference between group means, but what we are interested in is the probability of this difference in means occurring. To get this probability, we need to go to a table that shows the normal distribution of *t* values. Part of such a table is shown in Exhibit 8.8. Such tables are readily available online. Statistical software will compute both *t* and the probability of the *t* value occurring for you.

To understand fully and interpret a table of *t* values or the output that statistical software will give you, we need to understand two concepts—*degrees of freedom* and *one-tailed* versus *two-tailed* distribution of values.

As noted in Chapter 7, degrees of freedom (df) is an estimate of the number of independent pieces of information on which an estimate is based. In this case, it is calculated as the number of scores in group 1 (minus one) plus the number of scores in group 2 (minus one), so for our data, the calculation would be $(10 - 1) + (10 - 1) = 18$.

A **one-tailed test** means we are proposing that the differences between the groups will be in one direction—for example, that the mean score for the conservative group will be higher than for the liberal group. A **two-tailed test** proposes only that the groups will differ. The part of a *t* table shown in Exhibit 8.8 shows the probability of a *t* value occurring and how it varies according to degrees of freedom and whether the test is two-tailed or one-tailed.

The higher the *t* value, the lower the probability that it will occur. As described above, the result of our calculation for the above groups was $t = 1.35$ for 18 degrees of freedom. You can see from Exhibit 8.8 that, for a two-tailed test, the value needed to demonstrate a significant difference is 2.101 or greater at the 95% (.05) probability level. We have a *t* value less than that needed to demonstrate a significant difference between our two groups regardless of whether we are looking at a one- or a two-tailed test. Therefore, we conclude there is a 95% probability that the groups are not different.

Here is how we would think through the above analysis more formally and report it.

Initially, we have no reason to theorize that the liberal group would have higher scores than the conservative group or vice versa, so we propose a null hypothesis of no difference between the groups.

H_0: Scores on knowledge of world affairs will not differ between the liberal and conservative groups.

We will follow a social science convention and work to the .05 level of significance for hypothesis testing. The level of significance is a decision for you, the researcher. As the *t* table indicates, you could opt to test at the .01 or even at the .001 level of significance.

We calculated 1.35 as the *t* value with 18 degrees of freedom, and we look at the table of *t* values, selecting the two-tailed values because we hypothesized no difference between the two groups. The table tells us that for such a test, a *t* value of 2.101 is needed to reject the hypothesis that there is no difference between groups. Because our value of 1.35 is less than 2.101, we therefore accept the null hypothesis that there is no difference between the two groups. That is to say, the results we obtained could have been obtained by chance.

We report our findings as follows: There was no significant difference between liberal and conservative groups in the scores for knowledge of world affairs: $t(18) = 1.35$, $p < .05$.

t Test For Dependent Samples

The above *t* test is for independent samples, that is, for two separate groups of individuals. When test groups consist of the same individuals, we have dependent samples and must use a *t* test for dependent samples.

The classic "pretest–posttest" situation provides an example of dependent samples. Imagine advertisers testing a new advertising campaign. They might run a baseline study of consumer attitudes toward their client's product (pretest), expose these consumers to the test messages, and then run the study on the same group again (posttest). Any difference in attitudes would then be assumed to be a result of the exposure to the test messages. In this case, we are not comparing two groups; we are comparing the same group twice—"pre" and "post" exposure to the ad messages—and the *t* calculation gets amended to reflect this.

Analysis of Variance

One problem with the *t* test is that it compares only two groups. What if we wish to compare more than two groups, for example, how art, business, communication, and science majors score on some standardized test?

When it comes to multiple groups, we need multivariate statistics, of which **ANOVA** (ANalysis Of VAriance) is one example.

ANOVA is conceptually simple. ANOVA is based on variance, which you will recall is a measure of the extent to which the values for a variable differ. To calculate ANOVA is simply to compare the variance within groups with the variance among groups.

Think of three groups of individuals. One is composed of our siblings, a second is composed of our cousins, and a third is composed of our parents and grandparents. Each group is different in some way. Each individual is different in some way—eye color, dress, age, and so on—but each individual also has something in common with other members of his or her own group and also with members of the other two groups.

What defines each group is that its members more closely resemble one another than they do members of the other two groups. The variance within a group—its variety, if you will—is less than it is for the three groups overall.

If the individuals in a group vary more than the three groups considered together, we would assume that we are looking at one large group of individuals and that there are no distinctive groups. If the individuals in each group show less variety (variance) than the three groups overall, we assume that these individuals have more in common with others in the group than with the three groups overall and that there are consequently three distinct groups of people.

One-way ANOVA is the simplest member of the ANOVA family. It looks at one variable, but unlike the *t* test, it compares more than two groups. The formula is complicated in that it compares multiple groups, but it is also one of the easiest to comprehend.

Why not just do multiple *t* tests—comparing groups 1 and 2, 1 and 3, and 2 and 3, for example? The answer is that doing this would give you three tests rather than one and therefore change the odds of finding a statistically significant result. Repeated testing is analogous to retaking a test that you were not happy with until you get a good grade. We use statistical testing to discover what our sample is telling us at a given time, so repeated testing until a desirable result comes up is not our aim or interest.

The between-groups variance divided by the within-groups variance gives us an **F value**. From a table of *F* values, we can find the probability of *F* occurring and therefore whether we have a statistically significant difference among our sample groups.

ANOVA: Formula

The *F* test for analysis of variance is conceptually simple and computationally complex. The concept is shown below.

$$F = \frac{variance\ between\ groups}{variance\ within\ groups}$$

ANOVA: Example

Here we will work through the concept behind the calculations and interpretation of results. Suppose, for example, we have a question of whether there is a relationship between academic major (art, business, communication, and science) and use of social media (HSM). We have a group of students from each major, and each student has reported a value for HSM. If the variance for HSM within each group is less than the overall variance, we assume that we have four separate groups. If the variance within each group is greater than that for the groups overall, we assume that there are no separate groups.

The ANOVA calculation results in an *F* value. We can get the probability of that value occurring from a table of *F* values or from computer output. If our calculated value of *F* is greater than the table value for *F*, we would conclude that our *F* value is unlikely to have been obtained by chance. We would therefore reject the null hypothesis of no difference between groups and conclude that the difference between the four groups of majors with respect to time spent on social media is statistically significant.

Note that this is the only conclusion we are entitled to. Although it is tempting to look at whether specific majors differ in time spent on social media, that was not our original question. Our question was whether academic major as a variable interacts with time spent on social media, and the answer was that there is a statistically significant interaction. Whether communication majors differ from science majors in the use of social media is another question, and had we asked that question, we would have selected another test to answer it—most likely a *t* test.

ANOVA tests for relationships among two or more groups, but it is still a simple analysis of variance in that it explores the relationship between only two variables. Suppose we want to examine how academic major relates to multiple dependent variables, such as time spent on each of Facebook, YouTube, Twitter, and Instagram considered together. Now we would need MANOVA—multiple analysis of variance.

Note that we have not established any proof of causality. It may be tempting to think that one's academic major predicts time spent on social media. We might, for example, speculate that business majors are busy planning business start-ups and therefore spend time on social media. But the reverse reasoning equally explains our data; time spent on social media may predict academic major. For example, communication majors may have gravitated to the communication major as a consequence of spending time online and seeing the job opportunities that social media offer.

TESTING FOR RELATIONSHIPS BETWEEN AND AMONG VARIABLES

With the *t* test, chi-square test, and ANOVA, we examine differences between or among groups of people.

None of these tests tells us anything about the relationships between or among variables, a question of considerable interest to many researchers. Correlation and regression are two statistical techniques that answer this question.

Correlation

A frequent focus in communication research is the relationship between or among variables. For example, we might want to know whether a higher than average use of social media is associated with a lower than average level of interpersonal socializing; if there is an association between the amount of time spent online and academic performance; or if there is an association between viewing violent media content and antisocial behavior.

Correlation is used to assess such relationships between variables. It provides a measure of the strength of relationships between variables but will not tell us whether the relationship is causal.

One way to visualize correlation is to plot the values for one variable on a horizontal axis against the values for another variable on a vertical axis. If the values plot out close to a straight line horizontally or vertically, we infer that there is little relationship between the two variables because, as one changes in value, the other shows little change. On the other hand, a pattern that approximates a 45-degree line indicates a strong relationship between the two variables; for every unit change in one, there is a similar change in the other.

A **correlation coefficient** is a measure of the strength of association between variables. It is usually denoted as r_{xy}, where x and y are the two variables being examined for strength of association. Coefficients express the strength of the relationship between two variables and range between –1.0 and +1.0, indicating a 100% negative and a 100% positive correlation, respectively.

As a rule of thumb, social scientists get excited at correlations of .70 or better, find correlations between .30 and .70 moderate, and interpret correlations of less than .30 to be moderate to weak.

Note again that correlation does not indicate causality. If, for example, we found a strong correlation between time spent online and knowledge of world affairs, we would not know whether time spent online improves one's knowledge of world affairs or whether having a high knowledge of world affairs predicts that individuals are more likely to spend time online. While it might be tempting to assume that the more time we spend online the more we learn, it is equally plausible that a high level of knowledge predicts that an individual will spend more time online in order to add to that knowledge. To get an answer to the causality question, we need the experimental methods outlined in Chapter 10.

Regression

Correlation coefficients express the strength of relationships between two variables, but they do not predict the value of one variable given the value of another. Nor do they express the relationships among three or more variables, a common requirement in communication research. To address such needs, we have the tools of linear **regression** and multiple regression.

Unlike correlation, **linear regression** predicts a specific value for one variable (the **outcome** or **criterion variable**) given a value for a second, the **predictor variable**.

Because the values of the two variables are typically scattered and do not all plot out precisely on one line, there is almost inevitably an error (which can be calculated) in calculating the value of one variable from another.

Linear regression, by definition, assumes that the relationship between variables is best captured by a straight line. Some data distributions may be best captured by a curve rather than a line, and, yes, there are regression techniques that assume a **curvilinear relationship** rather than a linear one between variables.

If we wish to predict the value of one variable using two or more predictor variables, we use analogous formulae that take several variables into account, at which point we are doing **multiple regression**.

TWO FINAL DECISIONS

Accept or Reject My Findings?

Statistical testing offers you the probability, not the certainty, of a result occurring in the wider population. You, the researcher, still have to decide whether to accept that probability. Statistically based research errs on the pessimistic side. In a general sense, you are testing your ideas, hoping to be proven wrong. If there is a probability that your results could have occurred by chance, you dismiss your findings as not significant, in a statistical sense, and revisit your initial hypotheses or research questions.

Probability is an important concept. Consider that the trials of new drugs, drugs that could have a major impact on human health, are based on statistical probability. As a potential consumer, you would want to know the outcomes of such trials at a very high level of probability. But even at the highest level of probability, researchers still have to decide whether to accept or reject their findings. Conceptually, they have a chance of accepting a probability and being wrong or right, or rejecting it and being wrong or right.

In the language of statisticians, they face the possibility of committing either a **Type I error** or a **Type II error**. As shown in Exhibit 8.9, there are four possible outcomes from deciding to accept or reject a hypothesis.

EXHIBIT 8.9 ■ Type I and Type II Error		
	Accept Null Hypothesis	**Reject Null Hypothesis**
Null hypothesis is true in the wider population.	*No problem*	*Type I Error* Decided wrongly that there was a significant result.
Null hypothesis is false in the wider population.	*Type II Error* Decided wrongly that there was no significant result.	*No problem*

There are ways to reduce both Type I and Type II errors. Type I error—deciding that you have a significant finding when you do not—is under your control in that you can decide on the level of significance for accepting or rejecting hypotheses. That is why statistical tables typically show distributions of *t* and chi-square at the .10, .05, .01, and .001 levels of probability. Type II error—deciding that there is no significant result when there is—can be decreased by, for example, increasing sample size.

Statistically grounded research is an exercise in minimizing both types of error as far as possible. The standards applied are a function of the research culture, as well as of the individual researcher's judgment. Social scientists generally work to the .05 probability level; medical research may work to a .01 or even .001 level of significance given the implications of a false finding for human health. Statistical software provides an exact probability computation (e.g., .047) for any statistical test, but that final "accept/reject" decision remains with you, the researcher.

If It's Significant, Is It Significant?

Generally, published research is published because the findings are both significant and new.

Significance, in a general sense, is a matter of disciplinary judgment or, in the case of academic publications, editors' judgments. For quantitative studies, there is typically a further criterion—statistical significance. However, statistically significant findings may or may not be significant conceptually. Suppose we have a finding that proves to be statistically significant at the .10 (90%) level of significance. Conventionally, social science works to a .05 (95%) level of significance, so, by convention, our finding would not be regarded as significant statistically even though it might well be intellectually significant. Further, statistical significance is a function of sample size. With enormous random samples even tiny differences can pass standard tests of significance (Morin, 2014).

In the 2000s, new ideas challenged the relevance of statistical significance, the objectivity of researchers, and the research community's emphasis on new findings.

Notably, Ioannidis (2005) suggested that many research findings, particularly those based on tests of statistical significance, are refuted or not supported by subsequent studies. They are false positives—the finding of an effect when there isn't one.

Ioannidis's paper and others launched heated debates about replication—that is, the need for follow-up studies that use the same methods to measure the same variables in samples drawn from the same population as an original study. Replication advocates argue that "been there; done that" research is in fact necessary to address the problem of false positives and to test current hypotheses and theories. Results that are not statistically significant should be published because they put statistically significant results in context.

The replication debate continues, and it provides a useful reminder that studies, statistically significant or not, "breakthrough" or not, may add to our knowledge but not necessarily to our wisdom.

Exhibit 8.10 summarizes the statistical tests described in this chapter. See the recommended websites at the end of this chapter for details on the assumptions behind them, their specific applications, and their limitations.

EXHIBIT 8.10 ■ Summary of Advanced Statistics		
Statistical Tests	**Purpose**	**Example Research Question**
Tests for Differences		
t test for independent samples	To compare the mean score of two groups on the same variable.	Do communication majors differ from biology majors on knowledge of world affairs?
t test for dependent samples	To compare the mean scores of one group on two variables, e.g., to perform a pretest and posttest using the same group.	Did a group's attitudes change after exposure to a persuasive message?
ANOVA (Analysis of variance)	To assess differences among multiple groups on one variable.	Does time spent on social media differ among art, business, and communication majors?
MANOVA (Multiple analysis of variance)	To assess differences among multiple groups on more than one variable.	Does time spent on Facebook, YouTube, Instagram, and LinkedIn differ among art, business, and communication majors?
Tests for Relationships		
Correlation	To measure the strength of relationship between two variables.	What is the strength of the relationship between time spent on gaming and GPA?
Regression	To predict the value of one variable knowing the value of another variable.	What is an individual's predicted score on knowledge of world affairs, given the number of hours per week she spends on social media?
Multiple regression	To predict the value of one variable knowing the values of two or more other variables.	What is an individual's predicted score on knowledge of world affairs, given his number of international social media contacts, number of hours per week spent on social media, and the number of hours per week spent on traditional news sites?

* Revisit Chapter 5 for a discussion of nominal, ordinal, interval, and ratio variables. See the recommended websites at the end of this chapter for further details on statistical tests and their assumptions, specific applications, limitations, and use.

ETHICS PANEL
A COMMUNICATIVE TENSION

Two forces are at work when news media and other nonscholarly sources report statistics and research methods—simplification and selectivity.

Simplification occurs most commonly when journalists writing for lay audiences use their professional skills to report scientific research in a way that their audiences will understand. Most people are not familiar with and—dare we say—do not care about chi-square, *t* tests, or multiple polynomial regression, so there would be little point writing for most audiences in such terms. News writing, in most cases, has a "get to the point" style, so journalists understandably focus on a bottom-line "What's in it for the reader?" interpretation of research results.

It is easy to see the nature of this simplification. Just compare a scholarly research paper on media effects with any magazine article on such topics as "Is watching too much TV bad for your kids?"

Selectivity occurs when statistics are used to bolster an argument. For example, a political party may argue that it has reduced income taxes across the board for everyone by an average of 2%. The opposition will point out that because low-income people, by definition, are paying little tax, the effect of the tax cut on them is minimal in terms of absolute dollars. People in the top income bracket gain much more in terms of tax cuts. Which party is correct? Both. Neither is lying; each is merely selecting the most relevant statistic to make a point.

Questions

- How might simplifying research data mislead readers and thus violate professional standards of behavior for journalists, science writers, and researchers?

- A published research report is ultimately a researcher's personal summary and interpretation of his or her data collection and analyses. What ethical responsibilities, if any, do researchers have to make their nonpublished data and analyses accessible by interested parties? How might you be able to make such nonpublished content accessible?

- You have survey data indicating that 52% of respondents are in favor of a proposed legislative change. Your calculated margin of error is 3%. Which of the following might lead readers of your survey report to misunderstand your findings? Explain why.

  ○ Not reporting your margin of error

  ○ Reporting your result as

    - "almost half in favor of"

    - "nearly half in favor of"

    - "over half in favor of"

    - "approximately half in favor of"

Chapter Summary

- Inferential statistics help us estimate the probability that our sample data represent the population from which the sample is drawn.

- The two main uses of inferential statistics are assessing relationships among variables and assessing differences among groups.

- *z* scores standardize scores from different measures so that they can be compared.

- The normalized distribution of *z* scores allows us to calculate the probability of a result occurring.

- The *t* test compares two groups based on each group's scores on a continuous variable.

- The chi-square test compares two or more groups based on their distribution of scores on a categorical variable.

- Correlation is a measure of the strength of association between variables.

- Regression allows calculation of the value of one variable, given the value of a second variable.

- ANOVA compares values across multiple groups to help determine the probability that they are statistically different.

- Statistical significance is used to assess the probability that a study's findings are likely to have occurred by chance.

- Quantitative studies may be evaluated not only on the statistical significance of their results but also on the extent to which replication studies confirm the results.

Key Terms

ANOVA 165
bell curve 155
central limit theorem 155
confidence interval 159
correlation 167
correlation coefficient 167
curvilinear relationship 168
F value 166
inferential statistics 155
leptokurtic 154
linear regression 168

MANOVA 167
multiple regression 168
nonparametric statistics 160
normal curve 155
normal distribution 154
one-tailed test 164
outcome/criterion variable 168
parametric statistics 160
platykurtic 154
predictor variable 168
regression 168

sampling distribution 159
significance 153
skew 154
statistical significance 162
t test 163
t test for dependent samples 165
t test for independent samples 163
two-tailed test 164
Type I error 168
Type II error 168

Application Exercises

Statistical analyses typically relate to a group of people, so the following exercises are best done with a group.

Exercise 1: Predicting Group Wealth

Wealth is normally distributed, or is it? Ask one individual in your group to disclose the amount of cash he or she is carrying, and then ask group members how confident they are that this amount represents the group average. Ask a second individual, a third, and so on, recording each dollar amount from lowest to highest. As you record each new amount, calculate and record the mean value for the group, as shown in Exhibit 8.1. At what point does your group start to become confident about predicting the group average?

No cash? Try the same exercise with routine expenditures, for example daily expenditures on coffee or lunch, monthly expenditures on entertainment or transport, or annual expenditure on clothing.

Exercise 2: Generalizing From a Sample to a Population

Assume that the group you did Exercise 1 with is randomly selected from a wider student population. Use the formula for standard deviation to calculate the probabilities that the mean value for wealth you calculated from Exercise 1 will be found in that population.

Exercise 3: Occupation and Beverage Preferences

Back to the coffee bar. What test would you use to help decide whether beverage preferences are related to occupation—more specifically, whether faculty and students differ significantly in their drink preferences?

HINT 1: You will be dealing with two categorical variables here—occupation and type of beverage.

HINT 2: Before you can develop a table that sets out your data, you will first need to make a decision about how you will categorize beverages. For example, would tea, coffee, soda, and water be an appropriate set of categories? Or would cappuccino, latte, espresso, and Americano best capture your group's preferences?

Note also that here we can make a reasonable guess about direction of causality. Coffee drinking has many documented physiological effects, but, to date, demonstrable change in occupation is not one of them. If you find a significant difference between faculty and students in beverage preferences, it would be reasonable to assume that these preferences are predicted by occupation rather than vice versa.

Of course, it may not be occupation (faculty or student) that explains any observed difference in beverage preferences. What other variables might you need to consider in order to account fully for any differences you observe?

Exercise 4: "The Internet of Things" Revisited

Revisit Exercise 3, "The Internet of Things," from Chapter 7. Here, you were capturing responses to statements about the Internet of Things using Likert-type response options. Now you are in a position to compute the standard deviation for the responses you captured to each statement. What is the 95% confidence interval for the mean value of the responses you obtained to each question?

Recommended Reading

Diaconis, P., & Skyrms, B. (2018). *Ten great ideas about chance*. Princeton, NJ: Princeton University Press.

McEwan, B., Carpenter, C. J., & Westerman, D. (Eds.). (2018) Replications [Special issue]. *Communication Studies*, 69(3). Special issue on replication research in communication.

Nelson, L. D., Simmons, J. P., & Simonsohn, U. (2012). Let's publish fewer papers. *Psychological Inquiry*, 23(3), 291–293.

Simmons, J. P., Nelson, L. D., & Simonsohn, U. (2011). False-positive psychology: Undisclosed flexibility in data collection and analysis allows presenting anything as significant. *Psychological Science*, 22(11), 1359–1366. DOI: 10.1177/0956797611417632

Recommended Web Resources

The recommended readings and web resources provided in Chapter 7 are equally relevant for inferential statistics. See also the following:

GraphPad, QuickCalcs.......https://www.graphpad.com/quickcalcs/index.cfm

Online Statistics Education: An Interactive Multimedia Course of Study.......http://onlinestatbook.com/index.html

A course developed by Rice University, University of Houston Clear Lake, and Tufts University.

Probability and Statistics Ebook.......http://
wiki.stat.ucla.edu/socr/index.php/
Probability_and_statistics_EBook
*An open-access statistics book developed by the UCLA
Statistics Online Computational Resource (SOCR).*

Note: All of the above resources are searchable or have
headings on topics covered in this chapter.

t Distibution.......www.medcalc.org/manual/t-
distribution.php
A table of t distributions (two-tailed), with examples.

z Distribution.......www.medcalc.org/manual/values_of_
the_normal_distribution.php
*Shows different ways of displaying the distribution of z
scores and the area under the normal curve.*

References

Ioannidis J. P. A. (2005). Why most published research
findings are false. *PLoS Med, 2*(8). Retrieved
from e124. https://doi.org/10.1371/journal.pmed
.0020124

Morin, R. (2014, July 2). *Facebook's experiment causes a lot
of fuss for little result.* Washington, DC: Pew Research
Center Fact Tank. Retrieved from http://www
.pewresearch.org/fact-tank/2014/07/02/facebooks-
experiment-is-just-the-latest-to-manipulate-you-in-
the-name-of-research/

$SAGE edge™

Get the tools you need to sharpen your study skills. SAGE edge offers a robust online environment
featuring an impressive array of free tools and resources.

Access quizzes, eFlashcards, video, and multimedia at **edge.sagepub.com/treadwell4e**.

9

SURVEYS

Putting Numbers on Opinions

"They're pulling down the Hunter building!"

"Good! It's ugly!

"Yeah, but it's going to be a parking lot. You want that green part of campus bulldozed into a parking lot?

"It's not ugly; it's a great piece of architecture. They should be upgrading it not bulldozing it."

"Alumni will get steamed about the demolition—all the weddings and reunions and stuff there. Can't see any alumni support for that one."

"I like that building. I think we should protest."

"And your opinion matters, why?"

"It will, if we all get together on this."

"And if we get alumni on side, but they don't care any longer."

"They do so!"

"Don't"

"How do you know?"

"Well, um . . ."

"Who cares? It's the big donors that will swing the trustees' decision."

"So one of them can get a car park named after her? Give me a break!"

"Let's get some sanity here, folks. We don't actually know what anyone thinks. Correct?"

"Correct."

"So don't you think we should find out?"

"How?"

"Easy, just set up a web survey and ask everyone one simple question—'Are you in favor of bulldozing the Hunter building to make room for a parking lot?'"

"I hate to tell you this, but that's two questions, not one—Hunter building and parking lot are two separate questions."

"OK. OK. Anything else?"

"Yep! For starters, let's not assume that everyone can access a web survey. Second, what do you mean by 'everyone'? You don't want the entire world responding to the survey, do you? Third, how will the people you actually want to take your survey find out about it?"

"You don't like anything I'm doing, do you?"

"Sure, but go take a look at all the surveys out there. . . There are surveys, and then there are well-designed surveys."

"Sort of like there are surveys, and then there are 'read this chapter' surveys?"

"Sort of."

CHAPTER OVERVIEW

Surveys are frequently used in communication research for reasons of speed, coverage, and cost-effectiveness.

A **survey** is a series of formatted questions delivered to a defined sample of people with the expectation that their responses will be returned immediately or within a few days. The survey process starts with theoretically or pragmatically driven research questions or hypotheses and continues through question wording, formatting, and ordering; identifying and sampling potential respondents; pretesting; getting questions to respondents; collecting answers; and analyzing and reporting answers. Sampling is an important component of the survey process if survey results are to be generalized to a wider population. A **questionnaire** is the specific set of questions that respondents answer.

This chapter discusses the advantages and disadvantages of surveys, different types of surveys and survey methods, the important topic of wording questions, and some issues and considerations for web-based surveys.

CHAPTER OBJECTIVES

This chapter will help you

- Explain the advantages and disadvantages of surveys as a research method.
- Explain the advantages and disadvantages of mail, phone, face-to-face, and online surveys.
- Demonstrate with examples common ways of formatting survey questions.
- Describe with examples common problems in survey wording and how to correct them.
- Identify ways to improve survey response rates.
- Discuss the advantages and disadvantages of using other people's survey data.

INTRODUCTION: ADVANTAGES AND DISADVANTAGES OF SURVEYS

One advantage of surveys is that respondents can answer large numbers of questions rapidly. Typically, this is because surveys rely on formatted requests for information, such as yes-no or multiple-choice questions and the Likert and semantic differential formats discussed in Chapter 5.

A second advantage is that large numbers of people can be surveyed rapidly. Internet-based surveys with real-time processing of data permit national or global surveys of thousands of respondents to be run, analyzed, and reported within hours of the questions being finalized.

A third advantage is that, with appropriate sampling and the assumption of normally distributed attributes in the sampled population, you can make generalizations with a known level of confidence from your survey sample to a much larger population.

A major problem with surveys stems from the question formats. Questions with limited response options, such as yes or no or selecting a point on a scale, will give you numbers but little understanding of the "why" behind those numbers. For example, you may discover from a survey that 78% of voters would vote for candidate X, but you would not necessarily learn why the voters prefer candidate X. Even if you provide a series of possible answers such as "position on the environment" or "economic policy," you will have captured responses only to concepts that you have defined as important. You cannot be sure that you have captured all the reasons that your respondents think are important, or in fact that your respondents' understanding of "environment" or "economic policy" is the same as yours.

A second problem is that most survey designs do not allow us to assess causal relationships. For example, surveys indicating that overweight individuals are more likely to stream video does not permit us to conclude either that watching video causes obesity or the reverse. Correlation is not causality, as you will hear repeatedly in communication research. To make with confidence the statement that A causes B requires the experimental designs discussed in Chapter 10.

A third problem with surveys is that consumers are often unwilling to participate in them. Because marketing communications via phone, mail, and the Internet are often disguised as consumer research, consumers have grown increasingly resistant to anything resembling a survey. They use voice mail and caller ID to filter out phone surveys, and they may trash mail and e-mail surveys, unopened, as "junk."

A fourth problem, not unique to surveys, is having to decide whether or not the responses you received are valid; that is, do respondents' answers really match their behavior? People may report eating nutritionally balanced meals but may not do so, or they may provide researchers with answers they think the researcher is looking for. Especially for questions targeting personal behaviors and beliefs, researchers may well discover a gap between what they are told and what is happening in practice.

In this chapter, we will follow another student—Caroline—who finds herself in the middle of a campus controversy. Her university's administration is proposing to demolish the historic "Hunter" building in order to expand parking space on campus. The Hunter building has no special historic-site protections. Nonetheless, generations of students have strong and sentimental attachments to its "24-7" snack bar, idiosyncratic architecture, and sweeping campus views from the bell tower, site of many a first date. Caroline is a committed member of the "Save the Hunter" movement. She recognizes that the administration will likely decide the fate of Hunter based on the opinions of both the proponents and the opponents of the proposed demolition. A logical first step for her, then, is to run some campus surveys to find out what exactly those opinions are, so she can develop arguments in favor of preserving the building and countering any opposing views. The types of surveys she might run are outlined below.

TYPES OF SURVEYS

Cross-Sectional

Cross-sectional surveys are typically "a slice of life" or cross section in that they capture what is going on at one point in time. A public opinion poll capturing attitudes to a consumer product one day may produce remarkably different results the next day if, in between, there is a product recall, the launch of a better product, or adverse publicity about the product. Of course, there are occasions when a cross-sectional survey at a specific time would be expected to produce results unique to the time—after a major disaster, for example. Often, though, in opting for a cross-sectional survey, we are assuming that the opinions captured on Tuesday will not differ greatly from the opinions captured by the same questions put to the same people using the same method on the following Thursday or Sunday. Caroline is likely to run her public opinion surveys on this basis because there is no reason to expect dramatic day-to-day fluctuations in campus opinion.

If a "snapshot" from one point in time appears to be problematic, an alternative is to use **longitudinal studies**, which track people's changes in knowledge, attitude, or behavior over time. Some types of longitudinal study are outlined below.

Trend

Trend studies measure the same items over time using the same questions but drawing different samples from the population each time. The advantages of trend studies are that a researcher can maintain sample size as people move or drop out of the study and, obviously, that this type of survey tracks shifts in public opinion, for example, toward issues such as gun control or recycling. A disadvantage is that there is no assurance that new people in the sample will not differ in some way from the people they replaced.

Panel

In **panel** studies, a group of individuals is sampled and recruited, and the same individuals are retained to answer questions over time. The advantage of a panel is that there is no variation in the composition of the sample over time. The disadvantage is that because people die, move, or decide not to participate, panels can have a high attrition rate. Predictably, the number of individuals in a panel will decline over time. For example, Caroline may have initial success surveying a panel of resident students, only to find that maintaining the panel becomes impossible as its members graduate or transfer to other institutions.

Cohort

A **cohort** is a group of people defined, most typically, by having an event in common. Thus, all female corporate executives born in 1995 would be a cohort, as would the graduating class of 2020. Researchers study cohorts to see how, for example, career paths develop, how the health status of a particular age group changes over time, or how the political views of "Gen Xers," "Millennials," or the "iGeneration" change over the decades. Generally, cohort studies are long term and aimed at assessing broad shifts in the nature of a population. Individuals in each sample of a cohort will vary because sampling of the cohort takes place each time the cohort is surveyed.

Cross-Lagged

Cross-lagged surveys measure a dependent variable and an independent variable at two points in time and thus allow us to draw conclusions about causality. It is the only survey design that permits us to assess causality. More typically, we would use the experimental designs discussed in Chapter 10 for this.

One example would be surveying a cohort of children about their video-viewing habits and then surveying them as young adults with respect to their predispositions to violence. The researcher could then make some assessment of the relationship between exposure to violent video content and violence, and of causality, knowing that the measured exposure to video preceded any measured predisposition to violence.

 # SURVEY METHODS

This section provides a brief overview of survey methods, followed by a summary of advantages and disadvantages to help you put each method in context and decide which would be most appropriate to your survey needs.

Face-to-Face

A face-to-face survey typically means an interviewer in a one-on-one relationship with a respondent, asking questions and recording answers. Because these surveys are often done door to door, a major disadvantage is the cost of training and transporting interviewers. This cost can be reduced by using video conferencing or **intercept surveys**, in which interviewers survey passersby from a base, such as a shopping mall. Sampling becomes questionable, but for some consumer research this may not be an issue.

Telephone

Because landline area codes and exchange numbers are associated with specific geographic areas, sampling landline numbers makes sampling of defined geographic areas attractive and possible. After declining for years, response rates to telephone surveys appear to have now stabilized at around 9% (Keeter, Hatley, Kennedy, & Lau, 2017).

Smartphone numbers may not be associated with the owner's place of residence, so sampling smartphone numbers may not result in a defined geographic sample of respondents. Unlike landline numbers, which are associated with a household, smartphone numbers are associated with individuals. The more such phones at one address the more likely it is that that household will be oversampled.

Pushbutton surveys of the "Push 1 for yes; 2 for no" type automate the survey process but must be limited to a small number of brief questions with simple response options. They are inexpensive to run but have low response rates.

Mail

Mail surveys are good for delivering questions on complex issues that respondents may require time to think about, but they may be discarded as junk mail unless recipients have been alerted and motivated to participate in the survey.

Literacy can be a problem, not only in the sense that respondents have to be capable of reading but also in the more specific sense that survey questions must be written and pretested in a language appropriate to every group or subgroup being surveyed.

Random sampling of a defined population of street addresses is possible, although complicated by the fact that some households may use post office boxes rather than a street address—or both.

Online

Online methods offer the advantages of speed, low cost, wide geographic coverage, and the potential to present audio, video, and graphics and to interact with respondents.

The survey process itself can be analyzed. For example, researchers can analyze response patterns such as response time per question and the order in which respondents answered questions, if given that choice.

A problematic issue is Internet sampling frames. For example, because there is no universal list of e-mail addresses to sample, not every e-mail address has an equal chance of being sampled.

Internet users still differ demographically from nonusers, so it is questionable whether results from an online sample will be generalizable to a wider population that includes non-Internet users.

Similarly, social media platforms differ in member characteristics such as age, gender, education level, or ethnicity. It is therefore unlikely that results from any one social media platform will be generalizable to the wider Internet population.

Technology itself can be problematic in that any survey should appear identically to all respondents, but the appearance of an online survey can vary according to computer platform, operating system, browser, and the type of display. Also, a targeted population may be underrepresented or misrepresented if the survey technology filters out individuals with slow speed or unreliable Internet access.

Mobile

Mobile surveys—using smartphone technology—are attractive because respondents can access surveys anytime, anywhere they have Internet access.

As long as questions are formatted for easy use on small touchscreens, mobile responses can match computer-based online responses in quality; for example, smartphone respondents are equally likely to disclose sensitive information (Antoun, Couper, & Conrad, 2017). However, online surveys take longer on smartphones and can have a "**break-off rate**" 2–3 times that of PC surveys (Cook, 2014).

Most mobile devices can handle text, e-mail, audio, video, photography, sensors, and location tracking. This means that a researcher could combine contact and survey modes on one device—for example could dial or text a potential respondent, solicit her participation, and then switch her to the informed consent items and the survey while remaining accessible to answer any questions.

Accessing smartphone owners does not equate with accessing Internet users; fewer Americans own smartphones than use the Internet. However as smartphone use grows, researchers may finally have a way to random-sample Internet users because every smart phone has its own number. Random digit dialing (RDD) may become as applicable to sampling smartphone users as it is to sampling traditional landline users (Toepoel, 2016).

Online and Mobile Survey Design

Sampling and survey content aside, response quality will be largely a function of survey design.

Survey design begins with research objectives and defining the type of data to be collected. Design then becomes a question of how best to program respondents' experiences so that their interest is maintained from the introductory content and consent materials through to successful conclusion of the survey.

Online surveys offer design advantages not available in traditional print surveys. For example, branched questions can be completely hidden from respondents who do not need to answer them. Videos can be presented for a response and controlled to prevent respondents from skipping to the next question before the video finishes. Indicator bars can show respondents their progress through the survey and motivate them to complete it. Menu items, check boxes, and "click and drag" options can eliminate the need to type answers.

Specific response items include **radio buttons**; these permit one response only from a list of options. **Check boxes** allow respondents to select as many answers as they wish from a list. **Text boxes** allow respondents to type an answer in their own words, limited only by the size of the text box. Scales allow respondents to select their position on a semantic differential or Likert scale or, using a **slider**, to select a precise point on a scale.

The format and the content of response options influence response quality because they control how respondents express themselves. A topical example based on Facebook gender categories appears as an exercise at the end of this chapter.

Mobile surveys must be specifically designed to be legible on a small screen and to maximize the ease of entering responses. The two primary guidelines for mobile survey design are, first, prefer simple response options such as multiple-choice questions and, second, fit the content within the width of the device screen so that respondents do not have to scroll horizontally off their screens.

As with web surveys, mobile surveys should appear the same across all devices and platforms and operating systems.

Relative to traditional surveys, online surveys require many more decisions about sampling, design, and presentation. More detailed reporting of research methods is therefore required so that readers know exactly how the results were obtained and can distinguish between good and flawed research.

Ultimately, regardless of survey method, there is no substitute for pretesting to ensure that the survey does not present a problem for respondents.

EXHIBIT 9.1 ■ Advantages and Disadvantages of Specific Survey Methods		
Method	**Advantages**	**Disadvantages**
Face to Face	• Respondents may be less likely to refuse a face-to-face request. • Control over timing, pacing, and sequencing of questions. • Potential for longer interviews on complex topics. • Allows interaction with respondents. • Can assess respondents' non-verbal responses. • Can present content for interviewees to respond to. • Can administer via video link or be completely free of technology.	• Respondents may not feel that interviews are confidential. • Time consuming. • Expensive. • Time and money to train interviewers in interpersonal skills and/or cross-cultural communication. • Need for repeat visits if respondents not at home. • Interviewer resistance if interviewers are required to survey in locations they see as hazardous.
Phone	• Most U.S. households have phones and can be sampled. • Random sampling from a defined population. • Wide geographic coverage. • Survey large samples in a short time. • Lower cost than face-to-face survey. • Interviewer can control timing and sequencing of questions and clarify questions. • Push-button surveys can automate the survey process.	• Unwillingness of people to respond to unknown caller. • Call blocking. • Limited to a few short questions. • May compete with respondents' domestic activities and distractions. • No assurance that respondent is the member of the household targeted to answer questions. • "Cell only" households differ demographically from traditional landline users.
Mail	• Respondents have time to consider questions and can answer questions in any order. • Good for delivering questions on complex issues that require thought. • Suited to personal lifestyle questions, especially if respondents are guaranteed confidentiality and questions are seen to come from a reputable source. • May remain in front of respondents as a reminder. • May be seen as more legitimate than phone or e-mail surveys. • Lower cost than interviewer surveys. • Can random sample a defined population of street addresses.	• Low response rate. • Longer response times relative to telephone surveys. • May be trashed as "junk mail." • No way of knowing who completed the survey or if more than one person answered the questions. • Requires literate respondents. • Repeated contacts and incentives may be needed to increase rate and speed of returns.
Web, e-mail, and Social Media	• Can administer surveys quickly, flexibly, and inexpensively. • Wide geographic and demographic coverage. • Potential to access specific occupational or interest groups.	• Problem of Internet sampling frames; not every e-mail address has an equal chance of being sampled. • Results may not represent the opinions of Internet users in general or of the public as a whole.

• Can use snowball sampling to maximize respondent numbers. • Survey software facilitates design, pretesting, and experimenting with survey designs. • Can e-mail surveys or post to a website. • Can be asynchronous (completed in respondents' own time) or synchronous (respondents engaged in real-time chat or videoconferencing) or both. • Can present audio, video, and graphics. • May elicit sensitive information respondents would not provide face to face. • Results can be analyzed in real time as data come in. • Can analyze patterns in respondent answers (e.g., response time per question and question order). • Can analyze the survey process itself.	• Results from any one social media platform may not be generalizable because social media differ in membership characteristics. • Different browsers and computer platforms may display a survey differently. • May need mail, e-mail, or phone to drive respondents to survey website. • E-mail invitations can be overlooked or deleted as spam. • Requires more respondent effort than responding to a phone call. • Respondents may be involved in competing activities or multitasking when completing survey. • Low response rates. • Difficult for a survey to stand out from others. • Problem knowing or verifying who answered online questions. • Technology may filter out individuals with slow or unreliable Internet access.
Mobile (smartphone and tablet) • Smartphone users respond similarly to computer users. • Respondents can access survey anytime, anywhere they have Internet access. • Respondent privacy. • Respondents may feel less pressure to provide socially desirable answers. • Can present audio, video, and graphics. • Ability to combine contact and survey modes on one device—e.g., phone request, survey, and e-mail follow-up.	• Surveys must be (re)designed specifically for mobile device screens. • Users may not have the dexterity to complete mobile device surveys. • Sampling smartphone owners does not equal sampling Internet users. • Respondents taking survey in public areas may not disclose personal or sensitive information. • Respondents may take longer than with computer-based online surveys. • Survey may compete with distractions on the device itself.

WRITING, INTRODUCING, AND FORMATTING QUESTIONS

A survey is reciprocal communication between a researcher and respondents, but respondents first have to decide to become respondents. Think of a survey you might wish to run, identify potential respondents, and ask yourself what they would want to know about it. Why should they participate in it—or want to? Getting respondents to the first question requires that you first introduce and explain the survey in a way that will result in their informed participation.

Your introductory materials should flow logically into the first survey questions. If respondents have to make a confusing mental jump between the explanatory material and the survey itself, they may become unmotivated to continue with it.

Developing a successful survey—by which we mean one that captures the information you want to capture from the highest possible percentage of respondents—requires consideration of question formats, question wording, and question order. Any of these can influence respondents' answers and survey results, so time developing and pretesting questions is time well spent.

Most surveys seek to find out four things about respondents: demographic data such as age, gender, religion, income, and marital status; knowledge of an issue; attitudes toward the issue; and behaviors, if any, related to the issue.

The function of question formats is to clarify both the question and the response options as far as possible for respondents while giving researchers relevant categories of answers that will help them analyze results.

At one extreme, questions can be completely open ended so that respondents can reply as they see fit. At the other extreme, a question can be written to restrict respondents to one of only two available answers—for example, yes or no. The following section discusses some typical question formats and the advantages and disadvantages of each. Some of these formats will be familiar from Chapter 5, "Measurement."

Open-Ended Questions

Open-ended research questions allow respondents to answer in their own words but, in practice, may limit the number of words in the case of online surveys or printed survey forms.

Examples:

- In what building do you attend most of your classes?

- How do you feel about the proposed demolition of the Hunter building?

The advantage of this format is that you may get insights that you could not get with the highly structured questions shown below. Open-ended questions are generally avoided in survey research because they are time-consuming to code and analyze relative to multiple-choice and scaled questions. Answers in digital format can be analyzed to find the most frequent word occurrences or searched for specific words or word combinations the researcher is interested in. For survey research, the "In what building do you attend most of your classes?" question may be appropriate because it will generate relatively simple, brief responses. The second question—feelings about the proposed demolition—however, may elicit responses ranging from "OK" to a fulsome five-page essay and would be more appropriately used as a focus group or interview question rather than a survey question.

Dichotomous Questions

Dichotomous questions force respondents to select one of two possible answers.

Examples:

- What is your residence status?
  _____ Commuter
  _____ Resident

- Have you read the statistics chapters in this text?

  _____ Yes

  _____ No

This format has the advantage of simplifying data coding and analysis. The problem with such questions is that life is rarely yes-no simple. For example, when it comes to assessing the need for parking, the above residence status question could be problematic for a graduate student who rents a room on campus because she drives in from a distance once or twice a week. For a student who has read only part of the statistics chapters, neither "yes" nor "no" is an accurate answer.

Dichotomous response options are appropriate only when they provide a clear choice between two options and respondents will not be left wanting to respond with options that the researcher did not think to provide.

If there will be more than two possible responses to a question, other formats such as the multiple-choice questions and scaled questions discussed below become appropriate.

Multiple-Choice Questions

Multiple-choice questions provide respondents with several possible answers and ask them to select one or more answers or to rank order them.

Example:

If you are willing to help the "Save the Hunter" campaign, which of the following would you be most willing to do?

_____ Picket the building

_____ Contribute money

_____ Work on a publicity campaign

_____ Phone graduates

_____ Other (please identify)

This basic format may be used with different instructions, such as "Please check one option," "Please check as many answers as apply," or "Please rank order your choices by writing '1' after your first choice, '2' after your second choice, and so on."

The difference between "Select one" and "Select as many as apply" is the level of information the researcher needs. "Select one" questions force respondents to a single choice. This question format may be appropriate for political polling if a voter can vote for only one candidate and that one candidate is all the researcher is interested in knowing about: "Will you vote for candidate X, yes or no?" On the other hand, the researcher may be interested in looking for patterns of responses. Allowing multiple responses to the above "help save the building" question, for example, may tell the researcher whether or not the students who are willing to donate money are also willing to be campus activists and join a picket line.

Note that the above question begins with an "*If* you are willing." If you word it simply as "Which of the following are you willing to do?" you create a problem for respondents who are not willing to help the campaign. They would be unable to answer the question or might feel forced into checking an answer that does not reflect their true feelings. One way around this problem is to use branching and filter questions, as discussed below.

Rank order questions get around the problem of respondents checking every possible answer, in which case the researcher would have no understanding of which items are most important to respondents. With a rank order format, respondents are asked to assign each answer a score. The researcher adds the scores respondents assign to each answer to get the overall ranking of each answer.

Scale Questions

Revisit Chapter 5 for an overview of the Likert and semantic differential scales. Likert-scale questions are anchored at each end by "strongly agree" and "strongly disagree." Semantic differential scales are anchored at each end by words or phrases with opposite meanings. Caroline might use a Likert scale to capture responses to a statement such as "The Hunter building should be preserved at all cost." She might use a semantic differential scale anchored by "friendly" and "unfriendly" to capture respondents' feelings about the building.

While such scales appear superficially easy to construct, considerable work can be involved in ensuring that the words do capture the concepts that you want to capture (i.e., that the scales have high validity). A related point is that researchers should ensure that the word pairs chosen do represent true opposites. For example, which best captures the opposite of "works hard": "plays hard" or "lazy"?

SURVEY WORDING: "IF IT CAN BE MISINTERPRETED, IT WILL BE"

Misinterpretation occurs primarily because a question has been poorly worded and/or has not been pretested to see what misinterpretations are possible. Consider how even a simple question such as the following could be misinterpreted.

"What is your age?" _____

A respondent counting down the days to his 21st birthday could write in "as of today I am 20 years, 11 months, and 18 days old." Another respondent one day short of her 23rd birthday might conscientiously reply "22" when "23" would be more accurate. And because there's always someone out there with a sense of humor, you might get "Three—in dog years."

We can clarify the age question by rewording it to "What is your age as of your last birthday?" We could also reformat the question. Generally, we don't need to know people's ages to the nearest year (although specific age as it relates to driving, drinking, smoking, or voting might be exceptions). In most cases, categories of age will suffice, so we can ask respondents to check the age group within which they fall, as follows:

_____ 15–19

_____ 20–24

_____ 25–29

In this option, respondents don't have to think about how exactly to define their age, and for those who are reluctant to give a specific age, providing an age range may help them feel more comfortable answering the question.

Common Problems With Wording

Leading Questions

Leading questions lead respondents to a particular answer rather than letting them respond in their own terms.

Examples

- Why do you think the campus administration is unethical?

- When did you first start plagiarizing your research papers?

- When should the Hunter building be demolished?

These examples force respondents to agree that the campus administration is unethical, that the respondent is plagiarizing, and that the Hunter building will be demolished. None of these statements is necessarily true, but by answering the questions, regardless of their answers, respondents acknowledge that they are.

Check for leading questions and avoid them. For example, the first question above can be reworded so it is no longer a leading question—"Describe the ethical standards of the campus administration."

Double-Barreled Questions

Double-barreled questions ask two questions simultaneously but allow for only one answer.

Examples:

- Do you think the Hunter building is an asset to the campus, or should it be demolished?

There is no way anyone can answer this sample double-barreled question logically because it does not present an either-or choice. "Yes and no" might be my answer: yes (I think the building an asset) and no (I don't think it should be torn down). Deal with a double-barreled question by splitting it into two. In the case of the sample question, make two questions:

- Do you think the Hunter Building is an asset to the campus?

- Do you think the Hunter Building should be demolished?

Each of the above questions can be formatted as either a "yes-no" question or a Likert statement.

Framing Questions

Wittingly or unwittingly, researchers can influence respondents' answers to questions by framing or arranging questions in a particular way, in other words, by question content or question order.

For example, polls taken after the release of a Senate Intelligence Committee report on CIA interrogation practices indicated that a majority of Americans support torture. Blauwkamp, Rowling, and Pettit (2018) ran a study in which a torture question was asked with the question framed differently for different groups. They found that a small majority (51%) favored torture when the question was framed in the context of responding to the 9/11 terrorist attacks. However, support for torture dropped to 35% when the methods used on detainees were used to frame the question.

Whenever possible, avoid phrasing survey questions or statements as negatives. **Negative wording** may be simple and clear but still misunderstood by people reading in a hurry or misheard over the phone. For example, a simple question or statement such as "A course in statistics should not be required as part of the communication major" may be misread or misheard as "should be required." The solution is to phrase the question in the positive "should be required."

The Double Negative

A combination of negative wording and a double-barreled question results in the **double negative**. A classic "double negative" question in a 1992 Roper poll asked "Does it seem possible or does it seem impossible to you that the Nazi extermination of the Jews never happened?" What does this mean? What would you answer?

In a follow-up survey, Roper asked a clearer question, and the percentage of respondents expressing doubt that the Holocaust happened (which was the crux of the question) dropped from the original 22% to 1% (Rosenthal, 2006).

Language

In a global world, languages and dialects are inevitably a consideration in question design. Whether it is a local social services agency researching the health care status of immigrant communities or a multinational company researching consumer opinion in Lithuania, language use can make the difference between a successful survey and an unsuccessful one. For example, a question about a "program" will be met with puzzlement in countries that have "programmes." You would be well advised to seek a local consultant to ensure that subtle shades of meaning are translated successfully—for example, that the word *family* means the nuclear family living under one roof and not the extended family.

To minimize the possibilities for misinterpretation, check your questions at draft stage and then pretest them with a sample of the people you will be surveying.

Guiding Respondents Through Surveys

Generally, you have a choice of either a "**funnel**" or an "**inverted funnel**" format for overall questionnaire design. The funnel design starts with broad questions and progresses to specific questions. The inverted funnel does the reverse. For example, a funnel format may be used to first establish where respondents are on a broad liberal-conservative scale before moving to specific questions about broadcast regulation, abortion, or gun control. An inverted funnel format might start by asking respondents very specifically how many times a week they dine out; this would then be followed by broader questions focusing on why respondents dine out and their attitudes to online coupons and advertising for restaurants.

With mail surveys, respondents can answer questions in any order. This suggests that mail surveys need to begin with relevant questions that will hold the reader's attention. With phone and face-to-face surveys, the question order is determined by the interviewer, who might best begin with relatively easy questions, such as "How many tablet computers are in your household?" This gives respondents a comfort level that may predispose them to answer more difficult questions.

Generally, questions should move from general to specific, relevant to less relevant, and comfortable to less comfortable. Questions with the same format should be clustered together so that respondents do not bounce from format to format.

Questions related to the same theme should be grouped together, but sometimes sensitive questions related to drug use, sexual activity, or criminal background, for example, may be placed among questions with which respondents have a comfort level so that they feel more comfortable answering them. Generally, placing such questions toward the end of the survey increases the probability that respondents will answer them because at that point they have likely already answered difficult or sensitive questions. Meeting each of these requirements simultaneously can be difficult, which is why pretesting is so important.

A citizenship question proposed for the 2020 U.S. Census became contentious in light of claims that it would undermine the accuracy of the Census because immigrants would refuse to complete the form. The issue reinforces the need to be alert to the wording of any one question that may predispose respondents not to respond to a survey at all. See Cohn (2018) for the background of this issue.

Branching and Filter Questions

You may have questions that some respondents cannot or should not answer because they are irrelevant to those respondents.

For example, you may be studying the dynamics of family video viewing with a specific interest in how family characteristics influence viewing habits. For households with children, you would likely develop questions specifically related to the children and their viewing habits. Such questions will be irrelevant to households without children, so you need a way for these households to bypass the questions about children.

This can be done with a simple instruction, such as

- If one or more children under the age of 18 live in this household, please continue with Question 6. If no children under the age of 18 live in this household, please skip to Question 18.

Such questions are known as **branching** or **routing questions** because they route respondents around questions they do not need to answer.

Alternatively, you might use a **filter question** followed by an instruction, as in

- Do one or more children under the age of 18 live at this address?

    _____ Yes

    _____ No

    If you answered "yes," please continue with Question 6. If you answered "no," please go to Question 18.

Such questions filter out respondents who do not need to answer specific questions.

Branching questions can be made more conditional and more complex, but at the increased risk of respondents misunderstanding the question or dropping out.

In addition to the survey questions, there are four sets of messages you will need to plan: the introduction and explanation of the survey plus the incentives to complete the survey at a level appropriate to the respondents, the prompts and reminders that may be needed to ensure completion of the survey, instructions on how to complete each question, and the messages and any debriefings respondents will receive on completing the survey.

IMPROVING SURVEY RESPONSE RATES

All survey methods share the problem of an ever-increasing number of surveys targeting an ever-decreasing number of individuals willing to participate in them.

The willingness of respondents to participate in any survey is a function of the topic and its relevance; their interest in the topic; the perceived cost or benefit of doing the survey; the survey sponsor; interviewer characteristics, such as appearance, voice, and language if the interviewer and the potential respondent have direct contact; and incentives for doing the survey. Respondents' ability to complete a survey is affected by lifestyle issues that permit the time to participate; educational and cultural characteristics that may help or hinder comprehension of questions and instructions; and, for technology-based surveys, web literacy and the ability to access and use the relevant technology.

Intuitively, we can identify some of the tactics that might increase our willingness to participate in surveys. For any type of survey, we probably need to be reminded more than once, but not to the point of annoyance, to do the survey. We are also more likely to respond to a request from a credible source made in advance of the survey (see for example Groves, 2006).

We will likely prefer to complete a survey in our own time and at our convenience. We will also want some assurance that any sensitive information we provide will be kept confidential and that dropping out of a survey or refusing to do one will not penalize us in some way. We might also be interested in seeing the results of the research when the survey is completed. A small "thank you" would probably make us feel better about the time we contributed when we could have been doing something else. Perhaps a small reward offered in advance would make the difference between electing to do the survey or not.

Generally, response rates can be improved with a preliminary mailing or phone call to inform respondents about the survey and ask for their participation. Provide a phone number that respondents can call to verify the legitimacy of the survey and to ask questions about it. Follow-up reminder mailings and phone calls can also increase the response rate. Reply-paid envelopes are a must if you want mail questionnaires returned.

Traditional methods of response optimization apply for online surveys as well. People cannot go to a website they do not know about, so phone calls, postal solicitations, and e-mail may all be needed to drive individuals to the website hosting your survey.

Retail outlets that use phone surveys to assess consumer satisfaction may provide customers with a receipt that includes the number to dial and a code number good for a discount on a subsequent purchase. Such surveys are typically short, "push-button" surveys and will be described to customers as "brief" or "easy."

Generally, research finds that a combination of contact and follow-up methods coupled with incentives improves response rates.

The simplest way to calculate your survey's response rate is the percentage of completed returns. Thus, 900 completed returns from 1,200 participants is a 75% return rate.

USING OTHER PEOPLE'S SURVEYS

Before launching your own research, it is wise to check whether or not the answer to your question already exists. For scholarly research, this is, of course, one of the functions of a literature review. If you are seeking public opinion data, for example, a simple web search may reveal that the information you need is publicly available and reported by national media or available from any number of public opinion pollsters.

There are three potential problems with such data. First, they may be proprietary; this means you may not be able to access or use them without permission. Second, they may be from a source that has an agenda in conducting the research. This means that you will need to evaluate carefully the questions and how they were worded, together with the sample and how it was obtained. Third, you may not be able to process the data to meet your own needs. For example, you may find data categorized by gender but not by ethnicity.

One classic source of social research data is the General Social Survey (GSS); these data are available from the National Opinion Research Center (NORC) at the University of Chicago. The GSS includes demographic and attitudinal data on topical issues dating back to 1972. For more information, see the GSS website listed at the end of this chapter.

The Pew Research Center, whose Internet & Technology division has conducted surveys that inform several questions and exercises in this book, makes its raw survey data available so that you can do your own analysis of the data. To protect the privacy of respondents, telephone numbers, counties of residence, and zip codes are removed from all public data files.

An intermediate step between using such publicly available information and designing and running your own surveys is to hire a professional survey firm. Such firms will work with you to develop and test the questions and will analyze the results for you and help you interpret them. The cost may be less than that of doing the entire project on your own, especially if your questions can be "piggybacked" onto other surveys targeted at the sample that interests you.

BIG DATA AND THE END OF SURVEYS?

The slightly ominous term **big data** refers to data sets that are so huge, complex, or rapidly changing that traditional software or databases cannot process or manage the data. Big data can include personal data such as your Internet search histories and financial transactions, as well as device-generated data, such as the metadata and location tracking associated with your smartphone usage. It also includes nontext formats such audio, video, photographs, and sensor data. Because it cannot readily be put into traditional databases, new analytic techniques are necessary.

Big data offers researchers opportunities not otherwise available, such as exploring and visualizing social media networks or analyzing vast amounts of social media content. For example, Park, Baek, and Cha (2014) studied nonverbal cues in emoticons on Twitter using a data set of 1.7 billion tweets from 55 million users in 78 countries.

In communication research, major interest areas include Twitter, Facebook, *Wikipedia*, and search engines—how they are used and who uses them. Schroeder (2016) identifies practical and conceptual problems to be addressed with big data analysis of such sites. Practical problems include the fact that social media data sets are often proprietary. Access to these data is at the discretion of the social media company and may be granted only to researchers whose research interests align with those of the company. Researchers may not have access to all available data or know exactly how these data were generated. One exception to this is *Wikipedia*, a noncommercial site.

Conceptual problems include the fact that findings from proprietary social media platforms cannot be generalized to other social media or to Internet users more generally. A theoretical problem is how to integrate findings from big data with existing communication theories. For example, social media reach billions of people globally but are not mass media in the traditional sense; nor are they interpersonal media. Social media users communicate in something like a group setting, but not in groups as we have traditionally thought of them. A further concern is the potential for big data to be used for surveillance and, possibly, the manipulation of social media users.

Miller (2017) suggests that a survey might not be a first choice if the needed data are already available. If the most basic requirement of a survey—the ability to obtain a representative sample of respondents—is problematic due to declining response rates, then two alternatives can be considered. The first is using data from other sources such as government records. Big data and traditional surveys may be merged together to form data sets. The second alternative to a traditional probability survey is a nonprobability volunteer panel. Both sides of the debate have advocates over the extent to which volunteer panels might replace probability samples.

ETHICS PANEL
CLIENTS AND METHODS AS ETHICAL DECISIONS

Part I. Crespi (1998) distinguishes between professional standards and ethical standards in survey research. Professional standards are the standards of competence that govern sampling, survey design, and implementation. Ethical standards are the standards of responsibility to all parties affected by your research—clients, participants, those who will read your research reports, and society more generally. The two sets of standards are not necessarily related. For example, a professionally perfect survey may be ethically suspect. Or an ethically defensible survey may be professionally unsound, as when a judgment is made to conduct a needed low-budget survey rather than no survey at all.

Professional researchers have ethical and professional responsibilities to their clients and ethical obligations to respondents, their profession, and society.

Questions

Think of a survey you might design for a commercial client such as a software company or a restaurant:

- What are the ethical implications of using the survey results to publicize your own research firm?

- Why might you want to control how your clients publicize the survey results you obtained for them?

- Your client cannot afford a professionally designed and administered survey but can afford a less expensive survey based on convenience sampling. What is your advice to your client?

Part II. Surveys must not be morally objectionable, says Crespi. He finds it morally unacceptable to do surveys for a tobacco company, a right-wing and racist political party, or a military dictatorship.

- Is Crespi's position defensible? Why or why not? Or are researchers, be they academic or commercial, obligated to the highest standards of professionalism, regardless of client or topic? Why or why not?

- Why might you personally decline a potential client or research topic?

Refresh your thinking about ethics with a visit to Chapter 3. See also the American Association for Public Opinion Research Code of Professional Ethics and Practices (https://www.aapor.org/Standards-Ethics/AAPOR-Code-of-Ethics.aspx).

Chapter Summary

- Surveys are a "mainstream" method for capturing public opinion at a point in time.

- Surveys commonly use formatted questions such as multiple-choice checklists and scaled questions.

- Survey questions may be delivered to respondents by phone, mail, e-mail, websites, mobile technologies, or personal interview.

- Survey questions must be carefully written and pretested to ensure that they are not misunderstood.

- With proper sampling procedures, survey results can be generalized to a wider population with a known level of statistical confidence.

- Surveys can be fast and cost-effective.

- Most survey designs cannot assess causal relationships between variables.

- Online surveys can be fast and inexpensive but may misrepresent the population being sampled by excluding respondents who cannot or will not access online technologies.

- Survey interfaces must be adapted to mobile devices if these are to be used successfully for surveys.

Key Terms

big data 191
branching questions 189
break-off rate 181
check boxes 181
cohort 179
cross-lagged surveys 179
cross-sectional surveys 178
dichotomous questions 184
double negative 188

double-barreled questions 187
filter question 189
funnel 188
intercept surveys 179
inverted funnel 188
leading questions 187
longitudinal studies 178
multiple-choice questions 185
negative wording 188

panel 178
questionnaire 176
radio buttons 181
routing questions 189
slider 181
survey 176
text boxes 181
trend studies 178

Application Exercises

Exercise 1. Comparing Survey Methods

Many survey methods have advantages and disadvantages in common. To help you think about survey methods more critically, identify a *unique* advantage and disadvantage, not shared with any other methods, for each of the following survey methods: mail, face-to-face interview, e-mail, web interface, landline phone, smartphone.

Exercise 2. Survey Wording and Formatting

Are you in favor of _____? Yes / No

Fill in the blank in the above question with a topical or campus issue. Now take this basic question and rewrite it in open-ended, multiple-choice, semantic differential, and Likert-type formats so that you are capturing more subtle responses to the question. You may need several questions in each format. Check your wording carefully for any leading or double-barreled questions. Having written the questions, which, if any, would you now eliminate, and why? Remember that there may be good reasons for keeping questions that appear to duplicate each other. What additional questions will you need to capture information about your respondents as well as their knowledge of the issue and their possible actions toward it?

Exercise 3. Mobile Technologies

To use mobile technologies effectively for surveys, you must first successfully contact respondents and then present survey questions that will motivate respondents to begin the survey and continue with it until all questions have been answered honestly. Assume that you need to survey your campus community on a contentious issue. How would you initially contact respondents in the mobile community? What incentives, if any, might entice them to begin—and complete—your survey? To minimize the break-off rate for smartphone and tablet users, you will want to limit the number of questions and design all questions with those devices in mind. So how many questions do you think could be asked? What format(s) should they have?

Exercise 4. Balancing Respondent and Researcher Interests in an Age of Gender Fluidity

Traditionally, survey researchers provided two response options with respect to gender—male or female. Facebook now recognizes over 50 options. Suppose you are designing a survey and decide to collect information on respondents' gender identity. You have several options, in addition to the traditional male or female option:

- A list of each option along with a "check one" instruction.

- A list of each option along with a "check as many as apply" instruction.

- A text box with a "please enter your gender identity" instruction.

- A reduced number of options designed to meet your research interests.

- Not asking the question at all if gender is theoretically unimportant to your research.

Consider that you need to make the user experience relevant and comfortable for respondents, especially perhaps with how they would want to describe themselves. Consider also that you need to be able to record, store, and analyze all your survey data. If you do not intend to analyze 50 different response options why provide them? Consider also sample size. If a survey sample of 100 people had 50 gender categories equally represented, you would have only two people in each category.

How does your thinking about this issue change if you are designing your survey specifically for (a) the web or (b) smartphones?

For further explanation of the Facebook categories see, for example, Oremus (2014).

Recommended Reading

Antoun, C., Katz, J., Argueta, J., & Wang, L. (2017). Design heuristics for effective smartphone questionnaires. *Social Science Computer Review*, 36(%), 557–574. https://doi.org/10.1177/0894439317727072

See this article for design principles for mobile surveys and an example of a survey interface optimized for smartphones.

Kennedy, C. (May 14, 2018) Can we still trust polls? *Fact Tank: News in the Numbers*. Retrieved from http://www.pewresearch.org/fact-tank/2018/05/14/can-we-still-trust-polls/.

Explains why well-designed polls can be trusted.

Miller, P. V. (Ed.). (2017). Survey research, today and tomorrow [Special issue]. *Public Opinion Quarterly*, 81(S1), 205–404.

A special issue on the future of surveys.

Recommended Web Resources

American Association for Public Opinion Research, Education and Resources for Researchers . . . . www.aapor.org/Education-Resources/For-Researchers.aspx
See the material on survey research, which includes a discussion of response rates and response rate calculators. See also the AAPOR Code of Ethics.

Gallup . . . . www.gallup.com
A research company known for studies of the attitudes and behaviors of employees, customers, students, and the public.

General Social Survey, NORC at the University of Chicago . . . . gss.norc.org
The GSS contains demographic, behavioral, and attitudinal questions, plus questions about special interest topics such as civil liberties, crime, violence, morality, and national spending priorities.

The Harris Poll . . . . theharrispoll.com
Results of current surveys plus archived polling data from decades past.

National Centre for Research Methods, University of Southampton . . . . www.restore.ac.uk
An online research resource for the social sciences.

National Opinion Research Center at the University of Chicago . . . . www.norc.org
Known for its national public opinion surveys. See also the online booklet explaining surveys produced by the National Opinion Research Center at www.whatisasurvey.info.

Pew Research Center, Internet & Technology . . . . www.pewinternet.org/datasets
Visit this web address for information on downloading Pew raw survey data for your own analysis. Also view the methodology section of any of the survey reports for details on sampling, survey methods, and weighting of samples. Also useful is the "Datasets" page of the Pew Research Center, Media & News division (www.journalism.org).

Roper Center for Public Opinion Research . . . . www.ropercenter.uconn.edu
The Roper Center for Public Opinion Research is a leading archive of social science and public opinion data. The data range from the 1930s to the present. Most of the data are from the United States, but over 50 nations are represented.

Survey Research Laboratory (SRL) of the University of Illinois at Chicago . . . . www.srl.uic.edu
SRL links . . . . www.srl.uic.edu/Srllink/srllink.htm
The SRL links page provides links to research organizations, research ethics codes, and resources related to surveys, sampling, and data analysis.

Web Survey Methodology . . . . www.websm.org
A European university resource on web survey methodology.

World Association for Public Opinion Research . . . . http://wapor.org
See especially the WAPOR code of ethics at https://wapor.org/about-wapor/code-of-ethics/.

Survey Software Sites

Qualtrics . . . . www.qualtrics.com
QuestionPro . . . . www.questionpro.com
Snap Survey . . . . www.snapsurveys.com
SurveyMonkey . . . . www.surveymonkey.com
Zoomerang . . . . www.zoomerang.com

The above five sites provide the ability to create and host surveys and to collect and analyze data.

References

Antoun, C., Couper, M. P., & Conrad, F. G. (2017). Effects of mobile versus PC web on survey response quality: A crossover experiment in a probability web panel. *Public Opinion Quarterly, 81*(S1), 280–306. DOI: 10.1093/poq/nfw088

Blauwkamp, J. M., Rowling, C. M., & Pettit, W. (2018). Are Americans really okay with torture? The effects of message framing on public opinion. *Media, War & Conflict, 11*(4), 446–475. DOI: 10.1177/1750635217753655

Cook, W. A. (2014, June). Is mobile a reliable platform for survey taking? Defining quality in online surveys from mobile respondents. *Journal of Advertising Research, 54*(2), 141–148. DOI: 10.2501/JAR-54-2-141-148

Cohn, D. (2018, March 30). What to know about the citizenship question the Census Bureau is planning to ask in 2020. *Fact Tank*. Retrieved from http://www.pewresearch.org/fact-tank/2018/03/30/what-to-know-about-the-citizenship-question-the-census-bureau-is-planning-to-ask-in-2020/

Crespi, I. (1998). Ethical considerations when establishing survey standards. *International Journal of Public Opinion Research, 10*(1), 75–82. DOI: 10.1093/ijpor/10.1.75

Groves, R. M. (2006). Nonresponse rates and nonresponse bias in household surveys. *Public Opinion Quarterly, 70*(5), 646–675. https://doi.org/10.1093/poq/nfl033

Keeter, S., Hatley, N., Kennedy, C., & Lau, A. (2017, May 15). *What low response rates mean for telephone surveys* [Report]. Washington, DC: Pew Research Center. Retrieved from http://www.pewresearch.org/2017/05/15/what-low-response-rates-mean-for-telephone-surveys/

Miller, P. V. (2017). Is there a future for surveys? *Public Opinion Quarterly, 81,* 205–212. DOI: 10.1093/poq/nfx008

Oremus, W. (2014, February 13). Here are all the different genders you can be on Facebook. *Slate*. Retrieved from https://slate.com/technology/2014/02/facebook-custom-gender-options-here-are-all-56-custom-options.html

Park, J., Baek, Y. M., & Cha, M. (2014). Cross-cultural comparison of nonverbal cues in emoticons on Twitter: Evidence from big data analysis. *Journal of Communication, 64*(2), 333–354. DOI: 10.1111/jcom.12086

Rosenthal, J. (2006, August 27). Precisely false vs. approximately right: A reader's guide to polls. *New York Times,* The Public Editor. Retrieved from https://www.nytimes.com/2006/08/27/opinion/27pubed.html

Schroeder, R. (2016) Big data and communication research. *Oxford Research Encyclopedia of Communication*. DOI: 10.1093/acrefore/9780190228613.013.276

Toepoel, V. (2016). *Doing surveys online.* Los Angeles: Sage.

10

EXPERIMENTS

Researching Cause and Effect

"Heavy duty exams coming up folks. This weekend's big-time reading for me."

"That's how you study, Joe? I can't handle all that reading at the last moment. I do readings as they're assigned and get them all tucked into memory as I go."

"Doesn't work for me, Sofia. I read and then forget half the stuff by test time. Better to pull a couple of all-nighters just before the test and go in with it all fresh in your mind."

"Joe—read it all early and let it settle in, I say. Go in relaxed and not panicked about remembering everything."

"No way Sofia! Cram it all in a couple of nights before and then you've got your brain all topped up and ready to go."

"Which would get me a big fat F!"

"Help us out here, Luke. Who's right?"

"Don't know, but it's easy to find out. Sofia studies early. Joe does a last-minute all-nighter. Just compare their grades on the next exam."

"Except maybe the difference isn't study habits but something else altogether . . . like coffee. Joe drinks gallons of coffee, which does things to the brain. Sofia doesn't."

"So Joe would have to pull his all-night readathons without coffee?"

"Or Sofia would have to chug coffee all the time she's reading."

"So to see if coffee makes a difference, we'd need them studying like they both do now for one exam, then another exam where they're both drinking coffee, then another where neither of them is drinking coffee?"

"But then there's all the other stuff that might explains grades—like some people do better on written tests or have better recall or more test anxiety or get tutoring or whatever."

"So we need two groups—study-early and study-late—not just two people? Then we'll need to hope that the groups sort of balance each other out on coffee drinking, test anxiety, tutoring, and everything else."

"You've been reading the chapter."

"No. But I will!"

"Now, or the night before the exam?"

CHAPTER OVERVIEW

If the guiding thought for surveys is "let's ask people and see what they think," the guiding thought for experimental methods is "let's do something and see what happens."

This chapter introduces the principles of experimental method. All experimental designs have one thing in common: they focus on manipulating one variable to see what will happen to another variable as a result. In practice, **experiments** range from simple field observations that lack rigor to sophisticated designs in which all variables are rigorously controlled and measurable.

The major contribution of experimental method to communication research is its potential to identify variables that have a significant effect on other variables and to determine whether variables have causal relationships.

CHAPTER OBJECTIVES

This chapter will help you

- Identify the advantages and disadvantages of experiments as research methods.

- Describe the basic experimental design.

- Explain the concept of control in experimental design.

- Discuss the concept of random assignment in experimental design and why it is important.

- Explain the concept of factorial design in experiments.

- Compare and contrast between-subjects and within-subjects experimental design.

- Explain the concept of validity in experimental design and identify the threats to validity.

- Explain the advantages and disadvantages of online experiments.

INTRODUCTION: ADVANTAGES AND DISADVANTAGES OF EXPERIMENTS

Experimentation means manipulating one variable to see if another variable thought to be related to it changes as a result. In the context of communication research, this might mean exposing consumers to different versions of an advertisement to see which version is the most persuasive, asking web users to use different websites to determine which site is the most navigable, or asking groups to solve problems under different conditions of group size or leadership style to see which type of group performs most effectively.

In all such cases, the experimenters are doing something to see what happens rather than just asking people questions. The basic rationale for experimental design is summarized by Gilbert, Light, and Mosteller (1975): "We will not know how things will work in practice until we try them *in practice*" (p. 46).

One important purpose of experimental design is to determine which variables have an authentically **causal relationship**.

Causality can be the focus of intense political, regulatory, industrial, and academic interest. Parents and politicians want to know whether exposure to video games or violent or explicit sexual content causes some undesirable effect in children or adolescents. Educators want to know if a particular teaching method will improve student performance. Advertisers want to know if a particular advertising strategy will cause an increase in sales. The answers to such questions feed into often-contentious debates about media regulation, investments in educational technology, or where advertising dollars should be spent.

From a communication perspective, we might be interested in knowing whether heavy use of the Internet causes a change in the nature or frequency of interpersonal communication, or if exposure to alcohol advertising causes adolescents to drink more or to start drinking at a younger age than they might otherwise.

Generically, all such questions ask, "Does A cause B?"

To be satisfied that A (the **independent variable**) does cause B (the **dependent variable**) to change, we need to be assured of three things:

- A must precede B in time.

- A and B must vary together (**covariance**).

- B must demonstrably be caused by A and not by something else.

A must precede B if we are to argue that A causes B. We cannot argue that a new web microsite designed specifically for employees improved their morale if the only observed jump in morale occurred before the microsite was launched. To measure change in the variables we are interested in, we must measure them at "time 1" and then later at "time 2." This is a major weakness of surveys, which typically measure variables only once, at "time 1."

Also, A and B must vary together if we are to demonstrate causality. If we introduce our new microsite into an organization and employee morale remains unchanged, we cannot argue that the microsite had any effect on morale. We must be able to demonstrate that as the nature or frequency of communication with employees changed, so too did their level of morale.

However, knowing that A and B vary together is not in itself evidence of causality. We also need to eliminate the possibility that other variables might explain the effect(s) we see. For example, a human resources manager might observe that employee morale is indeed rising after the launch of an employee microsite and therefore conclude that the microsite caused the increase in morale. Suppose, however, the microsite had been launched as part of an employee benefit package that included additional benefits, salary increases, and profit sharing. In this case, there is indeed an apparent relationship between the introduction of the microsite and the increase in morale, but it may not be the causal relationship. If we investigated further, we might find that the improvement in morale is explained by the salary increases and not at all by the microsite. The particular strength of the experimental method is its potential to identify variables that have significant causal relationships, to assess the direction of causality, and to identify variables that have no significant effect on other variables.

The main disadvantage of experimental methods is the artificiality of the experimental conditions. Typically, participants in an experiment are invited into a lab or room to watch videos or a demonstration of a new product, to react to a message of some kind, or to work together solving a problem. The researcher may be trying to study how people watch sporting events, shop for products, or solve problems in groups, but experimental designs rarely capture the natural environments in which people watch sports, shop, or solve problems with colleagues. This problem is referred to as a lack of **ecological isomorphism**. The experimental condition is not the same as the conditions in the outside world it seeks to replicate, and, therefore, an experiment may have questionable validity.

A further problem with experiments is that more sophisticated designs may require large numbers of people who are willing to become experimental participants, perhaps for extended periods of time.

In this chapter, we will follow Professor Michaels, who is interested in the relationship between students' study conditions and their academic performance. We will see Professor Michaels move from basic to more and more sophisticated experimental designs as his thinking about this relationship develops, but first a detour through ethics.

In this discussion, we position Professor Michaels as thinking through experimental designs and their implications rather than implementing them. We do this for two reasons. First, experiments involving human subjects are inextricably related to formal institutional review board submissions and approvals—as you will recall from Chapter 3. Second, and related, ethical concerns can arise when students participate in faculty research. For example, Leentjens and Levenson (2013) argue that, at some institutions, students may be required or coerced into participation with no guarantee of educational gain or feel subject to influence that makes their participation less than fully voluntary. As the authors state, "Voluntary participation is only truly voluntary if not participating has no consequences for the student (p. 396)"

Can students truly be divorced from a classroom relationship with faculty when they are participants in faculty research? The question of whether Professor Michaels should have his students participating in his experiments is not necessarily a simple one, and you are invited to consider one aspect of this in an exercise at the end of this chapter.

Field Experiments and Ex Post Facto Designs

As often happens, Professor Michaels's interest in the relationship between group interaction and academic performance is sparked by a casual observation. On the first test of a semester, he notices that unlike the normal distribution of scores he usually sees, scores on this test appear to fall into two groups. (Remember bimodal distributions?) He sees a group of students with scores below the mean, a second group with scores above the mean, and relatively few scores hovering around the mean.

Why might this be? He does the obvious thing. He shows his students the bimodal distribution of scores and asks for their insights. Their answers are mixed, speculative, and include a large number of "dunnos," but at least one idea emerges that seems worth pursuing—study conditions. For example, some students study alone; others study in groups. Could different study conditions explain the difference in test scores?

Professor Michaels is getting the benefit of what we might call a natural experiment or **ex post facto design**. He did not design an experiment but merely observed after the fact that something seemed to have affected test results. Sometimes, that something is a known. For example, a natural catastrophe hitting campus provides the opportunity to observe student-faculty communication under emergency conditions and how it differs from normal, routine communication. A natural experiment can be diagrammed as follows:

Unique or unusual event → observation

Sometimes, as in Prof. Michaels's case, the something is an unknown that sparks his thinking about causality and relationships.

Intrigued, he envisages a simple experiment to test a tentative hypothesis about study conditions. Prior to the next test, he could ask student volunteers to form a study group and to study together. This basic design is a **field experiment** or simple observation. Here, he would be manipulating a variable (study conditions) and observing the results (test scores) for the study group versus the rest of the class.

This level of experimental design can be diagrammed as follows:

Study condition 1 (group study) → observation (test scores)

Study condition 2 (no group study) → observation (test scores)

If on the next test he discovered that the students who studied in a group scored higher than the students who did not, it might be tempting to recommend that students study together in a group if they want to improve their scores. Unfortunately, ex post facto designs and field experiments do not let him make that recommendation with any confidence. There are two reasons. The first is that he has no baseline measurement of student performance. The grouped and independent studiers may differ in test performance, but they may have differed before the experiment; in other words, the difference in scores may not be due to the grouped versus independent study conditions at all. He therefore needs to compare the students' performances before they studied under the two different conditions, as well as after they did this.

The second—and major—problem is that he has no idea how the individuals in the two groups differ outside of their study conditions—grouped or independent. It may well be that some attribute or a circumstance other than study condition best explains the difference in test scores.

For example, the high-scoring group consisted of volunteers. Could it be that something other than study condition—an extrovert personality type predisposed to volunteering, gender, age, or class year, for example—explains the difference in scores?

Nor can we be confident about the direction of causality. There may be an apparent relationship between study conditions and test performance, but in which direction does the causality run? Did the group study experience explain higher scores, or is it that students who score highly on quizzes anyway prefer to study together?

At this point in the research process, Professor Michaels is refining both his questions and his proposed experimental designs. Basically, he has started with a broad research question (*RQ*) such as this:

RQ: Is there a relationship between study conditions and test performance?

His simple field experiment suggested that this might be the case, and it is now time to review the relevant scholarly literature and arrive, if possible, at a more specific hypothesis.

His review of the literature suggests that studying as a member of a group can mean getting instant answers to questions, group support, shared resources, help from knowledgeable colleagues, and perhaps peer pressure to succeed. On the other hand, he suspects that any group also has the potential to degenerate into uncontrolled socializing and that studying by oneself offers distinct advantages such as no interruptions and the potential to study at any time and for as long as the individual needs to. He decides that the evidence is inconclusive; obviously, much depends on the nature of the study group and the individual student.

He decides that he now has enough evidence to propose a two-tailed hypothesis:

H_1: There is a relationship between study conditions and test performance.

(Recall from Chapter 2 that a two-tailed hypothesis proposes that a difference between two groups could be in any direction.)

What experimental design should Professor Michaels use to establish that there is such a relationship? There are several possibilities.

BASIC EXPERIMENTAL DESIGN

The different levels of experimental design are expressed as follows:

X = manipulation of a variable; what is done to the experimental group or groups. In Professor Michaels's case, it is manipulation of study conditions.

R = random assignment of individuals to groups, a key concept in experimental design.

O_1, O_2, etc. = observation 1, observation 2, etc.

One-Group Pretest–Posttest Design

A basic experimental design consists of a baseline observation (O_1), followed by exposure to an experimental condition (X), followed by postexperimental observation (O_2) to see if any change has occurred in the experimental group. It is diagrammed as

$$O_1 \qquad X \qquad O_2$$

With this design, we can see any changes that might occur as a result of the experimental condition. In the case of our example, Professor Michaels would get a baseline measure (O_1) of test performance of a group of students, place them in a group study session (X), and then measure their quiz performance again (O_2).

If he found a difference between the "before" and "after" measures $(O_1$ and $O_2)$, he might propose that the group study sessions are what caused it, but this design is not rigorous enough to answer the causality question.

To be certain that he has found a causal relationship, he needs to rule out two possibilities: first that any observed change in test scores might have occurred anyway for some reason and second that some influence other than the study conditions caused the change.

The problem with the one-group pretest–posttest design is that many other variables not in the experimental design—such as location of the group, students' major, class year, or residence status—might also be playing a part. Furthermore, the experiment itself is likely to have some effect on test scores. The one-group pretest–posttest design has a baseline quiz (O_1) followed by a second quiz (O_2) taken after the students study for that quiz under experimental conditions. If they have remembered anything from the first test, this in itself will almost inevitably have some effect on the second set of test scores.

We need to be sure that we have ruled out all other possible explanations before deciding that study conditions, *and only study conditions*, explain the difference in test scores. This means designing a level of control into experiments.

DESIGNING FOR CONTROL

In a general sense, **control** means to remove all other possible variables from the experimental design, so we can be sure that our treatment variable and only our treatment variable is causing any changes we see. **Control groups** are groups not exposed to any experimental variable. As shown in the following example, they are used as baselines against which to measure any changes in groups that are exposed to experimental variables.

Two-Group Pretest–Posttest Design

One way to be more certain that group study sessions do have an effect on test scores is to use two groups of students and to place only one of them into group study sessions. If the students in the group study sessions show a measurable change in test scores and students in the second group (the control group) do not, we can be more confident that the group study sessions did have an effect.

This design is diagrammed as

$$O_1 \qquad X \qquad O_2$$
$$O_1 \qquad \qquad O_2$$

Here, both groups' test scores are measured before and after one group participates in a group study session (X). Because the second group (the control group) has no exposure to this session, we would expect to find improved quiz performance only for the group of students who studied together. If we find a change in the control group, we have to accept that something other than group study is causing the observed changes in quiz scores.

The contribution of the O_1 observations is that even if the control group shows a change in scores, we can compare that change to any change in the scores of the experimental group. This lets us determine whether we are seeing a change in the experimental group scores that is significantly greater than the changes in scores for the control group.

If we determine that the study group had demonstrably higher test scores, we might now conclude that studying together does explain the improved test scores. Unfortunately, we could still be wrong because we have not accounted for other possible differences between the groups that might also explain our results. A yet more sophisticated experimental design is needed if we are to have full confidence in our results.

DESIGNING FOR RANDOM ASSIGNMENT

If we have more of one characteristic in one group than in another group, it may be *that* characteristic and not the experimental variable that is explaining the results. For example, variables that might differentially influence test scores could include a student's age, number of years at college, residence status, work commitments, attitudes to the major, and so on. Professor Michaels has considered none of these in his experimental design. We cannot fault him for this because he cannot possibly know in advance what all the relevant variables might be. Nor can he control all of them experimentally even if he is able to identify them.

This is where **random assignment** comes in. Your reading of Chapter 6, "Sampling," should have you thinking about the merits of randomly assigning participants into groups. In experimental design, random assignment becomes especially important. With random assignment, we can assume that the probability of some peculiarity occurring in one group is no greater or less than the probability of it occurring in another group. Any difference we observe between groups should then be due to the variable we are manipulating and not to something unique to one group.

For example, random assignment would mean that individuals with a particularly high GPA would be randomly assigned across both groups. Any effect of GPA is then equalized across both groups, and GPA can be eliminated as an explanation because, in principle, it affects both groups equally.

Two-Group Random Assignment Pretest–Posttest Design

The following design is essentially the same as a two-group pretest–posttest design but with the very important distinction that individuals are now randomly assigned to groups, as shown below. *R* denotes random assignment to groups.

$$R \qquad O_1 \qquad X \qquad O_2$$
$$R \qquad O_1 \qquad \qquad O_2$$

At this point, Professor Michaels would no longer be asking students to volunteer to study in a group; rather, he would be using **random numbers** (see Chapter 6) to assign students to a group. It is always possible that as a result of random assignment, he may end up, unknowingly, with coffee drinkers overrepresented in one group and underrepresented in another. But random assignment allows him to argue that such attributes have the same probability of occurring in each group. If his experimental group shows changes, he can reasonably argue that the change is due to the experimental variable.

With random assignment, a control group, and a pretest–posttest design, Professor Michaels would be well on the way to answering the causality question, but now this design has in itself created a problem. As noted above, it seems likely that taking a test on any topic must affect one's performance on a second test on the same topic. More generally, what is the possibility that the pretest or baseline measurement itself had some effect on participants?

To eliminate this possibility, Professor Michaels needs yet another group that has not been exposed to the pretest. These students will participate in group study sessions prior to the posttest (O_2), but to eliminate any possible influence of the pretest, there is no O_1.

The experimental design for this group would look like this:

$$R \qquad X \qquad O_2$$

Finally, to ensure that the experimental variable and only the experimental variable explains his results, he adds one further group to the design. It is a group of randomly assigned individuals to whom absolutely nothing happens except the final posttest. In the unlikely event that this group's posttest results are the same as for other groups, he would be forced to conclude that something other than the experimental variable is at work. This group's design is as follows:

$$R \qquad O_2$$

The Solomon Four-Group Design

Adding the above two groups to the experimental design results in an overall design known as the **Solomon Four-Group Design**, as shown in Exhibit 10.1.

With this design, we can compare pretest with posttest results, compare control groups with experimental groups, and take a look at a group to which nothing has happened except for a final test. Now we can be assured that the experimental variable preceded the posttest and that no other variable explains the changes we have observed.

We have now met two of the conditions needed to establish causality: **temporal ordering** (the causal variable must precede in time any effect) and the elimination of any other variables that might have caused the observed effect. If we can demonstrate that the independent variable and the dependent variable vary together (covariation), we will have met the third condition for demonstrating a causal relationship between them.

Covariation is usually expressed in the form of a correlation coefficient. Revisit Chapter 8 for a discussion of correlation.

EXHIBIT 10.1 ■ Solomon Four-Group Design	
Diagram	**Explanation**
$R \quad O_1 \quad X \quad O_2$	Random assignment, pre- and posttesting, subject to experimental variable. This is the "test group."
$R \quad O_1 \qquad\quad O_2$	Random assignment, pre- and posttesting, not subject to experimental variable. This control group shows what would have happened without the experimental variable.
$R \qquad\quad X \quad O_2$	Random assignment, posttesting only, subject to experimental variable. This control group checks that the pretest is not influencing the results.
$R \qquad\qquad O_2$	Random assignment, posttesting only, not subject to experimental variable. This control group checks that nothing other than the pretest and the experimental condition is influencing the experiment.

FACTORIAL DESIGNS

The experimental designs described so far in this chapter assess the relationship between two variables: study conditions and test scores. Analyses that examine the relationship among three or more variables are referred to as **multivariate analyses**, and experimental designs that manipulate two or more variables are referred to as **factorial designs**.

Professor Michaels considers a multivariate design as the next step in his thinking because intuition, observation, and his literature review all tell him that the relationship between study conditions and test performance might be influenced by other factors—residence status, for example. Is it possible that commuters and campus residents differ in their learning opportunities? After all, residential campuses tout the advantages of residence living, such as the ability to roll out of bed minutes before class and still get there on time. Perhaps a more important advantage would be the ability to meet helpful people, socialize, and discuss problems with others taking the same classes—an advantage less readily available to commuter students.

He formulates another hypothesis as follows (note that it is two-tailed because he has no specific evidence to suggest that residents will show a greater effect than commuters or vice versa):

H_2: The effect of study condition on test scores will differ between residents and commuters.

The experimental design to test this hypothesis now requires four groups of participants, as shown in Exhibit 10.2, along with some hypothetical experimental results.

Because there are two categories of residence (resident and commuter) and two study conditions (grouped and independent), the design is referred to as a 2 × 2 design. If there were three types of study condition such as group, individual, and online study, the design would be a 2 × 3.

Suppose the initial (bivariate) study showed that the average test scores for students who studied in a group were not significantly different from the scores for those who did not. Professor Michaels might conclude that group study sessions do not improve test scores, but suppose he runs the experiment as a 2 × 2 design and gets the results shown in Exhibit 10.2.

The pattern here suggests that commuter students score better under individual study conditions and that resident students do better under group study conditions. In other words, there is an interaction between residence status and study condition that influences test scores. Only when the study is run as a 2 × 2 design, with residence status as an additional variable, can we see that study condition *does* have an effect but that this effect varies according to residence status.

We can add more variables to the experiment at a cost of increasingly complex experimental design. Suppose Professor Michaels further hypothesizes that a student's major may also explain test scores. (Intuitively, students may be more motivated to study in their own subject area and with students in their own major than to study outside their subject area or with students having a different major than they do.) He proposes three hypotheses and from his reading and thinking to date is now prepared to make them one-tailed and directional, as follows:

EXHIBIT 10.2 ■ A 2 × 2 Factorial Design, Test Results by Residence Status and Study Condition, Showing Hypothetical Results		
	Average Score on 10-Point Test	
	Commuter	Resident
Individual Study	10	5
Group Study	5	10

EXHIBIT 10.3 ■ A 2 × 2 × 2 Experimental Design for Three Independent Variables				
	Group Study		**Individual Study**	
Resident	Major in test subject	Major in other subject	Major in test subject	Major in other subject
Commuter	Major in test subject	Major in other subject	Major in test subject	Major in other subject

H_3: Group study test scores will be greater than independent study test scores.

H_4: Group study test scores will be greater for residents than for nonresidents.

H_5: Group study test scores will be greater for majors in the test subject than for majors in other subjects.

How can he examine the interaction among residence status, major, and study conditions as they relate to test scores? Basically, he expands the number of cells in the experimental design. Let's assume that Exhibit 10.2 represents the results for majors. The same experimental design is essentially repeated with commuter and resident groups consisting of randomly assigned majors in subjects other than the test subject. As shown in Exhibit 10.3, this would now be a 2 × 2 × 2 design; the experiment looks at two levels of residence status by two types of study condition by two categories of major.

The design now has eight experimental groups (2 × 2 × 2 = 8). It offers the opportunity to explore the interaction of all three independent variables, for example to compare the scores of resident students studying together for a test outside their major with the scores of other groups, such as commuters studying together for a test in their major. But now we have a practical problem of recruitment into the experiment. As shown in Exhibit 10.3, eight different experimental groups are required, as is a sufficient number of participants assigned randomly to each cell in the experiment's design. Typically, we would be thinking of 10 to 15 participants per cell, with no fewer than 5 per cell. The design shown in Exhibit 10.3 has eight cells. At 10 to 15 participants per cell, this design would require 80 to 120 participants.

BETWEEN-SUBJECTS AND WITHIN-SUBJECTS DESIGN

One problem with experimental design is the number of participants that may be needed. The 2 × 2 × 2 experimental design discussed above could require in the order of 100 people if each person is exposed to only one experimental condition. If each person participates under only one set of conditions, such as "group study–resident–other major," the design is called a **between-subjects design**.

One way to reduce the number of participants required is to in effect use them twice, that is, to expose them to more than one experimental condition, for example to both group and individual study conditions. This is called a **within-subjects design**.

One obvious problem with within-subjects design is that one experimental condition may have an effect on another condition. Participants already exposed to a group study condition, for example, may have a different reaction to an individual condition than they would have if they had not been exposed to a group study condition. A second problem is that for some conditions, a within-subjects design is simply not possible. In our example, we cannot ask resident students to suddenly become commuters, or students to change their majors for the duration of the experiment.

TIME SERIES ANALYSIS

Even though experiments run over a period of time, that time typically is short, and we cannot know if the results obtained at the end of the experiment will still be true at some point in the future. We can address that problem with a procedure called **time series analysis**.

As the name implies, time series analysis is a series of observations made at intervals over time. In the context of experimental design, time series analysis can be diagrammed as shown below. Done before an experimental manipulation, these observations can check for the stability of the preexperimental condition. Done after an experimental manipulation, they can check whether an experimental result is stable over time.

$$O_1 \quad O_2 \quad O_3 \quad O_4 \quad X \quad O_5 \quad O_6 \quad O_7$$

VALIDITY AND EXPERIMENTAL DESIGN

Validity raises the question of whether the experiment yields results related to the concepts the researcher set out to investigate or whether something else has been captured in the findings. There are two types of validity to consider in experimental research: internal and external.

Internal Validity

Internal validity relates to questions of experimental design. In effect, it asks the "What could go wrong?" question. Unfortunately, many things can go wrong.

These include spurious relationships. Simply put, a **spurious relationship** is not a genuine relationship between two variables but one that only seems to exist. For example, Professor Michaels may assign students to groups based on their class years (freshman, sophomore, etc.). However, there is not a 100% relationship among class year, age, and number of credits. Two students, both in their third year, may differ significantly in number of credits if one of them is a full-time student and the other attends part time. Two seniors, both with the same number of credits, may differ significantly in age if one of them is beginning a degree program after a career in the workplace. Thus, although Professor Michaels may appear to find a relationship between class year and study condition, the relationship may actually be between student age and study condition or between student experience (whether full or part time) and study condition.

Selection bias occurs when the experimental groups are not comparable. For example, let's assume that one of Professor Michaels's experimental conditions—studying in a group—can take place only at night because of student schedules. This, arguably, requires more effort than the experimental condition of studying alone at any time. If a number of students cannot study at night, the nighttime group that studies together has, to some extent, become self-selecting. This group perhaps has a higher level of volunteer enthusiasm or a greater ability to volunteer, and so we now have a threat to internal validity because the two experimental groups are not the same, and the experiment's results are capturing a difference between willingness or ability to volunteer rather than a difference between the two study conditions.

Attrition occurs when people drop out of a study. In the case of our example, this may be due to boredom, a student suddenly realizing that he or she is not getting paid for the study, a change in the pace of academic life due to examinations, or a clash of personalities. Suppose in this case the attrition is due to the pressure of examinations. Even if Professor Michaels started his experiment with random assignment of individuals to pretest groups, he can no longer assume that his posttest groups are the same as the pretest groups. Any difference he finds between groups may be due to differences in ability to deal with stress while studying and not to differences between his two study conditions.

Repeated testing, almost by definition, can be a threat to internal validity. As group participants become more and more familiar with a test or its close relatives, they can be expected to perform better and better. The threat to internal validity in our example is that differences in group scores may reflect increasing levels of competence and/or confidence in test taking and not differences in the experimental study conditions.

A somewhat related threat to internal validity is **maturation**, which simply means that people change over time. If Professor Michaels runs his experiments over the course of a semester, his participants will be one semester older, one semester more experienced, and perhaps one semester more fatigued than they were at the beginning of the experiment. Again, there is a threat to internal validity because any difference in "pre" and "post" scores may be capturing maturation and not the level of exposure to studying in a group or alone.

Diffusion refers to a treatment effect spreading from group to group. Paradoxically, a problem for Professor Michaels as a communication researcher is that people communicate! Resident students talk to commuters, sophomores talk to seniors, pretest groups talk to posttest groups, and so on. In this case, an especially important problem may be that students who study alone do talk to students who study in groups. The experimental treatment (study condition) in effect gets "spread" across all groups. This threatens internal validity because the results of the study may be to suggest no difference between experimental groups when in fact there is one.

Some threats to internal validity may not be obvious to the researcher, for example the fact that the different experimental groups are spending a lot of time talking to each other. The researcher may be fully aware of other threats to internal validity but have no control over them. For example, you will recall from Chapter 3 that institutional review board (IRB) guidelines allow research participants to drop out of a study at any time without penalty.

What researchers can be attuned to, however, is **experimenter bias**, their own threat to internal validity. In addition to the ethical implications of using his students as experimental participants, if he were to do so, Professor Michaels would be in a problematic situation with respect to experimenter bias for a number of reasons. If he recruits participants from his own classes, his student participants would know his views about student behavior, including study habits. Unwittingly, he may have primed his research participants to behave in a particular way. If he were to offer extra credit for participating in his experiments, he will have biased his sample in favor of those students who are keen to get extra credit. Depending on when and where his individual students and study groups are studying, he may see more of one kind of student than another. This increased contact may be read as implicitly favoring one type of student over another.

You might think that sophisticated designs such as the Solomon Four-Group Design would rule out any problems with validity, but even the most sophisticated design is not immune to threats to internal validity.

External Validity

External validity relates to whether the experiment has in fact captured the external world that the researcher is investigating.

The ultimate test of external validity is that the findings of an experiment generalize to the wider population from which the experiment's participants are sampled. Professor Michaels would likely tell us that there are two important reasons he is running the experiments outlined in this chapter. The first is the driving force behind most scholarly research—an intellectual curiosity about the relationships among phenomena of interest. The second is the hope that he will gain ideas about effective study habits that will apply successfully to other students on campus and in the wider academic community. If the findings do not apply, his study will have a serious lack of external validity. Ideally, his research findings will be valid not only across "space" (as in from sample to population) but also across "time" (as in generalizable from now into the future).

Probably the most serious threat to external validity is the issue of ecological isomorphism introduced earlier in this chapter. The students briefed to study alone may find themselves in a realistic study scenario. However, if Professor Michaels directed a volunteer student group on where to study, when to study, and how long to study, it is unlikely that they would regard their study experience as typical. In other words, the **experimental situation** or setting may be a threat to external validity because it does not reflect external reality. The second obvious threat is the participant sample(s). By definition, all the students in this study are volunteers, which is not true for the wider population of students. To the extent that the sample does not fully capture the population's characteristics, there is a threat to external validity.

Another threat to external validity is the so-called **Hawthorne effect**, named after productivity studies conducted in the 1920s at the Hawthorne Works, a Western Electric plant. These studies were designed to see what changes in working conditions might improve worker productivity. An unanticipated conclusion from the studies was that observed increases in productivity seemed to be explained by the fact that the workers apparently interpreted the research as management and the research team taking an interest in them. There may well be some kind of Hawthorne effect with those students who are impressed by Professor Michaels taking a special interest in them (and who may then work hard to give him the research results they think he is looking for).

A further question arises with the operationalization of constructs and the need to develop measures that do in fact capture the concepts that the researcher intends to capture.

In the study example in this chapter, there are four variables of interest—major, residence status, test scores, and study conditions. Of these, residence status and major can be operationalized simply by asking students to identify their majors and themselves as a resident or a commuter.

Study conditions and test scores are more tricky. At one level, the study condition is simple; either students are in a study group, or they are not. However, student behavior within a study group can vary widely in terms of both attendance and participation. Conversely, students categorized as "independent" studiers may well be studying as members of a group by virtue of their participation in online discussions. They could be in a much larger and even more helpful and supportive study group online. The biggest question may be test scores. We would like to be able to make some general statements about academic performance, or perhaps even more generally "intellectual ability" as a result of our experiments, but Professor Michaels operationalized academic performance as "test scores," and test scores may or may not capture academic performance at a more general level outside of the classes he is studying.

Manipulation Checks

An experiment showing no relationship between an independent variable and a dependent variable may have correctly demonstrated no relationship. However, it is also possible that a relationship does exist but that participants did not interpret the experiment as the researcher intended.

A **manipulation check** is a check on how participants interpreted the manipulated variable—study conditions in the case of Professor Michaels. In this case, it should be abundantly clear to participants that they are responding to different study conditions, but in principle Professor Michaels would want to check that participants were responding to study conditions and not another perceived condition such as time of day, lighting, or room temperature.

A manipulation check can often take the form of a survey question that mirrors the experimental condition. For example, Professor Michaels might have his participants complete a survey that asks a number of questions about their study habits. Embedded in the survey might be a question that asks participants to rate their level of group activity during the experimental study session. Confirmation that the experiment was perceived as intended would come from seeing any difference in test scores between the two experimental groups also apparent between those who rated themselves high and low on group activity. As a bonus in this case, such a question could also shed light on whether individual study students saw themselves as engaged in group activity in some way.

Professor Michaels pours himself a coffee, reviews his thinking about experiments, and decides that they represent a good start at untangling the relationship among some of the variables that might influence his students' academic performance. His experimental designs would give him a level of insight beyond anything a survey would have provided, but he wonders if these experiments really would capture all the influences on students' test scores. He realizes, for example, that his thinking has completely ignored students' off-campus commitments. Students who have job commitments have less time to study than those who do not and therefore might be expected to do less well on quizzes. Then there are innate capabilities such as memory. All things being equal, we might expect that students with a greater ability to memorize relevant content would do better on quizzes.

As he contemplates the logistics of finding around 80 students who can be randomly assigned to experimental groups on the basis of major, residence status, and study conditions—let alone all the other attributes he is now identifying—he considers other approaches to answering his basic question. Recruiting students into an online experiment could solve the problem of numbers, but online experiments have their own disadvantages, as we will see.

On the other hand, he wonders if perhaps good, in-depth interviews with one or two students might not give him just as much understanding, or perhaps a different understanding, of the variables that influence academic performance.

We will discuss qualitative techniques such as interviews and focus groups in Chapter 13.

message /
artifact.

ONLINE EXPERIMENTS

To date, the Internet has been used to host surveys far more than experiments. Online experiments have been slower coming for two related reasons. First, experimental design often requires that participants do something more active than responding to questions. For example, a researcher might run an experiment to explore website "user friendliness" or navigability. Here, individuals would be randomly selected and assigned to one of two groups, each group interacting with a different site design and asked to perform a task such as an online search. Participants would be actively involved as they navigate through web links, perhaps audio-recording comments as they do so.

Second, the researcher would want to record such variables as the participants' mouse movements and response times as they navigate through an assigned task. Researchers may also want to record such **paradata** or **metadata** as respondents' computer or smartphone platforms, operating systems, browsers, Internet connection types and speeds, breaks in connection, number of attempts at a problem, dropouts, location, and time and date of signing on and off. Paradata and metadata are different kinds of data about data. Look at your smartphone for all the metadata associated with each "selfie" on your phone and see the glossary for fuller definitions.

Experimental data can therefore be much more complex and storage hungry than survey data. High-speed Internet connections and high bandwidth may be required to capture, for example, response times at the level of milliseconds, as well as the volume of data generated.

Greater levels of sophistication may also be demanded of the experimenter in terms of programming websites to host experiments and collect and process data. However, experiment software packages are increasingly facilitating web-based experiments. Typically, such packages allow user-defined experimental designs and the randomized distribution of participants to experimental conditions. They can present differing stimuli, such as text, images, video, and audio, and offer keyboard or mouse inputs, such as text input, radio buttons, and menus. Participants' paths through an experiment can be tracked to see where they faltered or dropped out. The software can display the experiment's design and procedures and may offer preloaded experiments and tutorials for user training.

Two such packages are WebExp and Wextor. Further information on each is available at their web addresses, which are listed at the end of this chapter.

Advantages and Disadvantages of Online Experiments

Online experiments offer automated administration of experiments, large pools of participants, the potential to get a required number of participants at low cost from a variety of different populations, and avoidance of time constraints and scheduling problems. Greater anonymity relative to classroom or lab settings means that participants may be more open to honest self-disclosure. Experimenter bias can be reduced, and there can be a greater openness of the research process, facilitating both replication and oversight of experiments.

Problems can include multiple submissions by the same individuals, loss of experimental control, self-selection of participants based on computer competencies, differing standards of Internet connection affecting responses, misunderstanding of instructions, lack of direct contact between participants and the researcher, dropouts, and difficulties with debriefing. Studies in other cultures require translation and pretesting prior to the experiment. Although

Internet results are often comparable to results from traditional methods, participants' lack of computer experience or computer anxieties may lead to results that differ from studies administered on paper. See Reips (2002) and Reips and Krantz (2010).

Running Online Experiments

The successful online experiment requires attention to technology, participant retention, and multiple submissions.

Online experiments should present content equally well across all platforms, operating systems, and browsers. If connection quality and speed are not the same for all participants, the experiment's results may be biased because data on "low tech" participants and "dropouts" frustrated with the connection quality will not be represented (Stieger, Lewetz, & Reips, 2017.)

Dropouts can be minimized by running the experiment on the least sophisticated technology that participants might have, but participants may also drop out for reasons related to the experiment's design. One approach to the dropout problem is to place seeming barriers such as instructions and practice tasks up front so that less-motivated participants drop out before the actual experiment begins (Reips, 2002). Another approach is to design experiments with online game features in order to maintain participant interest (Reips & Krantz, 2010). Overall, participants should experience the experiment website as attractive, trustworthy, and responsive, in terms of both speed and providing feedback.

Online experiments should be designed to track participants through the experiment and identify the points at which dropouts occur. Reips and Krantz (2010) argue that dropout information is an asset and should be reported because it provides feedback on the experiment's design as well as on whether the results can be generalized to a wider population.

The problem of multiple submissions can be partly addressed with instructions; by asking participants if they made multiple submissions; and by checking passwords, cookies, and computer addresses for multiple accesses to the experiment.

As discussed in Chapter 7, anomalous data also need to be examined with a view to deleting these data or analyzing them separately.

ETHICS PANEL
TWO FAMOUS AND CONTROVERSIAL EXPERIMENTS

Chapter 3 discusses codes of ethical behavior for human communication research. The many codes discussed converge on some important ideas about the treatment of research participants. Here are a few:

- Participants must be given the opportunity to choose what shall or shall not happen to them.

- Subjects must be fully informed, comprehend the study, and volunteer for the study.

- Participants should not be harmed.

- The research should maximize possible benefits and minimize possible harm.

- The researcher should systematically assess the risks and benefits from the study.

- The selection of research subjects should be fair and equitable; subjects ought not to be recruited simply on the basis of accessibility or manipulability.

Stanley Milgram's Experiments on Authority

In the 1960s, Yale University researcher Stanley Milgram found that most of his subjects were willing to give apparently harmful electric shocks to another person simply because a scientific "authority" told them to do so. Even though the other person was apparently in pain, many, though not all, participants continued to increase the level of shock at the command of the researcher. The overall objective of these experiments was to explain the conditions of obedience to authority. The "victim" was, in fact, an actor, and the "pain" was simulated, and this information was revealed to participants at the end of the experiment.

Philip Zimbardo's Stanford Prison Experiment

In 1971, Professor Philip Zimbardo randomly assigned 23 male student volunteers to two experimental groups. One group was to act as prisoners, the other group as guards, in a simulated prison environment that was to run for two weeks. Over the next few days, the "guards" became increasingly sadistic to the point that on day five Zimbardo felt obliged to discontinue the experiment. Zimbardo argues that such behaviors were born of boredom and that under such conditions good people are capable of turning bad.

See the "Recommended Reading" section of this chapter for more information about both of these studies.

Questions

Based on the principles summarized above,

- What criteria would you use to assess the ethical standards of these two controversial experiments?

- Where on a "completely ethical" to "completely unethical" continuum would you place each of these experiments, and why?

- Supposing both experiments were run online with the experimental conditions simulated. Does your thinking about the ethics of these experiments change? If so, how?

Chapter Summary

- Experimental methods range from simple observation to sophisticated factorial designs.

- Experimental design involves exposing participants to controlled conditions such as different versions of a persuasive message.

- Experimental methods can help determine whether there is a causal relationship between variables.

- Experimental methods can isolate the effect of different variables on a variable of interest.

- Good experimental design requires random assignment of participants to experimental and control groups.

- To determine the specific influence of a variable, researchers may need to use sophisticated experimental designs such as the Solomon Four-Group Design.

- Factorial designs examine the interaction among three or more variables.

- The basic weakness of experimental design is that experimental conditions rarely resemble real-life situations.

- Online experiments can recruit large numbers of participants rapidly at low cost, but results can be affected by self-selection, multiple submissions, dropouts, and lack of contact between participants and the researcher.

Key Terms

attrition 209
between-subjects design 207
causal relationship 199
control 203
control groups 203
covariance 199
dependent variable 199
diffusion 209
ecological isomorphism 200
ex post facto design 201
experimental situation 210

experimenter bias 209
experiments 198
external validity 210
factorial designs 205
field experiment 201
Hawthorne effect 210
independent variable 199
internal validity 208
manipulation check 211
maturation 209
metadata 212

multivariate analyses 205
paradata 212
random assignment 204
random numbers 204
repeated testing 209
selection bias 208
Solomon Four-Group Design 205
spurious relationship 208
temporal ordering 205
time series analysis 208
within-subjects design 207

Application Exercises

Exercise 1: Assessing the Effect of an Instructional Program

A Pew Research Center study (Mitchell, Gottfried, Barthel, & Sumida, 2018) explored people's ability to distinguish between factual and opinion statements in the news. This research topic is obviously important in our age of partisan politics, which has seen the denigration of the news media and accusations of "false news."

The study of some 5,000 U.S. adults asked participants to distinguish between five factual statements and five opinion statements. A majority of participants correctly identified at least three of the five statements in each set, but this result is only a little better than random guessing. Far fewer got all five correct and roughly a quarter got most or all wrong.

Assume that in response to such data your campus has initiated an across-the-curriculum program to ensure that all majors graduate with a basic ability to distinguish fact from opinion. Follow-up surveys of graduating seniors indicate that they have an acceptable ability to do this. However, as we know, surveys do not address causality.

What experiment(s) might you design to help assess whether the ability of graduating seniors to distinguish fact from opinion is a function of the campus instructional program and not of other relevant experiences such as being politically active or having taken other relevant courses such as philosophy, logic, debate, political science, or media criticism?

Assume that your dependent variable is the ability to distinguish a statement of fact from an opinion.

HINT: In this Pew study, a factual statement is defined as one that can be proven or disproven by objective evidence.

Exercise 2: Students and the "Opt Out" Question

Review your institution's IRB policies regarding student participation in faculty research. In this chapter's discussion of experimental design, Professor Michaels typically would have had two options regarding his research. One would be to seek IRB approval of his research; the other would be to seek an exemption of IRB review because his research is confined to the classroom and for educational purposes only.

Neither option is likely to shape the way his students would view a request for participation in his experiments. The "opt out" provisions in research codes of ethics apply as much to students as to any other experimental participants, but given the student-faculty relationship, few students are likely to refuse his request and opt out of the experiments.

Identify practical steps that Professor Michaels might take to reassure his students that opting out of his experiments truly would have no consequences.

HINT: Think anonymity.

Recommended Reading

Dreifus, C. (2007, April 3). A conversation with Philip G. Zimbardo: Finding hope in knowing the universal capacity for evil. *New York Times*. Retrieved from https://www.nytimes.com/2007/04/03/science/03conv.html

An interview with Professor Zimbardo in which he discusses both his Stanford Prison Experiment and Stanley Milgram's experiments. See also the Milgram (2004) recommended reading.

Milgram, S. (2004). *Obedience to authority: An experimental view*. New York: HarperCollins.

This 2004 edition of Milgram's 1974 book explains Milgram's obedience experiments and his findings.

Reips, U. (2012). Using the Internet to collect data. In H. Cooper, P. M. Camic, D. L. Long, A. T. Panter, D. Rindskopf, & K. J. Sher (Eds.). *APA handbook of research methods in psychology, Vol 2: Research designs: Quantitative, qualitative, neuropsychological, and biological* (pp. 291–310). Washington, DC: American Psychological Association. DOI: 10.1037/13620-017

This chapter shows the major steps in collecting data on the Internet.

Reips, U., Buchanan, B., Krantz, J., & Mcgraw, K. (2015). Methodological challenges in the use of the Internet for scientific research: Ten solutions and recommendations. *Studia Psychologica, 15*(2), 139–148.

Discusses solutions to ten common obstacles in Internet-based research.

Reips, U., & Krantz, J. H. (2010). Conducting true experiments on the web. In S. D. Gosling, J. A. Johnson, S. D. Gosling, & J. A. Johnson (Eds.). *Advanced methods for conducting online behavioral research* (pp. 193–216). Washington, DC, US: American Psychological Association.

See this for an example of using Wextor for online experiments.

Slater, M., Antley, A., Davison, A., Swapp, D., Guger, C., Barker, C., . . . Sanchez-Vives, M. V. (2006). A virtual reprise of the Stanley Milgram obedience experiments. *PLoS ONE, 1*(1), e39. DOI: 10.1371/journal.pone.0000039

A paper on replicating Milgram's experiments but using "virtual humans" as recipients of supposed electric shocks.

Recommended Web Resources

Dr. Philip Zimbardo's Stanford Prison Experiment.........www.prisonexp.org
Contains a presentation on the Stanford Prison Experiment and a link to Dr. Zimbardo's website.

Many websites discuss the Stanley Milgram "obedience to authority" experiments. One starting point would be YouTube for videos of the experiments and their many replications.

WebExp Experimental Software.........http://groups.inf.ed.ac.uk/webexp/index.shtml
Wextor.........http://wextor.org/wextor/en/index.php
WebExp and Wextor offer software packages for developing, managing, and visualizing online experiments.

The Web Experiment List.........www.wexlist.net
Hosts active and archived web experiments in psychology.

References

Gilbert, J., Light, R. J., & Mosteller, F. (1975). Assessing social innovations: An empirical base for policy. In C. A. Bennett & A. A. Lumsdaine (Eds.), *Evaluation and experiment: Some critical issues in assessing social programs* (pp. 39–193). New York, NY: Academic Press.

Leentjens, A. F. G., & Levenson, J. L. (2013). Ethical issues concerning the recruitment of university students as research subjects. *Journal of Psychosomatic Research, 75*(4), 394–398. DOI: 10.1016/j.jpsychores.2013.03.007

Mitchell, A., Gottfried, J., Barthel, M., & Sumida, N. (2018, June 18). *Distinguishing between factual and opinion statements in the news* [Report]. Washington, DC: Pew Research Center Journalism and Media. Retrieved from http://www.journalism.org/2018/06/18/ distinguishing-between-factual-and-opinion-statements-in-the-news/

Reips, U. (2002). Standards for Internet-based experimenting. *Experimental Psychology, 49*(4), 243–256. DOI: 10.1026//1618-3169.49.4.243

Reips, U., & Krantz, J. H. (2010). Conducting true experiments on the Web. In S. D. Gosling & J. A. Johnson (Eds.). *Advanced methods for conducting online behavioral research* (pp. 193–216). Washington, DC: American Psychological Association. DOI: 10.1037/12076-013

Stieger, S., Lewetz, D., & Reips, U.-D. (2017). Can smartphones be used to bring computer-based tasks from the lab to the field? A mobile experience-sampling method study about the pace of life. *Behavior Research Methods, 50*(6), 2267–2275. DOI: 10.3758/s13428-017-0991-6

$SAGE edge™

Get the tools you need to sharpen your study skills. SAGE edge offers a robust online environment featuring an impressive array of free tools and resources.

Access quizzes, eFlashcards, video, and multimedia at **edge.sagepub.com/treadwell4e**.

11

QUANTITATIVE UNDERSTANDING OF CONTENT

Content Analysis

"Hey Lee! Looks like you won't get your parking lot. Hunter building wins!"

"How do you know that, Caroline?"

"Easy. I counted the "Save Hunter" and the "More Parking" stickers on all the dorm windows. 'Save Hunter' wins in the court of public opinion."

"You've got a couple of problems there."

"Like what?"

"Like, I did the same with bumper stickers. 'More parking' wins by a mile in the parking lots."

"So we should pool our numbers to see what's going on overall. What's the other problem?"

"Neither of us has a clue how posting a sticker relates to action. Like I could post a 'vote for' sticker but not vote."

"True, but let's assume that if people put a sticker on their own property they believe in its message. So those stickers capture a belief at least, right James?"

"Absolutely! I've been looking at political stickers on faculty vehicles. I figure it's a way to figure out where faculty are at politically."

"OK. So we agree we can get a read on campus opinion from sticker content."

"Sure. And here's where I win, Caroline. The number of 'More Parking' stickers goes up every time I count cars—so the number of people saying they want more parking keeps going up."

"So you're tracking opinion change over time. Wish I'd thought of that with my windows. I suppose we could also see whether these two issues are actually the most important . . . like whether or not 'Hunter' and 'parking' are outnumbered by the 'boycott campus dining' stickers."

"One thing I like about this research is you don't need people—unlike surveys. You can sort of capture their opinions directly."

"Words can be tricky though. For every sentence with 'Hunter' or 'parking' in it you'd have to decide how to classify it as 'for,' 'against,' or 'neutral' on the subject. Plus with web content you'd have to think about fake content."

"But you can research web content any time, any place, right? Home at 3 a.m. sounds like my kind of research."

"Books too. You could analyze this chapter."

"I'd better read it first!"

CHAPTER OVERVIEW

Media for content analysis can include any recorded communication from papyrus document to podcast, published or unpublished. Approaches to studying media content are almost as diverse as the approaches to studying human communication behavior. In a general sense, any study of media content is a content analysis, but in communication research, the term has often implied a quantitative approach and a series of specific steps aimed at ensuring systematic sampling, coding, and counting of units of media content. This chapter introduces content analysis as a primarily quantitative procedure. Qualitative approaches to understanding content are discussed in Chapter 12.

CHAPTER OBJECTIVES

This chapter will help you

- Explain the advantages and disadvantages of content analysis.
- Identify settings in which content analysis might be used.
- Describe, with examples, the steps of a basic content analysis.
- Identify and explain the units that might be used in content analysis.
- Discuss, with examples, the use of content analysis in understanding human interaction.
- Explain the circumstances under which content analysis may have ethical implications.

INTRODUCTION: ADVANTAGES AND DISADVANTAGES OF CONTENT ANALYSIS

An early and influential definition of **content analysis** described it as a quantitative, systematic, and objective technique for describing the manifest content of communications (Berelson, 1952).

- Quantitative means we must count occurrences of whatever we are interested in.

- Systematic means that we must count all relevant aspects of the sample. We cannot arbitrarily pick what aspects get analyzed.

- Objective means that we select units for analysis and categorize them using clearly defined criteria.

- **Manifest** means tangible and observable. For example, we cannot count patriotism in consumer advertising because patriotism is ultimately an abstract or **latent** (hidden) notion. What we can count is the frequency with which the word *patriotism* occurs, the frequency with which a patriotic image such as a national flag appears, or perhaps the number of minutes that music defined as patriotic is played.

In this chapter, we introduce the systematic sampling, coding, and counting that is characteristic of quantitative content analysis and then explore the relationship between quantitative methods and the qualitative methods discussed more fully in Chapter 12.

Content analyses can be used with almost any form of content. It is possible to analyze almost any recorded medium—press, radio, video, web, billboards, T-shirts, license plates, lawn signs, photographs, love letters, maps, and tweets. Private or personal content such as personal letters or doctor-patient e-mails may be analyzed but may well require the consent of the owners or originators. More usually, the raw material of content analysis is readily accessible, be it presidential speeches, advertisements for liquid soap or lingerie, BBC foreign news coverage, comic strips, or editorials in *The New York Times*.

For example, Perrault (2018) analyzed the content of websites of university health centers and found that although they offered professional information about their health care providers, they gave very little information about staff members outside of the medical context. For example, information that might help a potential student patient relate more easily to the professional, such as a list of hobbies or interests, was not offered. Also, few such websites explained what health care credentials (e.g., PA-C) mean.

Mastro and Figueroa-Caballero (2018) examined depictions of body type in a random sample of prime-time U.S. television shows. They concluded from their analysis of 1,254 characters in 89 programs that, on television, women have become increasingly thin and that thinner characters were judged as more attractive than overweight characters.

Sarge and Knobloch-Westerwick (2017) analyzed the persuasive content in articles in five top-selling women's fitness and health magazines. They recorded the type of evidence (narrative or statistical), the message source (such as personal trainer, professional athlete, chef), and the efficacy of the advice given (ease of implementing the advice, the rapidity of achieving results, and the permanence of results). They concluded that such message variables may help promote realistic advice but also can be detrimental and instill false confidence in achieving unattainable results through impractical strategies and time periods.

The above examples illustrate a frequent communication research interest in the (mis)representations of demographic, occupational, and social groups, but content analysts' interests are wide ranging. Content analysts have studied user behavior in online shooter games (Ivory et al., 2017), rap lyrics (Epps & Dixon, 2017), political satire (Becker & Goldberg, 2017), online food marketing to children (Hurwitz, Montague, & Wartella, 2017), the use of tweets during Breast Cancer Awareness Month (Diddi & Lundy, 2017), and academic research itself (Šerić, 2018).

More generally, content analysis has been used to study representations in news, advertising, and entertainment media of demographic, social, minority, and occupational groups as well as of health, parenthood, food, religion, violence, gender, politicians, and politics. The contexts of content analysis range from an individual's communication through interpersonal, group, and organizational communication to social networks involving thousands of individuals.

On the plus side, content analysis is unobtrusive. Human participants are not involved. Human research approvals are typically not required though permission to access content and to publish content analysis studies may well be required if the content is unpublished or personal (e.g., diaries, psychiatric records, or e-mails) or proprietary (e.g., corporate records).

A strength of quantitative content analysis is its emphasis on systematic sampling, clear definitions of units, and counting. The procedures should be explicit, precise, and replicable so that other researchers can verify the results of the research. Content analysis can have 100% reliability if the researcher uses computers because content analysis software will automatically code all occurrences of a unit of text the same way. Ultimately, though, computers do nothing but recognize strings of characters.

Human coders can read for meaning, but because this involves judgments about content, the challenge is to have them code with 100% reliability. In principle, this can be accomplished with detailed coding manuals and training. By having each coder code the same content, we can compute intercoder reliability. If the level is unsatisfactory, we may need to train coders until their level of agreement reaches an acceptable level or revisit our coding scheme.

A limitation of content analysis is that it addresses only questions of content. For example, "Have movie representations of global warming changed since the year 2000?" is an appropriate question for content analysis. "Are movie representations of global warming causing more people to donate to environmental causes?" is not a question content analysis can answer (though it may contribute to an answer).

Another limitation is that the method mostly has application if used for comparisons. A "one-shot" survey indicating that 72% of voters would vote for candidate X if the election were held tomorrow produces a finding that is useful to a campaign manager. However, a content analysis indicating that candidate X used the term *patriotism* 17 times in the course of a campaign is not inherently useful information unless it has some point of reference. What we are interested in as content analysts are questions such as "How does the frequency of *patriotism* in candidate X's speeches compare with the frequency of that word in candidate Y's?" or "How do candidates' use of the term *patriotism* compare with their use of the term *environment*?" or "Has the frequency of use of the term *patriotism* increased or decreased over the course of the campaign?"

A further issue is validity. Validity in content analysis can be problematic in terms of relating its findings to the external world. Detecting that the frequency with which the word *patriotism* appears in a politician's speeches has increased over time does not entitle us to assume that the politician has become more patriotic over time; it tells us only that his use of the term has become more frequent. An impassioned speech against patriotism may reveal the same frequency of the word as an equally impassioned speech in favor of it.

In this case, the word *patriotism* needs to be examined in context. One way to do this is to define our units of analysis as sentences or paragraphs rather than words and then code each sentence or paragraph as positive, negative, or neutral with respect to patriotism.

A BASIC CONTENT ANALYSIS

Traditional content analysis can be summarized in one sentence. Simply, it is assigning units of content to predetermined categories and then counting the number of units in each category.

Accomplishing this requires successful completion of several specific steps, as follows:

- Develop a hypothesis or research question about communication content.
- Define the content to be analyzed.
- Sample the content.
- Select units for coding.
- Develop a coding scheme.
- Assign each occurrence of a unit in the sample to a code in the coding scheme.
- Count occurrences of the coded units.
- Report results, patterns of data, and inferences from data.

In this example, we follow a student—James—who has an interest in political biases on campus. He is aware of news media coverage of research suggesting that, overall, higher education faculty members are more likely to be liberal than conservative (see, for example, Jaschik, 2017). If true, a concern stemming from this finding would be that if there is an overt faculty political preference, students might be subject to subtle—or perhaps not-so-subtle—unbalanced political influence in the classroom.

James decides that this topic has both theoretical and practical significance. However, he reasons that interviewing members of the faculty on this topic may not be productive because many will not want to be interviewed or to go public with their political views if they are interviewed. He decides that he can get an unobtrusive measure of both the faculty's political views and willingness to express them by using content analysis.

He reasons that faculty vehicles often carry stickers supporting political candidates. A basic count of these stickers would be an indirect measure of faculty political bias, if the stickers can be linked to a political party, and also a measure of faculty members' willingness to express their views in public. Based on his reasoning and the above content analysis steps, his study might take the form outlined in the rest of the chapter.

Note that James's study is simplified in order to highlight the steps that are typically involved. As you read, you should be able to identify several questions about the study's design that would need to be addressed before James implements it. This study is also the basis of an end-of-chapter exercise. Some of these questions are addressed below under "A Basic Content Analysis: Further Questions."

Research Questions

Research questions or hypotheses are needed to guide or frame the analysis. Especially given the vast amount of content on the web, an implicit research question is needed at least—if only to define the context of the research and limit the content that will be analyzed. In James's case, two possible research questions might be

RQ_1. Do faculty members demonstrate a willingness to publicize their political views?

RQ_2. Do faculty vehicle stickers overall demonstrate a political preference?

Define the Content to Be Analyzed

The analyst needs to define the content of interest, both as a theoretical interest and as a practical matter of limiting the content to be studied.

James limits the content he is interested in to vehicle stickers that specifically support political candidates. These stickers may not identify a specific political party, but most of them will promote candidates whose affiliations he will be able to identify if necessary from party websites or the records of electoral commissions. Although "Save the Whales" and "Yes To Fracking" bumper stickers may each be associated with a political ideology, James reasons that individuals from any party could be in favor of fracking or saving whales and therefore elects not to sample such "cause" bumper stickers. He operationalizes party affiliation as his measure of political preference.

Sample the Content

James decides to sample faculty vehicles, which he defines as vehicles with faculty parking permits on them. He decides to sample faculty vehicles in employee parking lots from late morning through early afternoon, midweek. He reasons that this timing will maximize the number of faculty on campus. He decides on systematic probability sampling. That is, he will use a random number to identify his starting vehicle and will then select every nth vehicle until he has completed his sample of all faculty parking lots. A variety of sampling methods are possible, as discussed in Chapter 6.

Select Units for Coding

Vehicles with faculty parking permits are the sampling units, but they are not the primary focus of interest. What James will record—his recording or coding units—will be campaign stickers and, more specifically, the candidate names on these stickers. He decides to treat multiple names for one party on a sticker, for example a presidential and a vice presidential candidate, as one name because the ultimate objective is to code each sticker by party affiliation, not by candidate. In the event that one vehicle has two or more stickers, each for a different political party, the research question determines the coding. James would address his first research question by coding the vehicle as *having*—as opposed to *not having*—a sticker. To address his second research question, he would code each sticker separately because here he is interested in counting the party affiliation each sticker represents.

Develop a Coding Scheme

Developing a **coding scheme** means developing a classification system or categories into which each sampled unit can be placed. Content analysis requires that all sampled units be placed in a category. Vehicles, for example, can all be categorized by manufacturer, color, or state of registration. James's study is such that he cannot develop a coding scheme in advance of his study because he cannot predict all the candidate names that he is going to find. This means that he will start recording candidate names at the beginning of his study and may well be adding new names to his list at the end of his study. Ultimately, his coding scheme will be the list of candidate names he builds from his sampling of faculty vehicle campaign stickers.

Assign Each Occurrence of a Unit in the Sample to a Code in the Coding Scheme

The number of times each candidate sticker occurs will be counted. To simplify recording, James decides on a simple numbered list. The first name he records will be coded 1, the second name 2, and so on. The numbering will stop at the point where there are no new names to be added. Each repeat name that he finds will get coded with the number assigned to the first occurrence of that name. In this way, every candidate sticker will be coded.

Count Occurrences of the Coded Units

James will end up with a raw data sheet similar to that shown in Exhibit 11.1. For this study, he will have a further step to make and that is to recode each candidate name, as is

EXHIBIT 11.1 ■ Data Coding Sheet for Content Analysis of Political Campaign Stickers				
	Candidate Name	Tally	Count	Political Affiliation
1	Williamson	//////	6	Other
2	Chee	///	3	Other
3	Rowden	/////////	9	Other
4	McLeod	//////////////////	18	Republican
5	Szydlo	//////////	10	Democrat
6	Organ	////////	8	Democrat
etc.	etc.			
None		//////	6	–

necessary, into a party affiliation. He has two options for doing this. As he is interested in overall political affiliations, he may set up a simple three-part coding scheme in advance—"Democrat," "Republican," and "Other"—and assign each candidate name to one of these categories.

If he is planning to look at patterns of affiliation in more detail, another option is to develop categories of political parties that will emerge as he translates candidate names into party affiliation. This means he will end up with a coding scheme such as Democrat, Republican, Green, Rainbow, Communist, Libertarian, Independent, and so on, depending on the candidate affiliations he finds in his sample. Because this coding scheme will cover every party he identifies in his sample, the "Other" category will not be necessary.

In both cases, however, an additional category is necessary—"None"—because James is also interested in the percentage of faculty vehicles with no candidate stickers. In other words, as his systematic sampling takes him across the faculty parking lots, he is also recording the sampled vehicles that have no candidate stickers and coding those vehicles as "None."

The need for this "None" category relates directly to his research questions. James's first research question asked whether faculty were willing to express their political views and operationalized this willingness as the presence or absence of campaign stickers. Therefore, he is obliged to include in his sample both vehicles with stickers and those without them in order to get a measure of what percentage of these have campaign stickers. If he were looking for an answer to only his second research question about political affiliation, he could select only those vehicles with campaign stickers.

Report Results, Patterns of Data, and Inferences From Data

Data reduction is necessary to detect any patterns in the raw data and to make any such patterns comprehensible to readers of the final research report.

Exhibit 11.2 shows the summary data James is now in a position to interpret with respect to his research questions. Ninety percent of the vehicles he sampled have a candidate sticker on them. The answer to his first research question, then, is that the majority of faculty members on campus do appear to be willing to express a political preference publicly—at least on their vehicles. The second research question was whether there was an overall faculty affiliation with one political party more than others. His data for the 90% of vehicles with political stickers show an even split across all three categories—Republican, Democrat, and Other. James could reasonably conclude that his analysis of candidate stickers indicates no predominant political affiliation by faculty. His discussion of his findings would then center on the observation that while a majority of faculty members appear willing to go public with their political affiliations, it is unlikely that they have an overall political mind-set that campus critics should be concerned about.

EXHIBIT 11.2 ■ Summary Data From Exhibit 11.1	
Percentage of Vehicles With Campaign Stickers	54/60 = 90%
Campaign Stickers by Party Affiliation	
Democrat	18/54 = 33%
Republican	18/54 = 33%
Other	18/54 = 33%

A BASIC CONTENT ANALYSIS: FURTHER QUESTIONS

The above study sketches out the basic elements of a quantitative content analysis. As you will see from the academic literature, most content analyses are more complex in practice, for several reasons.

For starters, questions related to type of sample and size of sample become more complex. For example, James—reasonably—defined a faculty vehicle as any vehicle with a faculty parking sticker on it. If the campus parking stickers do not indicate faculty, employee, or student status, he would need another way to identify faculty vehicles specifically. Defining a faculty vehicle as any vehicle in a faculty parking lot would be a possibility, but not a totally defensible one; ask any student who can't find a space in the student parking lot!

If his institution's parking lots cater to all employees, he would be almost totally dependent on parking stickers to identify a faculty vehicle. If the stickers do not differentiate between faculty and staff vehicles, he might be obliged to redefine his population as all employees and sample all employee vehicles, analyze those bumper stickers, and then argue that any political preference he found overall reflects that for the faculty.

James might also want to know whether faculty vehicles belong to full-time or part-time faculty, reasoning that part-time faculty members have less contact with students and therefore less influence than full-time faculty. He would need to consider whether to include part-time faculty vehicles in his sample and, if he does, whether to analyze their bumper stickers separately from those of full-time faculty. A decision to sample the bumper stickers of part-time faculty would bring him full circle back to the "when" of sampling. If part-time professors are more likely to teach evening classes or early morning classes, his initial decision to sample from late morning to early afternoon could result in part-time faculty members being underrepresented in his sample. This is obviously a problem if he wants to include them.

Content analyses typically focus on more lengthy content than bumper stickers, for example, news articles, speeches, or social media exchanges. The content can also be more complex in that it may include graphics, animation, video, and audio. This complexity necessitates serious thinking and planning about units of observation and units of analysis.

For example, James's bumper sticker study has vehicles as units of observation; he is observing vehicles because he has an interest in vehicles that do and do not have political stickers. His units of analysis, however, are bumper stickers because the sticker content is what will answer his question about faculty political orientations.

Units of observation other than bumper stickers are of course possible. For example, James might elect to analyze faculty websites for political orientation, and, if he did, he would have further decisions about what content to sample and analyze. Sampling the institutional websites of faculty members would be theoretically defensible because these sites present the official campus "face" of faculty, but their personal social media accounts might well provide a better insight into their political leanings. If a representative sample of faculty were teaching online classes, and if James were able to access those classes, he might opt to define online classes as his focus of interest and argue that his content analysis of these classes provides a direct measure of faculty political bias (and one better than that obtained by sampling bumper stickers)—at least in the electronic classroom. Revisit Chapter 3 "Guidelines and Questions for Internet Research" to refresh your thinking on the ethics of accessing faculty websites and online classes for research purposes.

Analysts also have coding decisions. The first is whether to establish coding categories on the basis of theory prior to the study (for example, using a simple coding of "for" or "against" an issue) or whether to allow categories to emerge as the study progresses, as was the case with James's recording of candidate names.

Then there is the question of coding units. For example, James is coding a basic unit of language—names of political candidates. If he were analyzing more complex content, such as faculty social media posts, he might elect to code at sentence level and to develop a more nuanced coding scheme in which each sentence with a candidate name in it is assessed as positive, neutral, or negative with respect to the candidate. Similarly, he might code content in terms of major topical issues, such as immigration, taxes, the environment, or international relations, in order to determine which issues a faculty member most associates with a candidate.

Finally, there is the question of inference. The results of an analysis are important, but more important are the inferences drawn from these results. Content is ultimately nothing more than content. James's study, for example, provides no evidence one way or the other that professors might be prone to expressing political views in the classroom, or even that they vote. Making either connection requires much more than content analysis. Even if James had found an overall faculty political orientation, he would still have to develop the argument that willingness to go public by placing a candidate's sticker on one's vehicle translates in any way to a willingness to go public in the classroom. Indeed, a reverse argument might be made that if faculty members feel obligated to restrain their political views in the classroom, they are more likely to express their opinions outside of the classroom in the form of vehicle stickers.

More generally, analysts have to develop evidence and arguments that relate their content findings to a given theoretical interest—the ability of news and entertainment media to shape our views of minority groups, for example.

Important in this process are the prior steps an analyst has taken, such as conducting a literature review, seeking theoretical grounding, developing research questions and sampling procedures, and the like. These steps should all help support the inferences the analyst is trying to draw about the relationship between observed content and human behavior.

James's study has a number of assumptions and problems, some of which are raised in the exercises at the end of this chapter.

CONTENT ANALYSIS OF HUMAN INTERACTION

A conventional use of content analysis is in analyzing media content such as news, entertainment, or advertising (in part because of the ready availability of media content). It can also be applied in such areas as organizational communication and interpersonal communication, particularly as organizations and individuals live their lives on the web. Transcripts of interactions among people constitute texts and are open to content analysis just as much as television advertising, newspaper editorials, or State of the Union addresses.

For example, **interaction analysis**, pioneered by group dynamics scholar Robert Bales (1950), seeks to capture and understand interactions among members of a group and the different roles that group members play. He outlines three broad categories of group behavior: task-oriented, group-oriented, and self-centered behavior. Task-oriented individuals focus on the group's work—for example, asking if the group has all the information it needs or assigning specific tasks to members of the group. Group-oriented individuals work to ensure that the group remains cohesive—for example, by making jokes to relieve tension or by showing

EXHIBIT 11.3 ■ Sample Coding Sheet for Group Behaviors Over Time			
Behavior	**Frequencies of Appearance**		
	Time 1	**Time 2**	**Time 3**
Task-Oriented			
Reminds group members of deadlines			
Proposes solutions to problems			
Group-Oriented			
Makes statements supporting a group idea			
Makes statements approving of group's progress			
Self-Centered			
Refuses assignments			
Makes antagonistic statements			

supportiveness for other members' ideas. Self-centered individuals may refuse to participate or, at the other extreme, may dominate discussions.

Suppose we are looking at the transcripts or a video of a corporate team trying to develop a marketing strategy for a new product. The ebb and flow of discussion over the weeks leading up to the group's final decision can be coded using Bales's categories or subcategories as shown in Exhibit 11.3. Here, the group is the unit of analysis, and we are coding observed behaviors for three different meetings at Time 1, Time 2, and Time 3.

We could use the results of such an analysis to test a hypothesis that group behaviors change over time—for example, that group-oriented behaviors occur more frequently in the preliminary stages as group members clarify their roles and relationships before moving on to task-oriented behaviors. We could compare the results of such analyses for two different groups, one known to produce excellent decisions, the other known to produce mediocre decisions. This might then allow us to identify the characteristics of high-performing groups and provide a basis for training low-performing groups to do better. We could also use exactly the same criteria to analyze individual behaviors. For example, if we were to replace "Time 1," "Time 2," and "Time 3" in the chart with "Person 1," "Person 2," and "Person 3," we could record, analyze, and compare the behaviors of those individuals.

We could also combine both approaches and record individual behavior over time. Note that if we did record the behavior of each individual at different times, we would have a within-subjects design (Chapter 10). Such data are not statistically independent, and we would need a more sophisticated statistical test to assess any changes over time. By contrast, the data from the study of bumper stickers are statistically independent, and a simple chi-square test may serve to assess whether the distribution of bumper stickers shows significant variation.

CONTENT ANALYSIS OF THE WEB

The appeal of the web to content analysts is ready and inexpensive access to a huge diversity of content from a variety of media types and sources worldwide. Because web content includes communications within and between social networks, it offers the potential to analyze the dynamics of human interaction as well as traditional content such as documents. Analysts can generate a defined sample of content (say, a month of tweets on a given topic) or bypass sampling and analyze an entire population of content. Indeed, given the availability of software that can capture and analyze an entire population of content, the question of whether to sample at all arises. For example, Giglietto and Selva (2014) examined 2,489,669 tweets spanning an entire season (1,076 episodes) of talk shows. Web content may be ephemeral—for example, news sites constantly update their content—raising a further question of when to record and sample content. Once these decisions are made, however, sampling and coding can be programmed and automated using criteria the analyst selects.

Conventional analytic techniques face new challenges and opportunities because of the size, complexity, and ephemerality of web content. Size raises problems of sampling and archiving. Complexity raises problems of processing not only text but also audio, video, location data, and metadata. Ephemerality raises problems of data capture, sampling, and the possibility of the researcher missing important content altogether.

As discussed in Chapter 9, a concern with web sampling is not fully knowing the relationship between the sample and the population from which it is drawn. Web data may be incomplete from the researchers' point of view, for example, lacking information about the source of content, or these data may be inaccessible, as in the case of some e-mails. Samples may be biased for human reasons (e.g., some individuals are more active than others on social networks), for technical reasons (e.g., some individuals have differing levels of web access due to bandwidth, computer platforms, and operating systems), or for political reasons (e.g., citizen access to the Internet is controlled by a government).

A particular concern for content analysis is the ability of software to recognize and analyze the subtleties of human language and meaning, for example, humor. Against that is the potential for computer analysis to identify aspects of content that a human analyst with human biases may not identify.

Typically, analysis of web content involves acquiring, storing, and preparing data before analyzing it. These are the same generic steps that would apply to any computerized analysis of content, but when an analyst is dealing with the huge data sets available from the web, acquiring and storing data in particular demand additional attention.

There are two starting points for acquiring web content—use existing content or build your own body of content. Existing content should be familiar to you from your academic libraries. For example, LexisNexis provides a searchable database of news articles. The EBSCO newspaper source provides full-text newspaper articles as well as television and radio news transcripts.

Software tools for building your own body of data include **web crawling**, **web scraping**, and APIs, or application programming interfaces. Web crawling software starts with a given **URL** or web address and then searches for additional linked URLs, although not all websites will permit web crawling. Scraping software is then used to collect and store documents defined by the researcher. An **API** is software written to access web-based software such as social media platforms; it can be used for communication research such as monitoring and analyzing web content and activity.

Acquiring content may be more or less difficult depending on the nature of the source. For example, content aggregators such as Google News and Apple News offer ready access to content from thousands of publishers worldwide, as well as the ability to customize your flow of articles. Websites such as blogs and podcasts are mostly public, almost by definition.

Social network sites may be less accessible and have controls over who can or cannot access them. Some sites may allow partial but not whole access, which presents a sampling problem. For full access to content, a researcher may need to submit a special request or join a network as a member, which raises some of the ethical issues discussed in Chapter 3.

Storing or archiving data can be as simple as using the "Save Page" menu item for a web page, although this will not necessarily save all the content. An alternate action is to save the page as a **pdf** document. **Cloud storage** sites such as Dropbox and Google Drive offer web-based storage for web and other content. These sites are also offered by Microsoft, Apple, Amazon, and other hosting companies and may be free, up to a limit, if you have an account with the company.

Preparing and analyzing data are discussed below.

COMPUTER ANALYSIS OF CONTENT

Content, be it massive web data or more modest examples such as speeches or newspaper editorials, needs to be prepared for computer analysis. Hand in hand with this preparation, the analyst will need to train the analytic software to recognize content.

The power of software to process large amounts of content does not mean that the researcher can go on "autopilot" and avoid developing a defensible coding scheme, data analysis procedures, and careful software programming.

It can be a complex and finicky operation to train software. For example, many words such as *right*, *jam*, and *squash* have multiple meanings. **Disambiguation** is the process of examining a word in its context and assigning it the most appropriate out of several possible meanings. Without training in disambiguation, software will be unable to distinguish whether the word *right* is being used in the sense of "not wrong," "not left," or the verb form "to correct."

Without training with respect to hyphenation, compound words, capitalization, and foreign word equivalents, a computer will not know whether to regard *United States* and *united states* as four different terms, two terms, or the same term. Similarly, *nighttime, grasshopper, sunglasses,* and *low-profile* can each be read as one term or as two. *Neighbor* and *neighbour* can be read as two different words or as the same, depending on the software's programming.

Computer analyses may be simplified by **stemming**, **lemmatization**, and the removal of **stop words**. Stemming means changing all variations of a word to its basic stem. For example, *fish, fishing, fished, fisherman,* and *fisher* can all be stemmed to *fish*. This means instead of identifying five separate words, the software will count the occurrence of the basic term *fish* five times. Lemmatization works similarly by grouping words together based on their basic dictionary definition so that they can be analyzed as a single item—for example, *car* and *automobile* have no common stem, but both can be described by the term *vehicle*. Similarly, *trout, cod, shark,* and *marlin* cannot be stemmed, but all of them can be lemmatized under the basic dictionary definition of *fish*. Stop words are high frequency words such as pronouns (I, we, you) and prepositions (in, under). Ignatow and Mihalcea (2018) suggest that such words can provide insight on personalities and behaviors, but there are times when it is useful to remove them in order to focus on nouns and verbs.

Preparing content can be done with the variety of software that is available for both quantitative and qualitative analyses, but your word-processing software offers some of the functions of this software. For example, the "find and replace" command can perform many of the above functions, albeit using a more laborious process. If word frequency is your only interest, and your documents are short, you can simply use the "search" function to find how many occurrences of a word a document has. This will also show you how key words are used in context—**KWIC**, in content-analysis shorthand.

You might, for example, search this chapter for sentences containing *content analysis* to decide how many sentences refer to content as qualitative versus quantitative, whether the sentences describe content analysis or evaluate it, and whether the evaluative sentences are positive or negative. You can also request readability statistics, which will give you no insight on content as such but will give you measures of average word and sentence length as well as a readability score for documents.

Content acquisition, storage, and preparation provide the basis for traditional content analyses that study, for example, how news coverage of topics such as gender or global warming has changed over time. They are also a basis for simple tasks, such as finding information on a given topic; for more complex tasks, such as analyzing themes and narratives and identifying authors or author characteristics from their texts; and for solving challenging topical problems, such as identifying deceptive content and differentiating legitimate e-mail from spam.

The contexts of such analyses range from literary analysis to the analysis of human interactions to criminal and security investigations.

CONTENT ANALYSIS AS QUANTITATIVE AND QUALITATIVE

Every component of Berelson's (1952) concept of content analysis—as a quantitative, systematic, and objective technique for describing the manifest content of communications—has been contested. As we will see in Chapter 12, there are many qualitative approaches to the analysis of content, and analyses need not be systematic or objective.

Neuendorf (2017), for example, argues for a scientific, quantitative approach to the analysis of content, while allowing for qualitative, subjective analyses. She maintains that qualitative and quantitative approaches may coexist in any given study and that the dividing line between the two may be thin. She also proposes a distinction between the phenomena studied and the analyses applied to them. For example, one can use quantitative analysis to investigate qualitative phenomena such as emotional states; conversely, quantitative studies ultimately require qualitative interpretations.

Krippendorf (2013, p. 24) defines content analysis as "a research technique for making replicable and valid inferences from texts (or other meaningful matter) to the contexts of their use," a definition that contains none of the defining words listed at the beginning of this chapter—*quantitative, systematic, objective, manifest*. He proposes that quantification is not an end in itself; that using numbers is a convenience, not a requirement; and that qualitative analyses follow many of the steps of quantitative analyses, though perhaps less explicitly.

He questions the validity and usefulness of the distinction between quantitative and qualitative content analyses and notes that qualitative methods have proven successful in analyses of propaganda, psychotherapeutic assessments, ethnographic research, discourse analysis, and computer text analysis. "Ultimately, all reading of texts is qualitative, even when certain characteristics of a text are later converted into numbers (p. 22)."

Babbie (2013, p. 330) defines content analysis simply as "the study of recorded human communications"—about as wide-ranging a definition as one could get—and allows for qualitative analyses and the study of latent content.

Latent or hidden content is content to which the analyst assigns a meaning. For example, manifest content might be a cartoon character demonstrably waving a sword or gun. On the basis of such observable content, an analyst might code a character as "sword," "gun," "other," or "unarmed." In terms of latent content though, the analyst might opt to code characters as either "violent" or "nonviolent" using the presence of weapons as a criterion even though she sees no explicit acts of violence. Obviously, this is a subjective judgment. With latent content particularly, researchers bring their own meaning to the content rather than assuming that there is one specific identifiable common meaning manifest in the observable content.

Qualitative analyses become appropriate when the analyst seeks to interpret or critique a body of content or to investigate in depth beyond what some might argue is the superficial and reductive counting of quantitative analyses. That said, qualitative analyses that involve no explicit coding or counting may still have some quantitative basis in that they use quantifying expressions such as "often," "commonly," "absent," "rare," or "frequently" in their analyses.

Rather than making a qualitative-quantitative distinction, the researcher should more appropriately think of a family of methods for understanding human records. One important branch of that family is characterized by the scientific method. These analyses are designed in advance, systematic, and follow explicit rules and procedures. Conceptual aspects of the content are operationalized and measured in a way that can be replicated by other scholars. There is a concern for both reliability and validity of findings. Basically, a body of content is systematically sampled and coded in order to answer a pre-posed, theoretically informed research question—one often based on the relationship between some aspect of the content and some phenomenon external to it.

In contrast, another branch of the family of research methods may see the researcher engaging with the content and looking for patterns or themes to emerge during the research process. Often the researcher is a part of her research; that is, she is following her own theoretical or intuitive path that is theoretically defensible but not necessarily replicable.

Such analyses may involve a close reading of relatively small amounts of content rather than measuring predetermined variables. The analyst may be content to examine quotations or arguments that shed light on an author's motivations or that explain the personality behind the content or why the argument in a text is or is not effective. The analysis is an individual enterprise with no assumption that the results of the study will be generalizable. It is an exercise in understanding or explication rather than in testing for relationships among variables, and it may be more in depth with more complex reasoning than a quantitative study.

These differing approaches to researching content reflect the differing worldviews and the goals, values, and purposes of research familiar to you from Chapter 2. Specific qualitative approaches are discussed further in Chapter 12.

ETHICS PANEL
COULD CONTENT ANALYSIS RESULT IN HARM?

Content analysis methods generally focus on text and/or graphic media content and mostly do not require human research participants. Why, therefore, would such methods have an impact on individuals that might give rise to ethical concerns?

Consider the applications, overt or covert, of content analysis in the world of electronic communication.

Many software packages offer e-mail administrators a way of monitoring incoming e-mail for "spam," viruses, and attempts at "phishing." Outgoing e-mail can also be monitored and analyzed to prevent sensitive content leaving an organization or to identify potential policy violations and thus protect intellectual property, company reputation, and business relationships. Content analysis of employee e-mail is routine in many organizations for all such reasons. While we can be thankful for e-mail spam filters that themselves are based on the analysis of incoming e-mail message content, we might well see such monitoring as an invasion of privacy if applied to our own e-mail.

Content analysts face many of the ethical issues discussed in Chapter 3 when they use human coders to code visual content such as movies or comics that contain explicit sex, violence, or hate messages. Human coders may be part of the research team but can be expected to have the same responses as research participants exposed to such content as part of a study.

Potential ethical issues arise with personal or sensitive electronic content such as medical records or physician-patient e-mails. Although the content may appear anonymous, there is always the possibility that any embedded message data could be used to identify participants.

Questions

- In what ways could the knowledge that one's business or personal communications are being monitored and analyzed cause psychological distress?

- Should the institutional review boards (IRBs) responsible for the safety of human subjects be required to review content analysis studies even if no human participants are studied directly? Why or why not? Revisit Chapter 3 for more detail on IRBs.

- With respect to obtaining permissions, should content analysts treat personal or business e-mails, Internet discussion content, and correspondence differently from television commercials or newspaper pages? Why or why not?

- Should the ethical and legal protections offered to research participants exposed to disturbing graphic content also be offered to the members of a research team analyzing such content? Why or why not?

Chapter Summary

- Content analysis is a process of systematically sampling, coding, and analyzing media content.

- Content analysis techniques can be applied to both textual and visual content.

- The steps in a basic content analysis are as follows: define content to be analyzed; sample content; select units for coding; develop a coding scheme; code each occurrence of a unit; count occurrences of the coded units; and report results, patterns of data, and inferences from data.

- Content analysis software can analyze large data sets quantitatively or qualitatively but requires careful programming.

- Quantitative content analyses have qualitative interpretations and may be used to study qualitative phenomena.

Key Terms

API 229	KWIC 231	stop words 230
cloud storage 230	latent 220	URL 229
coding scheme 224	lemmatization 230	web crawling 229
content analysis 220	manifest 220	web scraping 229
disambiguation 230	pdf 230	
interaction analysis 227	stemming 230	

Application Exercises

Exercise 1: Warming Up With Wordle

Wordle (www.wordle.net) is a word cloud generator. Paste your selected content into Wordle to generate a word cloud that displays the most frequent words as the largest. Other generators, with varying levels of control, are easily found with a search for "word cloud generator."

Exercise 2: A Basic Content Analysis

Review the content analysis of vehicle campaign stickers outlined at the beginning of this chapter. What basic assumptions about faculty, vehicles, campaign stickers, sampling, and coding could be challenged? What problems can you identify with the sampling decisions made here? List the factors that might influence the composition of the sample.

Exercise 3: News Media Bias

Both ends of the political spectrum complain about biased reporting by the news media. Set out the basic elements of a content analysis project that would answer the question of whether a particular news medium is biased toward or against a political figure, government policy, or program. Identify the content you would sample from, the units of analysis, and the coding scheme you would use.

HINT: Visit the Rensselaer Polytechnic Institute NELA (News Landscape) Toolkit at http://nelatoolkit.science/. You can check online news for such attributes as objectivity and political impartiality.

Exercise 4: Stereotyping in Entertainment Media and Advertising

A criticism of advertising and entertainment media such as movies and television is the stereotyping of people by gender, ethnicity, occupation, or age, for example. Pick one of these types (for example, occupational stereotyping) and outline a content analysis study that would test for the presence or absence of stereotyping. Define the content you would sample from, the units of analysis, and the coding scheme you would use. Note that for this exercise you will need some operational definition of stereotyping so that you can identify it and code it when you see it.

Exercise 5: Analyzing Online Harassment: Quantitatively

A Pew Research Center study reported by Maeve Duggan (2014) asked respondents about six different forms of online harassment. The study also provides selected quotations about harassment from those surveyed at www.pewinternet .org/2014/10/22/online-harassment-experiences-in-their-own-words.

Using the steps described in this chapter, do a quantitative analysis of selected quotations from the above survey and report your conclusions. In Chapter 12, you will be invited to think about analyzing the same data qualitatively.

The full report, questionnaire, and respondent comments are available at www.pewinternet.org/2014/10/22/ online-harassment.

A 2017 update of this survey, which excluded the "In Their Own Words" content of the 2014 survey, is available at http://www.pewinternet.org/2017/07/11/online-harassment-2017/

Recommended Web Resources

Web-based resources for and about content analysis are many, ever changing, may or may not work across all platforms, and may or may not be free. For major social media sites, we recommend a search for current analytic software that will allow analysis of the site's traffic and content. Your own social media homepages will help with content search and retrieval strategies. You will be able to access many news sources, such as the EBSCO Newspaper Source, through your campus library.

Software for qualitative content analysis is listed at the end of Chapter 12.

Annenberg Robert Wood Johnson Media Health Coding Project.........www.youthmediarisk.org
An ongoing project analyzing media content for health-related behaviors. Look at the codebook and sampling procedures in particular.

Google Ngram.........https://books.google.com/ngrams/info
An online search engine that charts the frequencies of a search term in sources printed between 1500 and 2008.

Google Trends.........https://trends.google.com/trends/
Displays search terms over time by region; can compare with other search terms.

National Centre for Research Methods.........www.restore.ac.uk/lboro

A site on content analysis methods; it includes a comparison of software packages for qualitative data analysis.

Pew Research Center Content Analysis.........https://www.pewresearch.org/methods/about-content-analysis/
An overview of Pew Research Center's content analysis.

Text Analysis Overview.........www.textanalysis.info
Links and news on text analysis software.

Software

Evernote.........http://evernote.com
For archiving and organizing social media messages and other content.

Leximancer.........https://info.leximancer.com
For concept mapping and text and sentiment analysis.

Opinion Finder, MPQA (Multi-Perspective Question Answering).........http://mpqa.cs.pitt.edu/opinionfinder
For opinion mining.

Visual Web Ripper.........www.visualwebripper.com
For automated web scraping and content extraction.

Wordsmith 7.0..........https://lexically.net/wordsmith/version7
For keyword searches, word lists and statistics.

References

Babbie, E. (2013). *The practice of social research.* Belmont, CA: Wadsworth Cengage Learning.

Bales, R. (1950). *Interaction process analysis: A method for the study of small groups.* Reading, MA: Addison-Wesley.

Becker, A. B., & Goldberg, A. B. (2017). Entertainment, intelligent, or hybrid programming? An automated content analysis of 12 years of political satire interviews. *Atlantic Journal of Communication, 25*(2), 127–137. DOI: 10.1080/15456870.2017.1293670

Berelson, B. (1952). *Content analysis in communication research.* New York, NY: Hafner.

Diddi, P., & Lundy, L. K. (2017). Organizational Twitter use: Content analysis of tweets during Breast Cancer Awareness Month. *Journal of Health Communication, 22*(3), 243–253. DOI: 10.1080/10810730.2016.1266716

Duggan, M. (2014, October 22). *Online harassment* [Report]. Washington, DC: Pew Research Center, Internet & Technology. Retrieved from https://www.pewinternet.org/2014/10/22/online-harassment/

Epps, A. C., & Dixon, T. L. (2017). A comparative content analysis of anti- and prosocial rap lyrical themes found on traditional and new media outlets. *Journal of Broadcasting & Electronic Media, 61*(2), 467–498. DOI: 10.1080/08838151.2017.1309411

Giglietto, F., & Selva, D. (2014). Second screen and participation: A content analysis on a full season dataset of tweets. *Journal of Communication, 64*(2), 260–277. DOI: 10.1111/jcom.12085

Hurwitz, L. B., Montague, H., & Wartella, E. (2017). Food marketing to children online: A content analysis of food company websites. *Health Communication, 32*(3), 366–371. DOI: 10.1080/10410236.2016.1138386

Ignatow, G., & Mihalcea, R. (2018). *An introduction to text mining: Research design, data collection, and analysis.* Thousand Oaks, CA: Sage.

Ivory, A. H., Ivory, J. D., Wu, W., Limperos, A. M., Andrew, N., & Sesler, B. S. (2017). Harsh words and deeds: Systematic content analyses of offensive user behavior in the virtual environments of online first-person shooter games. *Journal of Virtual Worlds Research, 10*(2), 1–17. DOI: 10.4101/jvwr.v10i2.7274

Jaschik, S. (2017, February 27). Professors and politics: What the research says. *Inside Higher Ed.* Retrieved from https://www.insidehighered.com/news/2017/02/27/research-confirms-professors-lean-left-questions-assumptions-about-what-means

Krippendorff, K. (2013). *Content analysis: An introduction to its methodology* (3rd ed.). Thousand Oaks, CA: Sage.

Mastro, D., & Figueroa-Caballero, A. (2018). Measuring extremes: A quantitative content analysis of prime time TV depictions of body type. *Journal of Broadcasting & Electronic Media, 62*(2), 320–336. DOI: 10.1080/08838151.2018.1451853

Neuendorf, K. A. (2017). *The content analysis guidebook* (2nd ed.). Thousand Oaks, CA: Sage.

Perrault, E. K. (2018). Campus health centers' lack of information regarding providers: A content analysis of Division-I campus health centers' provider websites. *Health Communication, 33*(7), 860–866. DOI:10.1080/10410236.2017.1316635

Sarge, M. A., & Knobloch-Westerwick, S. (2017). Mechanisms of influence for weight loss in popular women's health media: A content analysis of health and fitness magazines. *Journal of Communication in Healthcare, 10*(4), 260–272. DOI: 10.1080/17538068.2017.1327128

Šerić, M. (2018). Content analysis of the empirical research on IMC from 2000 to 2015. *Journal of Marketing Communications, 24*(7), 647–685. DOI: 10.1080/13527266.2016.1184708

$SAGE edge™

Get the tools you need to sharpen your study skills. SAGE edge offers a robust online environment featuring an impressive array of free tools and resources.

Access quizzes, eFlashcards, video, and multimedia at **edge.sagepub.com/treadwell4e**.

12

QUALITATIVE UNDERSTANDING OF CONTENT

Rhetorical and Critical Analyses, and More

"Hey Mike! Wanna grab a cup of coffee?"

"Absolutely not!"

"I thought you loved coffee?"

"I do, which is why I absolutely refuse to grab one."

"What's the big deal with grabbing?

"'Grabbing is fast, pushy, in-a-hurry, slurp-it-down, don't-think-about-it coffee. Who wants that? I sit back and think about coffee—who grew it, where it came from. I appreciate taste, smell, appearance. Every bean tells a story, you know. My coffee's not for grabbing."

"That was eloquent, but what about the rest of us?"

"Easy! You can just drink a coffee, sample a coffee, enjoy a coffee . . . or we might even unwind over a coffee together. Anything but grab a coffee!"

"I'll settle for just drinking one right now. It's still the same coffee you know."

"Not true. Language defines coffee—as it does everything else. Relabel your basic cup of joe as barista-crafted, organic, aged, estate coffee and some people will pay twice as much."

"OK. Guilty as charged. Language does things to us and for us. How do you prove that though?"

"I'm not sure you can prove it with stats or anything like that, but you can easily demonstrate language at work."

"Like?"

"Like campus administrators referring to us all as 'community' or 'family.' Why would they do that?"

"Easy. Communities are supposed to have shared values and family members are supposed to get on with each other, right? That's what they want to see happening."

"Yeah, like all the orientation and commencement stories. They're all the same—work hard and succeed. It's like they're all modeling how we're supposed to behave."

"My reading of Chapter 2 tells me you're becoming a critical theorist."

"That aside, I bet there's a lot of language you could look at. Like what gets recognized or dropped out of our campus history or the arguments for and against changing the name of our sports teams or how the administration argues for a fee increase or. . . ."

"Or like what's in the rest of this chapter?"

"That too."

CHAPTER OVERVIEW

This chapter provides an overview of some primarily qualitative approaches to understanding and explicating content, including these:

- Rhetorical and dramatistic analyses—the study of argumentation and persuasion

- Narrative, discourse, and conversation analyses—the study of stories and talking

- Semiotics—the study of signs, interpretation, and meaning

- Critical analyses—the study of the forces behind the content

These approaches share a common interest in using words rather than numbers to understand, interpret, and report content, but the approaches can differ considerably in perspective. For example, conversation analysts look closely, second by second, at transcripts of conversations to understand human interaction whereas **rhetoricians** are more likely to step back and analyze the strategic use of language in order to assess the persuasive power of a speech or advertisement. This chapter in particular captures the concept behind the book's subtitle, "Paths of Inquiry." As you follow the examples in this chapter, you should see that qualitative analyses of text offer you many different paths to understanding and explaining communication content.

CHAPTER OBJECTIVES

This chapter will help you

- Describe the advantages and disadvantages of the qualitative analyses of content.

- Explain, with examples,
  - the main types of rhetorical analysis;
  - narrative, metaphor, and discourse analyses;
  - semiotic analysis; and
  - critical analyses and the assumptions underlying them.

- Describe the basic concepts and coding used in conversation analysis.

INTRODUCTION: ADVANTAGES AND DISADVANTAGES OF QUALITATIVE ANALYSES OF CONTENT

One advantage of the methods discussed in this chapter is that they offer a multiplicity of approaches to understanding text and image. Any text, image, or documented human interaction is potentially capable of being analyzed from multiple perspectives.

The analytic approaches outlined in this chapter are diverse but share a common interest in interpretation—that is, in understanding what content analysts might refer to as the latent content of communication. As you will recall from Chapter 11, the primary interest of traditional content analysis is in categorizing and counting manifest or observable content. The approaches in this chapter go beyond developing a taxonomy of content; they also seek to understand and interpret content. Suppose, for example, that a quantitative analysis of comedy television demonstrates that certain occupations are played predominantly by minority actors. The approaches in this chapter would help in the analysis of the same content but with a view to describing, understanding, and explaining, for example, how these minority characters interact with other characters; who the heroes and villains are and how we know which is which; how viewers' perceptions of minorities are shaped by language and image; what aspects of the characters' speech make them credible or not; or what interests are served by portraying minorities and occupations in a particular way.

The possibility of multiple interpretations for any given content can frustrate the interested reader seeking a definitive interpretation, but scholars using the approaches in this chapter are generally interested in interpretive possibilities. They accept that there can be more than one way of understanding content and that different interpretations may be equally valid, and they may well take the view that one definitive interpretation is impossible. To revisit the metaphor introduced in Chapter 1, researchers simply opt to use different modes of transport to get to their destinations.

If qualitative methods can be accused of being somehow less than precise, they can also be credited with providing close readings and multiple perspectives that enhance our understanding. These readings and perspectives result in a rich, ongoing discussion of how human communication should be understood and in insights that numbers alone cannot provide.

RHETORICAL ANALYSES

We begin this discussion with one of the oldest approaches to understanding human communication—rhetoric—and with a founding figure of communication theory—Aristotle.

Aristotelian Analysis

The Greek philosopher Aristotle (384–322 BCE) viewed **rhetoric** as the discovery of the available means of persuasion in any given situation. In this context, **rhetorical analysis** (or **Aristotelian analysis**) means examining communication content to identify and assess its persuasive strategies. Rhetorical analyses today can be used to assess the persuasiveness of advertising, editorial columns and blogs, social media, and the persuasive strategies of the corporations, nonprofits, government agencies, and individuals behind such content.

Aristotle proposed that the purpose of argumentation was not to discover verifiable absolute truths but rather to influence belief—to affect what people thought was true. Argumentation, therefore, was based on probability. It meant appealing to audiences in such a way that they were left with the highest level of certainty that the argument was valid.

It is unfair to distill the breadth and richness of Aristotle's writings down to just a few concepts, but his identification of **logos**, **pathos**, and **ethos** as keys to successful persuasion remain an enduring contribution to communication research in the 21st century.

- Logos addresses the use of fact and logic. The assumption is that audiences engage in rational decision making and so the speaker can lead audiences through such thought processes as induction and deduction (Chapter 2) to arrive at a conclusion.

- Pathos addresses the use of emotion. For better or worse, humans are not cold-blooded logic machines. Aristotle recognized that the variety of human emotions might also lead individuals to prefer one argument to another. He wrote about common human emotions, recognizing that an orator could draw on emotion to be persuasive.

- Ethos addresses the nature or character of the speaker. For Aristotle, ethos was the most important of these three modes of persuasion. Rational argument and appeal to emotions would have little or no effect unless the audience saw the speaker as credible and of good character.

Credibility and good character are, of course, in the mind of the beholder. A fourth and important consideration in Aristotelian rhetoric, therefore, was the audience and its characteristics. The nature of the audience was what drove the nature of the speech. Related, Aristotle identified sources or topics that might help an orator develop a persuasive argument. He identified special topics for use in legal settings, ceremonial settings, and deliberative or political settings. A speech appropriate to one setting would not be appropriate to another. We can see Aristotle's ideas at work in the 21st century. A politician, for example, tailors a speech to a specific audience and invests a great deal of effort in convincing voters of the speaker's good character.

Analyzing persuasive content such as speeches, advertising, and editorials using an Aristotelian framework gives us insight on whether the content might or might not be effective. In analyzing an advertisement, for example, we might examine the nature and character of the spokesperson, the use of fact and logic, and the use of emotion. While this can be done purely from the researcher's perspective, in principle, the assessment is done with respect to the effect of the content on the target audience.

Dramatistic Analysis

Kenneth Burke, a 20th-century literary theorist, devised an interpretive approach to communication behavior called dramatism or **dramatistic analysis**. He regarded communication essentially as performance, as actors acting out a drama against a particular background or scenario.

Burke's **dramatistic pentad** (five-part) analysis asks the following questions:

- **Act**—what act is taking place?

- **Agent**—who is taking this action?

- **Agency**—how or by what means did the act take place?

- **Scene**—where and when did the act take place?

- **Purpose**—why was the act done?

Burke believed that by examining the first four components of the pentad, one could obtain an answer to the question posed by the fifth—what was the purpose or motivation of the act?

Burke proposed that information about the dynamics and motivations of communication could be obtained by "ratio analysis." **Ratio analysis** means examining the relative significance of each pentad unit in any given situation, for example act-scene, act-agent, act-agency, act-purpose, agent-agency, agent-scene, and so on. By examining all of these ratios, we can gain insight into the motives behind the communication, uncover a dominant motivation, or reveal inconsistencies between elements.

In Chapter 13, we examine another approach to the study of human communication as performance—performance studies—more specifically.

Fantasy Theme Analysis

Fantasy theme analysis, pioneered by professor Ernest Bormann (1972), is a method of rhetorical analysis that provides a way of understanding group consciousness and the development of shared values. Fantasy themes are sagas, stories, or ideas shared by members of a group. These themes give members of the group a common perspective, motivate them, and provide a shared understanding of the group's accomplishments. As with Burke's dramatistic analysis, fantasies involve characters in a setting acting out a theme or plotline. Fantasies typically emerge out of uncertainty as to what the group is all about or how it should handle a new, problematic situation. Over time, competing stories emerge of how the group in its situation should be understood. Eventually, one **master narrative** gains credence with members to the point of **symbolic convergence** or an agreed-upon understanding of what unites group members, differentiates the group from other groups, and explains the group's successes or failures.

The role of the researcher using fantasy theme analysis is to identify the characters involved in the fantasy, the scene, the plotline, the rationale or logic behind the fantasy, and the **master analog** or deeper structure within the vision. Basically, the analyst seeks to uncover the collective vision that sustains the organization or group. The raw material for fantasy theme analysis can include interviews with group members, organizational histories, mission statements, and the like, as well as even seemingly minor items such as bumper stickers that capture and remind members of the fantasy in three or four words.

A strength of the method is its ability to explain what at first sight might seem to be illogical behaviors. For example, tax resisters or small start-up companies competing against giants in the marketplace might logically recognize that they are fighting against a superior force and will ultimately lose based on their relative lack of resources. A logical decision would be to quit while it is still possible to do so—and before arrest or bankruptcy happens.

It seems illogical to fight a losing battle, but from a careful analysis of documents, speeches, and policy statements, the fantasy theme analyst might discover that group members have adopted a David and Goliath fantasy—the notion that one individual "in the right" can beat a larger foe—and that this idea motivates them and explains an otherwise illogical behavior. For some such groups, a powerful vision is the fantasy of martyrdom—the vision that there can be no higher calling than to give up one's life for a worthy cause. In that context, a public defeat of the cause is not to be avoided but to be welcomed because of the reward of a blessed future that martyrdom will bring.

Fantasy theme analysis as the study of sagas and stories and visions has a close relationship to narrative analysis.

NARRATIVE ANALYSIS

Narrative analysis is an analysis of the formal properties of the stories that people tell and the social role that stories play. It generally attempts to identify the plot, setting, characters, and order of events in people's accounts of their lives.

Narratives take on a special meaning depending on the social context, and they provide meaning to members of that social context. Very likely, you will recall narratives told when you first moved into a dormitory, started work, or joined a sports team or social group. Typically, these narratives are important because they provide examples of the values of an organization and of the unofficial but important rules that govern its behavior. For example, a simple narrative from the workplace might describe how a new employee started work showing an impressive display of tattoos, was sent home by a supervisor to cover up, and returned to work wearing clothing that hid the tattoos (or possibly did not return to work). Such a narrative demonstrates expected standards of behaviors to new group members and shows who has the power to enforce them.

Similar narratives are told in informal settings such as families and transmit to family members the values and the attributes that make the family unique. The narratives make sense only in the social group within which they are told. The story of uncle Harry riding his bicycle in the snow has a meaning for Uncle Harry's family that it would not have for other families, and this narrative helps define how his family differs from others.

Narrative analysis pays specific attention to how stories play out over time and how events are sequenced from beginning to end. Analysts may be interested in how narratives are used to mark out the identities of a group and differentiate the group from others. They may focus on the formal properties of stories—that is, the plot, setting, characters, and order of events. They may analyze how stories are reproduced, change over time, change as a result of the settings in which they are told, or are used politically to influence attitudes and behaviors. Analysts may also be interested in identifying key events or "triggers" that flag a vital learning experience or the point at which an organization changed its vision or culture.

The raw material of narrative analysis includes organizational documents, such as mission statements and histories, and can also include interviews with organizational members who might be asked specifically to tell stories they have heard, describe key events, or perhaps even talk about the weirdest thing or the funniest thing that happened to them in their organization.

METAPHOR ANALYSIS

The vocabulary of any group includes the analogies and metaphors used by members to explain and interpret their group and to help simplify the complexities and ambiguities that are part of any organization. One such summary device is metaphor—a simple term used to categorize or summarize a more complex entity or concept. You hear metaphors on a daily basis: "This class is hell," "That music was heaven," or "On this campus, we are all family." None of these statements is literally true, but each captures in a brief, compelling way what the experience or organization behind it is all about. Thus, the "family"-type metaphor simplifies the complexities of a large organization so that its members can easily comprehend it. Metaphors include direction (he was "up" or "down"), color (she was "feeling blue" or "in the pink"), and activities (it's not "war" or "rocket science," but, until we got "cooking" it was like "herding cats").

Metaphor analysis includes a search for the basic or root metaphors that shape the way organizational members think. The raw materials of such research are once again documents and careful interviews with organizational members, as well as the answers to specific questions that probe for analogies and metaphors in use and for a **root metaphor** such as *family* or *team* that both explains and drives an organization.

The search for governing or root metaphors is inductive; it is built from specific observations of the language in use on up to a conclusion about metaphors. The root metaphor itself may not be apparent or in common use as a word or phrase. Researchers entering an organization and asking each member "Excuse me, are you a tree?" are likely to be met with looks of befuddlement or even propositions about the researcher's sanity. On the other hand, careful interviewing may reveal the fact that words such as *roots*, *branches*, *growth*, *decay*, and *change* are more commonly used than words such as *kill*, *defend*, *attack*, and *territory*. A reasonable conclusion from this observation is that the organization or group is best explained by a root metaphor of a living organism growing, changing, adapting, and perhaps being pacifist, at least relative to the root metaphor of war suggested by the second set of terms.

DISCOURSE ANALYSIS

From a research perspective, Curt (1994) refers to **discourse** as interest in the constructive, productive, or pragmatic uses of language. This interest in how language is used emerges from the recognition that "language can never neutrally describe the world, because language itself is an active part of the world" (p. 234). **Discourse analysis** focuses on how language shapes meaning and our understanding of events and how particular labels or concepts are developed and made powerful by the use of language.

Discourse analysis has several roots—sociology of knowledge, cultural analysis, rhetoric, the psychology of human interaction, and **conversation analysis** (introduced below). Predictably, then, there are a variety of approaches to discourse analysis, but most analysts would agree that they share a common interest in language as a social practice more than in the characteristics of the language itself. They are interested in the frameworks within which ideas are formulated and how ideas and concepts give meaning to physical and social realities.

For example, an analyst might ask what configurations of advertising, news coverage, consumer reviews, web content, and perhaps the writings and speeches of Steve Jobs and Bill Gates led to the perception of two "computer cultures"—Mac and PC. The raw data for discourse analysis often can be found in politics and contentious public issues. For example, an analyst might study how the language of the "right to life" movement versus that of the "reproductive rights" movement shapes public views about abortion, or how the language of the "defense hawks" versus that of fiscal conservatives shapes views—and decisions—on defense spending. Also about a political and contentious issue, a study by O'Regan and Riordan (2018) used critical discourse analysis to compare the representation of refugees, asylum seekers, and migrants in the Irish and UK press.

Discourse analysis is best understood as a field of research or an interest area rather than as a specific method. It has no specific, agreed-upon procedure, but typically discourse analysis involves starting with a research question and then selecting samples of news, videos, interview transcripts, social media, and such. Then comes coding, which unlike the coding in conventional content analysis is qualitative, and analysis. Coding and analysis are basically a search for patterns and variations in content. They vary according to the researcher's perspective on the research and may change as both the research and the analyst's thinking progress. Most discourse analyses, though, are based on how the discourse appears to be shaping our views of the world rather than on categories of language or frequencies of word occurrence, as with content analysis.

CONVERSATION ANALYSIS

Imagine a world with no rules, guidelines, or accepted ways of doing things. Imagine, for example, no traffic rules about what side of the road to drive on or stopping for red lights. And what would we do if there were no "right-of-way" rules? Now imagine an analogous scenario with respect to human interaction. The prospect of anyone being able to speak at any time to anybody on any topic may be an ideal of democracy, but it predicts conversational chaos.

One way around this problem is to produce formalized rules such as parliamentary procedures to control interaction and allow every participant a voice, but these formal rules apply only if groups of individuals agree to adopt them. That leaves most people living without any such rules. What, then, governs our daily interactions with other people? That is what conversation analysts seek to discover as they document, for example, physician-patient interaction, pilot-controller communications, business meetings, family discussions, political debates, and interactive journalism.

Document is an appropriate word here because the transcripts of conversations are the raw materials of conversation analysis. Researchers begin with a close reading of such transcripts, marking them up to show pauses in a conversation, the time lag between responses, words that get emphasized, where speakers overlap, and so on. From this marked up transcript, they are able to document, describe, and classify the unspoken agreements that govern conversations—for example, the mechanisms that govern **turn taking** or who speaks next in a conversation and the mechanisms that indicate possible types of responses to a question. These mechanisms are not formal rules with penalties attached to them for noncompliance; rather, they are the procedures that individuals follow in order to allow a conversation to take place.

If rhetorical and discourse analysts look for the broad sweep of ideas and how they are made persuasive, conversation analysts study the fine detail of human interaction on a second-by-second basis in order to identify the specific rules that allow a conversation to continue as a coordinated sequence of events rather than degenerating into chaos.

Analysts are interested in the mechanisms of a conversation rather than its content. Their focus is specifically on what a detailed analysis of the transcripts of conversations reveals rather than on the context (work or home, for example) in which the conversation takes place. If a variable such as the gender of a participant explains the nature of a conversation, that conclusion will be drawn from references to gender in the transcript, not from the analyst's prior knowledge of a participant's gender. There is, therefore, no need to work directly with the individuals involved in the conversation.

A fundamental concept in conversation analysis is that discrete units of a conversation can be recognized and categorized in order to understand the mechanisms that sustain the conversation. A major difference between content analysis and conversation analysis is that the analyst adds to the conversation's transcript a standardized series of codes that mark particular aspects of the conversation, such as the time between a speaker's utterances or the volume of an utterance.

Exhibit 12.1 shows an example of a transcript marked up with some of the basic conversation analysis annotations, which are explained in the right-hand column. The following section sets out some of the basic concepts in conversation analysis.

Utterances

Utterances are units of speech preceded by silence and followed either by silence or by another person speaking. They are not necessarily linguistic or grammatical units such as sentences or phrases.

Adjacency Pairs

Adjacency pairs are units of speech that occur together. They are one of the basic units of conversation analysis. Once the first utterance is heard, a second is required in response. Many adjacency pairs have been identified, such as the following:

Adjacency Pair	Utterance	Response
Question—Answer	What's the time?	Time for a coffee break.
Offer—Rejection	Do you need help with that homework?	Nope! Finished it already.
Compliment—Acceptance	You did a great job on that report.	Thanks. I used Ted's new software for the cover design.
Greeting—Greeting	G'day, mate.	Well, hello there.

Affiliative responses to a question, compliment, offer, or command maintain a link with the speaker; disaffiliative responses break the link with the speaker.

Turn Taking

Speaking out of turn is disruptive. If conversations are not to turn into chaos, individuals need to coordinate who speaks when.

Obviously, there must be some agreed-upon management system for turn taking, which conversation analysts conceptualize as having two parts—a transitional relevance place (TRP) and a turn constructional unit (TCU). A transitional relevance place is the point in the conversation at which turn taking may take place, and the norms of turn taking govern the conversation. For example, if the current speaker designates a second speaker to talk, the current speaker must then stop. If the current speaker does not select a second speaker, then any member of the group may self-select as the next speaker. A turn constructional unit is a sentence, word, or exclamation that signals a TRP—a point at which turn taking can occur.

EXHIBIT 12.1 ■ Example of Conversation Analysis Transcript

Annotated Transcript	Explanation of Annotations
13. Brian: What's the [time?]	*13, 14, 15, etc., indicate line numbers in transcript.* *] (right bracket) indicates Brian has stopped talking while Tshinta continues.*
14. Tshinta: [Almost time to get to our next class.	*[(left bracket) indicates where Tshinta's response overlaps with Brian's question.*
(0.3)	*(0.3) denotes timed length in seconds of a pause between speakers.*
15. Caroline: Yeah.	
16. Mike: What day's that guest speaker?	
(.)	*(.) denotes a just noticeable pause.*
17. Caroline: Tuesday.	*Line 17 shows an affiliative response to the question in line 16; no explanation is required.*
18. Mike: And. (.) Can you clear my campus mailbox tomorrow?	
19. Caroline: NOPE. No can do.	*Line 19 shows a disaffiliative response to the question in line 18. NOPE in capital letters indicates a much higher speaking volume.*
(0.5)	
20. Caroline: Sorry—uh—gotta go to my—uh—research site and—uh—do—ah—interviews.	*An explanation as in line 20 is required if the conversation is to continue.*
21. Mike: So when are we working on this project again?	*Line 21: Mike asks a question relevant to each individual in the group. Line 21 requires an answer, but Mike does not call on anyone to provide one.*
22. Elizabeth: How about Tuesday night? Tshinta?	*Line 22: Elizabeth self-nominates as the next speaker, then nominates Tshinta as speaker.*
23. Tshinta: Nope. We have that guest speaker, remember?	*Line 23: Tshinta speaks but does not designate the next speaker.*
(.)	
24. Caroline: How about Tuesday?	*Line 24: After a brief pause, Caroline self-designates as speaker and then engages in self-initiated self-repair of her error in line 24.*
25. >Oops. Sorry. Wasn't listening. Sorry.<	*Line 25: Inward arrows > and < indicate faster speech.*

Repair Mechanisms

There are four types of **repair mechanism** that might occur when a conversation is running into trouble. These are self-initiated–self-repair, self-initiated–other-repair, other-initiated–self-repair, and other-initiated–other-repair.

Self-initiated–self-repair means that the speaker identifies and corrects his own mistake. This is the preferred mechanism in that, being self-initiated, it gets the conversation back on track efficiently without other participants having to detour from the focus of the conversation to make sense of the mistake and correct it. At the other extreme, other-initiated–other-repair requires the work of other participants to get back on track, which may lead to further conversational difficulties.

Conversation analysis is distinguished by its attention to the microscopic detail of human interaction. You can see from Exhibit 12.1 that transcribing one minute of conversation requires considerably more than one minute of work. Transcription also requires a keen ear and a respect for what was actually said. Conversation analysts do not correct for errors in speech or grammar in the course of transcribing. Their mission is to record accurately and annotate what they heard. Transcriptions of real conversations are far more complex than the simple examples shown in Exhibit 12.1.

Visit the website at the end of this chapter for a conversation analysis of police–citizen conversations at traffic stops.

SEMIOTICS

"That which we call a rose by any other name would smell as sweet," according to Shakespeare's Juliet. On the basis of such thinking is the study of semiotics founded. At heart, semiotics is concerned with the relationship between language, and especially signs, and meaning.

Signs and language are arbitrarily connected to meaning and are culturally specific. You could call a book a "kkjtckl," and it would still be a book, as Shakespeare probably would not have said. *Book* can in fact be an action verb or an object that varies considerably in size, design, cost, and content. Stop signs have a commonly accepted meaning of "Stop—and then proceed when safe to do so." Taken literally, a stop sign says only "Stop!" It does not say anything else, so where did the "and then proceed when safe" meaning come from, and why do most of us agree to accept that meaning?

Semiotic analysis means exploring the relationships between signs and their meanings. It helps us understand how messages might be interpreted and misinterpreted. Note the plurals. If the relationships between signs and meanings are arbitrary, then multiple interpretations of the relationships are always possible. There are drivers who, at least by their behavior, appear to interpret a stop sign as "Slow down a bit . . . if you feel like it and you do not see a patrol car."

Semiotic Thinking: The Tobacco King and Sleeping Policemen

Edward Bernays, a pioneer of U.S. public relations in the 1920s, recalled that in his meetings with a major client, the president of American Tobacco, the president was always seated and always wore his hat in the office. To Bernays, a Freudian by background, this symbolized royalty seated on a throne and wearing a crown. The company president might well have been happy to have that hierarchical interpretation shared among the lesser beings he employed. **Semioticians**, however, would query the power of such monarchical symbolism in corporate America, post-1776, and indeed whether the hat should be interpreted as monarchical at all. They would want to question Bernays's interpretation further. For example, could the hat be read as a Lincolnian-style, presidential top hat generating respect for an American institution—American Tobacco—and its president?

Speed bumps in some countries are referred to as "sleeping policemen." This seems like a major putdown of the local constabulary—asleep in the middle of the road and driven over at frequent intervals by the motoring public. So what might be another interpretation? A more favorable meaning, at least from the point of view of the police, might be that there is a constant police presence on the roads, ready to "wake up" at any time. Drivers sensitive to the latter meaning would obviously drive with caution, a decision reinforced by the very real consequences of speeding over a tangible "sleeping policeman."

Much applied semiotic research centers on consumer products and the meanings that attach to them. In an applied setting, researchers may combine semiotic analyses of new products and product designs with other approaches, such as surveys and focus groups, to determine what meanings consumers assign to products and why they choose to affiliate with a particular brand. Semiotic researchers have studied the relationship between self-image and the shape of the perfume bottle a woman is likely to buy, the images conveyed by corporate logos such as those of IBM and Apple, and how the shapes of vehicles affect the memorability of vehicle brands.

The value of semiotic analysis is that the researcher explores the multiple possibilities for (mis)interpretation and so becomes alert to all the nuances and possibilities of interpretation associated with a product.

The following section demonstrates one of the many approaches to semiotic analysis and how it might be applied in practice.

Roman Jakobson Visits Sam's Car Lot

A classic telecommunications-based model of human communication, introduced in Chapter 1, has four major components—source, message, channel, and receiver.

Linguist and communication theorist Roman Jakobson expanded the model and assigned a **semiotic function** to each component. Jakobson's six semiotic functions identify how language functions for specific purposes.

Exhibit 12.2 shows how Jakobson's semiotic functions might be used to analyze and understand the advertising run by a hypothetical car dealer—Sam. For example, a statement such as "I have to be mad . . ." is an expressive statement establishing Sam's condition (it has an **expressive function**). "Come on down . . ." has a **conative function** establishing Sam's expectations of his advertising audiences. "Our deals are steals on wheels" has a **poetic function**; we can take pleasure in the alliteration even if we disagree with Sam's message. We might infer that Sam assumes that the poetic quality of his phrasing will make his advertising memorable. "We have the nation's best deals" has the **referential function** of establishing overall what the dominant message of Sam's advertising is. "Visit, phone, or e-mail" has a **phatic function**; it establishes how communication should take place between Sam and his potential customers. "Sam's cars are *the* cars" performs the **metalingual function** of establishing the preferred meaning, or at least Sam's preferred meaning, of the term *Sam's cars*.

Jakobson's six functions can be used for semiotic analysis in a number of ways. For example, Jakobson argued that one of the six functions is always dominant in a text. Determining which function is dominant would help you understand the motivation behind the message, as with Burke's ratio analysis. Or you could examine each function systematically to see how emotions, relationship messages, and the playful use of words help Sam establish an image of his dealership with his advertising audience.

EXHIBIT 12.2 ■ Jakobson's Semiotic Functions		
Communication Component	**Semiotic Function**	**Example**
Sender	Expressive. Describes or establishes the speaker's condition or emotional state.	"I have to be mad to sell at these prices."
Receiver	Conative. Establishes the sender's expectations of the receiver or what the receiver is expected to do as a result of receiving the message.	"Come on down—now!"
Message	Poetic. Uses language for pleasure, as in jokes, or uses alliteration because doing so is pleasurable in its own right.	"Our deals are steals on wheels."
Context	Referential. Establishes the communication context, dominant message, or agenda.	"We have the nation's best deals in used cars."
Channel	Phatic. Keeps communication participants "on track" and in contact by establishing how communication will take place.	"Visit, phone, e-mail; let's hear from you."
Code	Metalingual. Establishes agreed-upon meaning for a word—for example, by establishing that *Rose* refers to the name of a girl, not a flower.	Sam's cars are *the* cars."

CRITICAL ANALYSES

Critical analyses explore the way in which communication establishes, reinforces, and maintains power structures in society. As you might anticipate, there are many approaches to critical analysis. The ranks of critical theorists are drawn from a variety of disciplines, there are no widely agreed-upon theoretical assumptions or methods, and, as Curt (1994) points out, "writing produced from a critical theory perspective is often pretty impenetrable to the uninitiated" (p. 13). Nonetheless, critical scholars share a basic interest in identifying the power structures behind communication content and actions.

One way to understand this interest is to appreciate that all communication is based on having the resources with which to communicate. Any public communication—be it print media, broadcast media, websites, billboards, transit advertising, course syllabi, or sponsored Little League uniforms—requires resources in the form of time, money, and influence to produce. So do events such as halftime shows, religious rituals, initiation ceremonies, funeral services, and graduation ceremonies. We might argue, then, that much of the communication content to which we are exposed is a product of individuals and organizations with the power and resources (however defined) to communicate.

Although the Internet and social media may have democratized global communication to a degree, it remains true that your ability to maintain a social media presence is based on the fact that you have the resources to do so. Your presence on the Internet reflects a communicative power that those on the other side of the "digital divide" do not have.

Critical perspectives question the idea of objectivity and address social problems or inequalities in such a way as to provide more equitable access to society's collective resources. Critical scholars analyze communication with a view to determining whose voices are dominant in any given communication, the power structures behind the observed communication, and how communication is used by those in power to maintain the status quo.

In this section, we will revisit from a critical perspective some of the research approaches outlined in this chapter.

Rhetorical Analysis

From a critical perspective, the analysis of rhetoric seeks to establish how communication is used to maintain power relationships. The three rhetorical settings identified by Aristotle are formal settings for debate in any society—legal or judicial proceedings, ceremonial proceedings such as graduation, and deliberative proceedings such as political or policy debates. Rhetorical analysis can be understood from a critical perspective as an analysis of argumentation to win the assent of the powerful or how the powerful use argumentation to maintain their status. Similarly, Kenneth Burke's dramatistic analysis and narrative analysis can be seen as ways of understanding dramas and stories that tell of power relationships and the clash of values. Remember the AT&T "It Can Wait" campaign introduced in Chapter 1? A critical analyst would use the approaches suggested by Aristotle, Burke, and others to identify the arguments, narratives, and metaphors used by AT&T to maintain and promote its interests and to control and shape the discourse surrounding distracted driving.

Critical Discourse Analysis

Critical discourse analysis aims to explore the relationships between language and power. One assumption we can make about society is that societal elites and the powerful have the ability to interpret and describe the world in a way that favors them—and that implicitly or explicitly marginalizes minority voices. The basic aim of critical discourse analysis, then, is to uncover the ideological assumptions behind public discourse and to link communication content with underlying power structures. The interest of the critical analyst is in injustice and inequality. In examining discourse in this light, the researcher may look for taken-for-granted assumptions, use of evidence, style, use of rhetoric, media used, the ways in which text and graphics interact, and omissions—what is not said as much as what is. Because the discourse of the powerful may be countered by minority discourse, the critical discourse analyst may study both in order to see how one influences the other.

Unlike the content analyst who takes a primary interest in the frequency with which words occur, the critical analyst will take an interest in the words and phrases thought to be significant in promoting a viewpoint, not in their frequency.

Marxist Criticism

The **Marxist perspective** begins from a critique of capitalism and its attendant social relationships and values. From this perspective, critics examine communication content for the (often hidden) messages that reinforce the **ideology** or vision that guides those in power. A critical organizational scholar might, for example, analyze employee newsletters to determine the extent to which a management ideology dominates the content.

Class-based oppression is a significant area of study in Marxist critiques. Marxism considers the **base** and **superstructure**, two concepts that maintain and shape one another. The base is focused on production—how things are produced, who is producing them, what is the relationship between the people involved in that process. The superstructure is how society is built—ideas like politics, education, family, media, and government. It is the superstructure that is designed to support those already in power and keep the status quo.

For example, a Marxist criticism of a documentary on a political figure might ask questions of class and power structure. Questions about who was framed positively, who was framed negatively, who was ignored, and who paid for the whole production are all considerations for Marxist criticism (Hart, Daughton, and LaVally, 2017). A major goal of Marxist criticism is to prioritize oppressed voices and note why those voices have been oppressed.

From a critical Marxist perspective, metaphor analysis can reveal how language maintains and promotes organizational power structures. For example, suppose you are reading interview transcripts and documentation with a view to understanding why an organization is successful. As you read, it occurs to you that certain words and phrases appear repeatedly—*team*, *team player*, *plays*, *leader*, *goals*, *scored*, *captain*, *time out*, *rules*, and *coach*. It occurs to you that even though individual informants have not used the term *game* or *contest*, it appears that they are collectively viewing their organizational life as a game or contest. They would probably agree that there is a "captain" coordinating players, each of whom has specific responsibilities, an agreed-upon set of rules, and an overall objective to beat other teams playing the same game. In other words, there is a root "team" metaphor framing their thinking and perhaps shaping their behavior.

At one level, this metaphor implies a group of people working in harmony and coordinating their efforts toward a common goal. However, a critical analyst will point out that the team metaphor is capable of an alternative interpretation—that teams are hierarchical, with a captain and coach in charge and making the strategic decisions and an owner or league to whom these leaders report. Team members are expected to implement these decisions at a tactical level and to put their individuality aside for the good of the team. Members who persist in being individualistic at the expense of the team risk being thrown off the team for not being team players. From a critical viewpoint, then, the team metaphor promotes a message of obedience to authority, doing as one is directed, and maintaining the team's hierarchy. From a critical perspective, this is obedience not just to any authority but to authority rooted in historically identifiable forms of social, economic, or cultural power, which restrict participation by groups such as the disenfranchised.

With respect to organizational communication, the critical interpretation of such metaphors gains some additional validity in that such metaphors are typically found in new-employee materials, employee newsletters, recognition events, and the like. Who controls the content of such employee communications? Management!

Feminist Criticism

Criticism from a feminist perspective generally seeks to critique patriarchal hierarchies and ideologies and, in the context of communication research, the communication content and practices that reproduce and perpetuate such hierarchies and ideologies. **Feminist criticism** focuses on gender and, more specifically, on gender inequities and their portrayal, lived experiences, and replication. Critical approaches may range from determining the relative dominance of male versus female "voices" in media content to identifying sexism in language to analyzing such perceived masculine concepts as hierarchy. Media researchers, for example, would take an interest in how the relationships between men and women are portrayed in entertainment media, advertising, or employee communications. More specifically, they would investigate the power relationships between male and female characters, how male and female roles are defined, and how behaviors and roles perpetuate patriarchal behaviors and hierarchies in organizations and interpersonal relationships.

The role of the feminist critic is to disrupt hegemonic norms—the norms of the dominant social group—by analyzing and critiquing gender-based rhetoric. Rhetoric scholar Sonja Foss's hoped-for outcome is that "critics are able to discover ways in which artifacts can serve as models for creating alternatives to dominant ideologies and practices" (Foss, 2018, p. 154). Through such analyses, feminist criticism contributes to a wider understanding of hegemonic norms and how they might be challenged.

Often, feminist criticism looks at the language of feminist groups or marginalized populations, but this isn't the only option. Once the rhetorical artifact or content is chosen, the analysis has two stages. In the first stage, the goal is to disrupt hegemonic norms, for example, by creating multiple perspectives and cultivating ambiguities in interpreting the artifact. In the second stage, the critic should discuss how these perspectives and ambiguities function for the **rhetor**, or source, and the audience in creating new options for thinking, acting, and being (Foss, 2018).

For example, Ebben and Garza's (2017) analysis of Michelle Obama's rhetoric of inclusion in a campaign speech for Hillary Clinton challenges hegemonic norms. They note that in Obama's speech, "Her rhetoric of inclusion calls out injustices, affirms the authenticity of experiences that are marginalized under a regime of toxic masculinity, and constructs counter-hegemonic discourses that envision alternatives that afford agency" (p. 95). The authors summarize Obama's rhetoric of inclusion as a "RAVE" strategy: 1) resistance, 2) advocacy, 3) validation, and 4) empowerment. They note that First Lady rhetoric is understudied relative to studies of presidential rhetoric and argue for the importance of having a First Lady using and claiming feminist values.

The purposes and methods for analyzing and critiquing communication often overlap. For example, content analysis may be used to obtain a critical reading of advertising, and critical methods may be used to assess the effectiveness of advertising. Different methodologies may also be combined. For example, Holsanova, Holmquist, and Rahm (2006) combined a semiotic analysis of newspapers with eye-movement scans of newspaper readers.

ETHICS PANEL
RESEARCH AS MANIPULATIVE PRACTICE

This chapter has discussed approaches to research that focus on persuasion, argumentation, and the maintenance and shaping of relationships through communication. From a critical perspective, we can see that any and all of these approaches can reveal communication in the service of power and of power relationships.

The idea that communication research is manipulative has both theoretical and practical support. For example, Parker (1972) posits that most human relationships are manipulative and that rhetoric and argumentation fall under the "umbrella" of manipulation, along with political power, authority relationships, physical force, and rewards and punishments. Parker uses the term *manipulation* in an "ethically neutral sense" (p. 73). Nonetheless, from a critical perspective, one can argue that research participants are often manipulated into becoming participants and that research has a power component in that researchers use their research activities—if not for social change, then certainly for personal advancement.

This critical view of research is evidenced by what we know of some research in practice. For example, Lindlof and Taylor (2002) suggest that behind the myths of "researchers practicing universal informed consent, consistent empathy, honest disclosure, accurate reporting and unobtrusive observation . . . are the harsh realities of improvised consent, mutual dislike, strategic deception, creative reconstruction and intentional shaping of events" (p. 140).

Where the stakes are high, for example with respect to funding or being first to publish, research can be seen as a "winner-take-all game with perverse incentives that lead scientists to cut corners, and, in some cases, commit acts of misconduct" (Zimmer, 2012).

What has all this to do with the approaches to understanding communication content that we have outlined in this chapter? From a critical perspective, documents that seek institutional review board (IRB) approvals or funding, propose projects, solicit research participants, and report research findings, conclusions, and recommendations can all be regarded as manipulative. Research writing is not neutral, as we shall argue in Chapter 14.

Thinking of communication as persuasion and the exercise of power, answer the following questions.

Questions

Consider the following three research questions.

- What are the effects of fast-food advertising on children's food preferences?

- What is the relationship between social media use and the academic performance of college students?

- What communication behaviors facilitate the integration of new immigrant groups into society?

For each of the research topics suggested by the questions above, consider the following:

- What persuasive appeals might a researcher use to obtain research funding?

- How might the appeals to government agencies, private foundations, and citizen activist groups differ in their emphases, and why?

- What persuasive appeals might a researcher use in letters to individuals soliciting their participation in the research?

Chapter Summary

- Rhetorical analyses examine content to understand the nature of persuasion and argumentation.

- Narrative and discourse analyses focus on stories and their uses.

- Conversation analyses examine the details of human interaction to determine how conversations are coordinated among participants.

- Semiotic analyses focus on the meanings and interpretations of texts and signs.

- Critical analyses focus on the use of language as it promotes and maintains power in organizations and societies.

Key Terms

act 240
adjacency pairs 245
affiliative responses 245
agency 241
agent 240
Aristotelian analysis 239
base 251
conative function 248
conversation analysis 243
critical analyses 249
critical discourse analysis 250
disaffiliative responses 245
discourse 243
discourse analysis 243
dramatistic analysis 240
dramatistic pentad 240
ethos 240

expressive function 248
fantasy theme analysis 241
feminist criticism 252
ideology 251
logos 240
Marxist perspective 251
master analog 241
master narrative 241
metalingual function 248
metaphor analysis 243
narrative analysis 242
pathos 240
phatic function 248
poetic function 248
purpose 241
ratio analysis 241
referential function 248

repair mechanism 246
rhetor 252
rhetoric 239
rhetorical analysis 239
rhetoricians 238
root metaphor 243
scene 241
semiotic function 248
semioticians 247
superstructure 251
symbolic convergence 241
transitional relevance
    place (TRP) 245
turn constructional
    unit (TCU) 245
turn taking 244
utterances 245

Application Exercises

Exercise 1: Discourse Analysis

You will find competing discourses frequently in local and national news media. Often, the issue will be an environmental one as developers and investors compete with conservationists and historians over the proposed use of an historically or environmentally important site. Generically, the two competing discourses are likely to be jobs and economic growth versus nurturing and maintaining the local environment and its history. Another contested discourse especially at election time is the place of government in society—for example, the discourse of freedom and individual enterprise versus the discourse of care and fair treatment for all citizens.

Identify one such current discourse conflict and outline the media you would study; list specific techniques you might use to differentiate the competing discourses; and decide which discourse is the most powerful.

Exercise 2: Matching Method With Interest

Which of the methods outlined in this chapter would you prefer for researching the following interest areas? Why?

- Identifying the political agenda, if any, of a newspaper or television network.

- Identifying the agenda of management in internal organizational media.

- Explaining how a group makes its decisions.

- Explaining how two people make a decision.

Exercise 3: Analyzing Organizational Stories

Stories about organizations are frequently told informally to their new members. Whatever the motivation behind the storytelling, the stories often have the effects of explaining how to survive in the organization and of identifying the informal rules that members need to follow if they are to adjust successfully.

Identify stories that you and others heard during the first year of study at your institution. How do these stories differ from one another? What topics do they cover that are not addressed by the official student handbook or institutional policies? Which of the approaches identified in this chapter do you find the most useful for understanding these stories as a way of orienting newcomers to the institution?

Exercise 4: Analyzing Online Harassment: Qualitatively

Revisit the Pew Research Center survey of online harassment outlined in the Chapter 11 end-of-chapter exercises (Duggan, 2014). The study also provides several hundred selected quotations about harassment from those surveyed (www.pewinternet.org/2014/10/22/online-harassment-experiences-in-their-own-words).

Look at these quotations collectively and list the qualitative approaches that might provide the best understanding of harassment. For example, collectively, do they add up to a summary narrative that can be further analyzed? Looking at these statements, consider how valid the six specific types of harassment identified by Pew for its survey seem to be. If you had these statements before running a survey, how might your survey questions differ from the Pew questions?

The full report, questionnaire, and respondent comments are available at www.pewinternet.org/2014/10/22/online-harassment (Duggan, 2014); there is also a 2017 update (http://www.pewinternet.org/2017/07/11/online-harassment-2017/).

Recommended Reading

Aristotle

Boukala, S., & Dimitrakopoulou, D. (2017). The politics of fear vs. the politics of hope: Analysing the 2015 Greek election and referendum campaigns. *Critical Discourse Studies, 14*(1), 39–55. DOI: 10.1080/17405904.2016.1182933

Analyzes this Greek election using Aristotle's argumentation strategies.

Bormann

Gerl, E. J. (2016). Survivors and dreamers: A rhetorical vision of *Teen Voices* magazine. *Journal of Magazine and New Media Research, 17*(1), 1–26.

Using fantasy theme analysis and symbolic convergence, the article analyzes a teen-written magazine and finds four fantasy types: survivor, dreamer, activist, and can-do-anything.

Burke

Milford, M. (2015). Kenneth Burke's punitive priests and the redeeming prophets: The NCAA, the college sports media, and the University of Miami scandal. *Communication Studies, 66*(1), 45–62. DOI: 10.1080/10510974.2013.856806

A Burkean analysis of organizational adaptation to new circumstances.

Conversation Analysis

Kidwell, M., & Kevoe-Feldman, H. (2018). Making an impression in traffic stops: Citizens' volunteered accounts in two positions. *Discourse Studies, 20*(5), 613–636. DOI: 10.1177/1461445618760603

A conversation analysis of police officer / citizen conversations at traffic stops.

Discourse Analysis

Tangdall, S. (2017). The influence of popular culture on women's identities: A diachronic discourse analysis of *Vogue* magazine. *Southern Journal of Linguistics, 41*(2), 47–94.

Shows the shifting discourse in *Vogue* magazine throughout the last century and how it shaped the identities of upper-middle-class women.

Feminist Criticism

Griffin, R.A. (2015). Black feminist reflections on Michelle Obama's tribute to Maya Angelou. In E. J. Natalle & J. M. Simon (Eds.), *Michelle Obama: First Lady, American rhetor* (pp. 121–139). Landham, MD: Lexington Books.

Essay in an edited anthology studying Michelle Obama's speeches.

Marxist Criticism

Weaver, C. K. (2016). A Marxist primer for critical public relations scholarship. *Media International Australia, 160*(1), 43–52. DOI: 10.1177/1329878X16650735

Discusses the application of Marxist criticism to contemporary public relations practice.

Metaphor

Đurović, T., & Silaški, N. (2018). The end of a long and fraught marriage. *Metaphor & the Social World, 8*(1), 25–39. DOI: 10.1075/msw.17010.dur

Uses a marriage metaphor to study Brexit (Great Britain leaving the EU).

Narrative Analysis

Iannarino, N. T. (2018) "My insides feel like Keith Richards' face": A narrative analysis of humor and biographical disruption in young adults' cancer blogs. *Health Communication, 33*(10), 1233–1242. DOI: 10.1080/10410236.2017.1350909

Through narrative analysis, the author found that young adults' cancer blogs used humor to emphasize camaraderie with others, to discuss complex medical decisions, to help manage a loss of agency, and to manage changing social identities.

Semiotics

Keren, R. (2018). From resistance to reconciliation and back again: A semiotic analysis of the *Charlie Hebdo* cover following the January 2015 events. *Semiotica, 2018*(225), 269–292. DOI: 10.1515/sem-2015-0128

A semiotic analysis of the *Charlie Hebdo* cover in the issue after the attack on the magazine's cartoonists.

Recommended Web Resources

Daniel Chandler, University of Wales, Semiotics for Beginners. http://visual-memory.co.uk/daniel/Documents/S4B/semiotic.html

Online QDA (Qualitative Data Analysis). . . . . . . .http://onlineqda.hud.ac.uk/

Qualitative data analysis methods, resources, and a glossary from the Department of Behavioural Sciences, University of Huddersfield.

Professor Charles Antaki's conversation analysis tutorials. . . . . . . .http://ca-tutorials.lboro.ac.uk

Signo. . . . . . . .www.signosemio.com
> *Check out this site for more information on theoreticians such as Jakobson. Note that you can consult this page in English and French.*

TalkBank. . . . . .https://talkbank.org
> *At TalkBank, you can find downloadable conversation analysis transcripts linked to audio or video recordings, as well as other resources.*

References

Bormann, E. G. (1972). Fantasy and rhetorical vision: The rhetorical criticism of social reality. *Quarterly Journal of Speech, 58,* 396–407. DOI: 10.1080/00335637209383138

Curt, B. C. (1994). *Textuality and tectonics: Troubling social and psychological science.* Buckingham, UK: Open University Press.

Duggan, M. (2014, October 22). *Online harassment* [Report]. Washington, DC: Pew Research Center, Internet & Technology. Retrieved from https://www.pewinternet.org/2014/10/22/online-harassment/

Ebben, M., & Garza, T. (2017). When they go low, we go high: First Lady Michelle Obama's feminist rhetoric of inclusion. *Women & Language, 40*(1), 83–100.

Foss, S. K. (2018). Feminist criticism. In *Rhetorical criticism: Exploration and practice* (5th ed., pp. 141–179). Long Grove, IL: Waveland Press.

Hart, R.P., Daughton, S., & LaVally, R. (2017). *Modern rhetorical criticism.* (4th ed.). London: Taylor and Francis.

Holsanova, J., Holmquist, K., & Rahm, H. (2006). Entry points and reading paths on newspaper spreads: Comparing a semiotic analysis with eye-tracking measurements. *Visual Communication, 5*(1), 65–93.

Lindlof, T. R., & Taylor, B. C. (2002). *Qualitative communication research methods* (2nd ed.). Thousand Oaks, CA: Sage.

O'Regan, V., & Riordan, E. (2018). Comparing the representation of refugees, asylum seekers and migrants in the Irish and UK press: A corpus-based critical discourse analysis. *Journal of Language & Politics, 17*(6), 744–768. DOI: 10.1075/jlp.17043.ore

Parker, D. H. (1972). Rhetoric, ethics and manipulation. *Philosophy & Rhetoric, 5*(2), 69–87.

Zimmer, C. (2012, April 16). A sharp rise in retractions prompts calls for reform. *New York Times.* Retrieved from https://www.nytimes.com/2012/04/17/science/rise-in-scientific-journal-retractions-prompts-calls-for-reform.html

13

QUALITATIVE UNDERSTANDING OF COMMUNICATION BEHAVIOR

Interviews, Focus Groups, and Ethnography

"Hey Luke, how's your work-study job going this semester?"

"Good, Charlotte, I guess. It's quiet. Not a lot of students around."

"That's not what I'd expect in the Career Center."

"I know, right? It's strange. Actually, that's going to be my big assignment for next semester—trying to figure out why things are quiet. I'm going to help the director, Bonnie, find out how students see the center. What about you? Have you been there?"

"You know, I haven't this year. Last year I went there to get an internship, and people were really helpful. Now, I don't plan to apply for jobs 'til next year . . . I'll probably do that online anyway . . . so I haven't seen the need to go. How are you helping Bonnie?"

"Well, she's trying to get better information on how students see the Career Center. She sent out a survey last semester. Maybe you saw it on the e-mail blast? That gave us some information on what students saw as important, but it didn't give us a lot of in-depth information—like why they saw it as important."

"So how else are you getting information then?"

"Bonnie's starting some focus groups. You know, where there's a handful of people in the room answering questions."

"I did a focus group once, at the mall! It was a marketing thing though, testing out different movie trailers to see which ones people liked best."

"That's the same idea as Bonnie has. It's a lot of information gathering."

"I'd think that would be confusing—so many people talking at once. Why doesn't Bonnie just do interviews if she wants more information than surveys?"

"She did. She said the interviews helped shape her focus group questions. Obviously different methods can feed into each other. There's an overview of focus groups and a lot about other qualitative methods in this chapter."

"I should read it?"

"Well, Mike should read it because focus groups can involve food and beverages for participants. That aside, if you're interested in *understanding* communication—as opposed to just *measuring* it—yes!"

CHAPTER OVERVIEW

Not all human communication can be summarized satisfactorily as a "6" on a 7-point scale. Qualitative approaches to human communication may provide more insights and different insights than quantitative approaches. Intuitively, watching people and talking with them often seem preferable to measurement as research approaches, just as comprehension and understanding often seem preferable to simply being informed as research goals.

The methods discussed in this chapter are all essentially qualitative methods, and all may be used online as well as offline. More important, they share a common goal of trying to understand and interpret human behavior. This requires excellent listening, interviewing, and observational skills to obtain valid understandings of human communication, as well as excellent reporting skills to capture and convey to readers your research methods and what you have learned from your research participants.

CHAPTER OBJECTIVES

This chapter will help you

- List the advantages and disadvantages of qualitative research methods.

- Compare and contrast qualitative methods with quantitative methods.

- Explain, with examples, how to conduct the major methods of qualitative research.

- Compare and contrast online qualitative methods with traditional qualitative methods.

- Explain, with examples, the basics of coding qualitative data.

- Identify and discuss potential ethical issues related to interviews, focus groups, ethnography, and unobtrusive measures.

INTRODUCTION: ADVANTAGES AND DISADVANTAGES OF WATCHING AND LISTENING METHODS

This chapter covers some basic qualitative approaches to communication research—interviews, focus groups, ethnography, observational studies, unobtrusive measures, and performance studies.

Overall, these methods offer the opportunity to explore the thinking and communication behavior of individuals in depth.

Researching human communication in "full listening mode" is likely to be rewarded with insights, language, and unique logics and reasonings that surveys and experiments may not uncover. Such researchers are more likely to discover minority and dissident voices and to emerge with new understandings, perceptions, and critiques in contrast to the confirmation or disconfirmation of an idea that surveys and experiments largely provide. A performance study, for example, is often a critical method (see Chapter 2) as it critiques power structures in society.

Because many observational methods emphasize working with research participants in real-life settings, their findings are likely to have a much higher validity compared with the results of experimental research, which typically takes place in artificial settings.

At a practical level, interviews and focus groups can be set up quickly relative to experiments, which may take some time to organize. Interviews especially can take place immediately, sometimes as the fortuitous outcomes of fleeting opportunities. However, observational methods are not automatically more convenient than quantitative methods. For example, the fieldwork for a sound observational study may take months, if not years, whereas a survey—a predominantly quantitative method—can be completed in days if not hours.

Disadvantages of qualitative methods include the fact that the variability of human behavior over time puts a question mark over the reliability of findings. Because the participants in an interview or discussion are typically selected on the basis of the researcher's judgment rather than by random assignment, there can be questions about the validity of the selection and the extent to which participants represent a broader population.

The nature and level of interaction between the researcher and research participants affect what is observed and reported, so how to account for the researcher's own influence on the outcome of an interview or observation becomes an issue.

In summary, qualitative methods offer insight, understanding, and validity but not necessarily reliability or the ability to generalize with a high level of confidence.

QUALITATIVE AND QUANTITATIVE: SIMILARITIES AND DIFFERENCES

At first glance, the difference between the approaches discussed in this chapter and the surveys and experiments discussed in previous chapters is the difference between qualitative and quantitative research. It is important to realize, though, that the "qualitative or quantitative" question is neither the first nor the most important difference. Rather, as noted in Chapter 2, it is a secondary question that comes after the researcher has made basic assumptions about people and also about the basic purposes of her or his research.

Qualitative and quantitative researchers differ not so much on the use of words versus numbers as on the purpose of the research, its generalizability, and researchers' assumptions about human nature. **Quantitative** researchers look for relationships among phenomena; **qualitative** researchers look to understand phenomena as seen through the eyes of their research participants. As cultural anthropologist Clifford Geertz (1973) phrased it, the difference is between an experimental science in search of law and an **interpretive** one in search of meaning.

RESEARCHER-PARTICIPANT RELATIONSHIPS

A basic research decision is the level at which we engage with the people whose communication behavior we seek to understand. In principle, the closer we get to naturally occurring behaviors, the greater our understanding of them is likely to be. It is this basic assumption that leads researchers to observe or participate in communication in natural settings such as assembly lines, schools, hospitals, bars, or college campuses.

There is an interaction between the act of observation and what we observe and report. We can strive for distance and an impartial relationship with our informants and perhaps miss important insights, or we can decide that close personal involvement will produce more detailed accounts of our informants' lives, framed though the accounts may be by our own subjectivity. This basic decision about one's relationship with research participants is common to all of the research approaches outlined in this chapter.

Sociologist Raymond Gold (1958) described four possible relationships a researcher might have with research participants:

- The complete observer has no interaction with informants; they are not aware that they are being observed.

- The observer-as-participant role happens when the researcher makes short trips to a site for interviews or observations. Because the level of involvement is low, researchers may inadequately understand or misunderstand their informants.

- The participant-as-observer role happens when the researcher spends some time in a community. The researcher has a role in the community but is known to be studying it. Over time, mutual trust may develop between the researcher and research participants, but this trust has the potential to cause problems. For example, as the relationship approaches friendship, one or both parties may be reluctant to ask or to answer questions in a way that will hurt the friendship.

- In the complete-participant role, the researcher participates so closely in informants' lives that his or her research role may be unknown to them. A potential problem with this role is that researchers may become so involved in their participant role that they cannot function well as observers.

The precise balance between participant and observer is a function of how best to study the communication phenomena you are interested in, how each of the above roles might shape the nature of the data you gather and your reporting, and the ethical standards influencing your relationship(s) with research participants.

WATCHING AND LISTENING METHODS

In this chapter, we will follow a hypothetical research project focusing on students' use of social media. Bonnie—the observant director of a campus career services office—uses qualitative research methods to get some insight on a campus trend affecting her work. Her office has two major responsibilities. The first is preparing students for the world of employment by offering, for example, workshops in the art of the employment interview, networking, and résumé preparation. The second is alerting students to new employment opportunities.

Bonnie describes the effects that students' ever-increasing use of social media seems to be having on the services her office provides. For example, she is seeing a dramatic decline in the number of students using Career Center job search resources because, she thinks, they are directly accessing online search services. Similarly, workshops on networking and résumé preparation are poorly attended. She speculates that this is because students are actively networking via social media and see no need for workshops on how to do that. As for résumé workshops, one student has told her, "We don't need them. Every job application is online now. You just go online and answer the questions."

Bonnie tries to summarize the pluses and minuses of social media with respect to getting students successfully employed.

She hypothesizes that students who are active in the social media world will be more likely than less active students to be informed of the job market and to have good job search competencies. However, a second hypothesis is that they are more likely to lack such interpersonal skills as maintaining a face-to-face conversation, interviewing, problem solving with a team, cross-cultural communication, and superior-subordinate communication. In either case, there are practical implications for the Career Center, which may have to shift the type of services and training it offers. Of course, Bonnie may find no evidence to support her hypotheses. It may well be that students who are active social media users are highly competent in interpersonal skills, teamwork, and problem solving; it is just that they do it online rather than face to face.

A logical start to getting some answers would be to interview students.

Interviews

Essentially, an **interview** is a question-answer session between a researcher and **informants**, individuals selected because they can talk about others as well as themselves, or **respondents**, individuals who are regarded as speaking only for themselves.

Questions range in specificity and intent. An interview may consist of specific questions requiring nothing more than a simple "yes-no" response, or if an open-minded, exploratory approach is best, the researcher may use open-ended questions such as "I'm new to this; can you explain what's going on here?"

Structure

As Bonnie is at the beginning of her research and has hypotheses that are tentative for now, it is likely that she will start with unstructured interviews. But the question of how much to **structure** an interview will always arise.

Unstructured interviews come from the need to understand communication phenomena in informants' own terms. In this situation, interviews will likely begin with very broad, open-ended "tell me about . . ." questions. There is no predetermined set of questions, although, as the interview progresses, the questions will focus more on the researcher's basic interests.

Semistructured interviews dictate the broad questions to be asked but allow both the interviewer and the interviewee room to move. For example, Bonnie may decide that she has two broad questions: What sources of information do students use to find jobs, and where do they get advice on interview skills? Because there are only two basic questions, she has time for follow-up questions and for interviewees to volunteer information.

Fully structured interviews mean that the researcher has predetermined the questions, their format, and the order in which they will be asked. In our example, Bonnie would have a specific list of preformatted questions related to the use of specific social media, the role of friends in a job search, attitudes toward the Career Center, and the like.

Sequence

Sequence refers to the order in which questions occur. You will recall from Chapter 9 that questions may move in a funnel format from broad and general to narrow and specific or start with specific questions and move to broader questions. Most interviews begin with questions that informants can easily handle, such as class year or job title. Note, though, that seemingly harmless questions such as about age, religion, or even names may be intensely personal and emotional to interviewees and not a good starting point for an interview. Consider whether such questions are necessary if you sense that they might affect substantive aspects of the interview.

Question Types

You need different types of questions to elicit, probe, and interpret informants' understandings of the phenomena you are interested in. Anthropology professor James Spradley (1979) developed several often-used question categories as follows:

- **Descriptive questions** ask informants to describe phenomena. "Mini-tour" questions are one type of descriptive question; they ask for an overview of everyday occurrences. For example, "In a typical semester, how do you use social networking sites?"

- **Structural questions** explore the relationships among the terms informants use. For example, "Would you describe an online job search as part of your social networking?"

- **Contrast questions** help researchers understand the differences between and the relative importance of informants' concepts. For example, "You talk about 'job search' and 'career search.' Please explain the difference between these two." Another type of contrast question is a rating or ranking question. For example, "You talked about search engines, social media, and texting. Which of these two are most similar? Which one would you say differs most from the other two? Why?"

If you use all of the above question types, you can have some confidence that you have thoroughly explored your interviewees' views of their worlds and that you have an in-depth understanding of them.

Prompts

Interviewees may not respond to questions for many reasons. They may be naturally reticent, find the interviewer intimidating, or simply misunderstand the question.

What to do? Use **prompts**. Prompts are the follow-up questions that elicit more information and keep the interview progressing. Classic prompts include "tell me more" and the "5Ws + H" of journalism: for example, *Who* (else feels the same way that you do?), *What* (are the steps involved in ___?), *When* (do most people ___?), *Where* (did you first ___?), *Why* (do you say that?), and *How* (does ___ differ from ___?).

Reflecting interviewees' words back to them may get further responses. For example, "I heard you say that a job is not the same as a career; can you explain that?"

And then there is strategic silence. If you have ever noticed that someone in a discussion will ultimately fill a silence, you have noticed a basic interview technique. Keep silent in the hope that your interviewee will fill the silence.

Interviews need not be 100% talk. As part of an interview, respondents could be asked to demonstrate how they do something (for example, their online job search strategies), to describe what they see happening in a video, or to rank order photographs of different products or a series of statements describing their ideal political candidate.

Interviewee Considerations

It is important to develop trust and a rapport with **interviewees**. What kind of person might best accomplish this? Another person just like them; a high-powered PhD researcher; a newcomer hoping to learn from them; a compassionate, engaged, empathetic listener; or a dispassionate, neutral, nonjudgmental listener? We are all predisposed to respond differently to questions depending on who asks them.

In terms of presenting yourself successfully, honesty is the best policy for reasons of ethics, credibility, and maintaining a consistent persona, but note from the Ethics Panel in this chapter that positioning yourself as a different person may be necessary and may be approved by institutional review boards (IRBs).

The interview setting may also affect the interview. For example, workplace settings may constrain what employees feel they can tell you. Bonnie may have student interviewees come to her office; meet them in a dining area; or, moving into ethnographic mode, sit with them in campus apartments while she observes their use of social media. Interviews in Bonnie's office may free students from feelings of peer pressure but then have them feeling a need to provide the answers they think she is looking for. Students may feel more relaxed about meeting in a neutral space, such as a dining area.

Consider religious and cultural sensitivities when planning interviews. For cross-cultural interviews in particular, dress, body language, vocabulary, perceived status, and gender relations all need to be considered. For example, Xerri (2005) had his sisters set up interviews with women who for cultural reasons would have otherwise been reluctant to be interviewed by a male.

Recording

Audio- or video-recording interviews and focus groups (see below) can save you from taking notes and allow you to focus on the interview or behavior. Listening or viewing your recordings as soon as possible after making them allows you to update any notes while your memory is still fresh and gives you a second perspective on your observations.

People may "clam up" in front of a camera, may be nervous about what will happen to the recorded interview, or may decide to talk "for the record." In other words, what they say "on the record" may differ from what they might have told you "off the record." You have an ethical obligation to disclose that the interview will be recorded, if that is your plan, and you may have to negotiate whether recording will happen or not.

Focus Groups

A disadvantage of the one-on-one interview is that no matter how well informed and representative of others the interviewee may be, the interviewer is getting the views of only one person and no sense of how others might agree or disagree with those views.

A common method to elicit and test ideas that might arise outside the limits of the one-on-one interview is to bring a small group of people together in a **focus group**. Traditional "in-person" focus groups typically consist of 6 to 12 people in a discussion setting led by a **moderator** or **facilitator** to discuss a topic of interest. Focus groups can be used to explore such pragmatic issues as how people interpret and respond to political campaign messages or to help researchers operationalize theoretical constructs and hypotheses. They are often used before surveys to pretest survey questions, and they may be used after surveys to help researchers understand the survey results.

Focus groups are based on the assumption that the ideas that emerge from several people discussing a topic are of greater quality and diversity and provide more insight than the ideas generated by the same people interviewed separately as individuals. These groups should provide new insights, concepts, and vocabulary; a sense of why members think the way they do; and the ideas that members agree and disagree on. We hope for a "2 + 2 = 5" effect, noting, however, that a poorly selected group has the potential to provide a "2 + 2 = 3" effect, especially with an inept moderator.

Because focus group members most commonly are sampled judgmentally or on the basis of convenience, the method's major weaknesses are reliability and the ability to generalize to a wider population. Often the reliability question can be addressed by running a second focus group and comparing the results with those from the first group.

Generally, focus group participants are selected by the researcher to represent a defined demographic group such as college seniors looking for jobs. Within such groups, the researcher hopes to find a diversity of opinions on the topic by recruiting, for example, social media "geeks" and students who have yet to join a social networking site.

A focus group on students' use of social media would give Bonnie insight on the new "buzz words" and terminology that she needs to understand and, importantly, on the meanings that students associate with these words. Ideally, the group should generate new ideas she has not thought of and also show her areas where students agree and disagree.

Focus group moderators need the skills to encourage reticent members to speak and to control the more verbose members. They need to take a middle ground between allowing group members free expression and keeping the discussion focused on the topic at hand. To keep the discussion on track and to maintain order, the moderator should prepare in advance a discussion guide that lists key questions and the question order. The same prompts that help an interview along can be used to prompt a reticent focus group, but the ideal focus group has a level of interaction among its members such that prompting should be unnecessary.

Typically, the group's discussion will be audio or video recorded to provide transcripts for subsequent analysis. Professionally run focus groups often take place in a room with one-way mirrors so that observers can follow the discussion without their presence disrupting it. Group members may be offered drinks and snacks and may receive a small payment or a donation to a charity of their choice.

Online Focus Groups

Increasingly, focus groups are run online, especially in applied communication research areas such as marketing. Online groups offer the advantages of low cost, time saving, and the ability to link people internationally. Focus group software can record the discussion; offer anonymity to participants; and allow the moderator to contact participants individually and, if necessary, privately. Online groups can run for days or weeks as necessary and offer members the convenience of participating from their homes or offices.

The disadvantages of online focus groups include anonymity, the absence of nonverbal communication, and Internet technology itself. The same anonymity that can encourage free and frank discussion can also present a focus group moderator with the problem of not knowing who exactly is participating in a group. The technology itself can have a negative impact in that group members with poor Internet connections will be less able to participate. Even with high-speed, reliable connections, members with limited keyboard skills will be less able to participate and to express themselves spontaneously.

Online groups may be **asynchronous**, with members contributing in their own time, or **synchronous**, with members interacting in "real time." The asynchronous mode allows for a greater number of participants and may reduce feelings of pressure to respond to an idea. It may also reduce anxieties about answering sensitive questions and encourage in-depth responses because members can reply to questions in their own time. The synchronous mode is likely to be more efficient and to stimulate more interaction, but participants may be more likely to tire of discussions held in this mode rather than in the asynchronous mode.

Online focus group research can include the virtual world of **avatars**—users' online characters. Researching avatars can present problems, such as distributing and getting back completed consent forms, but, on the other hand, this type of research offers group members the advantages of anonymity and the opportunity to express opinions they might not express in the "real world" (Houliez & Gamble, 2012).

A theoretically and practically important question for moderators of virtual groups is the status of the avatar. Is the research interest in the avatar or the person behind the avatar? The question is further complicated by the fact that one "real" person may be the force behind several different avatars.

You can make your own good assessment of the relative advantages and disadvantages of online, offline, and perhaps virtual focus groups by thinking about your own experience with online and regular in-class discussions and identifying the factors that hindered and facilitated discussion in each case.

Any successful focus group has clear objectives, a membership appropriate to the research questions, carefully prepared questions and facilities (offline and/or online), and a moderator who facilitates an active, creative discussion that involves all members and remains focused on the topic.

Ethnographic Methods

Many varieties of watching and listening research take place under the umbrella of ethnography. **Ethnography** is basically the study of human social behavior or cultures. The term *ethnography* (from the Greek *ethnos* = people; *graphein* = writing) suggests that we are observing, describing, and interpreting people's behavior.

Kirsch (2001) identifies some principles of ethnographic research:

- Conduct research primarily in natural settings.

- Combine direct observation with interviews.

- Focus on local, subjective, knowledge, and categories.

- Engage directly with the community's members.

A number of important decisions must precede ethnographic research. These include defining the research questions, which may or may not be specific; identifying potential gatekeepers and informants; deciding whether to interview people individually or in groups; choosing between structured and unstructured interviews; and deciding what to observe and how to record, analyze, and present ethnographic data.

Whether the research interest is a village, a virtual world, a surgical team, a film studio, or a local pub, ethnographers seek to immerse themselves in its culture and natural setting. They seek to describe accurately the attitudes and the behaviors that define this culture and that differentiate it from other cultures. They seek to understand the culture's shared meanings that explain its behaviors and norms. While the generic research question is simple—"How and why do things get done in this culture?" or even more simply "What's going on here?"— getting answers and credible explanations of those answers may take months or years. Because the time available for research may be limited, some communication studies may be "ethnographically informed" rather than being full ethnographies, which can require a researcher's full immersion for a year or more. For example, it may be possible to study a group of students for only one semester, but not for the four years of their college careers.

In practice, ethnographies of all types begin with the formal and informal **gatekeepers** who make access to a community or culture possible. Formal gatekeepers are those individuals whose permission makes the access officially possible. Access to a work team, for example, will typically require a formal approval from management in return for which the researcher may have to provide written assurances that the organization and the individuals in it will not be identified, that no competing organization is involved in the study, and that no proprietary information will be published. Management approval can be a mixed blessing; you get access to employees but then may have to address employee suspicions about your management-approved research.

Formal approvals do not necessarily ease the way into the community to be studied. For a successful entry into the community, **key informants** are required. These are the individuals who are part of the study community and who for their own reasons have agreed to introduce the researcher to this community and legitimize the researcher's work as nonthreatening.

Some research requires that researchers work in disguise, for example as "fake" hospital patients or students (see the Ethics Panel in this chapter). It is more likely that researchers will identify themselves as what they are—researchers with a genuine interest in how and why the community or culture functions. Doing so reduces the potential for ethically suspect relationships and potential complications, such as being exposed as a phony when the members of a work team discover that their fellow employee is not actually an employee.

All ethnographies involve detailed observation and recording, typically in the form of voluminous written notes but increasingly with audio- and video-recording. Regardless of the recording media, the researcher typically will aim to capture a rich diversity of data—behaviors; dress; decor; rites and rituals; language and the meanings associated with specific words and phrases; greetings and salutations; respect for authority; relationships between men and women, old and young, and superiors and subordinates; use of time; work versus social behaviors; and so on.

Generally, ethnographers record at least three different kinds of notes. **Descriptive notes** are the primary records that detail the raw data of human interactions and the settings that are the focus of the ethnography. **Method notes** record the specific methods used to gather data on any given day—for example, direct observation, group interviews, video recording, screen capture, or reading social media content. Method notes are necessary because of the interaction between method and data. For example, individuals are likely to behave and speak differently in one-on-one interviews than they are in a group setting.

Analytic notes are the notes the ethnographer writes in order to interpret the raw data. They are reflexive in that the ethnographer will visit and revisit the notes repeatedly, and her theories and explanations will change as the study progresses and as more data are gathered. For example, she might initially see a power relationship between two individuals as best explained by an age difference or a respect for authority and then, as she gathers more data, come to understand the relationship as best explained by a difference in technical expertise. This interpretation would then trigger further observations and interviews. Such "looping back" through data, method notes, and analytic notes continues until the ethnographer is comfortable that there is no new information to be had and that she has considered all possible explanations and arrived at her best possible understanding of the culture she is studying.

At this point, the task becomes writing the best possible narrative that will explain to interested readers how life is lived as a member of the culture. One feature that distinguishes an ethnographic report is the use of the participants' own language. The availability of audio-visual media and hypermedia presents new challenges and opportunities for recording and reporting, as we shall see in Chapter 14.

Ethnographic Starting Points

"What specifically should I focus on?" can be a difficult question to answer for ethnographic studies because there are so many possible starting points. Sociolinguist Dell Hymes (1974) developed a system for examining communication as a cultural practice and proposed six basic units a researcher might study:

1. **Speech community**—a group of people who share common signs, a language that differentiates them from other groups, and rules governing their speech. Example: a group of communication majors.

2. **Speech situation**—the occasions within a speech community when people talk. Example: A class on research methods or an annual awards dinner.

3. **Speech event**—the specific speech activity that takes place. Example: a student presentation or an awards speech.

4. **Communicative act**—the smaller units of speech within a speech event. Example: asking a question or telling a joke.

5. **Communicative style**—the speech style that is characteristic of someone. Example: being habitually ironic or using "geek" jargon.

6. **Ways of speaking**—the styles of speech that may be used in specific situations and events or that are characteristic of a culture. Example: at the beginning of a class, the instructor speaks before students do.

After choosing one of the above units to study, you would then analyze it by asking a set of questions that Hymes developed. These questions are summarized in the acronym SPEAK-ING, and each item helps a researcher document the language and meanings in a speech community. The SPEAKING items are as follows:

- **Situation**—the setting where the activities take place and the overall scene of which they are a part. Example: a college classroom.

- **Participants**—the people present and their roles and relationships within the speech situation. Example: students and faculty.

- **Ends**—the ends or goals of the communication being studied. Example: mastering the language of communication research.

- **Acts**—the language and behaviors that convey meaning to the participants. Example: instructors demonstrating a specific research method.

- **Key**—the tone of speech. How the speech sounds. Example: formal or friendly.

- **Instrumentality**—the channels or methods used to communicate. Example: an online discussion group.

- **Norms**—the rules governing speech and its interpretation. Example: students cannot ask questions until after the instructor has spoken.

- **Genres**—the traditional types of speech found in most cultures. Examples: commencement speeches, election "stump" speeches, lectures, and funeral orations.

By working through Hymes's units of analysis, we can describe how people communicate, their patterns of communication, and how language is used and understood. This approach is far from being the only entry point into ethnography, but the emphasis on communication and the specific questions to be asked will help you with potential starting points for an ethnographic study.

Online Ethnography

The approaches and issues outlined in this chapter are all applicable to online ethnography, but online ethnography has some unique characteristics to be considered. For example, the online world provides no direct observation of human behavior, and the researcher is faced with data unique to the web such as **emoticons**, avatars, web pages, blogs, wikis, and hyperlinks.

Typically, online text, audio, graphics, and video can be easily recorded using screen-save software, so the effort of recording raw data is much reduced relative to traditional ethnographies.

Kozinets (2013) sees the differences between online and traditional ethnographies to be so evident that a new term—**netnography**—becomes necessary for online ethnographies. He defines netnography as "a specialized form of ethnography adapted to the unique computer-mediated contingencies of today's social worlds" (p. 1). According to Kozinets, netnography is an applied, interdisciplinary approach involving anthropology, sociology, and cultural studies, and whereas ethnography is entirely face to face, netnography is entirely online.

Kozinets's distinction notwithstanding, there is not necessarily a choice between offline and online ethnography because a research question may well imply both. For example, an exploration of how graduating seniors communicate with each other about employment would be seriously shortchanged if it were restricted to either web-only communication or interpersonal communication.

Ethnography at first sight may seem unstructured and unfocused, especially relative to the experimental method in which very specific research designs are proposed to test very specific hypotheses about human communication. It may conjure up the image of earnest explorers in pith helmets living with strange tribes in remote places. The image has some validity as a metaphor for serious, committed, and engaged inquiry into the communication behaviors of others, but ethnographers' interests are as modern as any other research interests today, just consider their focus on cyber-ethnography and the seemingly accepted neologism of "netnography."

Observational Studies

Observational studies typically record and interpret individual and group behaviors in their natural settings. Ethnography depends upon observation, but not every observational study is an ethnography. You could, for example, observe the behavior of music fans at a rock concert without doing any of the in-depth interviews or long-term observations that ethnography typically requires.

Many qualitative studies are observational without being ethnographies, for example observations of student-teacher interaction in the classroom or of small groups engaged in problem solving. In these two examples, observational methods will not necessarily provide an understanding of what it means to be a teacher, a student, or a member of a group, but they may well provide valid findings about communication and perhaps even reliable findings that will allow us to predict whether a particular teaching style will be effective with reticent students or what specific behaviors most facilitate or hinder a group's problem solving.

Observational studies use many of the methods described above and possibly even quasi-experimental methods, as in the observation of a group put together specifically to solve a problem assigned by the researcher under conditions defined by the researcher.

At the other extreme, a researcher may have no contact with the individuals being researched at all. This means using unobtrusive measures, as described below.

Unobtrusive Measures

Unobtrusive measures document people's behavior without them being aware of it. This can be important when we suspect that there may be a difference between words and action. For example, suppose research participants assure us in interviews or surveys that they would never text while driving and that they always wear their seat belts. True? Take a look at campus traffic to observe directly the extent of texting and seat belt usage. Interested in whether your informants' accounts of healthy eating match reality? You can unobtrusively observe campus dining behavior to get a sense of the cheeseburger-to-fruit ratio on cafeteria trays, or you can ask the dining services manager for data on what items are best sellers. Want a check on student alcohol consumption? Check out dormitory or apartment garbage, or campus police records. For a check on campus political sentiments, check out campaign stickers on employee and student vehicles, or graffiti. How might a car dealer decide which radio stations to advertise on? Have service staff record what station each car radio is tuned to when the vehicle comes in for service.

Most unobtrusive measures do not provide a direct check on any one individual's self-report, but they can provide a general sense of whether the self-reports you get of people's behaviors are credible.

Performance Studies

Often, when we discuss performance we think of numbers: golf scores, GPA, or income. None of those is what's being discussed here. Rather, in performance studies, researchers look at behavior performatively, or as a performance. For example, how does the identity of "student" get performed at your university? How does Bonnie perform the role of "Career Center director"? Or even, how does the "Career Center" perform?

Performance studies are multidisciplinary. Stemming originally from theatre and literary interpretation, it now includes communication, sociology, gender studies, critical race studies, and anthropology, among other disciplines. "Scholars in the field investigate storytelling, ritual, dance, music, and theater: live and mediated, professional and amateur. But they also deploy "performance" as a heuristic tool for examining practices of everyday life" (Hamera, 2018, p. 1). *Heuristic* refers to **heurism**, or the principle of enabling people to learn by making discoveries for themselves; in this context, the term means a practical or intuitive way of learning more about such practices. For example, shopping for groceries, ordering coffee, or doing a job interview—all could be opportunities for performance studies.

Much of performance is ritual. "Even when we think we're being original, most of what we do and utter has been said and done before—by us even" (Schechner, 2013, p. 52). Schechner argues that in liminal performances—those taking place in the in-between space as we're moving from one place to another in our lives—rites of passage and transformations can occur. For example, the process of graduating from a university and interviewing for and being offered a first professional job can be a liminal phase of ritual. Or think of your graduation—when graduates walk across the stage and move their tassel right to left. What might that ritual performance mean? How should it be interpreted?

For example, MacDonald (2018) writes about lighthouse keeping as tourism performance, and argues that the performance of lighthouse keeping has changed. In earlier times, keepers were required to keep the lighthouses functional and to save sailors from shipwrecks. Current performances can be understood as saving work, curating work, and advocacy work. Saving, as currently used, means to save lighthouses from destruction. Curating involves organizing displays, exhibits, and signage at lighthouses for tourists to engage with. Advocacy relates to educational and tourism performances—acts that show the public the importance of these sites. "Each of these presents a continuation of and departure from historical keeping. These departures mark and are marked as 'authentic' performances of keeping. Taken together, they create a performative repertoire beyond heritage tourism" (p. 27). Examples of performance studies range from oral interpretation to storytelling to cultural critique. See also Conquergood (2002) in the Recommended Reading section for an overview of performance studies.

Let's return to Bonnie and consider the Career Center's performance. For example, perhaps the Career Center's performance has changed over time: what was once an office with paper information, mock interview appointments, and a list of local internships now performs as a mostly online office hosting podcasts, online workshops, and interactive résumé builders, so the physical office now performs a secondary role for those who would like face-to-face help with interview prep.

We might also consider Bonnie's own performance as Career Center director. For example, might we see that her traditional performance as a university administrator managing "walk-in" services has changed over time to that of an online coach for students plus an entrepreneur promoting her Career Center's services?

Exhibit 13.1 shows a brief summary of the strengths and weaknesses of the methods discussed in this chapter.

EXHIBIT 13.1 ■ Summary of Qualitative Methods			
Method	**Summary**	**Advantages**	**Disadvantages**
Interviews	The process of asking questions of a respondent, usually face to face or by phone or video, to elicit information the researcher is interested in.	• Detailed information in participants' own words. • Understanding how participants frame their own experiences.	• Large amounts of data to analyze. • Can be time-consuming, particularly transcribing. • Can be influenced by moderator. • Participants' memories are sometimes inaccurate.
Focus Group	Small group of people brought together to discuss a topic of interest to the researcher.	• Varying opinions from people on the same topic. • Detailed information in participants' own words. • Can see interaction between participants.	• Some participants can take over discussion, limiting dialogue. • Can be influenced by moderator. • Too much data can be overpowering.
Ethnography	The study of human social behavior, typically with emphasis on description.	• Rich data. • Learn about people's experiences directly.	• Large amounts of data to analyze. • Not all locations are accessible. • Topics are usually very narrow. • Time-intensive method.
Unobtrusive Measures	Observations of people's behavior without them being aware of such observation.	• No researcher effect on those observed. • Can compare information to self-reports.	• Researcher's assessment might be inaccurate. • Potential validity problems. • Potential ethical problems related to privacy.
Performance Studies	Study of performance in ritual and situational contexts.	• Explores understudied topics. • Studies power and context.	• Topics very narrow. • Time-sensitive methods.

MAKING SENSE OF QUALITATIVE DATA

When you gather data on people's behavior by watching and listening, you record words and actions rather than numbers. The question then becomes how to establish a sense of order and interpret what may be hours of audio or video recordings or page after page and box after box of notes, transcripts, or observations.

The basis of many qualitative analyses is **categorization**—that is, identifying each piece of data as belonging to a particular category predetermined by the researcher or generated from the data itself. By analyzing these categories and the relationships among categories, researchers are able to see patterns of behavior or thinking that shed light on research interests.

Fundamentally, there are three ways of categorizing qualitative information. The first is to assign items to specific unchanging, preassigned categories (fixed coding). The second is to start with theoretically informed categories that may change as new data come in (flexible coding). The third is to start with no preconceived categories and to allow categories and theories to emerge as data analysis progresses (grounded-in-data coding).

Fixed Coding

Coding typically means assigning units of information to preassigned categories and then counting the frequency with which these different units occur. Suppose, for example, we are questioning students in an attempt to understand their use of social media. With **fixed coding**, we might, for example, hypothesize that four important factors will explain students' use of social media—convenience, relaxation, escape, and the opportunity for social interaction with friends. We would then develop a simple record sheet that records the number of times we find each of these mentioned in our data. Such a coding sheet would look like Exhibit 13.2.

Flexible Coding

A problem with fixed coding is that it provides no room for the inevitable "other" categories that will emerge as we read through our interview or focus group transcripts. Furthermore, one of the reasons we listen to people in the first place is to gain new insights. **Flexible coding** allows for new categories to emerge rather than forcing every piece of information into preconceived categories or perhaps one additional and less than useful "other" category.

EXHIBIT 13.2 ■ Sample Analysis Sheet for Qualitative Data: Predetermined Categories (Fixed Coding)		
Understanding Student Use of Social Media		
Categories Derived From Theory	**Number of Mentions**	**Reasons Item Is Considered Important**
Convenience		
Relaxation		
Escape		
Social Viewing		

For example, as we read though people's answers about social media, it appears that there are two broad reasons for using them—convenience and the opportunity to socialize. As we examine the explanations we have been given about convenience, we see that several different notions of "convenience" emerge—geographic (*I can stay home and socialize*), scheduling (*I can socialize anytime*), portability (*I can socialize on my smartphone*), and cost (*I don't need money to go to the movies or a restaurant*). All of these ideas seem to fit under the umbrella of "convenience," so we decide to set up four subcategories, as shown in Exhibit 13.3.

Similarly, "socializing," turns out to have three components. Two are perhaps predictable—"relaxation" and "social interaction." Also, it appears that online socializing is a social learning opportunity in the sense that students learn from other students and recently graduated friends about the social behaviors associated with careers and different types of employment. If students' definition of social media includes movie sites such as YouTube, they may even be learning about career behaviors specific to criminal justice, health care, business, and entertainment. They may even change courses or majors on the basis of what they learn from such sites. This is clearly a new concept, and it might be reasonable to set up a new "social learning" category called "career skills." For the moment, use of movie sites appears to be seen as part of socializing, but as our analysis progresses, we may decide that this is a major new concept related to career development and that we will be able to rationalize setting it up as a third major category, alongside "convenience" and "socializing."

Many qualitative analyses are grounded in an approach developed by Glaser and Strauss (1967) that considers theory as being "grounded in data." That is to say, rather than using data to test a theory or hypothesis, the theory itself emerges as the data analysis proceeds.

A basic of the **grounded theory** approach is the "constant comparative method." In this technique, we would look at statements and ideas that emerge from our observations and assign each statement to a category. The constant comparative method consists of testing each new statement or idea against the categories we have developed and reworking categories as necessary as our data analysis proceeds. In effect, we did this in previous paragraphs when we analyzed the data students provided on their use of social media and developed the summary table shown as Exhibit 13.3.

The above examples of coding might be regarded as an analytic approach in which the number and relationship of categories of data help build a theory about human communication. Another approach is interpretive; the researcher probes for the values and motivations that seem to be behind the observed data. The researcher tries to understand what it is that individuals are trying to achieve with, for example, their social media postings or what values define a community for its members and make it different from other communities.

Moving between analysis and interpretation, between data and hypotheses, and between different samples of data can help establish the relative importance of different observations and the relationships among them. Your hypotheses should change and evolve as a result. You can test your hypotheses by looking for data that contradict them. They should become less and less tentative to the point where you can have confidence in proposing a general theory about human communication in a particular setting.

There is no compelling reason to analyze all your data at once. Starting with a small judgmental sample of data may allow you to categorize and interpret it more readily. You can test your initial reading of your data by checking it against a further sample.

EXHIBIT 13.3 ■ Sample Analysis Sheet for Qualitative Data: Categories Emerge From Data (Flexible Coding)			
Understanding Student Use of Social Media			
Categories Emerge From Data			**Working Notes**
Convenience	geographic		1. *Which of these are most used as reasons to use social media?*
	scheduling		
	portability of medium		2. *Is there a difference between weeknight relaxation and weekend relaxation?*
	cost	money	
		time	3. *Am I hearing different words for the same concept?*
Socializing	relaxation	gaming	
		social planning	4. *Are residents and commuters telling me the same thing?*
	social interaction	keeping current	
		academic work	5. *Note: Need to be able to write an account that student would recognize as authentic.*
		networking	
	social learning	careers	
		work behaviors	

Qualitative Analysis Software

Just as there are statistical programs to handle numeric data, computer-assisted qualitative data analysis software (**CAQDAS**) handles qualitative data, including text, audio, graphics, video, and social media chat.

Basically, such programs allow the user to enter text such as interviews and then to search for words and phrases and pull together items that are flagged as belonging to a particular category. New coding categories can be created as new ideas emerge from examining the data. Typically, you will be able to search for terms, examine terms in context, display the frequencies of key terms, and produce graphic displays of the relationships among terms. Most programs offer tutorials, webinars, free trials, and user forums. Websites for some such programs are listed at the end of this chapter.

ETHICS PANEL
IN WHICH A PROFESSOR BECOMES A STUDENT

"Rebekah Nathan," a "50-something" professor of anthropology, decided that she needed to better understand her students and their lives. She took a sabbatical leave and, on the basis of her high-school transcript, enrolled as a freshman student at her own university for a semester. She moved into a dorm, took on a full course load, ate in the student cafeteria, joined student clubs, played volleyball and tag football, and, of course, attended class and completed (most) assignments.

To understand student life, she drew on interviews and conversations with classmates, as well as observations and interactions with professors and university staff. The issues she explored included friendships, race relations and social life, classroom participation, eating and sleeping in class, plagiarism, scheduling conflicts, dropping readings and assignments, holding down a job, not holding down food, and relations with faculty.

Nathan did not volunteer that she was a professor but did not lie if anyone specifically asked her. In day-to-day interactions, she allowed students to assume she was one of them. When conducting formal interviews, she identified herself as a researcher, explained her study, and obtained written permission to publish informants' words. She did reveal her identity to some students with whom she developed a close relationship.

On the one hand, Nathan has been criticized for enhancing her own academic career at the expense of students; on the other hand, she has been commended for following approved procedures such as obtaining informed consent and clearing her study through her university's IRB.

You can read the author's own views on ethics and ethnography in the Afterword to her book (Nathan, 2005).

Review Chapter 3—"Ethics: What Are My Responsibilities as a Researcher?"—and answer the following.

Questions

- Why would "Ms. Nathan" not want to be open about her status, occupation, and reason for being on campus?

- Do you feel that students involved in this study were exploited in any way?

- Do any aspects of this study strike you as ethically suspect? Why or why not?

- Nathan's research was approved by the campus IRB. Do you agree or disagree with the board's decision? Why?

Resources

American Psychological Association, Ethical Principles of Psychologists and Code of Conduct. . . . . www.apa .org/ethics/code

National Communication Association Code of Professional Ethics for the Communication Scholar/Teacher. . . . . .https://www.natcom.org/sites/default/files/ Public_Statement_A_Code_of_Professional_Ethics_ for_the_Communication_Scholar_Teacher_2017.pdf

Chapter Summary

- Qualitative methods are generally based on the assumption that people are idiosyncratic and have unique and subjective views of the world. The inability to generalize to a larger population is not therefore regarded as a problem.

- Qualitative researchers may begin with theoretically derived hypotheses or develop theories from research data as it is analyzed.

- Qualitative methods are generally preferred over surveys and experiments for their ability to elicit people's views in their own words.

- Qualitative research may be structured and ask questions predetermined by the researcher or be open ended and elicit ideas that informants volunteer.

- Participant or unobtrusive observation provides a check on whether people's words match their behaviors.

- Qualitative studies of online communication must deal with entities unique to the web such as avatars and emoticons and can be limited to the extent that online social behavior is mostly text and image based.

Key Terms

acts 269
analytic notes 268
asynchronous 266
avatars 266
CAQDAS 275
categorization 273
communicative act 268
communicative style 268
contrast questions 263
descriptive notes 268
descriptive questions 263
emoticons 269
ends 269
ethnography 266
facilitator 265
fixed coding 273
flexible coding 273
focus group 265

fully structured interviews 263
gatekeepers 267
genres 269
grounded theory 274
heurism 271
informants 262
instrumentality 269
interpretive 261
interviewees 264
interview 262
key 269
key informants 267
method notes 268
moderator 265
netnography 269
norms 269
observational studies 270
participants 269

performance studies 271
prompts 264
qualitative 261
quantitative 261
respondents 262
semistructured
    interviews 263
sequence 263
situation 269
speech community 268
speech event 268
speech situation 268
structural questions 263
structure 262
synchronous 266
unstructured
    interviews 262
ways of speaking 269

Application Exercises

Exercise 1: An Ethnographic Study

Review in this chapter the broad research question of how students use the Internet to find out about employment and apply for jobs. You decide that the best insights on student job hunting on the Internet will come from an in-depth ethnographic study of students as they do this online job search. Using the Dell Hymes questions outlined in this chapter, set out your plans for such a study. It should include key informants, an outline of the observations you would make, the questions you would ask your research participants, media content that you might want to read, and any permissions that you might need to obtain before your study begins.

Exercise 2: An Interview

You are interested in how exactly a student might go about using the Internet to locate jobs and apply for them. Assuming that a structured interview with specific questions is the best way to get this information, write out the specific questions you would want to ask a student whom you identify as being highly experienced in the art of the online job search.

Exercise 3: Performance Studies

You are interested in students' preparations for job interviews. If you were interested in studying this topic using the performance studies approach, where would you begin? What questions would you ask? How might performance studies questions and results differ from those for interviews or ethnography?

Recommended Reading

Conquergood, D. (2002). Performance studies: Interventions and radical research. *TDR: The Drama Review, 46*(2), 145–156.

Argues for the expansion of performance studies and what qualifies as performance studies.

Daymon, C., & Holloway, I. (2010). *Qualitative methods in public relations and marketing communications* (2nd ed.). New York, NY: Routledge.

A guide to planning, implementing, and writing research in the applied fields of public relations and marketing.

Krueger, R. A., & Casey, M. A. (2015). *Focus groups: A practical guide for applied research* (5th ed.). Thousand Oaks, CA: Sage.

Covers the practicalities of planning and running focus groups and analyzing and reporting results.

Lindlof, T. R., & Taylor, B. C. (2017). *Qualitative communication research methods* (4th ed.). Thousand Oaks, CA: Sage.

Shows with examples how qualitative studies are designed, conducted, and written.

Spradley, J. P. (1979). *The ethnographic interview.* New York, NY: Holt, Rinehart & Winston.

Describes 12 steps for developing an ethnographic study.

Recommended Web Resources

Ethnography of Communication.........www.cios.org/encyclopedia/ethnography/index.htm
An overview of Dell Hymes's ethnography of communications.

Forum: Qualitative Social Research.........www.qualitative-research.net
An open-access online academic journal of qualitative social research.

Qualitative Research Consultants Association.........www.qrca.org
Links to qualitative research practitioners.

University of Surrey, Social Research Update..........http://sru.soc.surrey.ac.uk/
A resource for interviewing, focus groups, study design and analysis, and more.

Qualitative Data Analysis Software

Atlas.ti.........www.atlasti.com/product.html
HyperRESEARCH.........www.researchware.com/products/hyperresearch.html
NVivo.........www.qsrinternational.com/products_nvivo.aspx
Transana.........www.transana.org

References

Conquergood, D. (2002). Performance studies: Interventions and radical research. *TDR: The Drama Review, 46*(2), 145–156.

Geertz, C. (1973). *The interpretation of cultures.* New York, NY: Basic Books.

Glaser, B. G., & Strauss, A. L. (1967). *The discovery of grounded theory: Strategies for qualitative research.* Chicago, IL: Aldine.

Gold, R. L. (1958). Roles in sociological field observations. *Social Forces, 36*(3), 217–223. DOI: 10.2307/2573808

Hamera, J. (2018, February 26). Performance studies in critical communication studies. *Oxford Research Encyclopedia of Communication* [Online publication]. DOI: 10.1093/acrefore/9780190228613.013.640

Houliez, C., & Gamble, E. (2012). Augmented focus groups: On leveraging the peculiarities of online virtual worlds when conducting in-world focus groups. *Journal of Theoretical and Applied Electronic Commerce Research, 7*(2), 31–51. DOI: 10.4067/S0718-18762012000200005

Hymes, D. (1974). *Foundations in sociolinguistics: An ethnographic approach.* Philadelphia: University of Pennsylvania Press.

Kirsch, S. (2001). Ethnographic methods: Concepts and field techniques. In R. A. Krueger, M. A. Casey, J. Donner, S. Kirsch, & J. N. Maack (Eds.), *Social analysis: Selected tools and techniques* (pp. 50–61)/ Social Development Paper #36. Washington, DC: World Bank. Retrieved from www.worldbank.org/reference

Kozinets, R. V. (2013). *Netnography: Doing ethnographic research online.* London: Sage.

MacDonald, S. M. (2018) Sentinels by the sea: Keeping as an alternative tourism performance. *Text and Performance Quarterly, 38*, 1–2, 19–37. DOI: 10.1080/10462937.2018.1457172

Nathan, R. (2005). *My freshman year: What a professor learned by becoming a student.* Ithaca, NY: Cornell University Press.

Schechner, R. (2013). *Performance studies: An introduction* (3rd ed.). New York, NY: Routledge.

Spradley, J. P. (1979). *The ethnographic interview.* New York, NY: Holt, Rinehart & Winston.

Xerri, R. C. (2005). *Gozitan crossings: The impact of migration and return migration on an island community.* Qala, Malta: A&M Printing.

$SAGE edge™

Get the tools you need to sharpen your study skills. SAGE edge offers a robust online environment featuring an impressive array of free tools and resources.

Access quizzes, eFlashcards, video, and multimedia at **edge.sagepub.com/treadwell4e**.

RESEARCH RESULTS IN PRINT AND ONLINE

Writing and Presenting for Scholarly and Other Publics

ASA Comments

Hello! The All-Seeing Authors are here to speak with you again. We hope you have come to appreciate the enthusiasm communication researchers have for their many interests, and have developed interests of your own and some sense of how to research them. We thank you for keeping us company and leave you with Charlotte, Lee, and Mike introducing the ideas that research is pointless unless published and that publication involves far more than the conventional scholarly paper.

"So, Charlotte . . . you're clubbing again tonight?"

"Can't decide, Mike. That comm. research I did on clubbing does keep dragging me back."

"Dragging you back? How so?"

"Well, every answer raises more questions, and I do get sort of involved in trying to find the answers. . . . But what worries me more right now is there's just so much detail in that club scene. You know, all those subtle little behaviors that mark you as one of the in-crowd—*or not*—and the clothes and the music and the dance moves, and, and, and . . . I've got all this information, and I still think I need more. That's why I might go back again tonight."

"You should have done content analysis like James did. He just counted up the "Republican" bumper stickers and the "Democrat" stickers and—boom—project done! Two pages max. See? You should have gone for counting not description."

"Not helpful, Lee. You know Prof. Michaels wants all that Intro–Lit Review–Research Questions–Method–Results–Conclusions stuff. And I'm starting to see why. Results are nothing without context. Two pages won't get you anywhere.

My problem is none of that helps me get that club culture across to readers. People would actually understand it better if I produced a movie or wrote a short story instead of writing it all up as a research project . . . or I at least got my audio and video records up on a website for them to access."

"Movies, fiction, websites? Doesn't sound like research to me, Charlotte. Next thing you know you'll have a dedicated website for your research and be posting social media updates."

"Lee, that's exactly where the action is now. You and James are too busy counting bumper stickers to notice?"

"So now I have to be a multimedia wiz as well as a writer? Now I really need that free lunch Mike offered us all back in Chapter 1."

"Empirical evidence clearly indicates that I did not make that offer."

"Yeah, Mike, but I'm in interpretive mode right now."

"Coffee is my best and final offer to get us through our project writing."

"You mean our project blog–podcast–interactive multimedia writing?"

"Sure! You can't sign up for communication research and not communicate!"

CHAPTER OVERVIEW

It would be inappropriate to conclude a book on communication research without discussing how research findings are communicated. Research cannot contribute to our wider knowledge unless people know about it. In this chapter, we look at scholarly writing and presentation, reaching interest groups and the media outlets to whom your research might be relevant, and the implications of **multimedia** and **hypermedia** for presenting research results.

CHAPTER OBJECTIVES

This chapter will help you

- Identify major publics for research findings and explain why each of them is important.

- Describe the format and style of a conventional scholarly research report.

- Explain why the format and style of scholarly reports are necessary when writing for a scholarly audience.

- Explain how writing for interest groups and news media differs from writing scholarly papers.

- Discuss the advantages and disadvantages of websites, blogs, and podcasts for disseminating and explaining research findings.

- Explain the advantages and disadvantages of graphics versus text for explaining research findings.

- Explain how reporting research findings can have ethical implications.

INTRODUCTION

As you reach the end of this book, you may have decided that there are two quite different research processes.

The first is the scholarly practice model in which research begins with a search of the relevant research literature and proceeds with straight-line logic to research design, implementation, analysis, interpretation, and reporting of results—all within the scholarly community.

Your own experience was probably different, and not nearly as simple. In the student experience model you probably talk with friends and social network contacts, search Google, and read anything you can find that is relevant. You talk with your sister who did the course three years ago, maybe read some scholarly literature, and maybe talk to faculty. You do all this because you want fast answers, social support, and contacts who could help you.

Rather than a linear progression, you probably bounce around between research questions, research methods, reading, and informal consulting—each aspect feeding into the other and getting more and more targeted until you become comfortable with and committed to your research questions, methods, and perhaps a finalized list of readings that form the basis of your literature review.

Then, you're into data collection—what everybody thinks of as research—and that stage is followed by data analysis, interpretation, and writing up your results. You want a good grade so you write your report as per your professor's instructions. But you also send a draft to your sister for comment, check with your class peers on their progress, monitor discussions on the class website, and maybe text your professor with specific questions or to clarify instructions. You submit your report and wait for a grade. But the process isn't over until grades come out, and even after that you might be given the opportunity to revise or at least to have the "who got what for a grade and why" discussion.

We're confident in thinking that the student experience model summarizes what you probably did in practice much better than the scholarly practice model.

Both models share expectations that you will produce an appropriately written and formatted body of work that meets the standards of the scholarly community you are writing for. The models differ, seemingly, in that the student experience model has a much greater emphasis on human motivations and informal connections—in other words, a greater sense of networking or community. It also recognizes that research is not necessarily a logical, ordered process and that it starts before the first steps of the scholarly model and continues on after that model's final step.

We suggest that the student experience model better captures the realities of research as a process and places an even greater emphasis on "community" or, more accurately, "communities"—plural. The advent of social media has increased the number, diversity, and interconnectedness of relevant communities. Add in research politics and funding to the student experience model, and we see a different model of research in which traditional scholarly publishing becomes just one of many methods for disseminating research findings.

This model of research practice differs from the traditional view in three important ways.

First, we recognize a preresearch phase during which our contacts' views, our readings, personal interests, worldviews, available time and resources, and method predispositions all feed into our thinking about research before we start on the formalities of a defined research project.

Second, communication about one's research needs to extend beyond the formal report to a scholarly public to addressing the information needs of a variety of publics such as news media and news sites, interest groups, funding sources, and institutions such as universities, each with their more specific publics such as alumni and administrators.

Third, thanks largely to digital media and social media, we are able to engage with almost any identifiable public using a variety of media and to do so interactively. This means we have the potential to build relationships with interested groups, to address critics, and to present our research to any group in a way that maximizes its understanding of our findings.

This view of the research process expanded in space, time, and complexity is captured by, for example, Mollett, Brumley, Gilson, and Willliams (2017) who propose a "research lifecycle" consisting of inspiration, collaboration, primary research, dissemination, public engagement, and impact.

Inspiration involves getting ideas about research from a variety of sources. Collaboration may range from collaborative writing with coauthors to working with community groups who may volunteer their time to run surveys, record the time they spend on gaming, or participate in your experiments or focus groups. Primary research is largely what this book is about—designing and implementing research. Dissemination is the process of getting your results not only to the scholarly community but also to funding sources, policy makers, and your own institution's administrators, faculty, and alumni. Public engagement means communicating with interest groups to demonstrate the relevance or application of your research or using that research to effect societal change at some level. Impact addresses the complex issue of measuring outcomes from your research and addressing the "so what" question. There may be personal outcomes such as promotion or additional research funding, policy outcomes such as having your research influence government regulations, and communication outcomes such as being able to demonstrate that your research was reported in major national newspapers or attracted millions of views on social media.

In this chapter, we consider the publics for research, the voices of research, and the media and methods that can make research accessible.

As shown in Exhibit 14.1, there are many foundational planning questions for reporting research. Here we discuss in more detail three basic publics for any scholarly research: scholars, the news media, and interest groups.

THE PUBLICS OF RESEARCH

Scholarly Publics

Publication is the way scholars engage in formal conversation with one another. The medium for this is the scholarly journal familiar to you from your literature review. One way to find out whether your research findings hold up is to publish them; doing so invites others to examine your research, critique it, and perhaps replicate it to see if they get the same results. Scholarly journals are a major arena for evidence-based and theoretically based arguments by members of the scholarly community.

Typically, communication journals are published quarterly. This schedule plus editorial and production time mean that scholarly articles may not see the light of day until months after their authors first submit their work for publication. The hiatus between journal issues is

Exhibit 14.1 ■ Foundation Questions for Reporting Research		
Who are your publics?		
scholarly	special interest	lay
What are your communication goals for each public?		
knowledge	attitude change	behavior
What do you know about each public?		
education level: _____		
language: _____		
interest in your research:high _____, moderate _____, low _____		
attitudes to your research:positive_____, neutral _____, negative_____		
What are their preferred information sources?		
social media	traditional news media	scholarly media
What feedback or interactivity do I want?		
visitor comments	online survey	visitor metrics
How much time do I have?		
Can I commit to a regular blog or podcast?		
What level of expertise might I need?		
Will I need professional help with web design, blogs, podcasts, infographics, or video production?		

now addressed by publishers making journal articles available online prior to their print publication and by academic social networking sites such as ResearchGate, Academia.edu, and Mendeley. Such sites offer participants the potential to share papers, ask and answer questions, browse for people with similar interests, and collaborate online. Web addresses for these sites are listed at the end of this chapter.

News Media

News media editors look for stories that are relevant to their readers, viewers, or listeners. A research story must clearly answer the "So what?" question before it will get a news editor's interest. Often, answering this question involves showing how your research relates to the concerns or interests of the general public. For example, the results of a study in cross-cultural communication might translate into a story on how to date someone from another culture, or the results of a study on families watching television might translate into a story on how to organize a family TV-viewing night.

As news veterans tell it, media audiences tune into only one station—WIIFM ("What's In It For Me?")—basically a "So what?" question. Relevance is one of several **news determinants** or aspects of a story that make it newsworthy, and it is one of the most important determinants. Other determinants include timeliness—the research findings are newsworthy just by virtue of being new or topical; proximity—the research or the researcher is local and known to local readers and viewers; and human interest—somewhere in all those data there is a story about "real people" to be told.

Adapting scholarly research reports to the needs of the news media implies two strategic tasks—answering the WIIFM question and writing to appropriate news media style, whether you are writing a quick news item or a feature story for print, broadcast, or web media.

In essence, news writing is characterized by a "get-to-the-point" style. Feature writing is characterized by rich description that maintains reader interest. Broadcast writing has a spoken, conversational style. As discussed later in this chapter, web writing uses **hyperlinks** and a layout that helps website visitors to navigate a site. The hyperlinks embedded in each page allow visitors to jump to more detail on a topic if they need it.

Because of the diversity of news media, researchers face the prospect of translating scholarly reports into print, radio, television, website, blog, and podcast formats, for example, as well as adapting the content for each medium to meet the interests and reading levels of each audience. This challenge can be met in a variety of ways. For example, science, technology, or psychology writers for magazines with a highly educated readership may prefer to get the original scholarly report and to interview its lead author, so they can do their own "translation" to meet their readers' needs. At the other extreme, a busy news editor may prefer a simple, brief, newsworthy news release that can be published without further rewriting.

Generally, you can facilitate the work of news editors by

- Providing content that meets their standards for news and relevance to their audiences,

- Providing content in the language of their news audiences and in a format that minimizes the time and effort required to turn scholarly communication into news, and

- Proactively ensuring that the research news reaches them.

Interest Groups

Communication research findings have potential relevance to corporations, nonprofit organizations, and government agencies generally and to sectors such as advertising, technology, education, and health care specifically. For example, a study giving new insights on how advertising can influence the food preferences of children may interest parents, nutrition advocates, the food industry, the advertising industry, and regulatory agencies.

Such entities may be interested in research from a policy perspective; that is, based on this research, they may want to promote, oppose, or change organizational policy or legislation. They will therefore be interested in getting research details, but only those details that are relevant to their purposes. Typically, their primary interest will be in research results and their implications—perhaps in some detail—but not in, for example, detailed descriptions of research methods or the theoretical background to research questions.

Funding agencies will have a specific interest in a research project if they have funded it. They will expect a full report detailing the results and their relevance for the funding agency, as well as how exactly the money was spent.

We will refer to the reports written for such interest groups as **professional reports** because, typically, they are written for professionals working in a particular sector. You may need to write research you have done or summarize the research of others in the form of a professional report for a client or an employer.

Professional reports, at their most basic level, have a three-part structure: introduction, body, and conclusion. The introduction summarizes the research and its relevance. The body summarizes the research methods and results. The conclusion summarizes the results and proposes any action that might be required, based on the research findings. Typically, there will be no literature review and no list of scholarly references. The focus of the report is on helping readers understand the results and their relevance and practical implications rather than their theoretical implications.

Because interest group members have a vested interest in the research topic, as well as some knowledge of it, the language of a professional report lies somewhere between formal, scholarly language and the lay language of most news media.

It is typical for research institutions to develop distribution lists of groups that are likely to be interested in their reports and to distribute news releases to these groups once a report becomes available online. It has also become standard practice for research institutions to post their research reports in full and summary forms to their websites. An example you will be familiar with is the Pew Research Center (www.pewinternet.org). You will see at this site that Pew makes available raw data, reports, presentations, interactive graphics, information on its researchers, and the opportunity to subscribe to newsletters and new report alerts.

Exhibit 14.2 shows the basic outline of a professional report. Because many of the components of a scholarly report are not required or expected in a professional report, the author has a much greater level of flexibility in what does and does not get reported.

In summary, writing for interest groups, news media, and other nonscholarly audiences means

- Writing to make research comprehensible,

- Writing to make research relevant, and

- Selecting appropriate media to reach relevant audiences.

THE VOICES OF RESEARCH

Scholarly Publications

Content aside, the overall "voice" of a scholarly publication comes from its combination of vocabulary, structure, use of quotations, use of passive or active style, and other details that all add up to knowing that you are reading *Journal A* and not *Journal B*. Two important components of a scholarly publication's voice are format and style.

One way to facilitate the understanding and discussion of published research papers is to **format** them in a way that allows for easy comparison. "Format" here refers to the standardized headings that most journal editors require for any paper they publish. The scholarly community basically expects that any published paper will have an informative title; an abstract that summarizes the paper; a literature review that provides a background to the study; a research question or questions; a method section; results, discussion, and conclusions; and a list of references. You will recall from Chapter 4 that it is this combination of features that distinguishes scholarly journals from popular and trade publications.

The precise nature and number of sections may vary, but, overall, this basic structure helps other scholars rapidly understand what a paper has to say and how it relates to other papers. Researchers working in the same area of interest and familiar with the relevant literature and the methods in use can skip directly to the results section to see how these published results compare with others. Researchers new to the field may want to spend more time reading the literature review and method sections to get ideas that will spark their own research.

Exhibit 14.2 shows a generic outline of a scholarly report.

EXHIBIT 14.2 ■ Scholarly and Professional Report Formats	
Scholarly Report	**Professional Report**
Title Page	Title Page
	Table of Contents (if necessary)
Abstract	Executive Summary
Introduction	Introduction
Goals and Significance of Research	Body of Report
Literature Review	
Research Questions and/or Hypotheses	
Method	*The headings used in a professional report depend on the length, purpose, and intended audience of the report.*
Participants or Media Sampling	
Procedures Used	*A professional report may or may not contain the sections expected for a scholarly report (left column).*
Measures Used (if quantitative study)	
Results	
Discussion	
Significance of Results	
Limitations and Flaws of Study	
Conclusions	
Recommendations for Future Research	Recommendations
References	
Appendices	Appendices

One way to ensure that all relevant aspects of your research are appropriately reported is to follow the appropriate style guide. The main ones, introduced in Chapter 4, are the *Publication Manual of the American Psychological Association* from the APA, the *Chicago Manual of Style* from the University of Chicago Press, and the *MLA Handbook* from the Modern Language Association. Such guides provide specific instructions for formatting scholarly papers, thereby ensuring before publication that all aspects of a scholarly paper are present.

Style guides provide an essential checklist for planning your research before you do it, specifications to ensure that you have reported everything a scholarly audience will want to read once you have completed your research and written it up, and details about applying a consistent style that will help readers. However, they are not necessarily the final word. For example, some scholarly journals have their own **house styles**, which are variations on a basic style such as APA style.

Help with the specifics of any style is also available in the form of journal editors and a variety of online sources. The specific style used by any given publication will typically be found on the publication's website. Look for a link such as "Author Guidelines" or "Submission Guidelines."

Citations (see Chapter 4) must be accurate because scholarly readers, and especially newcomers to the field, will want to be able to access the same material you did. Accurate citations help other scholars locate material you have found useful. In addition, you give the authors whose work has helped you the courtesy of public recognition, and you avoid potential issues of plagiarism.

The resources listed at the end of this chapter provide an overview of APA, Chicago, and MLA styles and how they differ.

The voice of any specific journal is further shaped by its editors and reviewers through an **editorial process** beginning after you submit your final research report to a journal's editor.

An editor's major decision is to either accept or reject your report for publication. This is not, however, an arbitrary decision by the editor. The final decision is based on peer review. Peer review means that the editor solicits the opinions of other scholars working in the same field to ensure that each submitted article meets scholarly standards and makes a contribution to scholarship.

Reviewers will want to see that your research makes a contribution to our understanding of human communication and that there is a match between your theories, the data you collect, and the method(s) used to collect and analyze your data. Peer review can be rigorous. If your paper is accepted for publication, there will inevitably be rewriting or the reworking of data to meet the requirements of reviewers. Published scholarly articles are therefore something of a collaborative process among authors, reviewers, and editors.

Many journals document the publication process for each published article by printing key dates such as first submission, revision, second revision, and so on.

Authors

Layered within the journal's voice and also shaping reader understandings of the research is the voice of the author.

The author's **voice** is shaped by three decisions about writing: where should my writing be on the qualitative-quantitative scale; should I use an active voice that shows me, the researcher, performing the research or a passive voice that emphasizes what is done and leaves the researcher (and author) out; and how will I make my language adequately reflect my interpretations while keeping a check on personal bias. Such author decisions together with specific style decisions made by a publication's editor are a major influence on the voice of a scholarly publication.

Qualitative—Quantitative

One advantage of quantitative studies is that the language of quantitative methods provides a convenient, commonly understood shorthand for authors and readers. Generally, the assumption is that one's peers doing research in the same field will know, for example, what regression, correlation, mode, and level of significance are and that these terms will not need explanation. The same is true with statistics and statistical tests. Reporting a chi-square value, with level of significance and degrees of freedom, can summarize an analysis and its results in about two lines. Paradoxically, this is one reason that style guides for quantitative studies are so specific. By identifying precisely what needs to be reported and how, you can eliminate a great deal of detail.

By contrast, reports of qualitative studies such as ethnography and participant observation need a greater level of explanation.

A quantitative researcher running a survey may report that her sample consisted of a stratified random sample of 120 people of a particular type and then describe the survey questions, the statistical analyses, and the results. This description will give readers with an understanding of survey research methods a clear idea of the research.

On the other hand, a researcher reporting an observational study will need to clarify his relationship to the participants and explain his selection of participants because the selection will have been based on judgment. In addition, he will need to describe and explain the types of data collected, the methods of collection, and the analyses used to make sense of the data.

This means that qualitative research reports will differ from quantitative reports not only in the obvious way of being nonstatistical but also in requiring relatively greater explanation of sampling, methods, analyses, and interpretation. Qualitative reports may also be more flexible with respect to their headings. Quantitative papers usually have explicit research questions or hypotheses that are answered or tested by statistical analyses of survey or experimental data. Qualitative papers written on the assumption that a new theory or insight will emerge out of the research as it progresses may report just a general line of inquiry rather than specific research questions or hypotheses.

Active—Passive

Scholarly writing inescapably aims at convincing readers that the author has made a significant contribution to our knowledge of human communication. One strategy is to distance the author as far as possible from the narrative by writing passively in the third person and avoiding personal commentary as far as possible so that the research methods and data speak for themselves. You will be familiar with this dispassionate "Three participants were interviewed" style from reading many scholarly reports.

Although this style may be regarded as a laudable attempt to remove the author's personal influence from the research and to allow the research data and results to speak for themselves, the question arises of whose voice is being heard. The answer is "basically nobody's." The author is identified at the beginning of the article but then disappears and becomes an abstract entity for the remainder of the paper. The researcher is not actually recorded as doing anything. We have what Alcoff (2008) calls an "erasure of responsibility" (p. 486).

One way to acknowledge the authors' presence and give them a voice is simply to shift to a first-person, active style of writing. So the "Three participants were interviewed" style becomes "I interviewed three participants." The paper becomes more interesting as a result because we now have a character—the author—on a quest to answer a question about human communication. There is a story to engage the reader. The author is now a specific presence and taking responsibility for the research reported. She may also opt to document her own biases, impressions, and opinions, thus permitting readers to allow for these in making their own interpretations of the reported research.

If the notion of the author as a character reporting on a research journey has you thinking that research writing itself can be analyzed using rhetorical, narrative, discourse, and dramatistic analyses and critical approaches, you are correct.

Researchers may also opt for what Van Maanen (1988) calls "impressionist writing," which uses a literary style to attract and engage the reader, and may well sacrifice objectivity in the interests of reader understanding. One such example is "A Small-Town Cop," in which organizational scholar and consultant Michael Pacanowsky (1983) experiments with using the style of fiction writing to describe a police officer's response to his partner being shot.

Subjective—Objective (Language and Bias)

Even when rigorously following the dictates of a style manual, every author decides what specific words will describe a method, sample, result, or conclusion.

In an often-cited example of rhetorical analysis of science writing, Gusfield (1976) points out that language for the scientist is supposed to be a "windowpane"—a panel of clear glass through which the external world can be seen clearly and without distortion.

No approach can be regarded as totally neutral, however. Given that research reporting is always an act of interpretation, it is questionable whether Gusfield's clear glass windowpane can ever exist. Regardless of overall style, writers wittingly or unwittingly shape readers' interpretations of research simply by choice of words.

Herbers (2006), a biologist who studies "slavemaking ants," warns against delusions of objectivity in science writing and argues that scientists have a responsibility for the rhetorical impact of their writing. By way of example, she discusses how she became uneasy with the implications of slavery as a metaphor and found a more accurate metaphor (*pirate*) for the ant behaviors she was studying.

APA guidelines for reducing bias in research reporting include mentioning participant's differences only when these are relevant to the research; for example, there is no need to identify marital status, sexual orientation, disabilities, race, or ethnicity unless this information is relevant to the study. A second guideline is being sensitive to labels and calling research participants what they prefer to be called—recognizing that this may change over time. A third is writing in a way that presents research participants as active rather than passive individuals (APA, 2015).

Research Participants

For research of the ethnographic and participant observation varieties, the voices of the research participants also need to be heard. Research papers coming out of the researcher's interaction with participants raise a further problem of voice.

APA style suggests that our writing should capture the idea that our research participants are active in their own right. This means, for example, preferring the active "Three participants completed the survey" to the passive "The survey was administered to three participants" or even "The survey was completed by three participants."

Then there's the question of the extent to which participant voices can be heard. This is limited by the conventional size of scholarly papers, but it is also a function of the researcher's assumptions about the nature of research. If the researcher is using, say, a focus group to identify opinions about a consumer product, there will be a need to describe those opinions but not as much need to focus on the people behind the opinions. Another researcher concerned with how a particular group of individuals uses language to define themselves and what they do will want to report examples of the language in the participants' own words, however incoherent, ungrammatical, and offensive those words may appear to others. A third researcher, doing action research aimed at improving the lives of the research participants, may want to communicate effectively with policy makers and those with influence in society and therefore choose to do so in professional language in a professional publication.

The question of participant voices arises particularly with "people-intensive" research, such as ethnography, and "people-first" research, such as action research, and it is a complex one (Alcoff, 2008). By electing to speak for others, "others" being typically a minority group in the case of action and some critical research, the researcher becomes a gatekeeper deciding what specific language—and whose—will or will not be heard as a result of publication. Thus the research itself can exemplify the very problem the research may have been intended to address—control of minority voices. One solution to the problem of enabling research participants to be heard is to facilitate their expression in their own nonscholarly media.

In terms of communicating research results effectively, decisions about voice can often be addressed by first considering potential audiences for the research. In other words, identifying the needs and interests of potential audiences for your research will tell you how best to present to those audiences the voices of both research participants and researchers.

A problem with disseminating the results of scholarly research beyond the academic world is that summary reports, news stories, blogs, podcasts, and even thorough, professional reports lose the detail and terminology that may have a specific meaning for scholars. In other words, as scholarly research findings become increasingly comprehensible to lay publics, they also become increasingly generalized to the point of losing what may be important detail to a scholar.

There are several ways we can make our research reporting comprehensible for all our potential publics.

Systematic reporting of research questions, literature review, method, and sampling decisions will help scholarly readers decide whether our results and conclusions are unbiased and defensible. Peer review processes help ensure that published papers meet scholarly standards and do not make unsubstantiated claims. We can aim not for the impossible goal of eliminating all our biases but for the achievable goal of making any biases explicit so that readers will have as full an understanding of our research as possible.

By working with news editors, journalists, and other professional writers and producers, we can maximize the chances that nonscholarly versions of our research will be both accurate and comprehensible to lay audiences. We can also use social media to tailor research findings to the interests and levels of understanding of specific audiences, as well as to respond directly to their questions, comments, and suggestions.

Finally, by making our original research data available on online, we can permit interested individuals to bypass our own interpretations of the data, and, in effect, do their own analyses and interpretations.

DISSEMINATING RESEARCH

While the Internet has allowed the proliferation of more interest and advocacy groups than a researcher might wish to deal with, it has also provided the means to address such groups—notably via targeted websites, blogs, podcasts, social media, and presenting research results in visual form.

Websites

The web allows the publication and archiving of content that cannot be presented via traditional print media. It can host large amounts of raw data, multimedia content, and hyperlinked documents that connect to other texts, visuals, and data. It has search capabilities that make it easy to search any such content.

Traditional print formats such as journal articles force researchers into a somewhat standardized, print-oriented presentation format. Traditional research papers are linear; they move logically from an initial research question to a method description and then to results and conclusions.

Websites, on the other hand, offer almost unlimited potential for customizing research presentations and the opportunity for nonlinear, branched reporting. For example, a scholarly research report can be hyperlinked to original raw data such as video interviews that present the voices of the research participants or to numeric data that can be opened up in public domain statistical software.

Hyperlinks provide alternate reading paths through a document but often provide no information about what reader or viewer experience each link will provide. How should an unexplained link be understood—"Visit this link for additional information that is not essential but is available if you want it" or "Here is essential information that is too detailed to fit into a standard report format" or even "Not that relevant to the research, but thought you might find this amusing"? Good web design therefore requires that we define the nature of hyperlinks for the reader or viewer.

Because the web is accessible to most scholars, it increases the possibilities for collaborative research and data analysis. Keeping experimental data and materials on a website after the experiment makes them available to other researchers and can offer a fuller explanation of the experiment. And web-based software not only permits authors to write and edit each other's work collaboratively but also enables readers to interact with the final document itself by annotating it and ranking comments about it. See for example Adema (2018).

Blogs

Think of a blog as a regular text communication with a web public via your own mini website. The defining feature is "regular"—that is, you are writing daily or weekly to provide relevant, topical commentary or information on a topic. Typically, a blog is around 800 words, shorter than a journal article and longer than a news release. You can opt for a formal or informal style as appropriate; link to graphics, audio, and video as appropriate; and link to social media and use these platforms to promote the blog. You can build in interactivity, so visitors can record their reactions to your blog postings; and you can capture usage metrics, so you know what aspects of your blog site are the most visited. Software such as WordPress and Blogger make it easy to set up a blog page. The primary cost is your time and a necessary commitment to blogging regularly.

A video blog or vlog uses video as its medium and may combine video or video links with text and images.

Podcasts

A podcast is an audio file made available via the web to be heard on an audio player, computer, or smartphone. Podcasts can range from an informal talk by the researcher edited on free audio processing software such as Audacity through to professionally produced interviews and lectures or fully scripted, hour-long productions with sound effects. Podcasts are, in effect, on-demand radio: informing and entertaining. They can be made available via audio distribution services such as iTunes or SoundCloud, or they can be posted on a host website, blog, or social media platform. In the form of participant interviews, they can be part of the research process itself and not just used for disseminating results. Video podcasts—"vodcasts"—include video clips.

Webinars

Webinars or web conferences allow live presentation to a web audience using a variety of presentation modes and typically allowing audience feedback. Webinars usually involve a speaker or moderator's presentation that may also include video, slideshow, and whiteboard presentations. Often, **screen sharing**, audio commentary, hyperlinks, and live text chat are available to all those connected to the meeting. Typically, the webinar is recorded and archived for access after the live presentation, and its producer or sponsor presents a survey to participants for feedback after the webinar.

Conference Presentations

A major forum where researchers engage in conversation is the academic conference. National associations such as the National Communication Association (www.natcom.org), the Canadian Communication Association (www.acc-cca.ca), and the International Communication Association (www.icahdq.org), as well as many regional associations, hold annual conferences.

Presentations at such conferences typically take two forms—**panel presentations** and **poster papers**.

A panel consists of six or so scholars with shared interests presenting the results of their research. Typically, each panelist presents for 10 or 15 minutes, and there is additional time for discussion among panelists and with audience members at the end of the presentations. The papers presented are often "works in progress." The feedback that presenters receive on their papers gives them ideas for improving their research or revising their papers before submitting them for publication.

The presentation time of 15 minutes or so for accepted papers means that the authors can present only key points, but in many cases, the full paper will be available for interested readers—often via a conference website—so the value of a panel is in the direct discussion with the author that it provides.

In poster sessions, presenters summarize their research on a display panel. There is no formal presentation, but anyone interested in a topic can meet and discuss the research informally with researchers alongside the poster papers. This more relaxed atmosphere gives a greater opportunity for discussion with the authors and gives the authors more feedback from a self-selected group of people who are specifically interested in their research. Poster papers need to communicate only summary points because the author can give the details personally and even provide a full research paper.

VISUALIZING RESEARCH

Visualizing research data and findings is an art and science in its own right and can be addressed here only briefly. There is a hierarchy of complexity beginning with the basic text "bullet points" of PowerPoint, Google Slides, or, more generically, **slideware**—the ubiquitous presentation software in classrooms, meetings, and academic conferences. PowerPoint has been criticized for its false simplicity, its rigid "bullet point" hierarchy, and the line-by-line logic it imposes on an audience (Tufte, 2006). Contemplate for a moment the power of metaphor and whether a "bullet" metaphor really captures the relationship you want to have with your audience.

Beyond basic bulleted text visuals are the classic line, bar, and pie charts and then infographics, familiar perhaps from major newspapers such as the *New York Times* and *USA Today*. **Infographics** can include charts, illustrations, photos, diagrams, and text. Kirk (2016) is a good starting point for data visualization.

Beyond slideware and infographics lies the opportunity to visualize research findings in more sophisticated and complex ways. For example, we can use the data in Exhibit 7.1 to draw a three dimensional plot using HSM, SMC, and PTI as axes. We'll put on our virtual reality headsets and take a walk through the data to see how our respondents cluster by gender and political preference. Maybe we'll select one or two of them and listen to the hyperlinked audio recordings they have consented to make public, so we can hear them talking about their political preferences and social media use.

In the age of social media, we can look back and see scholarly "absent authors," writing in the passive, third-person voice for their scholarly peer groups evolving into active first-person web presences with a need for multimedia skills to reach the many groups who have reason to be interested in, or to influence, their research.

For now, let's finish with an overview of some methods for disseminating research information. You can use Exhibit 14.3 to help select your methods—always referring to specific style guides such as APA, Chicago, and MLA for the details of scholarly writing and presentation.

EXHIBIT 14.3 ■ Research Reporting Methods: Advantages and Disadvantages		
	Advantages	**Disadvantages**
Scholarly Report	Scholarly voice addresses needs of scholarly communities. Full details of theories, methods, and analyses. Peer review ensures scholarly standards. Citations provide further information on topic. Contributes to knowledge and theory.	Scholarly voice may not be comprehensible outside scholarly communities. May require subscription or fee to access. Time lag between research and publication of results. May not contribute to policies or practices.
Professional Report	Narrative voice addresses nonscholarly audiences. Emphasizes relevance to audience. Meets needs of specific interest groups. Makes recommendations re policies or action. Minimal time between research and research report.	Lacks details of theories and research methods. May provide incomplete picture. Limited interest or relevance outside of targeted interest groups.
Conference Panel Presentation	Brief, timely update for scholarly colleagues. Interpersonal interaction and feedback from colleagues.	Accessible only by conference participants, unless recorded and archived. Omits detail. May not present the final data or report.
Conference Poster Paper	Instant summary of research. Brief, timely update for scholarly colleagues. Interpersonal interaction and feedback from those with specific interest in topic.	Accessible only by conference participants. Omits detail. May not present the final data or report.
News Story	News voice comprehensible to the news audience. Addresses the basic questions of an audience—Who? What? When? Where? How? "Get-to-the-point" writing. Emphasizes the relevance and implications of research.	First audience is the editor, then the news audience. Editor must see story as relevant and timely. Loss of control over content. Story may get distorted or misinterpreted. No information on theoretical background, sampling, or research methods.

Feature Story	Human interest voice captures reader interest. Devices such as metaphor, quotations, and background descriptions help reader retention, comprehension, and understanding. Feature length allows for full development and explanation of research.	First audience is the editor, then the feature audience. Editor must see story as relevant and timely. Loss of control over content. Story may get distorted or misinterpreted. Limited information on theoretical background, sampling, or research methods. Story length may have readers drop out.
Web Site	Audience opt-in predicts interest in site. A generally stable source of information for audiences worldwide. Can handle text, graphics, audio, and video. Can archive content for later retrieval. Can build in feedback in the form of surveys, visitor comments, and user metrics.	Recipients need web access. Recipients need web skills. Researcher needs web skills to design site and navigational aids for visitors. Site needs regular review to ensure home page is current and that hyperlinks are active and linked to current sites. Needs to be promoted with social and traditional media.
Blog	Audience opt-in predicts interest in topic. Can adopt blog voice to needs of audience. Can reach smaller, specialized audiences. Can address topical issues and research in progress. Can provide commentary or explanations of research. Can link to original research reports. Can capture visitor comments and feedback.	Recipients need web access. Needs to be promoted with social and traditional media. Commitment to regular updating.
Podcast	Audience opt-in predicts interest in topic. Conversational style of speech possible. Content accessible to the visually impaired. Can be self-produced and inexpensive. Can use researcher's own voice or multiple voices. Can bring voices of research participants direct to podcast audience. Can capture visitor comments and feedback.	Recipients need web access. May require professional production. Needs to be promoted with social and traditional media. Permissions and confidentiality or anonymity issues with podcast participants.
Webinar	Audience opt-in predicts interest in topic. Real-time interaction with participants. Audio, video, slideware, whiteboard presentation, and screen-sharing potential. Can be recorded and archived for later access.	Recipients need web access. Recipients need web skills for interaction with host. May require a specific web browser. Needs to be promoted with social and traditional media.

ETHICS PANEL

BALANCING BETWEEN SCHOLARLY AND POPULAR WRITING

Accounts of communication research become less specific and more general as they "move" from the original scholarly journals to popular media. They may also get embellished with metaphors, analogies, and commentaries as journalists try to interpret and explain the original research to lay audiences.

Questions

Based on your reading of this chapter

- To what extent could publishing a scholarly research paper limit the likelihood that all potentially interested publics will know about the research?

- To what extent is writing a news release, blog, or professional report on a research project an ethical decision about disseminating the results of your research?

- What responsibility do journalists and bloggers have to cite the original research papers they are reporting on so that interested readers and viewers can find them?

- What responsibility do researchers have for what journalists write when they interpret and report on scholarly research papers?

Chapter Summary

- Scholarly research papers present the theory behind the research, the research methods used, information on sampling, results, and conclusions.

- Style guides such from the APA, the University of Chicago Press, and the MLA give specific guidance on how to report scholarly research.

- The exact style and format of your research paper will be determined by the scholarly association or journal you are writing for.

- Interest groups and news media will be interested in your research only if it is timely and relevant.

- You can make your research relevant to news media and their audiences by writing in the appropriate news format and style.

- Research reports written for interest groups emphasize results, conclusions, and relevance to the reader.

- Web-based research presentations may be branched rather than linear and demand design and web-navigation skills in addition to writing skills.

- Social media allow targeting of very specific audiences, interactivity, and the opportunity to use audio, video, blogs, and podcasts.

Key Terms

editorial process 288
format 286
house styles 287
hyperlinks 285
hypermedia 281

infographics 293
multimedia 281
news determinants 284
panel presentations 293
poster papers 293

professional reports 285
screen sharing 293
slideware 293
style guide 287
voice 288

Application Exercises

Exercise 1: Readability

Your word-processing software should have an option to check the readability of your writing. Typically, this check will provide a number of indirect measures of readability, such as the average number of sentences per paragraph, words per sentence, characters per word, and percentage of passive sentences. You may also be able to get specific measures of readability such as the Flesch Reading Ease score and the Flesch–Kincaid Grade Level score.

Type or import sample paragraphs from a scholarly journal such as *Communication Monographs* into your word-processing software and obtain readability statistics, especially the Flesch–Kincaid Grade Level score. This latter statistic gives you the grade level of readers capable of reading the content. Repeat this exercise for an extract of science writing from the *New York Times* and from your local newspaper.

As a point of reference, 2017 U.S. Census data indicate that approximately 12% of U.S. citizens over the age of 25 have an advanced academic degree; 19% have a bachelor's degree. Cumulatively 88% are at least high school graduates (U.S. Census Bureau, 2017). Based on the readability scores you obtained, what percentage of the U.S. population is likely to be able to read successfully each of the articles you sampled?

What information is lost as you compare a scholarly article with a local newspaper account of scholarly research?

Exercise 2: Writing Styles

Compare the report of a conventional survey or experimental study from a scholarly journal with a narrative report such as Pacanowsky's "A Small-Town Cop" (1983). What differences do you find between the two reports with respect to

- your ability to relate to the individuals in each study,

- the level of insight each study provides you, and

- the ease with which policy makers could make policy decisions based on each study?

Exercise 3: Assessing Researchers' Community Engagement

A 2015 survey of members of the American Association for the Advancement of Science (AAAS) found that about 40% of them often or occasionally do at least two of four activities—talk with nonexperts, talk with the media, use social media, or blog (Rainie, Funk, & Anderson, 2015). Nearly half engage in one of these four activities either often or occasionally. These findings suggest that researchers need to move—and are moving—beyond traditional scholarly publishing and are engaging with the community at large.

You can use these four activities as a crude measure of community engagement by scholarly authors.

Use your online research skills to identify communication scholars in your area of interest and research their communication activities as far as possible. Assign each a score between 0 (*you find no evidence of the four activities listed above*) and 4 (*you find evidence of all four of these activities*). How do you rate these scholars for community engagement? What other measures of community engagement can you think of?

Recommended Reading

Bik, H. M., & Goldstein, M. C. (2013). An introduction to social media for scientists. *PLoS Biology, 11*(4). DOI: 10.1371/journal.pbio.1001535

Carrigan, M. (2016). *Social media for academics*. London: Sage

Two overviews of the uses of social media for academics.

Gusfield, J. (1976). The literary rhetoric of science: Comedy and pathos in drinking driver research. *American Sociological Review, 41*(1), 16–34.

A classic analysis of scientific writing as a persuasive literary form.

Kirk, A. (2016). *Data visualisation. A handbook for data driven design*. London: Sage.

Discusses the process and practices of data visualization, with examples of a variety of different data visualizations.

Knapp, A. (2012, March 15). ResearchGate wants to be Facebook for scientists. *Forbes*. Retrieved from https://www.forbes.com/sites/alexknapp/2012/03/15/researchgate-wants-to-be-facebook-for-scientists/#7dbe27415ddb

An overview of the development of ResearchGate and the reasons researchers should use social media.

Lipson, C. (2011). *Cite right: A quick guide to citation styles—MLA, APA, Chicago, the sciences, professions, and more* (2nd ed.) Chicago, IL: University of Chicago Press.

Important citation styles, all in one book.

Mollett, A., Moran, D., and Dunleavy, P. (2011). Using Twitter in university research, teaching and impact activities [Blog post]. *Impact of social sciences: Maximizing the impact of academic research*. London: London School of Economics and Political Science, LSE Public Policy Group.

A guide for academics and researchers to setting up and using Twitter.

Recommended Web Resources

Chicago-Style Citation Quick Guide........www.chicago-manualofstyle.org/tools_citationguide.html
The Chicago Manual of Style's free online guide to formatting citations (the full manual, which requires a subscription, may be available through your home library).

Citation Machine......................http://citationmachine.net
Easybib..www.easybib.com
EndNot..www.endnote.com
Learning APA Style....................www.apastyle.org/learn
The home page for APA style learning resources.

MLA Style Center: Writing Resources from the Modern Language Association.........www.mlahandbook.org/fragment/public_index
Provides access to writing resources from the MLA, including a free quick guide to MLA style.

Peter Norvig's Gettysburg PowerPoint Presentation.........http://norvig.com/Gettysburg
See this PowerPoint Gettysburg Address for a sense of how slideware can destroy an otherwise eloquent and moving presentation.

Refworks........www.refworks.com
Helps manage, store, and share information, as well as generate citations and bibliographies.

Infographics

Infogram..www.infogram.com
Piktochart..www.piktochart.com
Visme..www.visme.co
Visual.ly..www.visual.ly

You can sign up at the above sites for a free trial of infographics software and an overview of other services that may be provid ed such as video, e-books, reports, social media visuals, charts, maps and reports.

Scholarly Social Networks

Academia........www.academia.edu
Users can create a profile, share papers, and search for people with similar interests.

Mendeley........www.mendeley.com
A web-based program for managing and sharing research papers and collaborating online.

ResearchGate........www.researchgate.net
A large academic social network where researchers can share papers, ask and answer questions, and find collaborators.

References

Adema, J. (2018). Performative publications. *Media Practice & Education, 19*(1), 68–81

Alcoff, L. (2008). The problem of speaking for others. In A. M. Jaggar (Ed.), *Just methods: An interdisciplinary feminist reader* (pp. 484–494). Boulder, CO: Paradigm Publishers.

American Psychological Association. (2015). The basics of APA style. Retrieved from http://www.apastyle .org/learn/tutorials/basics-tutorial.aspx

Gusfield, J. (1976). The literary rhetoric of science: Comedy and pathos in drinking driver research. *American Sociological Review, 41*(1), 16–34.

Herbers, J. M. (2006, March 24). The loaded language of science [The *Chronicle* review]. *The Chronicle of Higher Education*, p. B5.

Kirk, A. (2016). *Data visualisation. A handbook for data driven design*. London: Sage.

Mollett, A., Brumley, C., Gilson. C., & Williams, S. (2017). *Communicating your research with social media. A practical guide to using blogs, podcasts, data visualisations and video*. London: Sage.

Pacanowsky, M. (1983). A small-town cop: Communication in, out, and about a crisis. In L. Putnam & M. Pacanowsky (Eds.), *Communication and organizations: An interpretive approach* (pp. 261–282). Beverly Hills, CA: Sage.

Rainie, L., Funk, C., & Anderson, M. (2015, February 15). *How scientists engage the public* [Report]. Washington, DC: Pew Research Center. Retrieved from http://www.pewinternet.org/2015/02/15/ how-scientists-engage-public/

Tufte, E. R. (2006). *The cognitive style of PowerPoint: Pitching out corrupts within* (2nd ed.). Cheshire, CA: Graphics Press.

U.S. Census Bureau. (2017). Table S1501: Educational attainment. *American Community Survey: 2013–2017 ACS 5-Year Estimates*. Retrieved from https://www .census.gov/acs/www/data/data-tables-and-tools/ subject-tables/

Van Maanen, J. (1988). *Tales of the field: On writing ethnography*. Chicago, IL: University of Chicago Press.

⑤SAGE edge™

Get the tools you need to sharpen your study skills. SAGE edge offers a robust online environment featuring an impressive array of free tools and resources.

Access quizzes, eFlashcards, video, and multimedia at **edge.sagepub.com/treadwell4e**.

GLOSSARY

Abduction. Reasoning from an observed effect to possible causes.

Act. In Burke's **dramatistic analysis**, the behavior that is taking place.

Action research. Research engaging with groups or communities specifically to solve problems.

Acts. In Hymes's ethnography of communication, the language and behaviors that convey meaning to the participants—for example, an instructor demonstrating a specific research method.

Address-based sampling (ABS). Survey sampling using address data provided by the U.S. Postal Service.

Adjacency pairs. In conversation analysis, units of speech that occur together and one of the basic units of conversation analysis—for example, question/answer.

Affiliative responses. In conversation analysis, responses to a question or statement that maintain a social link with the speaker. See also **disaffiliative responses**.

Agency. In Burke's **dramatistic analysis**, the means by which an act takes place.

Agent. In Burke's **dramatistic analysis**, the individual(s) taking the action.

Analytic notes. Notes an ethnographer writes as a way to make sense of or interpret the raw data or **descriptive notes**.

Anomalous data. Data that appear suspicious or are not anticipated by a researcher.

Anonymity. A way of protecting research participants in that the data collected from them does not identify them in any way. Typically, anonymity is ensured by instructing **respondents** not to put their names on any information they provide.

ANOVA. Analysis of variance. A comparison of the variance within groups with the variance among groups. See also **MANOVA**.

APA. American Psychological Association. APA is the standard style for many communication scholars when they reference other people's work. APA style uses an "author (date)" style in the body of the paper and places the full citation, alphabetized by author, at the end of the paper. APA is also relevant in terms of the American Psychological Association's Ethical Principles of Psychologists and Code of Conduct.

API. Application programming interface. Software for interaction with social media platforms.

Appeals. The bases of persuasion—for example, sex appeal and fear appeal in advertising.

Aristotelian analysis. Analysis of communication content for its persuasive effects, using Aristotle's concepts of rhetoric.

Asynchronous. Occurring at different times or uncoordinated—for example, members of a social media site contributing individually to it, in their own time. See also **synchronous**.

Attrition. The loss of participants from a study.

Authority. A way of knowing based on knowledge from a credible or respected source of information.

Autonomy. A *Belmont Report* principle that research participants should be treated with respect.

Avatars. Graphical representations of one or more computer users, such as icons or three-dimensional characters.

Base. From Marxist theory, the forces and relations of production.

Bell curve. See **normal curve**.

Belmont Report. A report by the National Commission for the Protection of Human Subjects of Biomedical and Behavioral Research. It outlines three basic ethical principles—**autonomy**, **beneficence**, and **justice**—covering research with human subjects.

Beneficence. A *Belmont Report* principle that human subjects research should maximize possible benefits and minimize possible harm to participants.

Between-subjects design. An experimental design in which subjects are exposed to only one experimental condition. See also **within-subjects design.**

Bibliographic. Pertaining to books and journals.

Bibliography. A list of sources (e.g., books, documents, and journal articles) about a particular topic or by a particular author or referred to in a scholarly work.

Big data. Data sets so large, complex, or rapidly changing that traditional software or databases cannot process or manage the data.

Bimodal distribution. Distribution of data that shows two values occurring with equal frequency.

Bivariate. Pertaining to two variables, as in bivariate analysis or bivariate statistics.

Boolean operators. Terms such as AND, OR, and NOT that allow one to fine-tune a database search.

Branching/routing questions. Route respondents around survey questions they do not need to answer.

Break-off rate. The proportion of respondents who fail to complete a survey once it is started.

CAQDAS. Computer-assisted qualitative data analysis software.

Categorical data. Data that fit into distinct categories such as zip code or academic major.

Categorical imperative. Philosopher Immanuel Kant's concept that a behavior is valid if one is willing to see it applied as a universal rule.

Categorization. The process of identifying an item of data as belonging to a category predetermined by the researcher or generated from the information provided by informants.

Causal relationship. A relationship between variables in which changes in one variable demonstrably result in changes in another.

Census. A study of every member of a population.

Central limit theorem. In summary, the proposition that the distribution of the average or sum of a large number of samples of a variable will be approximately normal, regardless of the underlying distribution.

Check boxes. A survey response format that allows respondents to select as many answers as they wish from a list.

Chi-square (χ). A statistical test for determining whether two groups differ significantly in their distribution of scores on the same variable.

Chicago. In the context of research reporting, a term referring to *The Chicago Manual of Style*.

Citations. The publication details of books, journal articles, or websites.

Closed-ended research questions. Questions that ask about the direction of the relationship between variables.

Cloud storage. Web-based data storage, typically offered by a hosting company.

Code/coding. The process of transforming data into a simplified form, usually for computer processing.

Coding scheme. A systematic way of classifying or categorizing units of analysis.

Cohort. A group of people defined most typically by having an event in common.

Common Rule. The Federal Policy for the Protection of Human Subjects. Shared standards adopted by federal agencies for the protection of human research subjects.

Communicative act. In Hymes's ethnography of communication, the smaller units of speech within a speech event—for example, asking a question or telling a joke.

Communicative style. In Hymes's ethnography of communication, the speech style that is characteristic of someone—for example, formal or informal.

Conative function. One of Jakobson's semiotic functions. Establishes the sender's expectations of the receiver or what the receiver is expected to do as a result of receiving the message.

Concurrent validity. Concurrent validity is demonstrated when a measure correlates highly with other measures designed to measure the same construct.

Confederates. Participants in a study who have been briefed by the researcher to behave in a particular way.

Confidence interval. A range of values estimated from a **sample**, within which a value for a **population** is estimated to fall.

Confidence level. The calculated probability of a value being true. Typically, for communication research, a confidence level of 95 is used, meaning that a reported value is estimated to occur 95 times out of 100 if a population is repeatedly sampled.

Confidentiality. The assurance given to research participants that the researcher will not release any information that will identify them. The researcher can link information that participants provide to the identity of the person providing it.

Construct validity. Construct validity is demonstrated when the measures of one concept or construct agree with the measures of other related concepts.

Constructed week sampling. A form of random sampling in which sample dates represent all seven days of the week to account for systematic variation.

Constructivist. The worldview that individuals construct their own views of the world in which they live, primarily through interaction with others.

Constructs. Abstract ideas or concepts.

Content analysis. Traditionally, a quantitative, systematic technique for describing the manifest content of communications.

Content validity. The extent to which a measure fully represents a given concept, typically as judged by a panel of experts. See also **face validity**, **expert validity**, and **panel validity**.

Contingency table. A table that shows how scores for two or more variables are related—for example, gender by income. See also **cross-tabs**.

Continuous data. Data with incremental values between the minimum and maximum. For example, age can have values of years, months, weeks, days, hours, minutes, or seconds.

Contrast questions. Questions that ask respondents to explain the difference between two or more things or concepts.

Control. In experimental design, *control* refers to an experimental group that does not receive any experimental treatment in order to provide a baseline for measuring changes that might occur in other groups. As a goal of research, *control* refers to gaining information about human behavior in order to be able to predict and control it.

Control groups. Experimental groups not exposed to any experimental variable.

Convenience sampling. Sampling based on convenience to the researcher.

Convergent validity. A demonstrable agreement between the concept or construct you are trying to measure and other related concepts.

Conversation analysis. A research approach that analyzes the rules governing conversational interactions.

Correlation. A statistical procedure for measuring the strength of association between two or more variables. More generally, the degree to which variables are related.

Correlation coefficient. Expression of the strength of the relationship between two variables; it ranges between −1.0 and +1.0 in value.

Covariance/covariation. A relationship between variables such that the values of one variable change as the values of another variable change.

Criterion validity. Criterion validity is demonstrated when a test or measure correlates highly with some tangible, external criterion.

Criterion variable. See **outcome/criterion variable**.

Critical. A communication research tradition that focuses on power and oppression so as to challenge common assumptions and effect emancipation.

Critical analyses/criticism. Studies that explore the way in which communication establishes, reinforces, and maintains power structures in society. More generally, these provide the processes by which assumptions can be challenged.

Critical discourse analysis. Explores the relationship between language and power. The basic aim is to uncover the ideological assumptions behind public discourse and to link communication content with underlying power structures.

Cross-lagged surveys. Surveys that measure the relationship between a **dependent variable** and an **independent variable** at two points in time.

Cross-sectional surveys. Surveys taken at one point in time, as opposed to **trend studies**.

Cross-tabs. Short for *cross-tabulations*. A cross-tab is a table that shows how scores for two or more variables are related. See also **contingency table**.

Curvilinear relationship. A relationship between two variables that, if plotted out, will show a curve rather than a straight line.

Cybernetic. A view of communication as the flow of information or a system of information processing and feedback.

Data points. The recorded values of each variable, one value for each individual.

Data reduction. The process of reducing "raw" data to a simpler form by using, for example, summary statistics, tables, or graphs.

Data set. All the data from a research project.

Databases. In the context of bibliographic research, collections of (mostly) scholarly articles that can be searched electronically.

Debriefing. The process of ensuring that research participants receive a follow-up explanation of the research when it is completed.

Declaration of Helsinki. The World Medical Association's international ethical guidelines for medical professionals researching human subjects.

Deduction. Reasoning from a theory to defining the observations you will make to test the theory.

Degrees of freedom (df). A measure of the number of ways data could be combined and still produce the same value for a statistic.

Demographic. Pertaining to such variables as age, marital status, income, and occupation.

Dependent variable. A variable whose values change as a result of changes in another (independent) variable.

Description. An account or documentation of observed conditions. One basic goal of research is to describe communication phenomena in such a way that others can understand it.

Descriptive notes. The primary, detailed records of the human interactions, language, and settings that are the focus of an ethnography.

Descriptive questions. Questions that ask informants to describe a phenomenon.

Descriptive statistics. Statistics that describe and summarize the data for a sample.

Dichotomous questions. Questions that offer a choice between two possible answers—for example, "yes" or "no."

Diffusion. In experimental design, the problem of a treatment effect spreading from group to group as people communicate.

Disaffiliative responses. In conversation analysis, responses to a question or statement that break the link with the speaker.

Disambiguation. The process in content analysis of assigning a word the most appropriate meaning out of all possible meanings.

Discourse. Generally, spoken or written communication. More specifically, a way of thinking about a topic or what can and cannot be said about it. See also **discourse analysis**.

Discourse analysis. Focuses on systems of meaning and how particular labels or concepts are developed and maintained by the use of language.

Divergent validity. Divergent validity is demonstrated when a measure of a construct or concept is shown to be unrelated to measures of unrelated concepts.

DOI. Short for *digital object identifier.* A string of characters used to uniquely identify a web-based document. Used in bibliographic citations.

Double negative. A combination of **negative wording** with a **double-barreled question**, almost guaranteed to confuse respondents.

Double-barreled questions. Questions that ask two questions simultaneously but allow for only one answer.

Dramatistic analysis. Analyzing communication as performance, as actors acting out a drama; sometimes called dramatism. For example, Burke's **dramatistic pentad** asks questions such as these: What act is taking place? Who is taking this action? How or by what means did the act take place? Where and when did the act take place? Why was the act done?

Dramatistic pentad. Kenneth Burke's core questions of **act**, **scene**, **agent**, **agency**, and **purpose** for analysis of motives.

Ecological isomorphism. The extent to which an experimental condition is similar to the real-world conditions it is attempting to simulate.

Editorial process. The process by which a manuscript becomes a published scholarly article or book. The three main phases are peer review, editing for style and accuracy, and production.

Emoticons. Typographic representations of emotional states or moods, most often used to indicate the mood of a message's sender or how the message should be interpreted.

Empiricism. The view that knowledge should be based on experience and observation, on empirical as opposed to theoretical knowledge.

Ends. In Hymes's ethnography of communication, the goals of the communication being studied—for example, to persuade an audience on an issue.

Epistemology. The study or theory of knowledge. Epistemology addresses such questions as "What is knowledge?" and "How do we know what we know?"

Established measures reliability. A measure of whether the results obtained from an instrument that you are developing match the results obtained from a known, tested instrument designed for the same purpose.

Ethnography. The study of human social behavior, typically with an emphasis on description.

Ethnomethodology. The study of how people make sense of their culture and communicate that understanding to others. Ethnomethodology seeks to describe and explain cultural understandings in terms of the culture's own language and concepts.

Ethos. Aristotelian concept of a source's character or credibility in argumentation.

Ex post facto design. An "after the fact" experimental design in which there is no **control** over experimental conditions.

Experimental situation. The setting experimental subjects are placed in. This setting may be a threat to external validity if it does not reflect external reality.

Experimenter bias. In experimental design, the problem of some kind of bias in an experimental group because of the way the researcher, knowingly or unknowingly, has selected its members.

Experiments. Research procedures carried out under controlled conditions and based on the technique of manipulating one or more variables in hopes of observing an effect. Typically, an experimental condition is applied to one group, and the results are compared with those from another group (**control group**) that has had no experimental treatment.

Expert validity. Validity as judged by relevant experts. See also **panel validity**.

Explanation. An attempt to account for the relationships observed among phenomena. A basic goal of communications research is to explain how and why communication phenomena occur.

Exploration. "Mapping out" a new area of research before proceeding to study it more specifically. This sort of research may lead down unknown paths as opposed to testing a specific hypothesis.

Expressive function. One of Jakobson's semiotic functions. Describes or establishes the speaker's condition or emotional state.

External validity. Relates to whether an experiment has in fact captured the external world that the researcher is investigating.

F **value.** Denotes an analysis of variance value.

Face validity. A question or measure that appears to capture the concept it is intended to capture. See also **expert validity** and **panel validity**.

Facilitator. The leader of a focus group who is responsible for running the group's discussion and ensuring that it keeps "on topic." See also **moderator**.

Factorial designs. Experimental designs that manipulate two or more variables at a time.

Fake news. Stories or information that take the form of news but have not been written, produced, or edited to traditional or professional news media standards.

Fantasy theme analysis. The process of searching for and analyzing fantasy themes, the sagas, stories, or ideas shared by members of a group and that give members a common perspective and a shared understanding of the group's accomplishments.

Feminist criticism. A diversity of critical approaches centered on the problem of implicit and explicit male-oriented ideologies in communication content and processes. Feminist criticisms examine gender politics, gender representations, and the marginalizing implications of male-centered language.

Field experiment. A less sophisticated level of experimental design, in which the effects of changes in one variable on another are observed under limited conditions of **control**.

Filter questions. Questions that determine whether respondents are qualified to answer an upcoming question and that typically redirect that respondent to another question if they are not.

Fixed coding. Assigning units of information to preassigned categories.

Flexible coding. Coding that allows new categories of data to emerge rather than using only preconceived categories.

Focus group. Small group of people brought together to discuss a topic of interest to the researcher.

Format. The structure of content required for a specific audience—for example, scholarly papers, news releases, and poster papers.

Frequency. The number of times a particular score or result occurs. Frequencies are commonly reported in the form of a **frequency table**.

Frequency tables. Tables that show categories of a variable by the number of times that category occurs.

Fully structured interviews. Interviews in which the researcher has determined what questions are important, the order in which they will be asked, and how they will be structured.

Funnel/inverted funnel. A set of questions that move from general to specific or vice versa.

Gatekeepers. Those who control access to research participants or the publication of research results—for example, employers and journal editors, respectively.

Genres. In Hymes's ethnography of communication, the traditional types of speech found in most cultures—for example, commencement addresses.

Grounded theory. A research approach that argues that theories should emerge from data analysis, not prior to data analysis.

Hawthorne effect. The effect that researchers themselves may have on an experimental group. The effect is named after an organizational study in which employees were found to be responding to the perceived interest of management rather than to the experimental condition itself.

Heurism. Knowledge gained from practical experience and empirical research.

Homogeneity. The degree of "sameness" in a population. Generally, the greater the homogeneity, the smaller the sample size required.

House styles. The publication styles of specific journals or publishers.

Hyperlinks. The web addresses embedded in a document that allow the viewer to open secondary—linked—documents, images, or other online material.

Hypermedia. Web-based documents and media that link to other media on the web. .

Hypothesis. A testable statement about the relationships one expects to find among variables of interest. A **two-tailed test** predicts relationships between two variables but does not specify the direction of the relationship. A **one-tailed test** specifies the direction of relationships between variables. **Null hypotheses** specify that there is no relationship between variables.

IBM SPSS® Statistics. One of several statistical software packages used in the social sciences.

Ideology. A broad set of ideas guiding behavior and expectations or a systematic scheme or body of knowledge and beliefs, especially about human life and culture, that guides groups and group members.

Idiographic. A research approach with an emphasis on understanding the subjectivity and individuality of human communication, rather than universal laws of human behavior.

Impact factor. In scholarly publishing, a measure of the number of times journal articles are cited by other scholarly articles.

Independent variable. A variable whose changes in values result in changes in another (dependent) variable.

Induction. Reasoning from observations to a theory that might explain the observations.

Inferential statistics. Statistics that estimate the values for a population from a sample of that population.

Infographics. Visual representations of data, often involving a combination of visual formats such as charts, photographs, and diagrams.

Informants. Interviewees considered capable of speaking on behalf of or about others.

Informed consent. The process by which potential research participants are informed of the nature of the research and given the opportunity to sign or not sign a voluntary agreement to participate.

Institutional review board (IRB). A panel established to review research proposals for their impact on human participants.

Instrumentality. In Hymes's ethnography of communication, the channels or methods used to communicate—for example, an online discussion group.

Inter-item reliability. A measure of whether the individual questions in a question set are consistent in their results. See also **internal reliability**.

Interaction analysis. Research that seeks to document and understand group roles and interactions among members of a group.

Intercept surveys. Surveys conducted from a base such as a shopping mall. Interviewers ask passersby to participate in the survey thus eliminating the cost of door-to-door surveys.

Intercoder or observer reliability. A measure of the extent to which two different coders code the same phenomenon the same way.

Internal reliability. A measure of whether all the questions in a question set are operationalizing the same concept and not different concepts. See also **inter-item reliability**.

Internal validity. Relates to experimental design. A study has internal validity when a cause-and-effect relationship between variables is clearly demonstrable and observed changes can be attributed to a defined causal variable and not to any other possible variables.

Interpretive. A descriptor used to indicate a perspective or research approach that seeks to understand how humans interpret or make sense of events in their lives. Interpretive studies can be understood as attempts to place oneself "in the other person's shoes."

Interquartile range. The range between the highest and lowest values for the middle 50% of values in a distribution.

Interval. Generally, the distance between points on a scale. In research terms, *interval* refers to a scale in which there is an assumption of equal intervals between points on the scale.

Interview. The process of asking questions of a respondent, usually face to face or by phone or video, to elicit information the researcher is interested in. See also **fully structured interviews**, **semistructured interviews**, and **unstructured interviews**.

Interviewees. Individuals who are interviewed.

Intuition. Refers to arriving at an answer without quite knowing how one arrived there; a hunch or "gut instinct."

Inverted funnel. See **funnel/inverted funnel**

Judeo-Christian ethic. In the context of human subjects research, the precept of not doing to others what you would not want done to yourself. This ethic is shared by many religions.

Justice. A *Belmont Report* principle that the benefits and risks of research should be distributed fairly.

Key. In Hymes's ethnography of communication, the tone of speech or how the speech sounds—for example, formal or friendly.

Key informants. The individuals who are part of a community being studied and who can introduce the researcher and legitimize the researcher's work to their community.

KWIC. Key word in context. This content analysis term refers to the display of a word and the words surrounding it.

Latent. Hidden; not apparent.

Leading questions. Questions worded to lead respondents to a particular answer rather than to the one they might have genuinely given.

Lemmatization. Content analysis procedure for grouping words according to a common dictionary definition.

Leptokurtic. A distribution of values that is peaked or high relative to the normal curve. Values in such a distribution have a narrower range.

Likert scale. An interval scale on which respondents record their reactions to statements by checking their level of agreement between, for example, "strongly agree" and "strongly disagree."

Linear regression. A calculation of the value of one variable given the value of another. Linear regression assumes that the relationship between variables is linear. See also regression.

Literature. In the context of communication and other research, academic publications such as refereed and published scholarly research reports.

Logos. Aristotelian concept of logic in argumentation.

Longitudinal studies. Studies that track people's changes in knowledge, attitude, or behavior over time.

Manifest. Apparent or observable.

Manipulation check. In experimental research, a check on whether the research participants interpreted the experimental conditions as the researcher intended.

MANOVA. Multiple analysis of variance. This procedure is used when there are multiple dependent variables. See also ANOVA.

Marxist perspective/criticism. The study of communication content aimed at assessing its political orientation or identifying messages that reinforce the ideology or vision of those in power.

Master analog. In fantasy theme analysis, a commonly understood theme or analogy that underpins a group fantasy—for example, space exploration, war, or detective work.

Master narrative. A covering story or fantasy that explains a group more readily or attracts more believers than other fantasies available to group members.

Maturation. In experimental design, the problem of individuals changing over time, most obviously by getting older.

Maximum. The highest value in a data set.

Mean. The average for a set of scores.

Measurement. The process of finding out whether people (or media content) have more or less of an attribute we are interested in. It is done by assigning numbers to the phenomena we are interested in.

Measures of central tendency. Measurements describing the central features of a data set rather than its outlying values. See mean, median, and mode.

Measures of dispersion. Measurements describing the range and variability of values in a data set. See range, variance, and standard deviation.

Median. The midpoint of a set of scores.

Metadata. Information that helps locate or identify data, for example, the search fields used in a bibliographic search—author, title, date. Smartphones record metadata such as time, date, and exposure level for each photograph. Web page examples include embedded dates and page headers. Numeric data files require the metadata "1 = rural," "2 = urban" to tell us what "1" and "2" actually mean.

Metalingual function. One of Jakobson's semiotic functions. Establishes the agreed-upon meaning for words—for example, by establishing that *Rose* refers to the name of a girl, not a flower.

Metaphor analysis. Analysis of the analogies and metaphors used by group members to explain and interpret their group and to help simplify the complexities and ambiguities that are part of any group.

Metatheory. A theory about theories or that embraces two or more theories; a basis for comparing, evaluating, and relating theories in a field.

Method notes. Records of the specific methods researchers use to gather data—for example, direct observation and interviews.

Metric. A quantitative measure for a concept or activity—for example, the impact factor in scholarly publishing as a measure of influence.

Minimum. The lowest value in a data set.

MLA. Modern Language Association. In the context of reporting communication research, the abbreviation refers to the *MLA Handbook,* a style guide.

Mode. The most frequent score in a set of scores.

Moderator. The leader of a focus group. A moderator is responsible for running the group's discussion and ensuring that it keeps "on topic." See also facilitator.

Multimedia. Media that present audio and video content.

Multiple regression. The use of more than one variable to predict the values for another variable. See also regression.

Multiple-choice questions. Questions that offer respondents a selection of answers from which they are instructed to select one or more.

Multistage cluster sampling. Sampling based on first sampling large units such as states or provinces and then sampling smaller units such as towns, city blocks, and so on.

Multivariate. Pertaining to three or more variables, as in multivariate analyses or multivariate statistics.

Multivariate analyses/statistics. Analyses that examine the relationship among three or more variables simultaneously.

Narrative analysis. The study of the formal properties of stories that people tell. It generally attempts to identify such aspects as plot, setting, characters, and order of events.

Negative wording. Questions phrased using a negative rather than a positive (e.g., "don't" rather than "do").

Netnography. A specialized form of ethnography adapted to computer-mediated social worlds.

Network/snowball sampling. Sampling using members of a network to introduce a researcher to other members of the network.

News determinants. Components of news stories such as timeliness, relevance, and proximity that make the stories newsworthy.

Nominal. A system of classification based on names rather than scales or rank ordering—for example, press, radio, and television.

Nomothetic. A research approach with an emphasis on measurement with a view to making generalizations about human behavior.

Nonparametric statistics. Statistics used with data that cannot be assumed to have a normal distribution.

Nonprobability sampling. Sampling based on a judgment by the researcher.

Normal curve. Curve resulting from the plot of values with a normal distribution. It is often called a bell curve because of its shape.

Normal distribution. Symmetrical distribution of values with the majority of scores "peaking" in the middle.

Norms. In Hymes's ethnography of communication, the rules governing speech and its interpretation—for example, students cannot ask questions until after the instructor has spoken.

Null hypotheses. Statements hypothesizing that no significant differences or relationships will be found between groups or variables in quantitative research. Testing the null hypothesis is a central task in quantitative communication research. See also hypothesis.

Numbers. Numbers assign value and relativity to phenomena. As contrasted with numerals, they can be calculated.

Numerals. Numerals are labels such as street numbers that cannot be computed.

Nuremberg Code. An international code emphasizing that research subjects must consent to the research in which they are involved and that the benefits of the research must outweigh the risks.

Observational studies. Studies based on the observation of behaviors, not necessarily as in-depth as ethnographies.

Observer reliability. See intercoder or observer reliability.

One-tailed hypotheses. Propositions stating that any statistical difference between two groups or variables will be in one direction.

One-tailed test. A test of the proposition that any difference between two groups will be in one direction; that is, one group will score higher than another. See also two-tailed test.

Ontology. The study of the nature of existence and what it is that language actually refers to.

Open-ended research questions. Questions to which respondents can reply in their own words.

Operationalize. To define a concept in such a way that it can be measured.

Ordinal. Scales with some measure of progression such as "Freshman, Sophomore, Junior, Senior."

Outcome/criterion variable. The variable whose value is predicted by the value of predictor variables in a regression analysis.

Panel. A group of the same individuals retained to answer questions over time.

Panel presentations. Small groups of researchers with shared interests presenting the results of their research.

Panel validity. Validity as judged by a group of relevant experts. See also expert validity.

Paradata. Data about the conditions or processes related to research data collection; also called *process data*. Paradata exist for each participant. For surveys and experiments, paradata might include length of text entered in response to a question, time taken to input the text, time and date the data were generated, type of contact (phone, e-mail, web), number of contacts a participant made with the study, participant dropout, reaction times to stimuli, and time to complete an experiment or survey.

Parameters. The values pertaining to a population rather than a sample.

Parametric statistics. Statistics used with data assumed to have a normal distribution (i.e., have parameters). See also nonparametric statistics.

Participants. Individuals who have volunteered to be in a research project, or in Hymes's theory, the people present in a speech situation and their roles and relationships.

Pathos. Aristotelian concept of emotion in argumentation.

pdf. portable document format. This file format is used to save documents, including images and formatting, independent of computer operating systems and application software.

Peer review. The process of having one's research reviewed by other researchers in the author's field prior to publication. See also refereeing.

Performance studies. Study of performance in situational or ritual contexts.

Phatic function. One of Jakobson's semiotic functions. Keeps participants in communication "on track" by establishing how communication will take place.

Phenomenology/phenomenological. A research approach that attempts to understand human behavior and consciousness from the individual, subjective point of view. The phenomenological tradition is part of communication research metatheory.

Phrenologists. Practitioners of a now discredited "science" based on the assumption that people's personalities could be assessed from the size and shape of their skulls.

Pilot/piloting. A prototype or pretest. A small study conducted prior to a full-scale study to ensure that the full-scale study will work successfully.

Platykurtic. A distribution of values that is flat or low relative to the normal curve. Values in such a distribution have a wider range.

Poetic function. One of Jakobson's semiotic functions. The use of language for its own pleasure—for example, jokes or alliteration because they are pleasurable in their own right.

Popular articles. Articles published without a refereeing process, typically in newspapers and magazines, and targeted to a consumer public.

Population. Every individual or item of a type you want to study. The entire set of individuals or items from which a sample is drawn.

Positivism. The idea that phenomena are governed by, and can be explained by, rules based on objective observation and generalizations from those observations.

Poster papers. Scholarly research set out in poster format for display at conferences and meetings.

Postpositive. A worldview that the world is governed by laws or theories that can be tested or verified, but recognizing that observations are fallible and that theories and findings are always subject to revision.

Pragmatism. A worldview focusing on solutions to problems and allowing a variety of approaches to understand a problem.

Prediction. One major goal of research; understanding human behavior in order to forecast the conditions under which it will occur.

Predictive validity. Predictive validity occurs when a measure successfully predicts a tangible outcome. For example, GRE scores should predict success in graduate school. See also criterion validity.

Predictor variable. Variable whose values are used in regression analysis to predict the value of outcome or criterion variables.

Primary source. An original article or book. See also secondary source.

Principle of utilitarianism. The principle of the greatest good for the greatest number.

Probability sampling. Sampling based on random selection of the sample units.

Professional reports. Reports written for groups with professional rather than scholarly interests.

Prompts. Questions that spark a response or further information from an interviewee—for example, "Why do you say that?"

Proprietary. Pertaining to data or research tools that are privately owned and therefore may not be used without the owner's permission.

Purpose. In Burke's dramatistic analysis, the reason or motivation that explains an act.

Purposive/judgmental sampling. Sampling based on specific criteria the researcher may have.

Q methodology. A research approach used to assess individuals' subjective understanding. Typically, participants rank a series of statements about a topic according to their perceived accuracy. Quantitative analysis of these rankings typically identifies factors that show the patterns of subjectivity within the participant group.

Qualitative. A research approach based on the use of language rather than numbers to understand and report human behavior.

Quantitative. A research approach based on measurement, counting, and, typically, statistical analysis.

Questionnaire. A set of questions to which **respondents** reply.

Quota sampling. Sampling that attempts to replicate in a sample the features that the researcher thinks are important in the population.

R. Open-source statistical software available at www .r-project.org.

Radio buttons. Choices presented in an online survey response format that permits only one response from a list.

Random assignment. The use of random selection to assign research participants to experimental groups.

Random digit dialing (RDD). A telephone survey method in which phone numbers are randomly dialed in hopes of reaching unlisted numbers.

Random numbers. Numbers that have an equal probability of occurring. Used to eliminate any researcher bias in selecting numbers.

Random numbers generator. A device for generating a sequence of numbers that has no pattern. Most typically a software program is used, but random numbers can also be generated by, for example, rolling dice.

Random sampling. Sampling in which every member of a population has an equal chance to be selected and in which selection is determined by "luck of the draw" rather than a decision by the researcher.

Range. The difference between the maximum value and minimum value in a data set.

Rank order questions. Questions that ask **respondents** to order items according to their perceived importance or preference.

Ratio. In measurement, refers to a scale that contains a "true" zero—for example, zero speed on a speedometer.

Ratio analysis. In Burke's **dramatistic analysis**, this means examining the relative significance of each pentad unit (**act**, **scene**, **agent**, **agency**, **purpose**) in any situation.

Rationalism. The view that knowledge is best acquired by reason and factual analysis rather than faith or emotion.

Refereeing. The process of other researchers in an author's field reviewing her or his research prior to its publication. See also **peer review**.

Referential function. One of Jakobson's semiotic functions. Establishes the communication context, dominant message, or agenda.

Regression. A statistical method for estimating the strength of relationships among variables.

Reification. Turning an abstract into a concrete thing—for example, assuming that because there are measures of intelligence, there is a unitary, tangible entity called intelligence.

Reliability/reliability coefficients. A measure of the extent to which a test or measure performs consistently.

Repair mechanism. In conversation analysis, a repair mechanism is an action that restores a conversation when it is in danger of breaking down.

Repeated testing. In experimental design, a threat to internal validity due to participants becoming more and more familiar with a test.

Research questions. Questions that help focus research. A research question is a researcher's basic research interest posed as a question. **Open-ended research questions** ask simply whether there is a relationship between variables. **Closed-ended research questions** ask about the direction of the relationship.

Respondents. Interviewees or survey participants considered capable of speaking only on behalf of themselves. The individuals responding to **survey** or **interview** questions.

Rhetor. Someone who teaches or practices rhetoric.

Rhetoric/rhetorical/rhetorical analysis. The study of the principles and means of persuasion and argumentation. The rhetorical tradition is part of communication research **metatheory**.

Rhetoric of place. Studies that examine how public places such as museums or memorials can shape public understandings of history and events.

Rhetorician. One who studies **rhetoric**.

Root metaphor. A basic metaphor such as *war, family,* or *team* that shapes the way group members think and that they may or may not be consciously aware of.

Routing questions. See **branching/routing questions**.

Sample. A set of individuals or items selected from a wider population.

Sampling distribution. The distribution of values in a sample.

Sampling frame. The master list from which a sample is selected.

Sampling interval. The interval selected in **systematic sampling** (e.g., every 10th or 100th unit).

Sampling units. The units selected for study.

Scaled questions. Questions in which **respondents** are asked to mark their answers on a scale.

Scales. Measurement devices used to locate an individual's ranking on some attribute. Classic scales in communication research are the **Likert** and **semantic differential scales**.

Scene. In Burke's **dramatistic analysis**, the location where an **act** takes place.

Scholarly articles. Research papers that have been **peer reviewed** and published in academic journals.

Scientific method. A research approach based on developing specific hypotheses or propositions that can then be tested using specific observations designed for that purpose.

Screen sharing. The ability of participants in a computer conference to share the content of their desktop screens.

Search engine. A device such as Google or Yahoo that retrieves information from the web.

Search fields. Searchable components of a database, such as *date, author*, and *title*.

Search term. A word typed into a database or search engine when searching for information.

Secondary source. An author's interpretation or summary of an original source—for example, a literature review.

Selection bias. A problem in experimental design stemming from the experimental groups not being comparable.

Semantic differential scale. A scale anchored at opposite ends by opposing words such as "strong–weak" or "hot–cold."

Semiotic function. In Jakobson's model of communication, an attribute of language that allows communication to occur.

Semiotic/semioticians. In communication research **metatheory**, the tradition of studying the relationships between signs and their interpretation and meaning; the researchers who conduct these studies.

Semistructured interviews. A set of interview questions that are largely predetermined but allow room for **interviewees** to add their own insights and views.

Sequence. The order in which questions are asked—for example from least to most difficult or general to specific.

Serials. Regularly published scholarly publications such as journals.

Significance. In general terms, importance or relevance, but see also **statistical significance**.

Situation. In Hymes's ethnography of communication, the setting where the activities take place and the overall scene of which they are a part.

Skew. Data distributions that, when plotted out, show an extended "tail." Skew is the "tail" of a distribution. Positive skew means the tail is in the high numbers; negative skew means that the tail is in the low numbers. For example, a quiz with a high percentage of scores in the 80s or 90s out of a possible 100 will produce a negative skew.

Slider. An online survey response option that allows respondents to drag a pointer to select a precise point on a scale.

Slideware. Generic term for presentation software such as PowerPoint and Keynote.

Snowball sampling. See **network sampling**.

Social scientists. Researchers who share the assumption that the methods of science can be applied to researching and understanding human behavior.

Sociocultural. A view of communication as producing and reproducing shared meanings and social order.

Sociopsychological. A view of communication as the interaction of individuals.

Solomon Four-Group Design. An experimental design using four groups. In a typical design, groups A and C receive an experimental treatment; groups B and D receive no experimental treatment; groups A and B receive a pretest and a posttest; and groups C and D receive only a posttest.

Speech community. In Hymes's ethnography of communication, a group of people who share a common language that differentiates them from other groups—for example, a group of communication majors.

Speech event. In Hymes's ethnography of communication, a specific speech activity—for example, an awards speech.

Speech situation. In Hymes's ethnography of communication, the overall scene of which activities are a part—for example, a college classroom.

Split-half technique. A way to determine **inter-item reliability** by correlating half the questions in a question set with the other half of the questions.

Spurious relationship. An apparent relationship between two variables that is actually caused by a third variable.

Standard deviation. A measure of the extent to which a set of scores vary on either side of their mean value. The square root of **variance**. See also **standard error**.

Standard error. For a **sampling distribution** (the distribution of scores for a **sample**), the standard deviation is called the **standard error**.

Statistical formulae. Formulae used to calculate statistics such as **mean**, **range**, and **variance**.

Statistical significance. The probability that a computed statistic such as a *t* test or correlation is not due to chance.

Statistics. Calculated numbers that summarize data and relationships among variables in a **sample**.

Stemming. Content analysis term for grouping different words by a common stem; for example, *fish* is the stem for *fisherman, fishy, fishtail, fishing,* and *fished*.

Stop words. High frequency words such as pronouns and prepositions that in content analysis may be removed in order to focus on nouns and verbs.

Stratified random sampling. Sampling in which randomly selected units from small or minority populations are forced into the sample to ensure that they are represented in proportion to their presence in the population.

Structural questions. Questions that ask interviewees to explain the relationships among different terms. For example, "Would you say that X is a part of Y?"

Structure. The extent to which an interview has a format. See also **fully structured interviews**, **semistructured interviews**, and **unstructured interviews**.

Style guide. A document detailing requirements for citation, heading levels, typography, and the like for such specific overall styles as **APA**, **Chicago**, and **MLA**.

Subjects. Individuals who participate in an experiment.

Superstructure. From Marxist theory. Ideologies that dominate a particular time and the systems that uphold those ideologies. The superstructure is dependent on the **base**.

Survey. A research method in which predetermined, formatted questions are distributed to relatively large numbers of people. Typically, **respondents** respond by phone, mail, e-mail, or website.

Symbolic convergence. The condition of group members being in agreement on the organizational symbolism or stories that unite them.

Synchronous. Coordinated communication—for example, focus group members interacting with each other in "real time."

Systematic sampling. Sampling by selecting every *n*th unit from a population.

***t* test.** A statistical test for assessing whether the mean scores for two groups are significantly different.

***t* test for dependent samples.** Test used when both groups consist of the same people, for example a pretest/posttest comparison.

***t* test for independent samples.** Test used when two different groups are being compared.

Tables. Arrangements of data displayed and summarized by rows and columns.

Temporal ordering. Ordering based on a time sequence. To determine that A causes B, A must precede B in time.

Tenacity. A way of knowing based on accepting knowledge, correctly or incorrectly, because it has stood the test of time.

Test-retest. To determine the reliability of a measure by testing and retesting it under the same conditions. If the measure is reliable, it will produce similar results each time.

Text boxes. An online survey response option that allows respondents to type responses in their own words, limited only by the size of the text boxes.

Time series analysis. Analysis of a series of observations made over time.

Trade publications. Journals published for particular industries. The articles are written by experts but not necessarily to the standards of an academic research publication.

Transformative. The worldview that argues for mixing research with politics to address social oppression and change lives for the better.

Transitional relevance place (TRP). In conversation analysis, a transitional relevance place is the point in a conversation at which **turn taking** may take place.

Trend studies. Studies that measure the same items over time but draw different samples from the population to do so.

Triangulation. The use of two or more research methods to address the same research question. If results from different methods agree, researchers can have greater confidence in their findings.

Trimodal distribution. Distributions of data having three values occurring with equal frequency

Turn constructional unit (TCU). In conversation analysis, a sentence, word, or exclamation that signals a **transitional relevance place**—a point at which **turn taking** can occur.

Turn taking. In conversation analysis, the mechanism of who speaks next in a conversation and the mechanisms that indicate possible types of responses to a question.

Two-tailed hypotheses. Propositions stating that there will be a difference between two groups but that this difference could be in either direction.

Two-tailed test. A test of the proposition that there will be a difference between two groups but that this difference could be in either direction. For example, you would use a two-tailed test to discover whether one class of high school seniors had higher or lower SAT scores than another. See also **one-tailed test**.

Type I error. Deciding wrongly that there was a significant result when in fact there was not.

Type II error. Deciding wrongly that there was no significant result when in fact there was.

Univariate analysis/statistics. Statistics that describe only one variable.

Unobtrusive measures. Observations of people's behavior without them being aware of such observation.

Unstructured interviews. Interviews with broad questions and a loose schedule of questions so that **interviewees** have the freedom to volunteer information and to explain their responses.

URL. Uniform Resource Locator. Commonly known as a web address, a URL is an Internet address that specifies an item's location on a computer network and a protocol for accessing it.

Utterances. In conversation analysis, units of speech preceded by silence and followed either by silence or by another person speaking.

Validity. A measure of whether a test measures what it is supposed to measure.

Variable. The aspects of a concept that are capable of being measured or taking on a value. The construct *academic performance* cannot be measured; the variable *grade point average* can.

Variance. A measure of the extent to which a set of scores vary on either side of their mean value. The square root of variance gives the **standard deviation**.

Veil of ignorance. Philosopher John Rawls's view that we take a dispassionate approach, reviewing all sides of a decision equally. We are asked to "wear a veil" that blinds us to all information about ourselves that might cloud our judgment.

Voice. The individual writing style of an author.

Volunteer sampling. Obtaining a sample by asking for volunteers.

Ways of speaking. In Hymes's ethnography of communication, the styles of speech that are characteristic of a culture or group; for example, at the beginning of a class, the instructor speaks before students do.

Web crawling. Compiling a list of websites by starting with a predetermined site and following the links to it.

Web scraping. Collecting documents from the web to download as text.

Within-subjects design. An experimental design in which participants are exposed to more than one experimental condition—for example, both democratic and autocratic managerial styles. See also **between-subjects design**.

Worldviews. Major conceptual frameworks for understanding the world. For example, one worldview might consider humans to be essentially similar, allowing their behavior to be measured and predicted, while another might view humans as individuals and unpredictable, making it possible to describe their behavior but not predict it.

z **score.** The number of units of standard deviation that any individual score is above or below the mean for a variable.

INDEX

ABOUT THE AUTHORS

Donald Treadwell earned his master's degree in communication from Cornell University and his PhD in communication and rhetoric from Rensselaer Polytechnic Institute.

He developed and taught communication research classes in classroom and online settings and also taught courses in organizational communication, public relations, and public relations writing. He is the coauthor of *Public Relations Writing: Principles in Practice* (2nd ed., Sage, 2005).

He has published and presented research on organizational image, consumer response to college names, health professionals' images of AIDS, faculty perceptions of the communication discipline, and employers' expectations of newly hired communication graduates. His research appears in *Communication Monographs, Journal of Technical Writing and Communication, Public Relations Review, Journal of Human Subjectivity,* and *Criminal Justice Ethics.*

He is professor emeritus, Westfield State University, and has international consulting experience in agricultural extension and health communication.

Andrea M. Davis is Associate Professor of Communication at Western New England University.

She regularly teaches research methods, small group communication, interpersonal communication, and public speaking. She also developed and taught courses in health communication and gender and communication.

She has published and presented research on sexual and relational health messages, critical pedagogy, and the performativity of space. Her research appears in *Cultural Studies↔Critical Methodologies, Journal of Teaching and Learning with Technology,* and *The Qualitative Report.*

She earned her master's from Saint Louis University and her PhD in communication studies from Bowling Green State University.